CHECKLIST OF THE BIRDS OF NEW ZEALAND

and the Ross Dependency, Antarctica

By
THE CHECKLIST COMMITTEE
(E. G. Turbott, Convener)
ORNITHOLOGICAL SOCIETY OF NEW ZEALAND

THIRD EDITION
1990

Random Century
in association with
ORNITHOLOGICAL SOCIETY OF
NEW ZEALAND INC.

Random Century New Zealand Ltd
(An imprint of the Random Century Group)

9–11 Rothwell Avenue
Albany
Auckland 10
NEW ZEALAND

Associated companies, branches and representatives throughout the world.

First published 1990
© Ornithological Society of New Zealand Inc. 1990
ISBN 1 86941 082 3
Printed in Malaysia
by SRM Productions Services Sdn Bhd

For enquiries about joining the Society, write to:
Membership Secretary
P.O. Box 12397
Wellington

Contents

Introduction

This *Checklist*, like its predecessors, provides a compact guide to the classification and distribution of the birds of the New Zealand region. Perhaps the main advance in New Zealand ornithology since the last (1970) *Checklist* is the growth of information on New Zealand's fossil and subfossil bird faunas, and the inclusion of as much material as possible on the fossil and subfossil distribution of both living and extinct forms is a special feature of the present list. To help the reader in this respect a brief survey of palaeornithology and of the impact of palaeornithological ideas on New Zealand ornithology in general, by a member of the Checklist Committee, Dr P. R. Millener, is given after this Introduction.

As with the two previous Ornithological Society of New Zealand checklists, a Committee was set up to carry out the task of preparation. The two previous checklists and the respective Checklist Committee conveners were: *Checklist of New Zealand Birds*, 1953 (C. A. Fleming, Convener); and *Annotated Checklist of the Birds of New Zealand*, 1970 (F. C. Kinsky, Convener). In addition, a revision entitled *Amendments and Additions to the 1970 Annotated Checklist of the Birds of New Zealand* was published in 1980 as a supplement to *Notornis*, volume 27 (F. C. Kinsky, Convener).

The following Committee was appointed by the Society's Council in 1980: E. G. Turbott (Convener), J. A. Bartle, D. H. Brathwaite, Dr P. R. Millener, R. J. Scarlett, R. B. Sibson, Dr J. Warham. Two additional members were later appointed by the Council: Dr B. J. Gill (1983) and Dr M. J. Imber (1985). In addition, Dr P. C. Bull was appointed to the Committee in an advisory capacity.

The Committee first agreed on style and format on the basis of proposals circulated by the Convener, and after this established a preliminary allocation of responsibility for the preparation of first drafts. Some changes in the allocations were required and those finally responsible for preparing drafts were the following:

Dinornithiformes: P. R. Millener
Apterygiformes: E. G. Turbott
Podicipediformes: E. G. Turbott and R. B. Sibson
Procellariiformes: M. J. Imber
Sphenisciformes: J. Warham
Pelecaniformes: D. H. Brathwaite
Ciconiiformes: E. G. Turbott and R. B. Sibson
Anseriformes, Falconiformes and Galliformes: E. G. Turbott
Gruiformes: B. J. Gill
Charadriiformes: R. B. Sibson
Columbiformes, Psittaciformes, Cuculiformes, Strigiformes, Caprimulgiformes, Apodiformes and Coraciiformes: B. J. Gill

Native Passeriformes (except for Pachycephalidae and
    Acanthizidae): E. G. Turbott
Pachycephalidae and Acanthizidae: B. J. Gill
Introduced Passeriformes: E. G. Turbott and P. C. Bull

The drafts were circulated to the Committee as prepared, and amendments and criticisms were referred back, where required, to draft compilers by the Convener. As far as possible the final text was brought up to date to the end of 1989.

Sectional compilers have not hesitated to refer difficult points, as required, to colleagues and to members of the Society with special knowledge, and the help received is gladly acknowledged. In addition, major help in the preparation of first drafts was given by: J. N. Jolly (Apterygiformes), Dr M. J. Williams (Anseriformes), and Dr J. L. Craig (Meliphagidae). B. D. Heather contributed substantially to the updating of distributional entries for the grebes, herons, waterfowl, and waders, and R. N. Holdaway commented on the draft on native passerines; Dr G. S. Dumbell also helped with updated information on the Brown Teal. Records on the transfer of threatened species and subspecies were checked and extended by C. R. Veitch and records of transfers to date of the South Island Saddleback were provided by A. Roberts.

Dr R. E. Fordyce, of the Geology Department, University of Otago, prepared the entries on fossil penguins and commented on the draft on the Pelagornithidae. The Committee has much pleasure in extending thanks to Dr Fordyce for his contribution to the *Checklist*.

As indicated earlier, Dr P. C. Bull prepared the distribution sections and lists of references for the introduced passerines, as well as providing general comments throughout the preparation of drafts and at the planning stage, and his help is gladly acknowledged by the Committee.

Thanks are also recorded on behalf of the Committee to Dr Ernst Mayr, who kindly read and commented on the draft on native passerines.

Format and Treatment

Letters for subspecies have been omitted: otherwise the format is essentially the same as in the 1970 *Checklist*, with subspecies arranged from north to south.

As mentioned above, information on fossil and subfossil distribution is included as appropriate in each entry, and forms known only as fossils or subfossils are shown in taxonomic sequence, numeration following consecutively throughout the *Checklist*. The fossil or subfossil forms are indicated, however, by a distinctive (sanserif) typeface. In the 1970 *Checklist*, fossil and subfossil forms were shown with their own numbers in Appendices. The addition of these, together with new records of living species, brings the species total for the present list to 379.

The Suspense List (Appendix A, 1970 *Checklist*) has been repeated, with the omission of Ruff *Philomachus pugnax*, now transferred to the main body of the *Checklist*.

Records of rare birds and stragglers have been mainly repeated from the 1970 *Checklist*; in a few cases alterations known to be required, or notified to sectional compilers, have been made. The Checklist Committee has kept in touch throughout with the Society's Rare Birds Committee, and new records accepted by the latter Committee since the 1970 *Checklist* were incorporated by the sectional compilers.

In addition to incorporating information on fossil and subfossil forms, it was decided to make two substantial innovations in the present *Checklist*. The new features are:

(a) The provision of original citations and synonymies for genera, species, and subspecies — partial synonymies only are given, i.e., names likely to be helpful to *Checklist* users when checking New Zealand ornithological literature.

(b) Lists of references for each species or subspecies, chosen to indicate recent trends in New Zealand ornithological research, advances in research on the biology of New Zealand species and especially references providing extensive literature lists. All references to the first published record of stragglers and rarer visitors are included.

Sectional compilers have differed considerably in their interpretation of what synonyms or references to include, and differences in this respect have been regarded flexibly by the Convener; it is hoped, however, that an overall consistency of treatment throughout the *Checklist* has been achieved.

Finally under this heading, notes on status are included in the distributional paragraphs where appropriate, especially in the case of rare or threatened species.

Classification and Nomenclature

Papers upon which taxonomic changes accepted by the Committee are based are included in the lists of references. For the shags, a modified version of the classification proposed by Siegel-Causey (*Condor* 90: 885–905, 1988) has been adopted, the main alteration to the 1970 *Checklist* being the elevation of the New Zealand forms of pink-footed shags (*Leucocarbo*), and *Stictocarbo featherstoni*, to full species.

The main change in major classification since the 1970 *Checklist* is the introduction of the families Pachycephalidae, Acanthizidae,

Monarchidae, and Eopsaltriidae. In this respect, the Committee's work was fortunately timed to coincide with the appearance of the final volume of Peters' *Checklist of Birds of the World* (volume XI, by Ernst Mayr, Melvin A. Traylor, Jr. and George E. Watson: 1986). This provides especially a reorganization of groups formerly included in the broad family Muscicapidae, carried out in consultation with Australian workers on these groups, and incorporates concepts arising from the DNA hybridizing techniques of Charles G. Sibley and co-workers. (For further information on recent views on the classification of Australian passerines, see Schodde, R. 1975. *Interim List of Australian Songbirds. Passerines.* Melbourne: RAOU.)

Through the kindness of Dr R. Schodde, the Committee has been able to keep up to date with any possible major discrepancies between the present *Checklist* and the list of Australian birds being prepared for the Australian Biological Resources Survey. In a few cases changes in the scientific names of Australian species occurring as stragglers in New Zealand have been applied; in addition, *Anas gibberifrons gracilis* (Grey Teal) has been replaced by *Anas gracilis* (monotypic species) as adopted for the Australian list.

European species established in New Zealand are shown in the present list as binomials only. The Committee believes that much remains to be done before subspecific identity can be established on grounds of either morphology or point of origin of the original stock; further, the introductions were in many cases of migratory species. The paper by Niethammer (*J. für Ornithol.* 112: 202–226, 1971) on the taxonomy of introduced European species quoted under a number of entries was based upon insufficient material to enable conclusions to be reached. A further consideration is that, as shown by Ross and Baker (*Can. J. Zool.* 60: 3316–3325, 1982) for the Starling, and by Baker and Moeed (*Can. J. Zool.* 57: 570–584, 1979; *Evolution* 41: 525–538, 1987) for the Common Myna, variation that would obscure the original subspecific characters is likely to have developed in introduced species.

The vexed question of whether or not to change *–ii* endings based on personal names to *–i* (*International Code of Zoological Nomenclature*, Articles 31a and 33d) is still unresolved, and accordingly the spelling of names in this category has been retained as in the 1980 *Amendments* (e.g. *Apteryx owenii*).

General References

Two important general works are not cited, or are referred to only occasionally, in the pres	ent *Checklist*. These are: Bull, P. C.; Gaze, P. D.; Robertson, C. J. R. (1985), *The Atlas of Bird Distribution in New Zealand*, Wellington: Ornithological Society of New Zealand; and *Reader's Digest Complete Book of New Zealand Birds* (1985),

Sydney: Reader's Digest. The *Atlas* provides the basis for distributional information on most New Zealand species and has been used extensively by sectional compilers in the preparation of the present *Checklist*. Outlines of distribution and life history by specialist authors are available in the *Reader's Digest* volume, to which reference should be made for up-to-date information on all species.

An additional recent book containing a survey of the taxonomy, biology, and status of a wide range of New Zealand birds is the late Sir Charles Fleming's work on the paintings of G. E. Lodge (Fleming, C. A. 1982. *George Edward Lodge: the Unpublished New Zealand Bird Paintings*. Wellington: Nova Pacifica).

Acknowledgements

A much appreciated contribution towards the cost of preparing this *Checklist* was made by Rank-Xerox (NZ) Ltd, who granted $500 towards typing costs and assisted with photocopying. This sponsorship, and matters relating to the publication of the *Checklist*, were negotiated by Dr B. J. Gill on behalf of the Society's Council.

The unmatched resources of the Auckland Institute and Museum Library have been used constantly over the period of preparation by Auckland members of the Committee, including the Convener, and thanks for providing access and help at all times are recorded to the Director, Mr G. S. Park, and to the Library staff.

Skilled typing by Gaye Powell, Dora Marsh, and Gloria Marsh has greatly furthered the work of preparing and circulating drafts.

Finally, the Society's Editor, Barrie Heather, has greatly improved the consistency and balance of the whole *Checklist*, and kindly undertook the demanding task of marking up the final manuscript for publication.

E. G. Turbott, Convener,
Auckland, March 1990.

Note
* An asterisk indicates introduced species.
Sanserif typeface indicates forms known only as fossils or subfossils.

New Zealand's avifaunal fossil record

In New Zealand, the avifaunal 'fossil' record from before the Late Pleistocene is very sparse, few taxa being represented (Procellariiformes, Sphenisciformes, Pelecaniformes, Anseriformes); however, far more taxa are known from last glacial and younger ('subfossil') deposits.

Throughout this checklist, the term 'fossil' is used for faunal remains from consolidated deposits (generally Early Pleistocene or older, and mostly marine), whereas the term 'subfossil' is applied for convenience to all remains from essentially unconsolidated, usually non-marine, sediments (dune sands, cave silts, buried soils, and fluvial/swamp deposits) typically of late glacial or post-glacial (Holocene) age.

Occupation 'middens' often contain the discarded or worked bones of the wide variety of birds hunted by the early Polynesians. Most such middens are on coastal dunes, but some are in inland rock shelters. Avian records from middens must, however, be interpreted with caution because, especially in eroding dune-midden sites, indisputable evidence is often lacking for direct association of the bird remains with human midden debris (see Coutts 1972; Millener 1981).

In recent years, the excavation of subfossil avian remains on oceanic island groups (including New Zealand) has allowed, for the first time, a direct detailed analysis of their prehistoric faunas (see Balouet & Olson 1989; Meredith 1985; Millener 1981, 1990, in press; Olson 1975, 1981; Olson & Hilgartner 1982; Olson & James 1982ab, 1984; Steadman 1985, 1986; Steadman & Olson 1985). The fossil remains collected (of extant and recently extinct species, including many previously unknown) have led to previous concepts of diversity and distribution of the endemic faunas being revised extensively and have cast doubt on the reliability of data used for (largely theoretical) considerations of island biogeography. The common conclusion derived from the subfossil discoveries on these various oceanic island groups (with New Zealand no exception) is that prehistoric human interference has been profoundly adverse, with typically as much as 40% of the prehistoric avifauna having been extirpated within a few hundred years of first human settlement.

References

BALOUET, J.C.; OLSON, S.L. 1989. Fossil birds from Late Quaternary deposits in New Caledonia. Smiths. Contrib. Zool. 469: 38 pp.

COUTTS, P. 1972. Interpretation of archaeological material eroded from coastal dune sites. J. Roy. Soc. NZ. 2: 407–412.

MEREDITH, C. 1985. The vertebrate fossil fauna of Norfolk Island and the phylogeny of the genus *Pterodroma*. Unpubl. PhD thesis (Zoology), University of Monash, Victoria. 255 pp.

MILLENER, P.R. 1981. The Quaternary avifauna of the North Island, New Zealand. Unpubl. PhD thesis (Geology). University of Auckland; xxviii + 897 pp., 2 vols.

MILLENER, P.R. 1990. The Quaternary avifauna of New Zealand. 28 pp. *in* Vertebrate Palaeontology of Australasia (Rich, P.V.; Baird, R.F.; Monaghan, J.M.; Rich, T.H. eds.). Chapman & Hall, London; Thomas Nelson, Melbourne.

MILLENER, P. R. (in press). The avifauna of the Chatham Islands: past and present. Notornis (Fleming Memorial volume).

OLSON, S. L. 1975. Paleornithology of St. Helena Island, South Atlantic Ocean. Smiths. Contrib. Paleobiol. 23: 49 pp.

OLSON, S. L. 1981. Natural history of vertebrates on the Brazilian islands of the Mid South Atlantic. Nat. Geogr. Soc. Res. Rep. 13: 481–492.

OLSON, S. L.; HILGARTNER, W. B. 1982. Fossil and subfossil birds from the Bahamas. *In* Olson, S. L. (ed.), Fossil vertebrates from the Bahamas. Smiths. Contrib. Paleobiol. 48: 22–56.

OLSON, S. L.; JAMES, H. F. 1982a. Fossil birds from the Hawaiian Islands: Evidence for wholesale extinction by man before Western contact. Science 217 (4560): 633–635.

OLSON, S. L.; JAMES, H. F. 1982b. Prodromus of the fossil avifauna of the Hawaiian Islands. Smiths. Contrib. Zool. 365: 59 pp.

OLSON, S. L.; JAMES, H. F. 1984. The role of Polynesians in the extinction of the avifauna of the Hawaiian Islands. Pages 768–780. *In* Martin, P. S. & Klein, R. G. (eds) Quaternary Extinctions. University of Arizona Press, Tucson.

STEADMAN, D. W. 1985. Fossil birds from Mangaia, Southern Cook Islands. Bull. Br. Ornithol. Club 105(2): 58–66.

STEADMAN, D. W. 1986. Holocene vertebrate fossils from Isla Floreana, Galapagos. Smiths. Contrib. Zool. 413: 103 pp.

STEADMAN, D. W.; OLSON, S. L. 1985. Bird remains from an archaeological site on Henderson Island, South Pacific: Man-caused extinction on an "uninhabited" island. Proc. Nat. Acad. Sci. USA. 82(18): 6191–6195.

P. R. Millener

Order **DINORNITHIFORMES**: Moas

Note: Cracraft (1974) proposed a monophyletic origin for the entire ratite–tinamou assemblage and united them within the single order Palaeognathiformes. Houde and Olson (1981), Olson (1985) and Houde (1986) provided compelling evidence that at least some palaeognathous birds (perhaps including ostriches, moas and kiwis) may have arisen independently (polyphyletically), by neotony, from neognathous ancestors (and are, thus, secondarily palaeognathous). Therefore, it seems prudent to revert to the more traditional arrangement (cf. Archey 1941, Brodkorb 1963, Kinsky 1970) of placing the moas (and kiwis) in their own orders.

Nomina nuda and names incorrectly applied to the taxon under consideration, through misidentification or incorrect referral of material, are not included in the partial synonymies which follow.

ARCHEY, G. 1941. The moa. Bull. Auck. Inst. Mus. No. 1.

BRODKORB, P. 1963. Catalogue of fossil birds, Part 1 (Archaeopterygiformes through Ardeiformes). Bull. Florida State Museum 7: 179–293.

CRACRAFT, J. 1974. Phylogeny and evolution of the ratite birds. Ibis 116: 494–521.

HOUDE, P.W. 1986. Ostrich ancestors found in the Northern Hemisphere suggest new hypothesis of ratite origins. Nature 324: 563–565.

HOUDE, P.W. 1988. Paleognathous birds from the early Tertiary of the Northern Hemisphere. Publ. Nuttall Ornithological Club. 22. viii + 148pp. Harvard University, Cambridge, Massachusetts.

HOUDE, P.W.; OLSON, S.L. 1981. Paleognathous carinate birds from the early Tertiary of North America. Science 214: 1236–1237.

KINSKY, F.C. (Convener). 1970. Annotated Checklist of the Birds of New Zealand. Wellington: OSNZ, Reed.

OLSON, S.L. 1985. The fossil record of birds. Pages 79–252 in Farner, D.S.; King, J.R.; Parkes, K.C. (eds), Avian Biology, Vol. 8. London: Academic Press.

Family **EMEIDAE**

Subfamily ANOMALOPTERYGINAE

Genus **Anomalopteryx** Reichenbach

Anomalopteryx Reichenbach, 1852, Avium Systema Naturale, p.xxx — type (by monotypy) *Dinornis didiformis* Owen.

Graya Bonaparte, 1856, C.R. Acad. Sci. Paris **43**(18): 841 — type (by subsequent designation) *Dinornis dromaeoides* Owen.

Anomalornis Hutton, 1897, Trans. NZ Inst. **29**: 543 — (new name for *Anomalopteryx* Reichenbach).

1   **Anomalopteryx didiformis** (Owen)

Dinornis didiformis (Owen), 1844, Trans. Zool. Soc. Lond. **3**(3): 242.
Dinornis dromaeoides Owen, 1844, Trans. Zool. Soc. Lond. **3**(3): 253.
Dinornis dromioides. Owen, 1848, Proc. Zool. Soc. Lond. **14**: 40.
Dinornis parvus Owen, 1883, Trans. Zool. Soc. Lond. **11**(8): 233.
Anomalopteryx oweni Haast, 1886, Trans. Zool. Soc. Lond. **12**(5): 171.
Anomalopteryx dromaeoides: Lydekker, 1891, Cat. Fossil Birds Brit. Mus: 266.
Anomalopteryx didiformis. Lydekker, 1891, Cat. Fossil Birds Brit. Mus. 275.
Anomalopteryx parva: Lydekker, 1891, Cat. Fossil Birds Brit. Mus: 278.
Anomalopteryx antiquus Hutton, 1892, Trans. NZ Inst. **24**: 124.

Anomalopteryx fortis Hutton, 1893, Trans. NZ Inst. **25**: 9.
Anomalopteryx antiqua: Hutton, 1893, Trans. NZ Inst. **25**: 14.
Anomalornis gracilis Hutton, 1897, Trans. NZ Inst. **29**: 546.
Anomalornis didiformis: Hutton, 1897, Trans. NZ Inst. **29**: 547.
Anomalopteryx parvus: Oliver, 1930, New Zealand Birds: 45.
Pachyornis oweni: Archey, 1941, Bull. Auck. Inst. Mus. **1**: 44.

Fossil: Late Pleistocene — subrecent; North Island (rare in the far North), South Island, Stewart Island; widespread subfossil (particularly in cave deposits) and midden.

ARCHEY, G. 1941. The moa. Bull. Auck. Inst, Mus. No.1.
MILLENER, P. R. 1981. The Quaternary avifauna of the North Island, New Zealand. Unpubl. PhD thesis (Geology), University of Auckland. 2 vols.
MILLENER, P. R. 1982. And then there were twelve: the taxonomic status of *Anomalopteryx oweni* (Aves: Dinornithidae). Notornis 29: 165–170.

Genus **Megalapteryx** Haast

Megalapteryx Haast, 1886, Trans. Zool. Soc. Lond. **12**(5): 161 — type (by monotypy) *Megalapteryx hectori* Haast.
Palaeocasuarius Rothschild, 1907, Extinct Birds: 219 — type (by original designation) *Palaeocasuarius haasti* Rothschild (ex *P. haasti* Forbes, nomen nudum).

2   **Megalapteryx didinus** (Owen)

Dinornis didinus Owen, 1883, Trans. Zool. Soc. Lond. **11**(8): 257.
Megalapteryx hectori Haast, 1886, Trans. Zool. Soc. Lond. **12**(5): 161.
Megalapteryx tenuipes Lydekker, 1891, Cat. Fossil Birds Brit. Mus: 251.
Anomalopteryx didina: Lydekker, 1891, Cat. Fossil Birds Brit. Mus: 277.
Anomalopteryx tenuipes: Andrews, 1897, Novitates Zoologicae: 188.
Megalapteryx hamiltoni Rothschild, 1907, Extinct Birds: 197.
Palaeocasuarius haasti: Rothschild, 1907, Extinct Birds: 220.
Palaeocasuarius velox Rothschild, 1907 Extinct Birds: 220.
Megalapteryx benhami Archey, 1941, Bull. Auck. Inst. Mus. **1**: 35.

Fossil: Late Pleistocene — subrecent; South Island only; subfossil and midden; common in northwestern and western areas, including subalpine zones; less common in eastern, lowland areas.

CRACRAFT, J. 1976. The species of moas (Aves: Dinornithidae). Smithsonian Contrib. Palaeobiology 27: 189–205.
WORTHY, T. H. 1988. A re-examination of the moa genus *Megalapteryx*. Notornis 35: 99–108.
WORTHY, T. H. 1989. Moas of the subalpine zone. Notornis 36: 191–196.

Genus **Pachyornis** Lydekker

Pachyornis Lydekker, 1891, Cat. Fossil Birds Brit. Mus: 316 — type (by original designation) *Dinornis elephantopus* Owen.

3   **Pachyornis elephantopus** (Owen)

Dinornis elephantopus Owen, 1856, Proc. Zool. Soc. Lond. **24**: 54.
Dinornis queenslandiae De Vis, 1884, Proc. Roy. Soc. Queensland **1**: 231.
Pachyornis elephantopus: Lydekker, 1891, Cat. Fossil Birds Brit. Mus: 321.

Pachyornis immanis Lydekker, 1891, Cat. Fossil Birds Brit. Mus: 343.
Euryapteryx ponderosus Hutton, 1891, NZ J. Sci. new issue **1**(6): 249.
Pachyornis rothschildi Lydekker, 1892, Proc. Zool. Soc. Lond. **33**: 249.
Eurapteryx elephantopus: Hutton, 1892, Trans. NZ Inst. **24**: 135.
Pachyornis inhabilis Hutton, 1893, Trans. NZ Inst. **25**: 11.
Pachyornis valgus Hutton 1893, Trans. NZ Inst. **25**: 12.
Euryapteryx immanis: Lambrecht, 1933, Handbuch der Palaeornithologie: 150.
Pachyornis murihiku Oliver, 1949, Dom. Mus. Bull. **15**: 67.
Pachyornis queenslandiae: Oliver, 1949, Dom. Mus. Bull. **15**: 80.
Dromiceius queenslandiae: Miller, 1963, Rec. S. Aust. Mus. **14**(3): 417.

Fossil: Late Pleistocene — subrecent; North Island (rare in the northern half), South Island, Stewart Island; subfossil and midden.

SCARLETT, R. J. 1968. A second North Island locality for *Pachyornis elephantopus* (Owen). Notornis 15: 36.
SCARLETT, R. J. 1969. On the alleged Queensland moa, *Dinornis queenslandiae* De Vis. Mem. Queensland Mus. 15: 207–212.

4   **Pachyornis australis** Oliver

Pachyornis australis Oliver, 1949, Dom. Mus. Bull. **15**: 70
Pachyornis elephantopus: Cracraft, 1976, Smithsonian Contrib. Palaebiology **27**: 196.

Fossil: Late Pleistocene — subrecent; South Island only; as yet, recognised only from a small number of subfossil and midden sites.

WORTHY, T. H. 1989. Moas of the subalpine zone. Notornis 36: 191–196.
WORTHY, T. H. 1989. Validation of *Pachyornis australis* Oliver (Aves: Dinornithiformes), a medium-sized moa from the South Island, New Zealand. NZ J. Geol. Geophysics 32: 255–266.

5   **Pachyornis mappini** Archey

Pachyornis mappini Archey, 1941, Bull. Auck. Inst. Mus. **1**: 41.
Pachyornis septentrionalis Oliver, 1949, Dom. Mus. Bull. **15**: 61.

Fossil: Late Pleistocene — subrecent; North Island only; widespread subfossil and midden.

MILLENER, P. R. 1981. The Quaternary avifauna of the North Island, New Zealand. Unpubl. PhD thesis (Geology), University of Auckland. 2 vols.
MILLENER, P. R. 1982. And then there were twelve: the taxonomic status of *Anomalopteryx oweni* (Aves: Dinornithidae). Notornis 29: 165–170.
WORTHY, T. H. 1987. Sexual dimorphism and temporal variation in the North Island moa species *Euryapteryx curtus* (Owen) and *Pachyornis mappini* Archey. Nat. Mus. NZ Rec. 3(6): 59–70.

Subfamily EMEINAE
Genus **Emeus** Reichenbach

Emeus Reichenbach, 1852, Avium Systema Naturale, p.xxx — type *Dinornis casuarinus* Owen.
Syornis Reichenbach, 1852, Avium System Naturale, p.xxx — type *Dinornis casuarinus* Owen.

Meiornis Haast, 1874, Trans. NZ Inst. **6**: 426—type *Dinornis casuarinus* Owen (designated by Archey 1941: 45).
Meionornis Haast, 1874, Ibis **3**(4): 212 (emendation).
Mesopteryx Hutton, 1891, NZ J. Sci. new issue **1**(6): 248—type (by monotypy) *Dinornis huttonii* Owen (referred to by Hutton, in error, as *D. didinus* Owen).

6   **Emeus crassus** (Owen)

Dinornis crassus Owen, 1846, Proc. Zool. Soc. Lond. **14**: 46.
Dinornis casuarinus Owen, 1846, Proc. Zool. Soc. Lond. **14**: 47.
Emeus crassus: Reichenbach, 1852, Avium Systema Naturale, p.xxx.
Syornis casuarinus: Reichenbach, 1852, Avium Systema Naturale, p.xxx.
Dinornis rheides Owen, 1870, Trans. Zool. Soc. Lond. **7**(2): 132.
Dinornis huttoni Owen, 1879, Extinct Birds of New Zealand: 430.
Anomalopteryx casuarina: Lydekker, 1891, Cat. Fossil. Birds. Brit. Mus: 257.
Syornis crassus: Hutton, 1891, NZ J. Sci. new issue **1**(6): 249.
Mesopteryx didinus (part): Hutton, 1892, Trans. NZ Inst. **24**: 129.
Euryapteryx compacta Hutton, 1893, Trans, NZ Inst. **25**: 11.
Mesopteryx didina: Hutton, 1893, Trans, NZ Inst. **25**: 13.
Mesopteryx casuarina: Parker, 1895, Trans. Zool. Soc. Lond. **13**(11): 377.
Mesopteryx species γ Parker, 1895, Trans. Zool. Soc. Lond. **13**(11): 378.
Meionornis didinus: Hutton, 1896, Trans. NZ Inst. **28**: 636.
Meionornis casuarinus: Hutton, 1896, Trans. NZ Inst. **28**: 636.
Euryapteryx crassus: Hutton, 1896, Trans. NZ Inst. **28**: 638.
Megalapteryx huttoni: Rothschild, 1907, Extinct Birds: 199.
? *Cela rheides*: Rothschild, 1907, Extinct Birds: 207.
Cela casuarinus: Rothschild, 1907, Extinct Birds: 207.
Emeus casuarinus: Oliver, 1930, New Zealand Birds: 48.
Emeus huttonii: Oliver, 1930, New Zealand Birds: 49.

Fossil: Late Pleistocene—subrecent; South Island only; subfossil and midden, more common in eastern, lowland areas.

CRACRAFT, J. 1976. The species of moas (Aves: Dinornithidae). Smithsonian Contrib. Palaeobiology 27: 189–205.

Genus **Euryapteryx** Haast

Cela Reichenbach, 1852, Avium Systema Naturale, p.xxx—type (by monotypy) *Dinornis curtus* Owen. Preoccupied by *Cela* Moehring, 1758; *Cela* Oken, 1816; *Cela* Illinger, 1826.
Celeus Bonaparte, 1856, C. R. Acad. Sci. Paris **43**(18): 841. Preoccupied by *Celeus* Boie, 1831.
Euryapteryx Haast, 1874, Trans NZ Inst. **6**: 427—type *Dinornis gravis* Owen, designated by Archey (1941: 53).
Zelornis Oliver, 1949, Dom. Mus. Bull. **15**: 117—type *Euryapteryx exilis* Hutton.

7   **Euryapteryx geranoides** (Owen)

Palapteryx geranoides Owen, 1848, Trans. Zool. Soc. Lond. **3**(5): 361.
Dinornis gravis Owen, 1870, Trans. Zool. Soc. Lond. **7**(2): 141.
Euryapteryx gravis: Haast, 1874, Trans. NZ Inst. **6**: 426.
Emeus gravipes Lydekker, 1891, Cat. Fossil Birds Brit. Mus: 297.
Emeus species γ Parker, 1895, Trans. Zool. Soc. Lond. **13**: 379.
Emeus species β Parker, 1895, Trans. Zool. Soc. Lond. **13**: 379.
Euryapteryx ponderosa Hamilton, 1898, Trans. NZ Inst. **30**: 445.
Emeus parkeri Rothschild, 1907, Extinct Birds: 210.

Emeus boothi Rothschild, 1907, Extinct Birds: 210.
Emeus haasti Rothschild, 1907, Extinct Birds: 210.
Euryapteryx crassa: Benham, 1910, Trans. NZ Inst. **42**: 354.
Dinornis expunctus Archey, 1927, Trans. NZ Inst. **58**: 152.
Euryapteryx kuranui Oliver, 1930, New Zealand Birds: 52.
Eurapteryx gravipes: Oliver, 1930, New Zealand Birds: 53.
Zelornis haasti: Oliver, 1949, Dom. Mus. Bull. **15**: 125.

Fossil: Late Pleistocene—subrecent; North Island, South Island, Stewart Island; widespread subfossil and midden, though less common in the northern North Island and western South Island.

CRACRAFT, J. 1976. The species of moas (Aves: Dinornithidae). Smithsonian Contrib. Palaeobiology 27: 189–205.
MILLENER, P. R. 1981. The Quaternary avifauna of the North Island, New Zealand. Unpubl. PhD thesis (Geology), University of Auckland. 2 vols.

8   Euryapteryx curtus (Owen)

Dinornis curtus Owen, 1846, Proc. Zool. Soc. Lond. **14**: 48.
Cela curtus: Reichenbach, 1852, Avium Systema Naturale, p. xxx
Dinornis geranoides Owen, 1866, Trans. Zool. Soc. Lond. **5**(5): 401.
Anomalopteryx geranoides: Lydekker, 1891, Cat. Fossil Birds Brit. Mus: 288.
Mesopteryx sp. α Parker, 1895, Trans. Zool. Soc. Inst. **13**(11): 378.
Euryapteryx exilis Hutton, 1897, Trans. NZ Inst. **29**: 552.
Euryapteryx tane Oliver, 1949, Dom. Mus. Bull. **15**: 105.
Zelornis exilis: Oliver, 1949, Dom. Mus. Bull. **15**: 121.

Fossil: Late Pleistocene—subrecent; North Island only; widespread subfossil (particularly in coastal areas) and midden.

CRACRAFT, J. 1976. The species of moas (Aves: Dinornithidae). Smithsonian Contrib. Palaeobiology 27: 189–205.
MILLENER, P. R. 1981. The Quaternary avifauna of the North Island, New Zealand. Unpubl. PhD thesis (Geology). University of Auckland. 2 vols.
WORTHY, T. H. 1987. Sexual dimorphism and temporal variation in the North Island moa species *Euryapteryx curtus* (Owen) and *Pachyornis mappini* Archey. Nat. Mus. NZ Rec. 3(6): 59–70.

Family DINORNITHIDAE
Genus Dinornis Owen

Dinornis Owen, 1843, Proc. Zool. Soc. Lond. **11**(121): 10—type (by monotypy) *Dinornis novae-zealandiae* Owen.
Megalornis Owen, 1843, Proc. Zool. Soc. Lond. **11**(122): **19** (*Dinornis* substituted for manuscript name *Megalornis* Owen in paper read at previous meeting; preoccupied by *Megalornis* Gray, 1841).
Palapteryx Owen, 1846, Proc. Zool. Soc. Lond. **14**: 46—type *Dinornis ingens* Owen, designated by Lydekker (1891: 224).
Movia Reichenbach, 1852, Avium Systema Naturale p.xxx—type (by monotypy) *Dinornis ingens* Owen.
Moa Reichenbach, 1852, Avium Systema Naturale p.xxx—type (by monotypy) *Dinornis giganteus* Owen.
Owenia Gray, 1855, Cat. Genera Subgenera Birds: 152—type *Dinornis struthoides* Owen.
Tylopteryx Hutton, 1891, NZ J. Sci. new issue **1**(6): 247—type *Dinornis gracilis*

Owen, designated by Richmond (1902: 720); *Dinornis torosus* Hutton, designated by Archey (1941: 61), in oversight of Richmond's action.

9   **Dinornis struthoides** Owen

Dinornis struthoides Owen, 1844, Trans. Zool. Soc. Lond. **3**(3): 244.
Dinornis struthioides: Lydekker, 1891, Cat. Fossil Birds Brit. Mus: 242 (emendation).
Dinornis torosus Hutton, 1891, NZ J. Sci. new issue **1**(6): 247.
Palapteryx plenus Hutton, 1891, NZ J. Sci. new issue **1**(6): 248.
Dinornis strenuus Hutton, 1893, Trans. NZ Inst. **25**: 8.
Dinornis novaezealandiae: Archey, 1927, Trans. NZ Inst. **58**: 155.
Dinornis dromioides: Oliver, 1930, New Zealand Birds: 41.
Dinornis gazella Oliver, 1949, Dom. Mus. Bull. **15**: 166.

Fossil: Late Pleistocene — subrecent; North and South Islands; widespread, subfossil and midden.

ARCHEY, G. 1941. The moa. Bull. Auck. Inst. Mus. No. 1.
CRACRAFT, J. 1976. The species of moas (Aves: Dinornithidae). Smithsonian Contrib. Palaeobiology 27: 189–205.
MILLENER, P.R. 1981. The Quaternary avifauna of the North Island, New Zealand. Unpubl. PhD thesis (Geology). University of Auckland. 2 vols.

10   **Dinornis novaezealandiae** Owen

Dinornis novaezealandiae Owen, 1843, Proc. Zool. Soc. Lond. **11**: 121.
Dinornis ingens Owen, 1844, Trans. Zool. Soc. Lond. **3**(3): 247.
Dinornis ingens var. *robustus* Owen, 1846, Proc. Zool. Soc. Lond. **14**: 48.
Dinornis gracilis Owen, 1855, Proc. Zool. Soc. Lond. **22**: 246.
Palapteryx ingens: Haast, 1869, Trans. NZ Inst. **1**(8): 84.
Dinornis firmus Hutton, 1891, NZ J. Sci. new issue **1**(6): 247.
Dinornis potens Hutton, 1891, NZ J. Sci. new issue **1**(6): 247.

Fossil: Late Pleistocene — subrecent; North and South Islands; widespread, subfossil and midden.

ARCHEY, G. 1941. The moa. Bull. Auck. Inst. Mus. No.1.
CRACRAFT, J. 1976. The species of moas (Aves: Dinornithidae). Smithsonian Contrib. Palaeobiology 27: 189–205.
MILLENER, P.R. 1981. The Quaternary avifauna of the North Island, New Zealand. Unpubl. PhD thesis (Geology). University of Auckland. 2 vols.
WORTHY, T.H. 1989. Moas of the subalpine zone. Notornis 36: 191–196.

11   **Dinornis giganteus** Owen

Dinornis giganteus Owen, 1844, Proc. Zool. Soc. Lond. **11**(129): 144.
Dinornis maximus Haast, 1869, Trans. NZ Inst. **1**: 87.
Dinornis altus Owen, 1879, Extinct Birds of New Zealand: 361.
Dinornis validus Hutton, 1891, NZ J. Sci. new issue **1**(6): 247.
Dinornis excelsus Hutton, 1891, NZ J. Sci. new series **1**(6): 247.

Fossil: Late Pleistocene — subrecent; North and South Islands; widespread, subfossil and midden.

ARCHEY, G. 1941. The moa. Bull. Auck. Inst. Mus. No.1.
CRACRAFT, J. 1976. The species of moas (Aves: Dinornithidae). Smithsonian Contrib. Palaeobiology 27: 189–205.
MILLENER, P.R. 1981. The Quaternary avifauna of the North Island, New Zealand. Unpubl. PhD thesis (Geology). University of Auckland. 2 vols.

Order **APTERYGIFORMES**: Kiwis
Family **APTERYGIDAE**: Kiwis
Genus **Apteryx** Shaw and Nodder

Apteryx Shaw and Nodder, 1813, Nat. Miscell. 24, pl.1057, 1058 — type (by monotypy) *Apteryx australis* Shaw and Nodder.
Pseudapteryx Lydekker, 1891, Cat. Fossil Birds Br. Mus.: 218 — type (by monotypy) *Pseudapteryx gracilis* Lydekker.
Stictapteryx Iredale and Mathews, 1926, Bull. Br. Orn. Cl. 46: 76 — type *Apteryx owenii* Gould (*nomen nudum*).
Kiwi Verheyen, 1960, Bull. Roy. Soc. d'Anvers 15: 10 — type *Apteryx owenii*. (New, though unnecessary, name for *Stictapteryx* Iredale and Mathews.)

12 **Apteryx australis** Shaw and Nodder

Brown Kiwi

New Zealand. Originally probably throughout forest and scrub areas in the North Island; forests (except apparently Banks Peninsula) and subalpine–alpine zones in the South Island; and forests and scrub in Stewart Island. Restricted since European settlement to residual forests and adjacent semi-cleared scrub and rough farmland; under suitable conditions has entered exotic forests.

Apteryx australis mantelli Bartlett

North Island Brown Kiwi

Apteryx Mantelli Bartlett, Proc. Zool. Soc. Lond. 1850 (1851), p.275 — North Island.
Highest density is now in Northland, but well established also in inland Taranaki, western slopes of Ruapehu, King Country, inland northern Hawke's Bay and Urewera (together with northern end of the central mountain chain); also Kapiti Island (hybrid stock)*, Coromandel, Ponui Island (introduced), Kawau, and Little Barrier Island (probably from both native and introduced stocks: J.N. Jolly). Studies of the substantial population in Waitangi State Forest, Northland, showed that, although mature exotic forest (*Pinus elliotti* and *P. radiata*) is occupied, the birds require, during management and logging, adequate areas of swamp and residual native bush within the forest area.

Subfossil and midden records at many sites from the Far North to Wellington.

CALDER, W.A.; ROWE, B. 1977. Body mass changes and energetics of the kiwi's egg cycle. Notornis 24: 129–135.

---

*Both *A.a. mantelli* and *A.a. australis* were introduced to Kapiti: the genetics of the present population suggest that it is derived mainly from *A.a. australis* (C.H. Daugherty).

COLBOURNE, R.: KLEINPASTE, R. 1983. A banding study of North Island Brown Kiwis in an exotic forest. Notornis 30: 109–124.
McLENNAN, J.A.; RUDGE, M.R.; POTTER, M.A. 1987. Range size and denning behaviour of Brown Kiwi, *Apteryx australis mantelli*, in Hawke's Bay, New Zealand. NZ J. Ecol. 10: 97–107.
REID, B.; ROWE, B. 1978. Management of kiwis in captivity. Otorohanga Zool. Soc. Prog. Rep. 27 pp.
TABORSKY, M. 1988. Kiwis and dog predation: observations in Waitangi State Forest. Notornis 35: 197–202.

Apteryx australis australis Shaw and Nodder
South Island Brown Kiwi (Tokoeka)

Apteryx australis Shaw and Nodder, 1813, Nat. Miscell. 24, pl.1057 — Dusky Sound, South Island.

Apparently, in view of subfossil distribution, originally mainly in higher rainfall districts of the South Island (from western Marlborough, Nelson, inland Canterbury, Westland and Fiordland, including Secretary and Resolution Islands, to eastern Otago and Southland); no historical records from Banks Peninsula. Now common only in Fiordland, and present in scattered localities in south Westland; in Fiordland still well established in subalpine and alpine zones. Introduced to Kapiti Island (hybrid stock).

Commonly identified in subfossil and midden sites throughout (including one record from Banks Peninsula), but because most bones of this species cannot be reliably differentiated from those of *A. haastii*, the subfossil distribution of these two species is not certain.

REID, B.: WILLIAMS, G.R. 1975. The kiwi. Pages 301–330 *in* G. Kuschel (ed.). Biogeography and Ecology in New Zealand. The Hague: Junk.

Apteryx australis lawryi Rothschild
Stewart Island Brown Kiwi (Tokoeka)

Apteryx lawryi Rothschild, 1893, Bull. Br. Ornith. Club 1: 61 — Stewart Island.

Stewart Island (main island, and Ulva Island in Paterson Inlet), in forest and scrub. Several midden records.

GUTHRIE-SMITH, H. 1914. Mutton Birds and Other Birds. Wellington: Whitcombe and Tombs.
SOPER, M.F. 1976. New Zealand Birds, 2nd ed. Christchurch: Whitcoulls.

13   **Apteryx owenii** Gould
Little Spotted Kiwi (Kiwi-pukupuku)

Apteryx Owenii Gould, 1847, Proc. Zool. Soc. Lond., 1847, p. 93 — New Zealand.
Apteryx mollis Potts, 1873, Trans. NZ Inst. 5: 196 — Martins Bay.
Pseudapteryx gracilis Lydekker, 1891, Cat. Fossil Birds Br. Mus.: 218 — New Zealand (? Waingongoro, North Island).
Apteryx oweni occidentalis Rothschild, 1893, Bull. Br. Ornith. Club 1: 61 — Dusky Sound.
Stictapteryx owenii Iredale and Mathews, 1926, Bull. Br. Ornith. Club 46: 76 — *nomen nudum*.

Kiwi owenii Verheyen, 1960, Bull. Roy. Soc. d'Anvers 15: 10 — New Zealand.

On European settlement rare in the North Island (a specimen from Mt Hector, Tararua Range; reported from head of Hutt River and from Wangapopo, King Country); in South Island throughout forest areas of Marlborough, Nelson, Westland and Fiordland. Subfossil and midden records indicate a pre-European distribution extending throughout the North Island and most of South Island — apparently absent from eastern Canterbury (except possibly Banks Peninsula) and from eastern Otago and eastern Southland. Over the past 50 years, the only verifiable mainland records are a specimen from Orepuki, Southland (1938) and bones from a specimen dead for some time from the Junction Burn, Fiordland (1974) identified by R. J. Scarlett and P. R. Millener. In addition, it survived on D'Urville Island. Common on Kapiti Island; although Kapiti birds were long believed to have been derived from introduced stock, the report of the introduction seems to have been in error as the result of confusion with an introduction of the South Island Brown Kiwi, and so they are likely to be native to Kapiti (J. N. Jolly). Successfully transferred from Kapiti to Red Mercury Island and to Hen Island in 1988 and 1989. The last known birds on D'Urville Island were transferred to Long Island, Queen Charlotte Sound, in 1982 and 1987, together with birds from Kapiti.

JOLLY, J. N. 1980. Little Spotted Kiwi. Wildlife — A Review 11: 5–9.
MILLENER, P. R. 1987. Fossil birds in the British Museum — corrections to Lydekker's (1891) catalogue. Bull. Br. Ornith. Club 107: 168–172.
SCARLETT, R. J, 1979. Avifauna and man. *In* Birds of a Feather (ed. A. Anderson): NZ Arch. Assn. Monograph 11, B.A.R. 62: 75–90.

14 **Apteryx haastii** Potts

Great Spotted Kiwi (Roa)

Apteryx Haastii Potts, 1872, Trans. NZ Inst. 4: 204 — Westland.

Original distribution probably throughout Westland (from Bruce Bay northwards) and northwest Nelson. Now common and widespread only in forests of northwest Nelson and Paparoa Range; present in some headwaters as far south as the Karangarua River but apparent gaps in distribution between Paparoas and upper Grey and between Taipo River and Smyth River; extends across the divide (in high altitude beech forest) at various points between Arthur's Pass and Hope River. Subfossil from Pyramid Valley, North Canterbury (see under subfossil distribution of *A.a. australis*). Not recorded from the North Island, living or subfossil.

McLENNAN, J. A. in press. The Great Spotted Kiwi. *In* E. Fuller (ed.). A Monograph of Kiwis. Seto Publishing, Auckland.
REID, B.; WILLIAMS, G. R. 1975. The kiwi. Pages 301–330 *in* G. Kuschel (ed.). Biogeography and Ecology in New Zealand. The Hague: Junk.

Order **PODICIPEDIFORMES**: Grebes
Family **PODICIPEDIDAE**: Grebes
Genus **Podiceps** Latham

Podiceps Latham, 1787, Gen. Syn. Birds Suppl. 1: 294—type (by subsequent designation) *Colymbus cristatus* Linnaeus.

15   **Podiceps cristatus** (Linnaeus)

Great Crested Grebe

Colymbus cristatus Linnaeus, 1758, Syst. Nat. ed. 10, 1: 135—Sweden.
Europe, much of Asia, Africa south of the Sahara, Australia and New Zealand. Three subspecies.

Podiceps cristatus australis Gould

Australasian Crested Grebe (Puteketeke)

Podiceps australis Gould, 1844, Proc. Zool. Soc. Lond., p.135—Australia and New Zealand (error = New Zealand *apud* Mathews).
Australia (mainly southeast and southwest) and New Zealand. In New Zealand breeding South Island only; lowland lakes west of the Southern Alps; subalpine and alpine lakes within and east of the main ranges, with the greatest density in Canterbury. After a decline in Nelson, Marlborough, Otago and Southland has recolonised Marlborough. Some local movement between lakes; but seldom reported from salt water. Breeding population fewer than 100 pairs.

North Island: few acceptable records since European colonisation. One at Rotorua, December 1975—June 1976.
Subfossil from Taupo (cave) and Poukawa (swamp). Three North Island midden records (Tairua, Taupo, Paremata); only one South Island record (Lake Grassmere, dune/? midden).

O'DONNELL, C. F. J. 1981. Head plumage variation and winter plumage of the Southern Crested Grebe. Notornis 28: 212–213.
SAGAR, P. M. 1981. The distribution and numbers of Crested Grebe in New Zealand 1980. Notornis 28: 301–310.
SAGAR, P. M.; O'DONNELL, C. F. J. 1982. Seasonal movements and population of the Southern Crested Grebe in Canterbury. Notornis 29: 143–149.
WESTERSKOV, K. E. 1972. History of distribution of the Crested Grebe (*Podiceps cristatus*) in the North Island and Nelson–Marlborough. Notornis 19: 74–82.

Genus **Poliocephalus** Selby

Poliocephalus Selby, 1840, Cat. gener. subgen. Types Aves: 47—type (by monotypy) *Podiceps poliocephalus* Jardine and Selby.

16   **Poliocephalus rufopectus** (Gray)

New Zealand Dabchick (Weweia)

Podiceps (Poliocephalus) rufopectus G. R. Gray, 1843, *in* Dieffenbach's Trav. New Zealand, 2, p. 198—North Island, New Zealand.

New Zealand only. North Island: coastal and sand-dune lakes from North Cape to lower Waikato; and from southern Taranaki to Paraparaumu; lakes and dams of Volcanic Plateau south to Lakes Rotopounamu and Rotoaira: lakes and dams of Gisborne, Hawke's Bay and Wairarapa, with post-nuptial flocks forming especially in Wairarapa and Manawatu.

South Island: formerly sparingly distributed on lowland lakes, but declined rapidly in the 19th century; last proved breeding early 1940s (Eglinton Valley); only one recent record (Lake Elterwater, June 1987), presumably a vagrant from the North Island.

Total population, perhaps 600–700 breeding pairs.

Subfossil from one North Island site (Poukawa) and three South Island sites (Lake Grassmere, Waikari Cave, Pyramid Valley). Only one midden record (Whakamoenga Cave, Taupo).

Storer (1971) considered the New Zealand Dabchick to be closely related to the Australian Hoary-headed Grebe *Poliocephalus poliocephalus* and that the two forms differ both in behaviour and in morphology from the "true" dabchicks or little grebes (*Tachybaptus*). However, the relationship is not here considered close enough to be subspecific. (See also Fleming 1982, *George Edward Lodge: the Unpublished New Zealand Bird Paintings*, p. 69.)

BUDDLE, G. A. 1939. Some notes on the breeding habits of the Dabchick. Emu 39: 77–84.
HEATHER, B. D. 1988. A South Island puzzle—where have all the Dabchicks gone? Notornis 35: 185–191.
LUSK, C. H.; LUSK, J. R. 1981. The New Zealand Dabchick on Lake Rotoiti. Notornis 28: 203–208.
STIDOLPH, R. H. D.; HEATHER, B. D. 1978. Notes on post-breeding movements of the New Zealand Dabchick in the southern North Island. Notornis 25: 84–88.
STORER, R. W. 1971. The behaviour of the New Zealand Dabchick. Notornis 18: 175–186.
STORER, R. W. 1987. Morphology and relationships of the Hoary-headed Grebe and the New Zealand Dabchick. Emu 87: 150–157.

17 **Poliocephalus poliocephalus** (Jardine and Selby)
Hoary-headed Grebe

Podiceps poliocephalus Jardine and Selby, 1827, Illus. Orn. 1: pl. 13—New South Wales.

Australia, mostly south of 25°, and Tasmania; an irregular visitor elsewhere throughout much of Australia.

First New Zealand records: Boat Harbour, The Snares, one, February 1975; Lake Horowhenua, one, July 1975; Te Anau district, two, November 1975. One then two pairs bred in Southland, 1976 to 1978; breeding not known in North Island. Widely scattered sightings in 1977–1978, mostly of single birds, in North and South Islands north to Aupouri Peninsula. Few records since; apparently has not established in New Zealand.

BARLOW, M. L. 1976. Breeding of Hoary-headed Grebe in Southland. Notornis 23: 183–187.
BEST, H. A. 1976. First sightings of the Hoary-headed Grebe (*Podiceps poliocephalus*) in New Zealand. Notornis 23: 182–183.
FJELDSA, J. 1983. Social behaviour and displays of the Hoary-headed Grebe. Emu 83: 129–140.
STORER, R. W. 1987. Morphology and relationships of the Hoary-headed Grebe and the New Zealand Dabchick. Emu 87: 150–157.

Genus **Tachybaptus** Reichenbach

Tachybaptus Reichenbach, 1852 (1853), Avium Syst. nat.: 3 — type (by monotypy) *Colymbus minor* = *Colymbus ruficollis* Pallas.

The genus includes the four Eastern Hemisphere species *novae-hollandiae, ruficollis, pelzelni* and *rufolavatus* (Storer, 1963. Proc. XIII Int. orn. Congress 1: 562–9).

18   **Tachybaptus novaehollandiae** (Stephens)
Eastern Little Grebe

Indonesia, southern New Guinea, New Caledonia, New Hebrides, Australia, Tasmania and New Zealand.

Tachybaptus novaehollandiae novaehollandiae (Stephens)
Australasian Little Grebe

Podiceps novaehollandiae Stephens, 1826, Shaw's Gen. Zool. 13: 18 — New South Wales.

Australia (mainly northern, southwestern and eastern) and Tasmania.

First New Zealand records: near Arrowtown, one, 1968; near Dargaville, two, 1972 (attempted breeding); Lake Okareka, one, 1973. North Island: by early 1980s, breeding on small sheltered ponds from Aupouri Peninsula to southern Kaipara, forming small flocks in autumn (maximum 20 on Lake Rotokawau, Karikari Peninsula, 1983); has apparently declined, the only recent breeding reports being of a pair on Lake Kereta, southern Kaipara, but may still breed elsewhere in Northland. South Island: pairs or family parties seen until mid-1980s on at least eight widely scattered small lakes from Elterwater, Marlborough, to Redcliff, Southland, and on both sides of the Southern Alps (maximum groups five at Redcliff in 1978 and six adults with four young at St Anne's Lagoon, northern Canterbury, in 1980). Has apparently declined, breeding still on St Anne's Lagoon and probably Lake Rotoiti, Kaikoura.

CHANCE, G. R. 1969. A new bird for New Zealand — Australian Little Grebe, at Arrowtown. Notornis 16: 3–4.
LAUDER, C. S. 1978. Breeding of Australian Little Grebe. Notornis 25: 251–252.
LYLE, G. W. 1973. Australian Little Grebe on Lake Okareka. Notornis 20: 279–280.

MARCHANT, S.; FULLAGAR, P.J.; DAVEY, C.C. 1989. Nesting of the Australian Grebe, *Tachybaptus novaehollandiae*. Aust. Birds 23: 2–6.
MILLER, P. 1973. Second record of the Australian Little Grebe in New Zealand. Notornis 20: 272–75.

Order **PROCELLARIIFORMES**: Tube-nosed Birds
Family **DIOMEDEIDAE**: Albatrosses, Mollymawks
Genus **Manu** Marples

Manu Marples, 1946, Trans. Roy. Soc. NZ 76: 133—type (by monotypy)
Manu antiquus Marples.

19   **Manu antiquus** Marples

Manu antiquus Marples, 1946, Trans. Roy. Soc. NZ 76: 133—Duntroon.
Fossil (Middle/Late Oligocene); Duntroon in North Otago.
MARPLES, B.J. 1946. Notes on some neognathous bird bones from the Early Tertiary of New Zealand. Trans. Roy. Soc. NZ 76: 132–134.

Genus **Diomedea** Linnaeus

Diomedea Linnaeus, 1758, Syst. Nat., ed. 10: 132—type (by subsequent designation) G. R. Gray, 1840, List Gen. Birds: 78, *Diomedea exulans* Linnaeus.
Phoebastria Reichenbach, 1853, Avium Syst. Nat. (1852): 5—type (by original designation) *Diomedea brachyura* Temminck = *Diomedea albatrus* Pallas.
Thalassarche Reichenbach, 1853, Avium Syst. Nat. (1852): 5—type (by original designation) *Diomedea melanophrys* Temminck.
Thalassogeron Ridgway, 1884, *in* Baird, Brewer, and Ridgway, Mem. Mus. Comp. Zool. 13: 345, 357—type (by original designation) *Diomedea culminata* Gould = *Diomedea chrysostoma* J. R. Forster.
Nealbatrus Mathews, 1912, Birds Aust. 2: 274—type (by original designation) *Diomedea chlororhynchos* Gmelin.
Diomedella Mathews, 1912, Birds Aust. 2: 275—type (by original designation) *Diomedea cauta* Gould.
Rhothonia Murphy, 1917, Bull. Am. Mus. Nat. Hist. 37: 861—type (by original designation) *Diomedea (Rhothonia) sanfordi* Murphy = *Diomedea epomophora* Lesson.
Julietata Mathews, 1943, *in* Mathews & Hallstrom, Notes Order Procellariiformes: 27—type (by original designation) *Diomedea irrorata* Salvin.
Galapagornis Boetticher, 1949, Beitr. Gattungssystematik Vögel: 27—type (by original designation) *Diomedea irrorata* Salvin.
Laysanornis Boetticher, 1949, Beitr. Gattungssystematik Vögel: 27—type (by original designation) *Diomedea immutabilis* Rothschild.
Penthirenia Boetticher, 1949, Beitr. Gattungssystematik Vögel: 27—type (by original designation) *Diomedea nigripes* Audubon.

20   **Diomedea exulans** Linnaeus

Wandering Albatross

Diomedea exulans Linnaeus, 1758, Syst. Nat., ed. 10, 1: 132—Cape of Good Hope.
The southern oceans, breeding on islands between 37°S and 55°S, wandering south to about 65°S, north to about 25°S, and circumpolar. Stragglers have entered the North Atlantic.

As a review by C.J. R. Robertson and J. Warham, including the description of new subspecies from New Zealand, is in preparation, this species is treated monotypically. In the New

Zealand area, breeds on Macquarie, Auckland, Antipodes and Campbell Islands.

Subfossil and midden material of this and/or the following species has been found in numerous North, South and Chatham Island sites but, in most cases, specific assignation cannot be made with certainty.

21 **Diomedea epomophora** Lesson

Royal Albatross (Toroa)

The southern oceans, breeding in southern New Zealand and on nearby islands, ranging into New Zealand and Australian seas, migrating to seas off western and southeastern coasts of South America, and the Falkland Islands, but rare in the Indian Ocean and in the southeast Atlantic Ocean.

Diomedea epomophora epomophora Lesson

Southern Royal Albatross

Diomedaea(sic) *epomophora* Lesson, 1825, Ann. Sci. Nat., Paris 6: 95 — no locality given.
Diomedea regia Buller, 1891, Trans. NZ Inst. 22: 230 — Campbell Island.
Diomedea epomophora mccormicki Mathews, 1912, Birds Aust. 2: 261 — Enderby Island.
Diomedea epomophora longirostris Mathews, 1934, Bull. Br. Ornith. Club 54: 112 — South Atlantic Ocean.

Breeds on Campbell Island (up to 8000 pairs) and on Enderby, Adams and Auckland Islands (about 60 pairs). Ranges into New Zealand seas north to Cook Strait, and to Australia. Migrates to seas off western and southeastern coasts of South America, and the Falkland Islands. Recorded widely in subantarctic seas, and strays to 20°S in the Pacific Ocean.

BAILEY, A. M.; SORENSEN, J. H. 1950. Subantarctic Campbell Island. Denver: Denver Mus. Nat. Hist.
ROBERTSON, C.J.R.; KINSKY, F.C. 1972. The dispersal movements of the Royal Albatross (*Diomedea epomophora*). Notornis 19: 289–301.
RUDGE, M. R. 1986. The decline and increase of feral sheep (*Ovis aries* L.) on Campbell Island. NZ J. Ecol. 9: 89–100.
TAYLOR, R. H; BELL, B. D.; WILSON, P. R. 1970. Royal Albatross, feral sheep and cattle on Campbell Island. NZ J. Sci. 13: 78–88.

Diomedea epomophora sanfordi Murphy

Northern Royal Albatross

Diomedea (Rhothonia) sanfordi Murphy, 1917, Bull. Am. Mus. Nat. Hist. 37: 861 64 km off Corral, Chile.

Breeds at the Chatham Islands on The Sisters (about 2700 pairs) and The Forty Fours (about 5000 pairs), and at Taiaroa Head, Otago Peninsula (about 25 pairs). Ranges particularly east of the North Island as far north as East Cape during the breeding season. Migrates east to the coasts of South America, particularly off Chile, Argentina and the Falkland Islands.

RICHDALE, L. E. 1950. The pre-egg stage in the albatross family. Biol. Mono. 3: the author.
RICHDALE, L. E. 1952. The post-egg period in albatrosses. Biol. Mono. 4: the author.
ROBERTSON, C. J. R. 1971. The Royal Albatross at Taiaroa Head. Wildlife — A Review 3: 46–49.
ROBERTSON, C. J. R. 1973. Royal Albatross. Wildlife — A Review 4: 10–12.

22   **Diomedea nigripes** Audubon
Black-footed Albatross

Diomedea nigripes Audubon, 1839, Ornith. Biog. 5: 327 — Pacific Ocean 30°44′N, 146°W.
Phoebastria nigripes reischekia Mathews, 1930, Bull. Br. Ornith. Club 51: 29 — New Zealand.

North Pacific Ocean, breeding on the Leeward Hawaiian Islands and on Tori Shima, Izu Islands; ranging mainly into the north-eastern Pacific. Only one NZ (and Southern Hemisphere) record: Dusky Sound, July 1884, A. Reischek collection.

RICE, D. W.; KENYON, K. W. 1962. Breeding cycles and behavior of Laysan and Black-footed Albatrosses. Auk 79: 517–567.

23   **Diomedea melanophrys** Temminck
Black-browed Mollymawk

The southern oceans, circumpolar, breeding on islands between 46°S and 56°S, ranging extensively between 30°S and the coasts of Antarctica: furthest north in winter, furthest south in summer. Occasional vagrant far into the North Atlantic, where it has prospected nest sites, and to the central Pacific.

Diomedea melanophrys melanophrys Temminck
Black-browed Mollymawk

Diomedea melanophris Temminck, 1828, Planches Color., livr. 77, pl.456 and text — Cape of Good Hope. (Spelling corrected to *melanophrys* by Temminck, 1839, Planches Color., Tableau Method., livr. 102: 76.)
Thalassarche melanophris belcheri Mathews, 1912, Birds Aust. 2: 271 — Kerguelen.
Thalassarche melanophris richmondi Mathews, 1912, Birds Aust. 2: 272 — west coast of South America.

Breeds abundantly on islands off southern Chile (Diego de Almagro, Ildefonso, Evout, Diego Ramirez), on Staten Island, at the Falklands, South Georgia, Crozets, Kerguelen, Heard and Macquarie (Bishop and Clerk), with about 150 pairs on Bollons Island (Antipodes Islands) and a few on the Western Chain (The Snares) and Campbell Island.

Ranges widely between 30°S and Antarctic coasts in all oceans, including seas off mainland New Zealand, particularly in winter months.

CLARK, G. S.; GOODWIN, A. J.; von MEYER, A. P. 1984. Extension of the known range of some seabirds on the coast of southern Chile. Notornis 31: 320–324.

PRINCE, P. A. 1980. The food and feeding ecology of the Grey-headed Albatross *Diomedea chrysostoma* and Black-browed Albatross *D. melanophris*. Ibis 122: 476–488.
PRINCE, P. A. 1981. The Black-browed Albatross *Diomedea melanophris* population at Beauchêne Island, Falkland Islands. Com. Nat. Franc. Rech. Antarct. 51: 111–117.
TICKELL, W. L. N. 1976. The distribution of Black-browed and Grey-headed Albatrosses. Emu 76: 64–68.
TICKELL, W. L. N.; PINDER, R. 1975. Breeding biology of the Black-browed Albatross *Diomedea melanophris* and Grey-headed Albatross *D. chrysostoma* at Bird Island, South Georgia. Ibis 117: 433–450.

Diomedea melanophrys impavida (Mathews)
New Zealand Black-browed Mollymawk

Thalassarche melanophris impavida Mathews, 1912, Birds Aust. 2: 267, pl.96—Tasmania.

Breeds only on the northern coasts of Campbell Island (c.24 000 pairs). Ranges widely in New Zealand seas and the Tasman Sea to eastern Australia; north to about 16°S in the Pacific Ocean, particularly in winter. Not reported from other oceans.

BAILEY, A. M.; SORENSEN, J. H. 1950. Subantarctic Campbell Island. Denver: Denver Mus. Nat. Hist.

24 Diomedea cauta Gould
White-capped (Shy) Mollymawk

Diomedea cauta Gould, 1841, Proc. Zool. Soc. Lond. (1840): 177—Bass Strait.

Breeds in the southwest Pacific between 40°S and 50°S, ranging mainly in the South Pacific between 35°S and 55°S, but migrating to seas off South Africa, Peru, Chile and Argentina. Vagrant to the northeast Pacific.

Four subspecies, three breeding in the New Zealand region. Widespread subfossil and midden records: not distinguishable to subspecies.

Diomedea cauta steadi Falla
New Zealand White-capped (Shy) Mollymawk

Thalassarche cauta steadi Falla, 1933, Rec. Auck. Inst. Mus.1: 179—Foveaux Strait.

Breeds on Disappointment, Auckland and Adams Islands of the Auckland Islands (c. 64 000 pairs). Ranges north into seas off mainland New Zealand. Immatures may reach South African seas, but movements not well known.

BOURNE, W. R. P. 1977. Albatrosses occurring off South Africa. Cormorant 2: 7–10.

Diomedea cauta salvini (Rothschild)
Salvin's Mollymawk

Thalassogeron salvini Rothschild, 1893, Bull. Br. Ornith. Club 1: 58—New Zealand.
Diomedea cauta peruvia Mathews, 1933, Bull. Br. Ornith. Club 53: 185—western Peru.

Diomedella cauta atlantica Mathews, 1933, Bull. Br. Ornith. Club 53: 213–35°44'S, 53°W, southwest Atlantic Ocean off Argentina.

Breeds on the Bounty Islands (c. 76 000 pairs) and on the Western Chain of The Snares (c. 650 pairs). Ranges throughout New Zealand seas, particularly eastern side, and migrates to seas off Peru, Chile and Argentina. A few pairs recently discovered breeding on Penguin Island (Crozet Islands).

MISKELLY, C. M. 1984. Birds of the Western Chain, Snares Islands 1983–84. Notornis 31: 209–223.

ROBERTSON, C. J. R; VAN TETS, G. F. 1982. The status of birds at the Bounty Islands. Notornis 29: 311–336.

Diomedea cauta eremita (Murphy)

Chatham Island Mollymawk

Thalassarche cauta eremita Murphy, 1930, Am. Mus. Novit. 419: 4—The Pyramid, Chatham Islands.

Breeds on The Pyramid at the Chatham Islands (c. 4000 pairs). Ranges to Bass Strait, seas off mainland New Zealand, and the central South Pacific Ocean, but rarely seen away from The Pyramid.

FLEMING, C. A. 1939. Birds of the Chatham Islands. Part I. Emu 38: 380–413.

25   Diomedea chrysostoma Forster

Grey-headed Mollymawk

Diomedea chrysostoma J. R. Forster, 1785, Mem. Math. Phys. Acad. Sci., Paris, 10: 571, pl.14—vicinity of the Antarctic Circle and in the Pacific Ocean.

Thalassogeron desolationis Salvadori, 1911, Boll. Mus. Zool. Anat. Comp. Univ. Torino 26 (no.638): 2—Desolation Island, Tierra del Fuego, 52°S, 74°W.

Thalassogeron chrysostoma harterti Mathews, 1912, Birds Aust. 2: 280—46°52'S, 85°E.

Diomedea culminata mathewsi Rothschild, 1912, Bull. Br. Ornith. Club 29: 70—Campbell Island?

Thalassogeron chrysostoma alexanderi Mathews, 1916, Austral Avian Rec.3: 55—west coast of Australia.

Circumpolar, breeding at Diego Ramirez Islands, South Georgia, Marion and Prince Edward Islands, Crozet, Kerguelen, Macquarie and Campbell Islands. At least 5 800 pairs breed on the northern coasts of Campbell Island.

Ranges particularly in higher latitudes between 35°S and the edge of the pack-ice. Frequently wrecked on New Zealand coasts but, other than during storms, not often seen off the mainland. Vagrant (possibly human-assisted) to Northern Hemisphere.

PRINCE, P. A. 1980. The food and feeding ecology of the Grey-headed Albatross *Diomedea chrysostoma* and Black-browed Albatross *D. melanophris*. Ibis 122: 476–488.

TICKELL, W. L. N. 1976. The distribution of Black-browed and Grey-headed Albatrosses. Emu 76: 64–68.

TICKELL, W. L. N.; PINDER, R. 1975. Breeding biology of the Black-browed Albatross *Diomedea melanophris* and Grey-headed Albatross *D. chrysostoma* at Bird Island, South Georgia. Ibis 117: 433–450.

26   Diomedea chlororhynchos Gmelin
Yellow-nosed Mollymawk

Breeds in the South Atlantic and Indian Oceans between 37°S and 47°S, and between 13°W and 78°E, on four archipelagoes. Ranges mainly between 30°S and 50°S in the Atlantic and Indian Oceans, and in Australian seas, but reaches northern New Zealand regularly. Straggler to the North Atlantic.

Diomedea chlororhynchos chlororhynchos Gmelin
Atlantic Yellow-nosed Mollymawk

Diomedea chlororhynchos Gmelin, 1789, Syst. Nat. 1: 568; based on "Yellow-nosed Albatross" of Latham, 1785, General Synop. Birds 3: 309, pl.94—Cape of Good Hope.
Thalassogeron eximius G.E. Verrill, 1895, Trans. Conn. Acad. Arts Sci. 9: 440, pl.8—Gough Island.
Diomedea melanoptera Miranda-Ribeiro, 1928, Bol. Mus. Nacn. Rio de Janeiro 4 (part 4): 45—no locality but restricted to Tristan da Cunha by Mathews, 1948, Bull. Br. Ornith. Club 68: 162.

Breeds on the Tristan da Cunha Islands (Inaccessible, Nightingale, Tristan da Cunha, Gough), and ranges widely in the South Atlantic Ocean. One vagrant found prospecting on Middle Sister Island, Chatham Islands, on 21 January 1975.

BROOKE, R.K.; SINCLAIR, J.C.; BERRUTI, A. 1980. Geographical variation in *Diomedea chlororhynchos* (Aves: Diomedeidae). Durban Mus. Novit. 12: 171–180.
ROBERTSON, C.J.R. 1975. Yellow-nosed Mollymawk (*Diomedea chlororhynchus*) (*sic*) recorded in the Chatham Islands. Notornis 22: 342–344.
ROWAN, M.K. 1951. The Yellow-nosed Albatross *Diomedea chlororhynchos* Gmelin, at its breeding grounds in the Tristan da Cunha Group. Ostrich 22: 139–155.

Diomedea chlororhynchos carteri (Rothschild)
Yellow-nosed Mollymawk

Thalassogeron carteri Rothschild, 1903, Bull. Br. Ornith. Club 14: 6—Point Cloates, Western Australia.
Diomedea bassi Mathews, 1912, Novit. Zool. 18: 206—southeast Australian seas.

Breeds on Prince Edward Island, Crozet Islands (Penguin Island), and on Amsterdam and St Paul Islands. Ranges mainly between 22°S and 50°S in the Indian Ocean and Australian seas. Now a regular visitor to seas of northern North Island and Bay of Plenty, usually in winter (non-breeding season). A little-studied Mollymawk.

(*Note*: C.J.R. Robertson has examined the holotype of *T. carteri* and found that it is of the Indian Ocean form.)

CLASSIFIED SUMMARISED NOTES 1979–1985 Yellow-nosed Mollymawk Notornis 26–32.
LATHAM, P.C.M. 1980. Yellow-nosed Mollymawks in the Bay of Plenty. Notornis 27: 393–394.
SERVENTY, D.L.; SERVENTY, V.; WARHAM, J. 1971. The Handbook of Australian Sea-birds. Sydney: Reed.

27   **Diomedea bulleri** Rothschild
                                           Buller's Mollymawk
Breeds only in the New Zealand region on The Snares, Solander
Islands, Chatham Islands and Three Kings Islands. Ranges in
the Pacific Ocean from eastern Australian seas to the coasts of
Chile and Peru. Subfossil and midden records probably include
both subspecies.

Diomedea bulleri bulleri Rothschild
                                     Southern Buller's Mollymawk
Diomedea bulleri Rothschild, 1893, Bull. Br. Ornith. Club 1: 58 — New Zealand.
Breeds on The Snares (c.5550 pairs) and on Solander Islands
(c.5000 pairs). Ranges from seas off the South Island to the
Auckland Islands and to seas off southeastern Australia; migrates
to eastern South Pacific Ocean off Chile and Peru.
COOPER, W.J.; MISKELLY, C. M.; MORRISON, K.; PEACOCK, R.J. 1986.
Birds of the Solander Islands. Notornis 33: 77–89.
RICHDALE, L. E. 1949a. Buller's Mollymawk: incubation data. Bird-banding
20: 127–141.
RICHDALE, L. E. 1949b. The pre-egg stage in Buller's Mollymawk. Dunedin: the
author.
WARHAM, J.; BENNINGTON, S. L. 1983. A census of Buller's Albatross *Diomedea
bulleri* at the Snares Islands, New Zealand. Emu 83: 112–114.
WEST, J.A.; IMBER, M.J. 1986. Some foods of Buller's Mollymawk *Diomedea
bulleri*. NZ J. Zool. 13: 169–174.

Diomedea bulleri platei Reichenow
                                     Northern Buller's Mollymawk
Diomedea platei Reichenow, 1898, Ornith. Monatsber. 6: 190 — Cavancha, Chile.
Breeds on The Sisters (c.2000 pairs) and The Forty Fours
(c.24 000 pairs), Chatham Islands, and on Rosemary Rock,
Three Kings Islands (c.15 pairs). Ranges mainly about the
Chatham Islands and in seas east of New Zealand; migrates to
seas off Chile and Peru. Absent from Chatham Islands seas from
late June to early September.
FLEMING, C.A. 1939. Birds of the Chatham Islands. Part 1. Emu 38: 380–413.
McCALLUM, J.; BROOK, F.; FRANCIS, M. 1985. Buller's Mollymawks on
Rosemary Rock, Three Kings Islands, in 1985. Notornis 32: 257–259.
WEST, J.A.; IMBER, M.J. 1986. Some foods of Buller's Mollymawk *Diomedea
bulleri*. NZ J. Zool. 13: 169–174.
WRIGHT, A.E. 1984. Buller's Mollymawks breeding at the Three Kings Islands.
Notornis 31: 203–207.

Genus **Phoebetria** Reichenbach

Phoebetria Reichenbach, 1853, Avium Syst. Nat. (1852): 5 — type (by original designation) *Diomedea fuliginosa* Gmelin = *Diomedea palpebrata* J. R. Forster.

28   **Phoebetria palpebrata** (Forster)
                          Light-mantled Sooty Albatross

Diomedea palpebrata J.R. Forster, 1785, Mem. Math. Phys. Acad. Sci., Paris,
10: 571, pl.15 — south of Marion and Prince Edward Islands, *fide* Mathews, 1934,
Novit. Zool. 39: 157.
Phoebetria palpebrata huttoni Mathews, 1912, Birds Aust. 2: 297 — New Zealand seas.
Phoebetria palpebrata antarctica Mathews, 1912, Birds Aust. 2: 302 — South Georgia.
Phoebetria palpebrata auduboni Nichols and Murphy, 1914, Auk 31: 531 — mouth of
the Columbia River, Oregon.
Phoebetria palpebrata murphyi Mathews and Iredale, 1921, Manual Birds Aust.: 50
(in text) — new name for *antarctica*.

Breeds at South Georgia, Marion and Prince Edward Islands,
Crozet Islands, Kerguelen, and Heard, Macquarie, Auckland,
Campbell and Antipodes Islands. Recorded subfossil on
Chatham Island. Circumpolar, ranging mainly between 40°S
and the coasts of Antarctica but occasionally north to within
30°S to 40°S. Possible straggler north of the equator.

BERRUTI, A. 1979. The breeding biologies of the sooty albatrosses, *Phoebetria fusca*
and *P. palpebrata*. Emu 79: 161–175.
MOUGIN, J.-L. 1970. Les albatros fuligineux *Phoebetria palpebrata* et *P. fusca* de l'île
de la Possession (Archipel Crozet). L'Oiseau Rev. fr. Ornith. 40 (no. spécial):
37–61.
POWLESLAND, R. G. 1985. Seabirds found dead on New Zealand beaches in 1983
and a review of albatross recoveries since 1960. Notornis 32: 23–41.
SORENSEN, J. H. 1950. The Light-mantled Sooty Albatross at Campbell Island.
NZ DSIR, Cape Exped. Ser., Bull. 8: 30pp.
THOMAS, G. 1982. The food and feeding ecology of the Light-mantled Sooty
Albatross at South Georgia. Emu 82: 92–100.
THOMAS, G.; CROXALL, J. P.; PRINCE, P. A. 1983. Breeding biology of the
Light-mantled Sooty Albatross (*Phoebetria palpebrata*) at South Georgia, J. Zool.
(Lond.) 199: 123–135.

Family **PROCELLARIIDAE**: Shearwaters, Diving
Petrels, Fulmars, Prions and Gadfly Petrels
Subfamily PROCELLARIINAE: Shearwaters and
Diving Petrels
Genus **Calonectris** Mathews and Iredale

Calonectris Mathews and Iredale, 1915, Ibis (1915): 590, 592 — type (by original
designation) *Procellaria leucomelas* Temminck.

29   **Calonectris diomedea** (Scopoli)
                          North Atlantic Shearwater

Procellaria diomedea Scopoli, 1769, Annus I Hist. Nat. p.74 — no locality (Tremiti
Islands, Adriatic Sea, designated by Committee on Nomenclature, Br. Ornith.
Union, 1946, Ibis 88: 534).

Breeds on islands in the Mediterranean Sea and in the eastern
North Atlantic between 15°N and 40°N. Ranges widely in those

seas and migrates to the South Atlantic Ocean and southwest Indian Ocean. Probably three subspecies, only one having reached New Zealand.

Calonectris diomedea borealis (Cory)
North Atlantic (Cory's) Shearwater

Puffinus borealis Cory, 1881, Bull. Nuttall Ornith. Club 6: 84 — off Chatham Island, Massachusetts, U.S.A.

Puffinus kuhli fortunatus Bannerman, 1915, Bull. Br. Ornith. Club 35: 120 — Isla Graciosa, Canary Islands.

Breeds on The Berlengas (Portugal), Madeira, Porto Santo Islands, Desertas, Salvages, The Azores and Canary Islands. Ranges extensively in the North Atlantic Ocean and migrates south to Argentina and seas off southern Africa. One New Zealand record: Foxton Beach, January 1934 (specimen).

JOUANIN, C.; ROUX, F.; ZINO, P. A. 1977. Sur les premiers résultats du baguage des Puffins Cendrés aux îles Selvagens. Oiseau Rev. fr. Ornith. 47: 351–358.

OLIVER, W. R. B. 1934. Occurrence of the Mediterranean Shearwater in New Zealand. Emu 34: 23–24.

ZINO, P. A. 1971. The breeding of Cory's Shearwater *Calonectris diomedea* on the Salvage Islands. Ibis 113: 212–217.

Genus **Puffinus** Brisson

Puffinus Brisson, 1760, Ornith. 1: 56, 6: 129–130 — type (by tautonymy) *Puffinus = Procellaria puffinus* Brünnich.

Nectris Kuhl, 1820, Beitr. Zool. vergl. Anat.: 146 — type (by subsequent designation) *Procellaria puffinus* Brünnich.

Thyellas Gloger, 1827, Froriep's Notiz.: 279 — new name for *Puffinus* Brisson.

Rhipornis Billberg, 1828, Syn. Faun. Scand. 1: tab. A — new name for *Puffinus* Brisson.

Cymotomus Macgillivray, 1842, Man. Br. Ornith. 2: 13 — type (by monotypy) *Procellaria puffinus* Brünnich.

Ardenna Reichenbach, 1853, Avium Syst. Nat. (1852): 4 — type (by original designation) *Puffinus maior* Faber = *Puffinus gravis* O'Reilly.

Thyellodroma Stejneger, 1888, Proc. U.S. Nat. Mus. 11: 93 — type (by original designation) *Puffinus sphenurus* Gould = *Puffinus chlororhynchus* Lesson.

Zalias Heine and Reichenow, 1890, Nom. Mus. Hein. ornith.: 362 — type (by subsequent designation) *Puffinus chlororhynchus* Lesson.

Reinholdia Mathews, 1912, Austral Avian Rec. 1: 107 — type (by original designation and monotypy) *Puffinus reinholdi* Mathews = *Procellaria gavia* J. R. Forster.

Neonectris Mathews, 1913, Austral Avian Rec. 2: 12 — type (by original designation) *Puffinus brevicaudus* Gould = *Procellaria tenuirostris* Temminck.

Hemipuffinus Iredale, 1913, Austral Avian Rec. 2: 20 — type (by original designation) *Puffinus carneipes* Gould.

Alphapuffinus Mathews, 1913, Austral Avian Rec. 2: 110 — type (by original designation) *Puffinus assimilis* Gould.

Microzalias Mathews and Iredale, 1915, Ibis (1915): 597 — type (by original designation and monotypy) *Puffinus nativitatis* Streets.

Cinathisma Hull, 1916, Emu 15: 205 — type (by monotypy) *Cinathisma cyaneoleuca* Hull = *Procellaria gavia* J. R. Forster.

Paranectris Iredale, 1930, Austral. Zool. 6: 115—type (by original designation) *Procellaria grisea* Gmelin.

Subgenus **Ardenna**

0 **Puffinus creatopus** Coues

Pink-footed Shearwater

Puffinus creatopus Coues, 1864, Proc. Acad. Nat. Sci. Philadelphia (1864): 131—San Nicolas Island, California.

Breeds on Mas-a-Tierra and Santa Clara (Juan Fernandez Islands), and on Mocha Island, Chile. Migrates to eastern North Pacific as far as Alaska and wanders to Hawaiian and Line Islands. Ranges mainly over continental shelf seas.

One New Zealand record: outer Canterbury Bight, 7–9 June 1979, at least 2 seen.

MURPHY, R. C. 1936. Oceanic Birds of South America. Vol.II. New York: Am. Mus. Nat. Hist.

TUNNICLIFFE, G. A. 1982. First sightings of the North Atlantic (Cory's) Shearwater *Calonectris diomedea* (Scopoli, 1769) in Australasian seas. Notornis 29: 85–91.

TUNNICLIFFE, G. A. 1984. Correction: North Atlantic Shearwater to Pink-footed Shearwater. Notornis 31: 130.

31 **Puffinus carneipes** Gould

Flesh-footed Shearwater

Puffinus carneipes Gould, 1844, Ann. Mag. Nat. Hist. 13: 365—Seal Island, Cape Leeuwin, Western Australia.

Puffinus carneipes carbonarius Mathews, 1912, Birds Aust. 2: 90—off Three Kings Islands, New Zealand (*ex* Solander MS). Renamed *P.c. zealandicus* 1926, Bull. Br. Ornith. Club 46: 76; and *P.c. neozealandicus* 1926, Bull. Br. Ornith. Club 46: 93.

Puffinus carneipes hakodate Mathews, 1912, Birds Aust. 2: 90—seas off Japan.

Puffinus carneipes hullianus Mathews, 1912, Birds Aust. 2: 90—Norfolk Island (error) = Lord Howe Island.

Breeds on St Paul Island (Indian Ocean), on many islands off the south coast of Western Australia from Cape Hamelin to the Recherche Archipelago, on Lord Howe Island, and in New Zealand on islands off the North Island and in Cook Strait (Hen and Chickens – particularly Coppermine, Mercury group, The Aldermen, Karewa, Saddleback off New Plymouth, Trio and Titi Islands in Cook Strait). Ranges mainly over the North Island continental shelf but south as far as Foveaux Strait in the west and Banks Peninsula to the Chatham Islands in the east. Subfossil and midden records, North Island; subfossil in Chatham Island dunes.

Western populations migrate northwestwards to the Arabian Sea. Eastern (Lord Howe Island and New Zealand) birds migrate to the North Pacific, mainly to seas east of Korea and off Japan but also across to the west coast of North America.

FALLA, R. A. 1934. The distribution and breeding habits of petrels in northern New Zealand. Rec. Auck. Inst. Mus. 1: 245–260.

GUZMAN, J. R.; MYRES, M. T. 1983. Occurrence of shearwaters (*Puffinus* spp.) off the west coast of Canada. Can. J. Zool. 81: 2064–2077.
HINDWOOD, K. A. 1945. The Fleshy-footed Shearwater (*Puffinus carneipes*). Emu 44: 241–248.
WARHAM, J. 1958. The nesting of the shearwater *Puffinus carneipes*. Auk 75: 1–14.

Subgenus **Thyellodroma**

32   **Puffinus pacificus** (Gmelin)

Wedge-tailed Shearwater

Breeds on islands in the Indian and Pacific Oceans, mainly between 30°N and 30°S, and ranges widely in adjacent seas. Some subtropical populations migrate transequatorially. Two subspecies accepted here.

Puffinus pacificus pacificus (Gmelin)

Wedge-tailed Shearwater

Procellaria pacifica Gmelin, 1789, Syst. Nat. 1: 560 (based on "Pacific Petrel" of Latham, 1785, General Synop. Birds 3: 416 — Pacific Ocean) — restricted to Kermadec Islands by Mathews, 1912, Birds Aust. 2: 80.
Puffinus chlororhynchus iredali Mathews, 1910, Bull. Br. Ornith. Club 27: 40 — Sunday = Raoul Island, Kermadec Islands.
Puffinus pacificus whitneyi Lowe, 1925, Bull. Br. Ornith. Club 45: 106 — Kadavu, Fiji Islands.

Breeds on Kermadec (probably all), Norfolk (probably all), Fiji (Kadavu, Mamanuca, Yasawa, Lau groups and other islets) and some Tonga Islands.

Ranges widely in adjacent seas to about 35°S and straggles to North Island coasts: Auckland west and east coasts, November to April, about 8 beach-wrecked. Migrates apparently to the southeastern area of the North Pacific Ocean.

CROCKETT, D. E. 1975. Kermadec Islands Expedition reports: The Wedge-tailed Shearwater (*Puffinus p. pacificus*) in the northern Kermadecs. Notornis 22: 1–9.
JENKINS, J. A. F. 1979. Observations on the Wedge-tailed Shearwater (*Puffinus pacificus*) in the south-west Pacific. Notornis 26: 331–348.
JENKINS, J. A. F. 1986. The seabirds of Fiji. An account based on the literature and recent observations. Austral. Seabird Group Newsl. 25: 1–70.
MURPHY, R. C. 1951. The populations of the Wedge-tailed Shearwater (*Puffinus pacificus*). Am. Mus. Novit. 1512: 1–21.
PITMAN, R. L. 1986. Atlas of seabird distribution and relative abundance in the eastern tropical Pacific. National Marine Fisheries Service, SW Center, Admin. Rep. LJ-86-02C.

Puffinus pacificus chlororhynchus Lesson

Wedge-tailed Shearwater

Puffinus chlororhynchus Lesson, 1831, Traité d'Ornith., livr. 8: 613 — no locality given but type from Shark Bay, Western Australia.
Puffinus sphenurus Gould, 1844, Ann. Mag. Nat. Hist. 13: 365 — Abrolhos Islands, Western Australia.
Proc(ellaria) carbonaria Gray, 1844, Genera Birds 3: 647 (synonym of *P. chlororhynchus* Lesson).

Puffinus cuneatus Salvin, 1888, Ibis (1888): 353 — "Krusenstern Islands" = mythical islands designated by the collector, actually one of the Leeward Hawaiian Islands (Murphy 1951).
Puffinus pacificus hamiltoni Mathews, 1912, Birds Aust. 2: 82 — The Cousin, Seychelles Islands.
Puffinus pacificus alleni Mathews, 1912, Birds Aust. 2: 83 — San Benedicto, Revilla Gigedo Islands.
Puffinus pacificus laysani Mathews, 1912, Birds Aust. 2: 83 — Laysan Island.
Puffinus pacificus royanus Mathews, 1912, Birds Aust. 2: 85, pl.75 — Bondi Beach, New South Wales.

Breeds on islands of the tropical and subtropical Indian and Pacific Oceans, including Australian islands and Lord Howe Island, and ranges widely in adjacent seas. Relatively sedentary, but southeast Australian birds migrate to the western North Pacific. Vagrant to New Zealand: Makara Beach, January 1962; Otaki Beach, June 1962; Cook Strait, November 1965; Taranaki, September 1983.

FALLA, R. A. 1962. A Wedge-tailed Shearwater in New Zealand. Notornis 9: 278–279.
JOUANIN, C.; MOUGIN, J.-L. 1979. Order Procellariiformes. Pages 48–121 *in* Check-list of Birds of the World. Vol.1, 2nd edn. (Mayr, E.; Cottrell, G. W. eds) Cambridge, Mass.: Mus. Comp. Zool.
KING, W. B. 1974. Wedge-tailed Shearwater *Puffinus pacificus*. Smithson. Contrib. Zool. 158: 53–95.
MURPHY, R. C. 1951. The populations of the Wedge-tailed Shearwater (*Puffinus pacificus*). Am. Mus. Novit. 1512: 1–21.

33 **Puffinus bulleri** Salvin

Buller's Shearwater

Puffinus bulleri Salvin, 1888, Ibis (1888): 354 — New Zealand (Waikanae Beach).
Puffinus zealandicus Sandager, 1890, Trans. NZ Inst. (1889) 22: 291 — Mokohinau Islands.

Breeds on 7 of the 12 Poor Knights Islands (c. 2.5 million birds). Seen flying over Three Kings Islands. Ranges mainly over the North Island continental shelf, particularly from Kaipara Harbour to North Cape to East Cape, but reaches Foveaux Strait, seas off Fiordland and the Chatham Islands. Vagrant to eastern Australia. Migrates to the North Pacific (mid-ocean and seas off Japan, Alaska to California) and reaches seas off west coast of South America (pre-breeders?).

Subfossil and midden records from North Island, subfossil from South Island and Chatham Island.

GUZMAN, J. R.; MYRES, M. T. 1983. Occurrence of shearwaters (*Puffinus* spp.) off the west coast of Canada. Can. J. Zool. 81: 2064–2077.
HARPER, P. C. 1983. Biology of the Buller's Shearwater (*Puffinus bulleri*) at the Poor Knights Islands, New Zealand. Notornis 30: 299–318.
JENKINS, J. A. F. 1974. Local distribution and feeding habits of Buller's Shearwater (*Puffinus bulleri*). Notornis 21: 109–120.
MURPHY, R. C. 1936. Oceanic Birds of South America. Vol.II. New York: Am. Mus. Nat. Hist.

WAHL, T. R. 1985. The distribution of Buller's Shearwater (*Puffinus bulleri*) in the North Pacific Ocean. Notornis 32: 109–117.

Subgenus **Puffinus**

34   **Puffinus griseus** (Gmelin)

Sooty Shearwater (Muttonbird, Titi)

Procellaria grisea Gmelin, 1789, Syst. Nat.1: 564 (based on "Grey Petrel" of Latham, 1785, General Synop. Birds 3: 399)—between 35°S and 50°S = New Zealand, as designated by Mathews, 1912, Birds Aust. 2: 95.
Procellaria tristis Forster, 1844, Lichtenstein's Descr. Anim.: 205—New Zealand.
Nectris chilensis Bonaparte, 1857, Consp. Gen. Avium 2: 202—Chile.
Nectris gama Bonaparte, 1857, Consp. Gen. Avium 2: 202—(name for pl.56 in Smith, 1840, Ills Zool. S.Afr. Aves)—off Chile.
Nectris amaurosoma Coues, 1864, Proc. Acad. Nat. Sci. Philad.: 124—Cape St. Lucas, Lower California.
Puffinus stricklandi Ridgway, 1884, Baird, Brewer and Ridgway's Mem. Mus. comp. Zool. Harv. 13: 390—North Atlantic Ocean.
Neonectris griseus pescadoresi Mathews and Iredale, 1915, Ibis (1915): 602—Pescadores Islands.
Neonectris griseus missus Mathews and Iredale, 1915, Ibis (1915): 603—Kurile Islands.
Neonectris griseus nutcheri Mathews, 1916, Austral Avian Rec.3: 54—Bondi Beach, New South Wales.

Breeds on Chilean islands (Guafo, Guamblin, Wollaston, Bayly, Deceit), on Kidney Island (Falkland Islands), on c.12 islands off Tasmania and southeastern Australia, on Macquarie Island, and in New Zealand—on Three Kings, Cavalli, Hen and Chickens, Mokohinau, Aldermen, Rurima, Whale, White, Kapiti and Mana Islands off North Island; on Stephens, Trio, Titi, Open Bay, Green, Taieri, and islands in Fiordland, off South Island and decreasingly on several headlands (Banks Peninsula, Cape Wanbrow, Otago Peninsula, west coast); on islands in Foveaux Strait, on Solander Islands and on Stewart Island and almost all adjacent islands (large colonies on Codfish, Big South Cape); on The Snares (c.2.75 million pairs); on Antipodes, Campbell, Auckland and Chatham Islands.

May range south to the edge of pack-ice (sightings only). The majority from New Zealand migrate to the North Pacific from about 35°N to the Bering Sea. South American birds are only partly migratory. Common, both subfossil and midden, from North, South and Chatham Islands.

GUZMAN, J. R.; MYRES, M. T. 1983. Occurrence of shearwaters (*Puffinus* spp.) off the west coast of Canada. Can. J. Zool. 81: 2064–2077.
OGI, H. 1982. Feeding ecology of the Sooty Shearwater in the western subarctic North Pacific Ocean. Proc. Pacific Seabird Group Symp., Seattle, 6–8 Jan. 1982: 78–84.
RICHDALE, L. E. 1963. Biology of the Sooty Shearwater *Puffinus griseus*. Proc. Zool. Soc. Lond. 141: 1–117.

WARHAM, J.; WILSON, G. J. 1982. The size of the Sooty Shearwater population at the Snares Islands, New Zealand. Notornis 29: 23–30.
WARHAM, J.; WILSON, G. J.; KEELEY, B. R. 1982. The annual cycle of the Sooty Shearwater *Puffinus griseus* at the Snares Islands, New Zealand. Notornis 29: 269–292.

35 **Puffinus tenuirostris** (Temminck)
Short-tailed Shearwater (Tasmanian Muttonbird)

Procellaria tenuirostris Temminck, 1835, Planches Color., livr. 99: text to pl.587 — seas north of Japan and shores of Korea.
Puffinus brevicaudus Gould, 1847, Birds Aust. 7: pl.56 — islands of Bass Strait.
Puffinus intermedius Hull, 1911, Emu 11: 98 — Cabbage Tree Island, New South Wales.
Neonectris tenuirostris grantianus Hull, 1916, Emu 15: 206 — Ulladulla, New South Wales.
Neonectris tenuirostris hulli Mathews, 1916, Bull. Br. Ornith. Club 36: 82 — Great Barrier Reef, Queensland.

Breeds on islands off southern Australia from Figure-of-Eight Island, Western Australia, to Bateman's Bay, New South Wales, on Bass Strait islands and on the coast of Tasmania and adjacent islands. Ranges south to the edge of the pack-ice. Migrates to the North Pacific, mainly from 45°N to the Bering Strait. Found along mainland New Zealand coasts mainly as wind-drifted migrants in spring and autumn. Subfossil and midden records from North, South and Chatham Islands.

NAARDING, J. A. 1980. Study of the Short-tailed Shearwater *Puffinus tenuirostris* in Tasmania. Tasmania: Nat. Parks & Wildl. Serv. 78 pp.
SERVENTY, D. L. 1967. Aspects of the population ecology of the Short-tailed Shearwater *Puffinus tenuirostris*. Proc. 14 Internat. Ornith. Congr.: 165–190.
SERVENTY, D. L.; SERVENTY, V.; WARHAM, J. 1971. The Handbook of Australian Sea-birds. Sydney: Reed.
SKIRA, I. J. 1986. Food of the Short-tailed Shearwater, *Puffinus tenuirostris*, in Tasmania. Aust. Wildl. Res. 13: 481–488.

36 **Puffinus nativitatis** Streets

Christmas Island Shearwater

Puffinus (Nectris) nativitatis Streets, 1877, Bull. U.S. Nat. Mus. 7: 29 — Christmas Island, Pacific Ocean.

Breeds on the Marshall, Leeward Hawaiian, Johnston, Line, Phoenix, Marquesas, Austral, Gambier, Oeno and Easter Islands. Not known to migrate. One New Zealand record: Dargaville Beach, February 1976.

AMERSON, A. B.; SHELTON, P. C. 1976. The natural history of Johnston Island, central Pacific Ocean. Atoll Res. Bull. 192. 178–187.
CROCKETT, D. E. 1977. First record of the Christmas Island Shearwater in New Zealand. Notornis 24: 285–286.
JOUANIN, C.; MOUGIN, J.-L. 1979. Order Procellariiformes. Pages 48–121 *in* Check-list of Birds of the World. Vol.1, 2nd edn. (Mayr, E.; Cottrell, G. W. eds) Cambridge, Mass.: Mus. Comp. Zool.

37   **Puffinus puffinus** (Brünnich)

Manx Shearwater

Six well-defined subspecies or allopatric species. Breeds on islands in the North Atlantic and in the Mediterranean Sea, on the Hawaiian and Revilla Gigedo Islands, and on islands west of Baja California. Some forms are migratory.

Puffinus puffinus puffinus (Brünnich)

Manx Shearwater

Procellaria puffinus Brünnich, 1764, Ornith. Borealis: 29—Faeroes and Norway.
Procellaria anglorum Temminck, 1820, Man. Orn. 2: 806—St Kilda.
Puffinus arcticus Faber, 1822, Prodromus isl. Orn.: 56 (new name for *P. anglorum* Temminck).
Puffinus scotorum Partington, 1837, Br. Cycl. nat. Hist. 3: 429 (new name for *P. anglorum*).
Puffinus manksii Coues, 1864, Proc. Acad. nat. Sci. Philad.: 125 (new name for *P. anglorum*).
Puffinus puffinus bermudae Nichols and Mowbray, 1916, Auk 33: 195—Bermuda.

Breeds in the North Atlantic on islands off Massachusetts, Newfoundland, Iceland, the British Isles and Brittany, and on the Faeroes, Azores and Madeira Islands. Migrates mainly to seas off Brazil and Argentina; reaches southern Africa; straggles to Australasia. Two New Zealand records (both beach-wrecked): Pukerua Bay, June 1972, and Waikanae Beach, January 1985.

HARRIS, M. P. 1966a. Breeding biology of the Manx Shearwater *Puffinus puffinus*. Ibis 108: 17–33.
HARRIS, M. P. 1966b. Age of return to the colony, age of breeding and adult survival of Manx Shearwaters. Bird Study 13: 84–95.
KINSKY, F. C.; FOWLER, J. A. 1973. A Manx Shearwater (*Puffinus p. puffinus*) in New Zealand. Notornis 20: 14–20.
TENNYSON, A. J. D. 1986. Second record of a Manx Shearwater in New Zealand. Notornis 33: 59–61.

38   **Puffinus gavia** (Forster)

Fluttering Shearwater (Pakaha)

Procellaria gavia J. R. Forster, 1844, Descr. Animal. Itinere Maris Australis Terras: 148—Queen Charlotte Sound, New Zealand.
Puffinus reinholdi reinholdi Mathews, 1912, Birds Aust. 2: 47 (in key), 74, pl.74—New Zealand and east Australian seas.
Reinholdia reinholdi byroni Mathews, 1913, Austral Avian Rec. 1: 187—Byron Bay, New South Wales (error) = Five Islands, NSW (Mathews, 1916, Bull. Br. Ornith. Club 36: 89).
Cinathisma cyaneoleuca Hull, 1916, Emu 15: 205, pl.32—Ulladulla, New South Wales.
Reinholdia reinholdi melanotis Mathews, 1916, Bull. Br. Ornith. Club 36: 89—Kaipara Beach = Muriwai Beach, New Zealand.
Reinholdia reinholdi montaguei Mathews, 1922, Austral Avian Rec. 5: 3—New Caledonia.

Breeds only in New Zealand on Three Kings (major colony), Moturoa, Stephenson, Cavalli, Poor Knights, Bream, Hen and Chickens, Mokohinau, Saddle (formerly), Channel, Little Tiri, Mercury, Aldermen, Slipper, Plate, Rurima, Whale (formerly), East, Stephens, Trio and Chetwode Islands, and islands in Queen Charlotte Sound and off the east coast of Marlborough. Ranges mainly over the continental shelf, as far south as Westland and South Canterbury Bight in autumn and winter. Prebreeders visit eastern Australian seas. Straggles to New Caledonia and Vanuatu.

Identified from numerous subfossil and midden sites in North, South and Chatham Islands. (Some may be of the following species, since the post-cranial bones of the two cannot be reliably distinguished).

FALLA, R. A. 1934. The distribution and breeding habits of petrels in northern New Zealand. Rec. Auck. Inst. Mus. 1: 245–260.
SERVENTY, D. L.; SERVENTY, V.; WARHAM, J. 1971. The Handbook of Australian Sea-birds. Sydney: Reed.

39 **Puffinus huttoni** Mathews

Hutton's Shearwater

Puffinus reinholdi huttoni Mathews, 1912, Birds Aust. 2: 47 (in key), 77—Snares Islands.
Puffinus leptorhynchus Mathews, 1937, Bull. Br. Ornith. Club 57: 143—Bunbury, Western Australia.

Breeds only in New Zealand in the Seaward Kaikoura Mountains between 1200 m and 1800 m above sea level. Formerly bred also in the Inland Kaikoura Mountains. Ranges mainly east of the South Island at least as far as 300 km southeast of Banks Peninsula, and into Cook Strait. Migrates to seas off northwestern Australia between April and August. Probably wind-drifted to northern North Island and Queensland. Supposed subfossil and midden records from the South Island (R.J. Scarlett) should be treated with caution (see note under *P. gavia*).

FALLA, R. A. 1965. Distribution of Hutton's Shearwater in New Zealand. Notornis 12: 66–70.
HALSE, S. A. 1981. Migration by Hutton's Shearwater. Emu 81: 42–44.
HARROW, G. 1965. Preliminary report on discovery of nesting site of Hutton's Shearwater. Notornis 12: 59–65.
HARROW, G. 1976. Some observations of Hutton's Shearwater. Notornis 23: 269–288.
IMBER, M.J.; CROCKETT, D. E. 1970. Sea birds found dead in New Zealand in 1968. Notornis 17: 223–230.
WEST, J.; IMBER, M.J. 1985. Some foods of Hutton's Shearwater (*Puffinus huttoni*). Notornis 32: 333–336.

40   **Puffinus assimilis** Gould
Little Shearwater

Breeds on islands in the North Atlantic and at Tristan da Cunha, Gough and St Paul Islands; on islands off southwestern Australia; at Lord Howe, Norfolk, and Kermadec Islands, off northern New Zealand, at Rapa Island, and at Antipodes and Chatham Islands. Seven subspecies; all but the subantarctic one seem non-migratory. Assignment to subspecies of subfossil and midden material must be considered tentative.

Puffinus assimilis assimilis Gould
Norfolk Island Little Shearwater

Puffinus assimilis Gould, 1838, Synop. Birds Australia, pt.4, append.: 7 — New South Wales = Norfolk Island (*fide* Mathews, 1912, Birds Australia 2: 50).
Puffinus australis Gould, 1848, Birds Aust. 35: text pl. 59 — *ex* Eyton; synonym of *P. assimilis* Gould.
Puffinus assimilis howensis Mathews, 1915, Austral Avian Rec. 2: 125 — Lord Howe Island.

Breeds at Lord Howe (Roach) and Norfolk (Philip, Nepean, Bird Rocks) Islands. Straggles to west coast of North Island.

FLEMING, C.A.; SERVENTY, D.L. 1943. The races of *Puffinus assimilis* in Australia and New Zealand. Emu 43: 113–125.
FLEMING, C.A.; SERVENTY, D.L. 1952. On the specific name of the Little Shearwater. Emu 52: 17–23.
TARBURTON, M.K. 1981. Seabirds nesting at Norfolk Island. Notornis 28: 209–211.
WARHAM, J. 1955. Observations of the Little Shearwater at the nest. W. Aust. Nat. 5: 31–39.

Puffinus assimilis kermadecensis Murphy
Kermadec Little Shearwater

Puffinus assimilis kermadecensis Murphy, 1927, Am. Mus. Novit. 276: 3 — Herald Islets, Kermadec Islands.

Breeds on the Kermadec Islands (Herald Islets, possibly still on Raoul itself, Macauley, Haszard, Curtis, Cheeseman). Ranges to seas off west coast of North and South Islands.

FLEMING, C.A.; SERVENTY, D.L. 1943. The races of *Puffinus assimilis* in Australia and New Zealand. Emu 43: 113–125.
MERTON, D.V. 1970. Kermadec Islands Expedition reports: a general account of birdlife. Notornis 17: 147–199.

Puffinus assimilis haurakiensis Fleming and Serventy
North Island Little Shearwater

Puffinus assimilis haurakiensis Fleming and Serventy, 1943, Emu 43: 119 — Lizard Island, Mokohinau Islands.

Breeds on Moturoa, Stephenson, Cavalli, Poor Knights, Hen and Chickens, Mokohinau, Mercury and Aldermen Islands.

Ranges south into Bay of Plenty and occasionally to Hawke Bay, reaching Castle Point. Sedentary. Subfossil and midden, North Island.

FALLA, R.A. 1934. The distribution and breeding habits of petrels in northern New Zealand. Rec. Auck. Inst. Mus. 1: 245–260.

Puffinus assimilis elegans Giglioli and Salvadori
Subantarctic Little Shearwater

Puffinus elegans Giglioli and Salvadori, 1869, Ibis (1869): 68 — 43°54'S, 9°20'E.
Nectris munda Salvin (*ex* Solander ms), 1876, *in* Rowley, Ornith. Misc. 4: 236 — 48°27'S, 93°00'W.
Puffinus assimilis kempi Mathews, 1912, Birds Aust. 2: 69 — Chatham Islands.
Puffinus kuhliana Mathews, 1933, Bull. Br. Ornith. Club 54: 25 (new name for Solander's *Nectris munda*).

Breeds on Inaccessible, Nightingale, Tristan da Cunha and Gough Islands in the South Atlantic, and on Chatham Islands (Star Keys, Little Mangere) and Antipodes Islands (Bollons, Archway, Inner Windward, probably Outer Windward and Leeward) (major colony). Ranges in subantarctic seas, reaching seas off east coast of South Island, Auckland and Bounty Islands, and southern Chile. Subfossil and midden, South Island, Stewart Island and Chathams.

IMBER, M.J. 1983. The lesser petrels of Antipodes Islands, with notes from Prince Edward and Gough Islands. Notornis 30: 283–298.
JEHL, J.R. 1973. The distribution of marine birds in Chilean waters in winter. Auk 90: 114–135.
WARHAM, J.; BELL, B.D. 1979. The birds of Antipodes Island, New Zealand. Notornis 26: 121–169.

Genus **Pelecanoides** Lacépède*

Pelecanoides Lacépède, 1799, Tableaux Mammifères Oiseaux, p.13 — type (by monotypy) *Procellaria urinatrix* Gmelin.
Halodroma Illiger, 1811, Prodromus: 274 — type (by monotypy) *Procellaria urinatrix* Gmelin.
Onocrotalus Rafinesque, 1815, Analyse Nat.: 72 — new name for *Pelecanoides*.
Puffinuria Lesson, 1828, Man. Ornith. 2: 394 — type (by monotypy) *Puffinuria Garnotii* Lesson.
Porthmornis (subgen.) Murphy and Harper, 1921, Bull. Am. Mus. Nat. Hist. 44: 502, 503 (in key), 513 — type (by monotypy) *Puffinuria garnotii magellani* Mathews.
Pelagodyptes (subgen.) Murphy and Harper, 1921, Bull. Am. Mus. Nat. Hist. 44: 502, 503 (in key), 519 — type (by monotypy) *Pelecanoides georgica* Murphy and Harper.

* Rejection of family status based on Cracraft, 1981, Auk 98: 681–714; Sibley *et al.*, 1988, Auk 105: 109–123.

41   **Pelecanoides urinatrix** (Gmelin)
Common Diving Petrel

Circumpolar, breeding on islands between 34°S and 55°S and staying mainly in adjacent seas. Sedentary. There are about four subspecies, two in this region.

Pelecanoides urinatrix urinatrix (Gmelin)
Common Diving Petrel (Kuaka)

Procellaria urinatrix Gmelin, 1789, Syst. Nat. 1: 560—Queen Charlotte Sound, New Zealand (based on "Diving Petrel" of Latham, 1785, General Synop. Birds 3: 413).
Pelecanoides urinatrix belcheri Mathews, 1912, Austral Avian Rec. 1: 84—Australian seas = Victoria.
Pelecanoides urinatrix chathamensis Murphy and Harper, 1916, Bull. Am. Mus. Nat. Hist. 35: 65—Chatham Islands.

Breeds on islands off Tasmania and in Bass Strait; and many islands off New Zealand—from Three Kings Islands to Bay of Plenty, off Taranaki, in Cook Strait and off Marlborough Sounds, off southern South Island and Stewart Island, Codfish Island, Solander Islands, The Snares and Chatham Islands (now almost extinct on Chatham and Pitt Islands). Ranges in adjacent seas, mainly in coastal waters. Sedentary. Abundant in subfossil and midden deposits: North, South and Chatham Islands.

FLEMING, C. A. 1939. Birds of the Chatham Islands. Part I. Emu 38: 380–413.
RICHDALE, L. E. 1965. Biology of the birds of Whero Island, New Zealand, with special reference to the diving petrel and the white-faced storm petrel. Trans. Zool. Soc. Lond. 31: 1–86.
THORESEN, A. C. 1969. Observations on the breeding behaviour of the diving petrel *Pelecanoides u. urinatrix* (Gmelin). Notornis 16: 241–260.

Pelecanoides urinatrix exsul Salvin
Subantarctic Diving Petrel

Pelecanoides exsul Salvin, 1896, Cat. Birds Br. Mus. 25: 437 (in key), 438—Kerguelen Island, as determined by Murphy and Harper, 1921, Bull. Am. Mus. Nat. Hist. 44: 544.

Breeds on islands mainly in the subantarctic zone: South Georgia, Prince Edward, Crozet group, Kerguelen, Heard; and on Auckland and Antipodes Islands. Formerly bred on Marion Island (recently exterminated by cats), Macquarie and Campbell Islands. Probably still breeds on islets off Macquarie and Campbell Islands. Apparently sedentary, ranging mainly in seas near the breeding places.

IMBER, M. J. 1983. The lesser petrels of Antipodes Islands, with notes from Prince Edward and Gough Islands. Notornis 30: 283–298.
JOUVENTIN, P.; MOUGIN, J.-L.; STAHL, J.-C.; WEIMERSKIRCH, H. 1985. Comparative biology of the burrowing petrels of the Crozet Islands. Notornis 32: 157–220.
PAYNE, M. R.; PRINCE, P. A. 1979. Identification and breeding biology of the diving petrels *Pelecanoides georgicus* and *P. urinatrix exsul* at South Georgia. NZ J. Zool. 6: 299–318.

WARHAM, J.; BELL, B.D. 1979. The birds of Antipodes Island, New Zealand. Notornis 26: 121–169.

42 Pelecanoides georgicus Murphy and Harper

South Georgian Diving Petrel

Pelecanoides georgica Murphy and Harper, 1916, Bull. Am. Mus. Nat. Hist. 35: 66 — Cumberland Bay, South Georgia.

Pelagodyptes georgicus novus Mathews, 1935, Novit. Zool. 39: in key — Macquarie Island.

Breeds on South Georgia, Marion, Prince Edward, Crozet group, Kerguelen and Heard Islands; and on Codfish Island, New Zealand (c.40 breeding pairs); formerly on Macquarie and Auckland Islands (Enderby, 1840; Dundas, 1943). Stays mainly in seas near the breeding islands, but has straggled once to the east coast of Australia.

DOWNES, M.C.; EALEY, E.H.M.; GWYNN, A.M.; YOUNG, P.S. 1959. The birds of Heard Island. ANARE Reps., Ser. B, 1: 1–96.

EALEY, E.H.M. 1954. Analysis of stomach contents of some Heard Island birds. Emu 54: 204–210.

IMBER, M.J.; NILSSON, R.J. 1980. South Georgian Diving Petrels *Pelecanoides georgicus* breeding on Codfish Island. Notornis 27: 325–330.

PAYNE, M.R.; PRINCE, P.A. 1979. Identification and breeding biology of the diving petrels *Pelecanoides georgicus* and *P. urinatrix exsul* at South Georgia. NZ J. Zool. 6: 299–318.

WEST, J.; IMBER, M.J. 1989. Surveys of South Georgian Diving Petrels on Codfish Island. Notornis 36: 157–158.

Genus **Procellaria** Linnaeus

Procellaria Linnaeus, 1758, Syst. Nat., ed. 10, 1: 131 — type (by subsequent designation, G.R. Gray, 1840, List Gen. Birds p. 78) *Procellaria aequinoctialis* Linnaeus.

Priofinus Hombron and Jacquinot, 1844, C.R. Acad. Sci., Paris, 18: 355 — type (by subsequent designation, Mathews and Iredale, 1920, Austral Avian Rec. 4: 111) *Procellaria aequinoctialis* Linnaeus.

Majaqueus Reichenbach, 1852 (1853), Vollst. Naturgesch., 2 Vogel, 1 Avium Syst, nat.: iv — type (by original designation) *Procellaria aequinoctialis* Linnaeus.

Adamastor Bonaparte, 1856, C.R. Acad. Sci., Paris, 43: 595 — type (by original designation) *Procellaria haesitata* J.R. Forster = *Procellaria cinerea* Gmelin.

Cymbatobolus Heine and Reichenow, 1890, Nom. Mus. Hein. Ornith.: 363 — new name for *Majaqueus* Reichenbach.

43 Procellaria cinerea Gmelin

Grey Petrel

Procellaria cinerea Gmelin, 1789, Syst. Nat. 1: 563; based on "Cinereous Fulmar" of Latham, 1785, General Synop. Birds 3: 405 — within the Antarctic Circle = New Zealand seas at 48°S, *fide* Mathews, 1912, Birds Aust. 2: 123.

Procellaria gelida Gmelin, 1789, Syst. Nat. 1: 564 — inter 35° and 50° south.

Procellaria haesitata J.R. Forster, 1844, Lichtenstein's Descr. Anim.: 207 — South of 42°S, Pacific Ocean.

Procellaria pallipes Mathews, 1912, Birds Aust. 2: 123 — New Zealand (*ex* Solander MS).

Priofinus cinereus dydimus Mathews, 1916, Austral Avian Rec. 3: 54 — New Zealand.
Breeds on Tristan da Cunha, Inaccessible and Gough Islands, on Marion and Prince Edward Islands, on Crozet Islands (Possession, East), at Kerguelen, (formerly on Macquarie Island), on Campbell Island (including Dent and Jacquemart) and Antipodes Islands. The last is a major colony. Circumpolar, ranging widely between about 25°S and 60°S, and to seas off Peru. More common east of New Zealand than in the Tasman Sea. Tentatively identifed (W. R. P. Bourne) subfossil on Chatham Island.

BARRAT, A. 1974. Note sur le Pétrel gris *Procellaria cinerea*. CNFRA 33: 19–24.
IMBER, M. J. 1983. The lesser petrels of Antipodes Islands, with notes from Prince Edward and Gough Islands. Notornis 30: 283–298.
JOUVENTIN, P.; MOUGIN, J.-L.; STAHL, J.-C.; WEIMERSKIRCH, H. 1985. Comparative biology of the burrowing petrels of the Crozet Islands. Notornis 32: 157–220.
WARHAM, J.; BELL, B. D. 1979. The birds of Antipodes Island, New Zealand. Notornis 26: 121–169.

44   **Procellaria parkinsoni** Gray

Black (Parkinson's) Petrel

Procellaria parkinsoni G. R. Gray, 1862, Ibis (1) 4: 245 — New Zealand.
Breeds on Little Barrier Island (c. 100 pairs) and on Great Barrier Island (c. 800 pairs), New Zealand; formerly also on coastal ranges of North Island and northwestern South Island. Ranges mainly between 30°S and 42°S near New Zealand while breeding but reaches seas off New South Wales. Migrates to the eastern tropical Pacific Ocean, from Guatemala to Peru and off the Galapagos Islands. Subfossil from Far North dunes and from cave deposits in both the North and South Islands.

IMBER, M. J. 1976. Comparison of prey of the black *Procellaria* petrels of New Zealand. NZ J. Mar. Freshwat. Res. 10: 119–130.
IMBER, M. J. 1987. Breeding ecology and conservation of the Black Petrel *Procellaria parkinsoni*. Notornis 34: 19–39.
JEHL, J. R. 1974. The near-shore avifauna of the Middle American west coast. Auk 91: 681–699.

45   **Procellaria westlandica** Falla

Westland Petrel

Procellaria parkinsoni westlandica Falla, 1946, Rec. Cant. Mus. 5: 111 — Barrytown, west coast of South Island, New Zealand.
Breeds only near the type locality, south of the Punakaiki River in hills below c. 200 m (total population 9000+). Ranges mainly in adjacent seas between Cape Egmont and Foveaux Strait, through Cook Strait to between East Cape and Banks Peninsula, but has reached eastern Australia and Chile. Post-breeding movements not known, although common near the Chatham Islands in December.

Subfossil from cave deposits near Punakaiki and from dunes and one cave on Chatham Island.

BAKER, A.J.; COLEMAN, J.D. 1977. The breeding cycle of the Westland Black Petrel (*Procellaria westlandica*). Notornis 24: 211–231.

BARTLE, J.A. 1974. Seabirds of eastern Cook Strait, New Zealand, in autumn. Notornis 21: 135–166.

BEST, H.A.; OWEN, K.L. 1976. Distribution of breeding sites of the Westland Black Petrel (*Procellaria westlandica*). Notornis 23: 233–242.

46 **Procellaria aequinoctialis** Linnaeus

White-chinned Petrel (Shoemaker)

Circumpolar in southern oceans, breeding at South Georgia, Falkland Islands, Inaccessible Island, Marion and Prince Edward Islands, Crozet Islands (Possession and East), Kerguelen, and at Auckland, Campbell and Antipodes Islands. Ranges between 30°S and 65°S but to 15°S west of South America and Africa, furthest north in winter. Two subspecies recognised; only one known in this area.

Procellaria aequinoctialis aequinoctialis Linnaeus

White-chinned Petrel

Procellaria aequinoctialis Linnaeus, 1758, Syst. Nat., ed. 10, 1: 132—Cape of Good Hope.

Procellaria aequinoctialis steadi Mathews, 1912, Birds Aust. 2: 107, 112—Antipodes (type) and Auckland Islands.

Breeds at South Georgia, Falkland Islands, Prince Edward Islands, Crozet Islands, Kerguelen and on Auckland Islands (Auckland, Adams, Disappointment), Campbell Island (including Dent, Jacquemart) and Antipodes Island. Ranges mainly south and east of New Zealand. Recorded subfossil in Chatham Island dunes and from middens at Kaikoura, South Island.

IMBER, M.J. 1983. The lesser petrels of Antipodes Islands, with notes from Prince Edward and Gough Islands. Notornis 30: 283–298.

MOUGIN, J.-L. 1970. Le Pétrel à menton blanc *Procellaria aequinoctialis* de l'île de la Possession (Archipel Crozet). Oiseau Rev. fr. Ornith. 40: 62–96.

WARHAM, J.; BELL, B.D. 1979. The birds of Antipodes Island, New Zealand. Notornis 26: 121–169.

Genus **Pseudobulweria** Mathews

Pseudobulweria Mathews, 1936, Ibis 1936: 309—type (by original designation) *Thalassidroma (Bulweria) macgillivrayi* G.R. Gray.

47 **Pseudobulweria rostrata** (Peale)

Tahiti Petrel

Procellaria rostrata Peale, 1848, Proc. U.S. Explor. Exped. 8: 296—mountains about 6000 feet on Tahiti, Society Islands

Pterodroma rostrata Trouessarti Brasil, 1917, Bull. Mus. Nat. Hist. Nat., Paris 23: 432—New Caledonia.

South Pacific Ocean, breeding in New Caledonia, possibly Fiji
(Taveuni, Gau), Society Islands (Tahiti, Moorea) and Mar-
quesas Islands (Hiva-oa, Tahuata, Nuku Hiva). Visits tropical
North Pacific as a non-breeder. Reaches the east coast of Aus-
tralia and the Indian Ocean off northwest Australia. One New
Zealand specimen (Glinkes Gully Beach, June 1988) and four
possible sightings (Bay of Plenty, July–August 1988; east of Poor
Knights, August 1988).

HANNECART, F.; LETOCART, Y. 1980. Oiseaux de Nouvelle Calédonie et des
Loyautés. Vol. I. Noumea: the authors.
MURPHY, R.C. 1928. Birds collected during the Whitney South Sea Expedition.
IV. Am. Mus. Novit. 322: 1–5.
PITMAN, R. L. 1986. Atlas of seabird distribution and relative abundance in the
eastern tropical Pacific. U.S. National Marine Fisheries Service, SW Center,
Admin. Rep. LJ-86-02C.
THIBAULT, J.C.; RIVES, C. 1975. Birds of Tahiti. Papeete: les éditions du
Pacifique.

Subfamily FULMARINAE: Fulmars, Prions
and Gadfly Petrels
Genus **Lugensa** Mathews

Lugensa Mathews, 1942, Emu 41: 305—type (by original designation) *Procellaria
brevirostris* Lesson = ? *Procellaria lugens* Kuhl.

48   **Lugensa brevirostris** (Lesson)

Kerguelen Petrel

Procellaria brevirostris Lesson, 1833, Traité d'Ornith., livr. 8: 611—Cape of Good
Hope.
Aestrelata kidderi Coues, 1875, Bull. U.S. Nat. Mus. 2: 28—Kerguelen Island.
Pterodroma kidderi okahia (sic) Mathews, 1935, Bull. Br. Ornith. Club 56: 37—
Ohakea, New Zealand.

Breeds on Gough, Marion, Prince Edward, Crozet (Possession,
East, Penguin, Apostles) and Kerguelen Islands; possibly also
on Tristan da Cunha and Inaccessible Island. Ranges between
40°S and 70°S, to about the edge of the pack-ice, but less
common in the Pacific Ocean. Irregular winter-spring wind-
drifted visitor to New Zealand, mainly when immature (largest
numbers dead on beaches: 300+ in 1981, 600 in 1984).

IMBER, M.J. 1984. The age of Kerguelen Petrels found in New Zealand. Notornis
31: 89–91.
IMBER, M.J. 1985. Origins, phylogeny and taxonomy of the gadfly petrels
Pterodroma spp. Ibis 127: 197–229.
JOUVENTIN, P.; MOUGIN, J.-L.; STAHL, J.-C.; WEIMERSKIRCH, H. 1985.
Comparative biology of the burrowing petrels of the Crozet Islands. Notornis
32: 157–220.
MOUGIN, J.-L. 1969. Notes écologiques sur le Pétrel de Kerguelen *Pterodroma
brevirostris* de l'île de la Possession (Archipel Crozet). Oiseau Rev. fr. Orn. 39 (no.
spécial): 58–81.

SCHRAMM, M. 1983. The breeding biologies of the petrels *Pterodroma macroptera*, *P. brevirostris* and *P. mollis* at Marion Island. Emu 83: 75–81.
SCHRAMM, M. 1986. The diet of chicks of Greatwinged, Kerguelen and Soft-plumaged Petrels at the Prince Edward Islands. Ostrich 57: 9–15.

Genus **Pagodroma** Bonaparte

Pagodroma Bonaparte, 1856, C. R. Acad. Sci., Paris 42: 768 — type (by monotypy) *Procellaria nivea* Forster.

49 **Pagodroma nivea** (Forster)

Snow Petrel

Breeds in Antarctica on nunataks, coasts and adjacent islands, and on some high latitude islands. At sea, mainly in the pack-ice zone. Two subspecies, hybridising freely and extensively (at South Orkney, South Sandwich and Proclamation Islands, Casey, Dumont d'Urville, Capes Hunter, Denison, Adare and Hallett, and probably at other places where both forms have yet to be recognised).

Pagodroma nivea nivea (Forster)

Greater Snow Petrel

Procellaria nivea G. Forster, 1777, Voyage Round World, 1: 96, 98 — 51°50′S, 21°03′E.
Pagodroma confusa Mathews, 1912, Birds Aust. 2: 177 — Cape Adare.

Breeds on the Balleny Islands, and hybridising with *minor* at numerous colonies named above. Range at sea presumably similar to that of *minor*.

References: Those after *P.n. minor* apply to both forms.

Pagodroma nivea minor (Schlegel)

Lesser Snow Petrel

Procellaria nivea minor Schlegel, 1863, Mus. Hist. Nat. Pays-Bas, Rev. Méthod. Crit. Coll., livr. 4, Procellariae: 16 — "Glaces du Pole Sud".
Pagodroma nivea (novegeorgica) von der Steinen, 1890, Internat. Polarforsch. Deutsche Exped. 2: 250 — South Georgia.
Pagodroma nivea candida Mathews, 1912, Birds Aust. 2: 177 — Cape Adare.

Breeds on South Georgia, South Shetland, South Orkney, South Sandwich, Bouvet and Scott Islands, and on Antarctica, including Ross Sea localities (Edisto Inlet, Cape Hallett, Cape Adare; Franklin, Possession and Ross Islands). Rarely ranges north of 60°S.

BROWN, D. A. 1966. Breeding biology of the Snow Petrel *Pagodroma nivea* (Forster). ANARE Sci. Rep., ser. B, 89: 1–63.
COWAN, A. N. 1981. Size variation in the Snow Petrel (*Pagodroma nivea*). Notornis 28: 169–188.
COWAN, A. N. 1983. "Large" Snow Petrels (*Pagodroma nivea*) breeding at the South Sandwich Islands. Notornis 30: 250–252.
CROXALL, J. P. 1982. Sexual dimorphism in Snow Petrels *Pagodroma nivea* Notornis 29: 171–180.

GUILLOTIN, M.; JOUVENTIN, P. 1980. Le pétrel des neiges à Pointe Géologie. Gerfaut 70: 51–72.
JOUVENTIN, P.; VIOT, C.R. 1985. Morphological and genetic variability of Snow Petrels *Pagodroma nivea*. Ibis 127: 430–441.
MAHER, W.J. 1962. Breeding biology of the Snow Petrel near Cape Hallett, Antarctica. Condor 64: 488–499.
PRÉVOST, J. 1969. A propos des pétrels des neiges de la Terre Adélie. Oiseau Rev. fr. Ornith. 39 (no. spécial): 33–49.

Genus **Daption** Stephens*

Daption Stephens, 1826, *in* Shaw, General Zool. 13(1): 239 — type (by original designation) *Procellaria capensis* Linnaeus.
Calopetes Sundevall, 1873, Meth. nat. Avium dispon. Tentam.: 142 — new name for *Daption*.
Petrella Mathews, 1914, Auk 31: 91 — type (by monotypy) *Procellaria capensis* Linnaeus.

50   **Daption capense** (Linnaeus)

Cape Pigeon

Circumpolar, breeding from Antarctic coasts and islands to temperate islands at 44°S. Ranges widely in southern oceans, reaching the tropics and straggling north of the equator. Two subspecies.

Subfossil and midden records (not subspecifically distinguished) from the North Island and the Chathams.

Daption capense capense (Linnaeus)

Cape Pigeon

Procellaria capensis Linnaeus, 1758, Syst. Nat., ed. 10, 1: 132 — based chiefly on "The white and black Spotted Peteril" of Edwards, 1747, Nat. Hist. Birds: 90, pl. 90 right fig. — Cape of Good Hope.
Procellaria pardela Oken, 1816, Lehrb. Naturgesch. 3: 533 — Cape seas.
Procellaria naevia Bonaparte, 1857, Consp. Gen. Avium 2: 188 — synonym of *Procellaria capensis* Linnaeus.

Breeds on the coasts and islands of Antarctica and its Peninsula; on South Georgia, South Shetland, South Orkney, South Sandwich, Bouvet, Crozet, Kerguelen, Heard, Balleny and Peter I Islands. Ranges throughout southern seas to Tropic of Capricorn, and further north off west coast of both South America and Africa. Common in New Zealand seas in winter-early spring, especially east of the South Island.

BECK, J.R. 1969. Food, moult and age of first breeding in the Cape Pigeon, *Daption capensis* Linnaeus. Br. Antarct. Surv. Bull. 21: 33–44.
MOUGIN, J.-L. 1968. Etude écologique de quatre espèces de pétrels antarctiques. Oiseau 38 (no. spéc.): 1–52.

* The view of some committee members, including the compiler of this section, is that *Daption* and *Thalassoica* will become junior synonyms of *Fulmarus*.

PINDER, R. 1966. The Cape Pigeon, *Daption capensis* Linnaeus, at Signy Island, South Orkney Islands. Br. Antarct. Surv. Bull. 8: 19–47.
POWLESLAND, R. G. 1986. Seabirds found dead on New Zealand beaches in 1984 and a review of fulmar recoveries since 1960. Notornis 33: 171–184.

Daption capense australe Mathews

Snares Cape Pigeon

Daption capensis australis Mathews, 1913, Austral Avian Rec. 1: 187 — New Zealand.

Breeds on The Snares, Bounty, Antipodes, Auckland (Beacon Rock), and possibly Campbell Islands; in 1987 found breeding on The Forty Fours and probably on The Pyramid and The Sisters, Chatham Islands (range extension). Ranges in New Zealand seas and perhaps further but not usually distinguished at sea from *capense*.

HORNING, D. S.; HORNING, C. J. 1974. Bird records of the 1971–1973 Snares Islands, New Zealand, expedition. Notornis 21: 13–24.
SAGAR, P. M. 1979. Breeding of the Cape Pigeon (*Daption capense*) at the Snares Islands. Notornis 26: 23–26.
SAGAR, P. M. 1986. The sexual dimorphism of Snares Cape Pigeons (*Daption capense australe*). Notornis 33: 259–263.

Genus Thalassoica Reichenbach

Thalassoica Reichenbach, 1853, Avium Syst. Nat. (1852): 5 — type (by original designation) *Procellaria antarctica* Gmelin.
Aeipetes Forbes, 1882, Rep. Scient. Results Challenger Exped.: 59 — type (by original designation) *Procellaria antarctica* Gmelin.

51 Thalassoica antarctica (Gmelin)

Antarctic Petrel

Procellaria antarctica Gmelin, 1789, Syst. Nat. 1: 565 — based on "Le Pétrel antarctique ou Damier brun" of Buffon, 1783, Hist. Nat. Générale 24, Hist. Nat. Oiseaux 9: 311 (*ex* "Antarctic peterel" of Cook, 1777, Voyage South Pole 1: 252) — within the Antarctic Circle, 35–45°E.
Procellaria lugubris Tschudi, 1856, J. Ornith. 4: 185 — *fide* Mathews, 1934, Novit. Zool. 39: 161.

Breeds on Antarctic islands, coasts and nunataks in Dronning Maud, Enderby, MacRobertson, Princess Elizabeth, Wilkes and Marie Byrd Lands, and on the Theron and Rockefeller Mountains. Range circumpolar in the pack-ice and irregular north of 50°S. First recorded in New Zealand in September 1973; 73 beach-cast mainly on Auckland west coast, and numerous sightings in Foveaux Strait — Stewart Island area in August–September 1978; only four records since, until 1987 when nine were beach-cast.

BARLOW, M. 1979. Antarctic Petrels around Foveaux Strait. Notornis 26: 313.
MOUGIN, J.-L. 1975. Ecologie comparée des Procellariidae antarctiques et subantarctiques. Com. Nat. Franc. Rech. Antarct. 36, 199 pp.
VEITCH, C. R. 1980. Seabirds found dead in New Zealand in 1978. Notornis 27: 115–124.

Genus **Fulmarus** Stephens

Fulmarus Stephens, 1826, *in* Shaw, General Zool. 13(1): 236 — type (by subsequent designation, G. R. Gray, 1855, Cat. Gen. Subgen. Birds Br. Mus.: 129) *Procellaria glacialis* Linnaeus.
Halohippus Billberg, 1828, Syn. Faun. Scand. 1: 192 — type (by monotypy) *Procellaria glacialis* Linnaeus.
Rhantistes Kaup, 1829, Entwick. — Gesch. eur. Thierw.: 105 — type (by monotypy) *Procellaria glacialis* Linnaeus.
Wagellus Gray, 1840, List Gen. Birds: 78 — type (by original designation) *Procellaria glacialis* Linnaeus.
Priocella Hombron and Jacquinot, 1844, C. R. Acad. Sci., Paris 18: 357 — type (by monotypy) *Priocella garnotii* Hombron and Jacquinot = *Procellaria glacialoides* A. Smith.

52   **Fulmarus glacialoides** (Smith)

Antarctic Fulmar

Procellaria glacialoides A. Smith, 1840, Illus. Zool. South Africa, Aves: pl.51 — seas off Cape of Good Hope.
Priocella garnotii Hombron and Jacquinot, 1844, C. R. Acad. Sci., Paris 18: 357 — Cape seas.
Procellaria smithi Schlegel, 1863, Mus. Pays-Bas 6, Procell.: 22 — new name for *Procellaria glacialoides* Smith.
Thalassoica polaris Salvin, 1896, Cat. Birds Br. Mus. 25: 394 — synonym of *Procellaria glacialoides* Smith.
Priocella antarctica addenda Mathews, 1915, Austral Avian Rec. 2: 125 — New Zealand seas.

Breeds at many places on the coast of Antarctica and on adjacent islands, and on South Sandwich, South Orkney, South Shetland, Bouvet, Balleny and Peter I Islands. Circumpolar, ranging to about 40°S, but further north off west coast of South America. Regular straggler to New Zealand seas, mainly from July to October, with larger numbers beach-wrecked in 1975 and 1978. Recorded beach-wrecked, but also subfossil on Chatham Islands.

MOUGIN, J.-L. 1967. Etude écologique des deux espèces de fulmars: le fulmar atlantique (*Fulmarus glacialis*) et le fulmar antarctique (*Fulmarus glacialoides*). Oiseau Rev. fr. Ornith. 37: 57–103.
POWLESLAND, R. G. 1986. Seabirds found dead on New Zealand beaches in 1984 and a review of fulmar recoveries since 1960. Notornis 33: 171–184.
PRÉVOST, J. 1953. Notes sur la réproduction du Fulmar antarctique; *Fulmarus glacialoides* (A. Smith). Alauda 21: 157–164.

Genus **Macronectes** Richmond

Macronectes Richmond, 1905, Proc. Biol. Soc. Washington 18: 76 — type (by original designation) *Procellaria gigantea* Gmelin. (New name for *Ossifraga* Hombron and Jacquinot, 1844, C.R. Acad. Sci., Paris 18: 356 — preoccupied by Wood, 1835, Analyst 2: 305.)

53   **Macronectes giganteus** (Gmelin)

Southern Giant Petrel

Procellaria gigantea Gmelin, 1789, Syst. Nat. 1: 563—based on "Giant Petrel" of Latham, 1785, General Synop. Birds 3: 396, pl.100—Staten Island.

Proc(ellaria) Basilia Kuhl, 1820, Beitr. Zool. vergl. Anat. 2: 140—synonym of *Procellaria gigantea* Gmelin.

Procellaria ossifraga Forster, 1844, Lichtenstein's Descr. Anim.: 343—Tierra del Fuego.

Procellaria gigas Huxley, 1867, Proc. Zool. Soc. Lond.: 431—error for *Procellaria gigantea* Gmelin.

Ossifraga .alba Potts, 1874, Trans. N.Z. Inst. 6: 152—off Centre Island, Foveaux Strait.

Macronectes giganteus solanderi Mathews, 1912, Birds Aust. 2: 187—Falkland Islands.

Macronectes giganteus forsteri Mathews, 1912, Birds Aust. 2: 189—Valparaiso Bay, Chile.

Macronectes giganteus wilsoni Mathews, 1912, Birds Aust. 2: 189—Ross Sea, Antarctica.

Macronectes giganteus dovei Mathews, 1916, Austral Avian Rec. 3: 54—Sydney, New South Wales.

Procellaria maxima fusca Mathews (*ex* Anderson MS), 1933, Emu 33: 138—Tierra del Fuego and Kerguelen.

Breeds on the coasts of Antarctica, at Islas Noir and Islas Diego Ramirez (Chile), Falkland Islands, South Georgia, South Sandwich, South Orkney, South Shetland, Bouvet?, Gough, Marion, Prince Edward, Crozet, Kerguelen, Heard and Macquarie Islands. Ranges from Antarctic coasts to about 30°S, straggling occasionally further north. Wind-drifted juveniles are common in New Zealand seas from August to October.

CONROY, J.W.H. 1972. Ecological aspects of the biology of the giant petrel *Macronectes giganteus* (Gmelin) in the maritime Antarctic. Sci. Rep. Br. Antarct. Surv. 75: 1–74.

JOHNSTONE, G.W. 1974. Field characters and behaviour at sea of giant petrels in relation to their oceanic distribution. Emu 74: 209–218.

JOHNSTONE, G.W. 1977. Comparative feeding ecology of the giant petrels *Macronectes giganteus* (Gmelin) and *M. halli* Mathews. Pages 647–668 *in* Llano, G.A. (ed.) Adaptations within Antarctic Ecosystems. Washington: Smithsonian Institution.

WARHAM, J. 1962. The biology of the Giant Petrel *Macronectes giganteus*. Auk 79: 139–160.

54   **Macronectes halli** Mathews

Northern Giant Petrel

Macronectes giganteus halli Mathews, 1912, Birds Aust. 2: 187—Kerguelen.

Breeds on South Georgia, Marion, Prince Edward, Crozet, Kerguelen, Macquarie Islands, on islands in Port Pegasus at Stewart Island, and on Auckland, Campbell, Antipodes and Chatham (Sisters, Forty Fours) Islands. Ranges widely over Southern Hemisphere seas, mainly in the subantarctic zone. Subfossil and midden records from the North Island and Chatham Island.

BOURNE, W. R. P.; WARHAM, J. 1966. Geographical variation in the giant petrels of the genus *Macronectes*. Ardea 54: 45–67.
HUNTER, S. 1983. The food and feeding ecology of the giant petrels *Macronectes halli* and *M. giganteus* at South Georgia. J. Zool., Lond. 200: 521–538.
WARHAM, J. 1962. The biology of the Giant Petrel *Macronectes giganteus*. Auk 79: 139–160.

Genus **Pachyptila** Illiger

Pachyptila Illiger, 1811, Prodromus Syst. Mammalium Avium: 274—type (by subsequent designation, Selby, 1840, Cat. Gen. Sub-gen. Types Class Aves: 49) *Procellaria forsteri* Latham = *Procellaria vittata* Forster.
Prion Lesson, 1828, Man. Ornith. 2: 399—type (by monotypy) *Procellaria vittata* Forster.
Pseudoprion Coues, 1866, Proc. Acad. Nat. Sci. Philad.: 164—type (by original designation) *Procellaria turtur* Kuhl.
Fulmariprion Mathews, 1912, Birds Aust. 2: 215—type (by original designation) *Pseudoprion turtur crassirostris* Mathews.
Heteroprion Mathews, 1912, Birds Aust. 2: 222—type (by original designation) *Heteroprion belcheri* Mathews.
Attaprion Mathews, 1933, Bull. Br. Ornith. Club 54: 25—type (by original designation) *Procellaria desolata* Gmelin.
Salviprion Mathews, 1943, *in* Mathews & Hallstrom, Notes Order Procellariiformes: 30—type (by original designation) *Prion vittatus salvini* Mathews.

55   **Pachyptila turtur** (Kuhl)

Fairy Prion (Titi Wainui)

Procellaria turtur Kuhl, 1820, Beitr. Zool. Vergl. Anat., Abth. 1: 143—no locality. *Nomen conservandum* based on an indeterminable drawing by Parkinson in the Banks Library, British Museum (Natural History), labelled "Feb. 1st. 1769. Lat.59.00" (Lysaght, 1959, Bull. Br. Mus. (Nat. Hist.), Hist. Ser., 1: 274).
Procellaria velox Kuhl, 1820, Beitr. Zool. Vergl. Anat., Abth. 1: 143—synonym of *Procellaria turtur* Kuhl.
Prion brevirostris Gould, 1855, Proc. Zool. Soc. Lond.: 88, pl.93—Madeira (locality doubtful).
Pseudoprion turtur solanderi Mathews, 1912, Birds Aust. 2: 220—southern Chile.
Pseudoprion turtur huttoni Mathews, 1912, Birds Aust. 2: 220—Chatham Islands.
Pseudoprion turtur eatoni Mathews, 1912, Birds Aust. 2: 220—Kerguelen Island.
Pseudoprion turtur nova Mathews, 1916, Austral Avian Rec. 3: 55—Sydney, New South Wales.
Pachyptila turtur fallai Oliver, 1930, NZ Birds: 114—Otago, New Zealand.
Pseudoprion turtur steadi Mathews, 1932, Bull. Br. Ornith. Club 52: 146—Stewart Island, breeding on Cundy, Woman's and Betsy Islands.
P.(seudoprion) t.(urtur) oliveri Mathews, 1932, Bull. Br. Ornith. Club 52: 147—Motunau Island, Canterbury, NZ.
Pseudoprion turtur dertrum Mathews, 1938, Emu 37: 281—Bunbury, Western Australia.
Pseudoprion turtur mangarei Mathews and Hallstrom, 1943, Notes Order Procellariiformes: 23—Mangere Island, Chatham Islands.
Pseudoprion turtur benchi Mathews and Hallstrom, 1943, Notes Order Procellariiformes: 23—Poor Knights Islands, NZ.
Pseudoprion turtur armiger Mathews and Hallstrom, 1943, Notes Order Procellariiformes: 23—Poor Knights Islands, N.Z.

Pachyptila turtur subantarctica Oliver, 1955, NZ Birds, 2nd ed.: 119—Antipodes Island.

Breeds on Beauchêne Island (Falklands), Bird Island (South Georgia), Marion and Prince Edward, Crozets (Hog, Penguin, East), Kerguelen, Roche Quille (St Paul), 2 stacks off Macquarie, and on Antipodes Islands, and probably on islets off Campbell Island. Breeds on about 14 islands in or near Bass Strait; on many islands around New Zealand, notably Poor Knights, Stephens, Trios, Brothers, Motunau, Banks Peninsula islets, Open Bay, in Foveaux Strait, off Stewart Island, The Snares, and on Chatham Islands (Mangere, Little Mangere, Rabbit, Kokope, Murumurus, Star Keys, The Sisters). Ranges in subantarctic and subtropical seas, including the Tasman Sea, throughout New Zealand seas and east into the South Pacific. Reaches further north in winter, and straggles to New Guinea, Kermadec Islands, South America and South Africa. Subfossil and midden, North, South, Stewart and Chatham Islands.

FLEMING, C. A. 1941. The phylogeny of the prions. Emu 41: 134–155.
HARPER, P. C. 1976. Breeding biology of the Fairy Prion (*Pachyptila turtur*) at the Poor Knights Islands, New Zealand. NZ J. Zool. 3: 351–371.
HARPER, P. C. 1980. The field identification and distribution of the prions (genus *Pachyptila*), with particular reference to the identification of storm-cast material. Notornis 27: 235–286.
IMBER, M. J. 1981. Diets of stormpetrels *Pelagodroma* and *Garrodia* and of prions *Pachyptila* (Procellariiformes). *In* Cooper, J. (ed.) Proc. Symp. Birds Sea Shore, 1979: 63–88. Cape Town: African Seabird Group.
RICHDALE, L. E. 1944. The Titi Wainui or Fairy Prion *Pachyptila turtur* (Kuhl). Trans. Roy. Soc. NZ 74: 32–48, 165–181.
RICHDALE, L. E. 1965. Breeding behaviour of the Narrow-billed Prion and Broad-billed Prion on Whero Island, New Zealand. Trans. Zool. Soc. Lond. 31: 85–155.

56 **Pachyptila crassirostris** (Mathews)

Fulmar Prion

Breeds at Chatham, Bounty, Snares, Auckland and Heard Islands. Apparently remains in adjacent seas but may be storm-drifted further away. Two subspecies accepted here.

Pachyptila crassirostris crassirostris (Mathews)

Fulmar Prion

Pseudoprion turtur crassirostris Mathews, 1912, Birds Aust. 2: 221—Bounty Islands.
Fulmariprion crassirostris antipodes Mathews and Hallstrom, 1943, Notes Order Procellariiformes: 26—Antipodes Islands.

Breeds on Bounty Islands, Western Chain of The Snares (? subspecies), Auckland (Rose, Ewing, Ocean) and Heard Islands. Presumed to remain in adjacent seas, but some storm-drifted to New Zealand coasts in winter.

DOWNES, M.C.; EALEY, E.H.M.; GWYNN, A.M.; YOUNG, P.S. 1959. The birds of Heard Island. ANARE Rep., Ser. B, 1: 1–96.
EALEY, E.H.M. 1954. Analysis of stomach contents of some Heard Island birds. Emu 54: 204–210.
ROBERTSON, C.J.R.; VAN TETS, G.F. 1982. The status of birds at the Bounty Islands. Notornis 29: 311–336.

Pachyptila crassirostris pyramidalis Fleming
Chatham Fulmar Prion

Pachyptila (Pseudoprion) eatoni pyramidalis Fleming, 1939, Emu 38: 400 — The Pyramid, Chatham Islands.

Breeds on The Pyramid and The Forty Fours (Chatham Islands). Presumed to remain in adjacent seas but occasionally storm-drifted to New Zealand coasts in winter, notably in 1985. Subfossil records from Chatham Island are referred to this subspecies.

FLEMING, C.A. 1939. Birds of the Chatham Islands. Part 1. Emu 38: 380–413.
POWLESLAND, R.G. 1987. Seabirds found dead on New Zealand beaches in 1985 and a review of *Pterodroma* species recoveries since 1960. Notornis 34: 237–252.

57   Pachyptila belcheri (Mathews)
Thin-billed Prion

Heteroprion belcheri Mathews, 1912, Birds Aust. 2: 215, 224 (text-figures) — Geelong, Australia.
Heteroprion belcheri serventyi Mathews, 1935, Bull. Br. Ornith. Club 55: 160 — Cottesloe, Western Australia.
Pachyptila (Heteroprion) belcheri orientalis Falla, 1937, B.A.N.Z.A.R.E. Rep., ser. B, 2: 200 — Royal Sound, Kerguelen.
Heteroprion belcheri lalfa Mathews, 1939, Bull. Br. Ornith. Club 59: 103 — Kapiti Island, NZ.
Heteroprion belcheri falklandicus Mathews, 1939, Bull. Br. Ornith. Club 59: 104 — Falkland Islands.

Breeds on Isla Noir (Chile), Falkland Islands (New Island and about 12 other colonies), East Island of Crozet group (rare), and at Kerguelen. Ranges extensively within subantarctic seas, across all the oceans. Regular winter–early spring visitor to New Zealand seas. Straggler to Kermadec Islands.

CLARK, G.S.; GOODWIN, A.J.; Von MEYER, A.P. 1984. Extension of the known range of some seabirds on the coast of southern Chile. Notornis 31: 320–324.
HARPER, P.C. 1972. The field identification and distribution of the Thin-billed Prion (*Pachyptila belcheri*) and the Antarctic Prion (*Pachyptila desolata*). Notornis 19: 140–175.
STRANGE, I.J. 1980. The Thin-billed Prion, *Pachyptila belcheri*, at New Island, Falkland Islands. Gerfaut 70: 411–445.

58   Pachyptila desolata (Gmelin)
Antarctic Prion

Circumpolar, breeding on subantarctic and antarctic islands. Ranges between about 35°S and the pack-ice or the coasts of Antarctica. Two subspecies accepted here.

Pachyptila desolata desolata (Gmelin)

Antarctic (Kerguelen) Prion

Procellaria desolata Gmelin, 1789, Syst. Nat. 1: 562 (based on "Brown-banded Petrel" of Latham, 1785, Gen. Synop. Birds 3: 409) — Desolation Island = Kerguelen.
Procellaria fasciata Bonnaterre, 1791, Tabl. encycl. méth. Orn. 1: 79 — synonym of *Procellaria desolata* Gmelin.
Prion rossi Bonaparte, 1857, Consp. Gen. Avium 2: 193 — Kerguelen Island.
Heteroprion desolatus mattingleyi Mathews, 1912, Birds Aust. 2: 223 (in key), 226 — Geelong, Australia.
Heteroprion desolatus alexanderi Mathews and Iredale, 1921, Manual Birds Aust. 1: 42 — Cottesloe Beach, Western Australia.

Breeds mainly on Kerguelen Islands; also a few hundred pairs on Crozet Islands (East, Penguin). Ranges mainly in the southern Indian Ocean, reaching the southeast coast of Africa, mainly the southwest coast of Australia, and rarely the west coast of New Zealand in winter-early spring.

DERENNE, P.; LUFBERY, J.X.; TOLLU, B. 1974. L'avifaune de l'archipel Kerguelen. C.N.F.R.A. 33: 57–87.
HARPER, P.C. 1980. The field identification and distribution of the prions (genus *Pachyptila*), with particular reference to the identification of storm-cast material. Notornis 27: 235–286.
JOUVENTIN, P.; STAHL, J.-C.; WEIMERSKIRCH, H.; MOUGIN, J.-L. 1984. The seabirds of the French subantarctic islands and Adélie Land: their status and conservation. ICBP Tech. Publ. 2: 609–625.

Pachyptila desolata banksi Smith

Antarctic Prion

Pachyptila banksi A. Smith, 1840, Illus. Zool. South Africa, Aves, 9: pl.55 — seas off Cape of Good Hope.
Heteroprion desolatus macquariensis Mathews, 1912, Birds Aust. 2: 227 — Macquarie Island.
Heteroprion desolatus peringueyi Mathews, 1912, Birds Aust. 2: 230 — Pondoland coast, South Africa.
Heteroprion desolatus alter Mathews, 1912, Birds Aust. 2: 231 — Auckland Islands.
H.(eteroprion) d.(esolatus) georgia Mathews, 1932, Bull. Br. Ornith. Club 52: 147 — Stromness Bay, South Georgia (= *Pachyptila vittata georgicus* Mathews, 1933, Bull. Br. Ornith. Club 53: 214).
Heteroprion desolatus dispar Iredale, 1938, Emu 37: 244 — Heard Island (= *Heteroprion desolatus heardi* Mathews, 1942, Emu 41: 264).

Breeds on South Georgia, South Sandwich, South Orkney, South Shetland, Bouvet(?), Heard, Macquarie, Auckland and Scott Islands; possibly on islets off Campbell Island; formerly at Cape Denison, Antarctica. A few prospecting at Tristan da Cunha (Inaccessible I.) and Chatham Islands (Houruakopara, Star Keys). Ranges between about 35°S and the pack-ice or the coast of Antarctica; scarcer in the South Pacific Ocean. Regular visitor to seas off mainland New Zealand, mainly in winter. Straggler to Kermadec Islands and Vanuatu.

EALEY, E.H.M. 1954. Analysis of stomach contents of some Heard Island birds. Emu 54: 204–211.
HARPER, P.C. 1972. The field identification and distribution of the Thin-billed

Prion (*Pachyptila belcheri*) and the Antarctic Prion (*Pachyptila desolata*). Notornis 19: 140–175.
HARPER, P. C. 1980. The field identification and distribution of the prions (genus *Pachyptila*), with particular reference to the identification of storm-cast material. Notornis 27: 235–286.
PRINCE, P. A. 1980. The food and feeding ecology of Blue Petrel (*Halobaena caerulea*) and Dove Prion (*Pachyptila desolata*). J. Zool. (Lond.) 190: 59–76.
TICKELL, W. L. N. 1962. The dove prion, *Pachyptila desolata* (Gmelin). Falk. Is. Dep. Surv. Sci. Rep. 33: 1–55.

59   **Pachyptila salvini** (Mathews)

Salvin's Prion

Breeds on Marion, Prince Edward, Crozet and St Paul (Roche Quille) Islands. Ranges widely in the southern Indian Ocean and eastwards in winter, reaching New Zealand regularly. Two subspecies.

Pachyptila salvini salvini (Mathews)

Salvin's Prion

Prion vittatus salvini Mathews, 1912, Birds Aust. 2: 212 — Crozet and Marion Islands.
Heteroprion desolatus crozeti Mathews, 1932, Bull. Br. Ornith. Club 52: 147 — Crozet Archipelago.
Pachyptila gouldi maui Mathews, 1937, Emu 37: 118 — Kapiti Island, NZ.
Pachyptila gouldi whittelli Mathews, 1938, Emu 37: 282 — Bunbury, Western Australia.
Pachyptila salvini muriwai Mathews and Hallstrom, 1943, Notes Order Procellariiformes: 23 — Muriwai Beach, NZ.

Breeds on Marion, Prince Edward, and Crozet (Hog, Penguin, Apostles, Possession, East) Islands. Ranges mainly in the Indian Ocean south of 40°S, reaching the coasts of South Africa, Australia and New Zealand, mainly in winter. Immature birds are regular, probably wind-drifted, winter visitors to the Tasman Sea. Identified, subfossil, from North Island dunes.

DERENNE, P.; MOUGIN, J.-L. 1976. Les Procellariiformes à nidification hypogée de l'île aux Cochons (archipel Crozet, 46°06′S, 50°14′E). CNFRA 40: 149–175.
DESPIN, B.; MOUGIN, J.-L.; SEGONZAC, M. 1972. Oiseaux et Mammifères de l'île de l'Est, archipel Crozet (46°25′S, 52°12′E). CNFRA 31: 1–106.
FLEMING, C. A. 1941. The phylogeny of the prions. Emu 41: 134–155.
JOUVENTIN, P.; MOUGIN, J.-L.; STAHL, J.-C.; WEIMERSKIRCH, H. 1985. Comparative biology of the burrowing petrels of the Crozet Islands. Notornis 32: 157–220.

60   **Pachyptila vittata** (Forster)

Broad-billed Prion (Parara)

Procellaria vittata G. Forster, 1777, Voyage Round World 1: 91, 98 (note) — Anchor I., Dusky Sound (type locality nominated by Mathews & Hallstrom, 1943; 24, after drawing by G. Forster, plate 87, in the British Museum).
Procellaria Forsteri Latham, 1790, Index Ornith. 2: 827 — New Zealand.
Procellaria latirostris Bonnaterre, 1791, Tabl. encycl. méth. Orn. 1: 81 — New Zealand.

(Prion) lamellirostris Bonaparte, 1856, C. R. Acad. Sci., Paris 42: 768—synonym of *Procellaria vittata* Forster.

Prion magnirostris Gould, 1862, Proc. Zool. Soc. Lond.: 125—Dusky Sound.

Prion australis Potts, 1873, Ibis (3) 3: 85—New Zealand.

Prion vittatus gouldi Mathews, 1912, Birds Aust. 2: 203 (in key), 211—Bass Strait.

Prion vittatus missus Mathews, 1912, Birds Aust. 2: 203 (in key), 212, pl.92—Perth, Western Australia.

Prion vittatus keyteli Mathews, 1912, Birds Aust. 2: 210—Tristan da Cunha.

Pachyptila vittata balaena Mathews, 1938, Emu 37: 281—Cottesloe, Western Australia.

Breeds on Tristan da Cunha, Nightingale, Inaccessible and Gough Islands, and on many islands about southern New Zealand: in Fiordland and Foveaux Strait, on Solander Islands, islands and stacks around Stewart Island and Codfish Island, The Snares, and on most of the Chatham Islands. Ranges close to the subtropical convergence (37–49°S) from the South Atlantic to the central South Pacific Oceans. Storm-drifted further north. Subfossil and midden records, North, South and Chatham Islands.

FLEMING, C. A. 1939. Birds of the Chatham Islands, Part I. Emu 38: 380–413.

HARPER, P. C. 1980. The field identification and distribution of the prions (genus *Pachyptila*), with particular reference to the identification of storm-cast material. Notornis 27. 235–286.

IMBER, M. J. 1981. Diets of stormpetrels *Pelagodroma* and *Garrodia* and of prions *Pachyptila* (Procellariiformes). *In* Cooper, J. (ed.) Proc. Symp. Birds Sea Shore, 1979, 63–88. Cape Town: African Seabird Group.

RICHDALE, L. E. 1965. Breeding behaviour of the Narrow-billed Prion and Broad-billed Prion on Whero Island, New Zealand. Trans. Zool. Soc. Lond. 31: 85–155.

Genus **Halobaena** Bonaparte

Halobaena Bonaparte, 1856, C. R. Acad. Sci., Paris 42: 768—type (by monotypy) *Procellaria caerulea* Gmelin.

Zaprium Coues, 1875, Bull. U.S. Nat. Mus. 2: 34—type (by monotypy) *Procellaria caerulea* Gmelin.

61 **Halobaena caerulea** (Gmelin)

Blue Petrel

Procellaria caerulea Gmelin, 1789, Syst. Nat. 1: 560 (based on "Blue Petrel" of G. Forster, 1777, Voyage Round World 1: 91)—Southern Ocean at 58°S.

Procellaria similis J. R. Forster, 1844, Descr. Animal. Itinere Maris Australis Terras: 59—Antarctic Ocean.

Halobaena caerulea victoriae Mathews, 1916, Austral Avian Rec. 3: 54—Victoria, Australia.

Halobaena murphyi Brooks, 1917, Bull. Mus. Comp. Zool. 61: 146—Stromness Bay, South Georgia.

Breeds on Cape Horn and adjacent islands of the Hermite and Wollaston groups, Islas Diego Ramirez, South Georgia, Marion, Prince Edward, Crozet group (East, Penguin, Apostles), Kerguelen, and stacks off Macquarie Island. Ranges from Antarctica to about 40°S, sometimes further north. Regular winter-spring visitor to New Zealand seas; hundreds beach-wrecked in 1981, 1984 and 1985. Tentatively identified (R.J. Scarlett) from one North Island midden site.

DELL, R. K. 1952. The Blue Petrel in Australasian waters. Emu 52: 147–154.
JOUVENTIN, P.; MOUGIN, J.-L.; STAHL, J.-C.; WEIMERSKIRCH, H. 1985. Comparative biology of the burrowing petrels of the Crozet Islands. Notornis 32: 157–220.
POWLESLAND, R. G. 1986. Seabirds found dead on New Zealand beaches in 1984 and a review of fulmar recoveries since 1960. Notornis 33: 171–184.
PRINCE, P. A. 1980. The food and feeding ecology of Blue Petrel (*Halobaena caerulea*) and Dove Prion (*Pachyptila desolata*). J. Zool. (Lond.) 190: 59–76.

Genus **Pterodroma** Bonaparte

Pterodroma Bonaparte, 1856, C.R. Acad. Sci., Paris 42: 768 — type (by subsequent designation, Coues, 1866, Proc. Acad. Nat. Sci. Philadelphia 18: 137) *Procellaria macroptera* A. Smith.
Aestrelata Bonaparte, 1856, C. R. Acad. Sci., Paris 42: 768 — type (by subsequent designation, Bonaparte, 1856, C.R. Acad. Sci., Paris 43: 996) *Fulmarus meridionalis* Lawrence = *Procellaria hasitata* Kuhl.
Cookilaria Bonaparte, 1856, C.R. Acad. Sci., Paris 43: 994 — type (by subsequent designation, Coues, 1866, Proc. Acad. Nat. Sci. Philadelphia 18: 137) *Procellaria cookii* G. R. Gray.
Oestrelatella Bianchi, 1913, Faune Russie, Aves 1 (pt.2): 521, 719 — type (by original designation) *Oestrelata hypoleuca* Salvin.
Hallstroma Mathews, 1943, *in* Mathews and Hallstrom, Notes Order Procellariiformes: 35, 37 (in keys) — type (by original designation) *Procellaria neglecta* Schlegel.
Proaestrelata (subgenus) Imber, 1985, Ibis 127: 219 — type (by original designation) *Oestrelata axillaris* Salvin.

Subgenus **Cookilaria**

62   **Pterodroma longirostris** (Stejneger)

Stejneger's Petrel

Aestrelata longirostris Stejneger, 1893, Proc. U.S. Nat. Mus. 16: 618 — Mutzu Province, Honshu, Japan.
Pterodroma (Aestrelata) cooki masafuerae Lönnberg, 1921, *in* Skottsberg, Nat. Hist. Juan Fernandez Easter Islands 3: 14 — Mas Afuera Island.

Breeds on Mas-a-fuera Island (Isla Alejandro Selkirk), Juan Fernandez archipelago. Migrates to the subtropical North Pacific Ocean between Hawaiian Islands and Japan. Non-breeding vagrant to seas around North Island, November to January: Baring Head 1961, Ohope Beach 1962 (2), Turakina Valley 1963, east of Hawke Bay 1978, Ruakaka beach 1980, Northland 1981, Ninety Mile Beach 1983 (3).

BROOKE, M. L. 1987. Population estimates and breeding biology of the petrels *Pterodroma externa* and *P. longirostris* on Isla Alejandro Selkirk, Juan Fernandez Archipelago. Condor 89: 581–586.

FALLA, R. A. 1962. New Zealand records of *Pterodroma longirostris* (Stejneger) and a new record of *Pterodroma leucoptera* (Gould). Notornis 9: 275–277.
MURPHY, R. C. 1936. Oceanic Birds of South America. Vol. II. New York: Am. Mus. Nat. Hist.
TANAKA, Y.; KANEKO, Y.; SATO, S. 1985. Distribution and migration of smaller petrels of the genus *Pterodroma* in the Northwest Pacific. J. Yamashina Inst. Ornith. 17: 23–31.

53   Pterodroma pycrofti Falla

Pycroft's Petrel

Pterodroma pycrofti Falla, 1933, Rec. Auck. Inst. Mus. 1: 176 — Hen Island.

Breeds only in New Zealand on Stephenson, Poor Knights (Aorangi), Hen and Chickens (Lady Alice, Whatupuke, Copper-mine), and Mercury (Red Mercury, Korapuki, Kawitihu, Double, Stanley) Islands. Range at sea uncertain but extends east and west of northern North Island. Probably migrates to the North Pacific Ocean. Subfossil at Norfolk Island and Lord Howe Island.

BARTLE, J. A. 1968. Observations on the breeding habits of Pycroft's Petrel. Notornis 15: 70–99.
DUNNET, G. M. 1985. Pycroft's Petrel in the breeding season at Hen and Chickens Islands. Notornis 32: 5–21.
FLEMING, C. A. 1941. Notes on Neozelanic forms of the subgenus *Cookilaria*. Emu 41: 69–80.
MEREDITH, C. A. 1985. The vertebrate fossil fauna of Norfolk Island, and the phylogeny of the genus *Pterodroma*. Ph.D. thesis, Monash University, Victoria.

64   Pterodroma leucoptera (Gould)

Gould's Petrel

Procellaria leucoptera Gould, 1844, Ann. Mag. Nat. Hist. 13: 364 — Cabbage Tree Island, New South Wales.

Breeds on Cabbage Tree Island, NSW, and on New Caledonia. Ranges in the south-west Pacific and in the Tasman Sea to seas off Tasmania, and migrates to the eastern tropical Pacific Ocean.

Pterodroma leucoptera caledonica Imber & Jenkins

New Caledonian Petrel

Pterodroma leucoptera caledonica Imber and Jenkins, 1981, Notornis 28: 151, 152 — Muriwai Beach, New Zealand.

Breeds on New Caledonia. Ranges north to the Solomon Islands and far south in the Tasman Sea to seas off Tasmania and to the west of Foveaux Strait. Migrates to the eastern tropical Pacific, especially to southwest of Galapagos Islands. About 25 records as far south as Dunedin (1988) but mainly from the North Island west coast, November to June.

BULL, P. C. 1943. The occurrence of *Pterodroma leucoptera* in New Zealand. Emu 42: 145–152.
HAWKE, D. 1989. Gould's Petrel from Dunedin City. Notornis 36: 189–190.

IMBER, M.J.; JENKINS, J.A.F. 1981. The New Caledonian Petrel. Notornis 28: 149–160.
NAKAMURA, K. 1982. Distribution of gadfly petrels of the genus *Pterodroma* in the antarctic and subantarctic regions of the Australian sector, austral summer 1981. Trans. Tokyo Univ. Fish. 5: 203–211.
PITMAN, R.L. 1986. Atlas of Seabird Distribution and Relative Abundance in the Eastern Tropical Pacific. U.S. National Marine Fisheries Service, SW Center, Admin. Rep. LJ–86–02C.

65   Pterodroma cookii (Gray)

Cook's Petrel (Titi)

Procellaria Cookii G.R. Gray, 1843, *in* E. Dieffenbach, Travels New Zealand 2: 199 — New Zealand.
Pterodroma cookii orientalis Murphy, 1929, Am. Mus. Novit. 370: 5 — 200 miles west of Callao, Peru.

Breeds on Little Barrier (major colony), Great Barrier (a few pairs) and Codfish (c.100 pairs) Islands. Ranges mainly east of New Zealand but also into the Tasman Sea. Migrates to the eastern Pacific Ocean, mainly between 34°S and 30°N, straggling further north. Subfossil and midden records from North Island, subfossil from South Island.

FALLA, R.A. 1934. The distribution and breeding habits of petrels in northern New Zealand. Rec. Auck. Inst. Mus. 1: 245–260.
PITMAN, R.L. 1986. Atlas of Seabird Distribution and Relative Abundance in the Eastern Tropical Pacific. U.S. National Marine Fisheries Service, SW Center, Admin. Rep. LJ–86–02C.

Subgenus Oestrelatella

66   Pterodroma nigripennis (Rothschild)

Black-winged Petrel

Oestrelata nigripennis Rothschild, 1893, Bull. Br. Ornith. Club 1:57 — Kermadec Islands.
Oestrelatella nigricollis Bianchi, 1913, Faune Russie, Oiseaux 1: 727 — (error) synonym of *Oestrelata nigripennis* Rothschild.
Cookilaria hindwoodi Whitley, 1938, Austral. Mus. Mag. 6: 297 — Norfolk Island.

Breeds at Lord Howe, Norfolk and Philip Islands, on islets of New Caledonia, at Kermadec Islands, Three Kings (Great King, South West, West?, North East?), East and Portland Islands, Chatham Islands (South East, Mangere, possibly Star Keys), probably in Tonga, and on Rarotonga, islets off Rapa Island and possibly Bass Rocks (Austral Islands). Prospecting at Mutton-bird Island (New South Wales), Heron Island (Queensland), Cape Maria van Diemen and North Cape, possibly other headlands in Northland, at Poor Knights and Cuvier Islands, and on other Chatham Islands (Forty Fours, Pitt Island). Ranges throughout the north Tasman Sea and subtropical southwest Pacific Ocean. Migrates to the subtropical North Pacific Ocean, from Japan to Mexico. Subfossil in Chatham Island dunes.

EAGLE, M. 1980. Black-winged Petrels on Portland Island. Notornis 27: 171–175.
JENKINS, J. A. F.; CHESHIRE, N. G. 1982. The Black-winged Petrel (*Pterodroma nigripennis*) in the South-west Pacific and the Tasman Sea. Notornis 29: 293–310.
OLIVER, W. R. B. 1955. New Zealand Birds. 2nd ed. Wellington: Reed.
PITMAN, R. L. 1986. Atlas of Seabird Distribution and Relative Abundance in the Eastern Tropical Pacific. U.S. National Marine Fisheries Service, SW Center, Admin. Rep. LJ-86-02C.
TANAKA, Y.; KANEKO, Y.; SATO, S. 1985. Distribution and migration of smaller petrels of the genus *Pterodroma* in the Northwest Pacific. J. Yamashina Inst. Ornith. 17: 23–31.

67 **Pterodroma axillaris** (Salvin)

Chatham Petrel

Oestrelata axillaris Salvin, 1893, Bull. Br. Ornith. Club 1: 33 — Chatham Islands.

Breeds now only on South East Island, Chatham Islands. Range at sea unknown; probably migrates to the North Pacific Ocean from June to November. Subfossil in cave and dune deposits on Chatham Island, and in soil deposits on Mangere Island.

FLEMING, C. A. 1939. Birds of the Chatham Islands, Part I. Emu 38: 380–413.
IMBER, M. J. 1985a. Origins, phylogeny and taxonomy of the gadfly petrels *Pterodroma* spp. Ibis 127: 197–229.

68 **Pterodroma inexpectata** (Forster)

Mottled Petrel (Korure)

Procellaria inexpectata J. R. Forster, 1844, Descr. Animal. Itinere Maris Australis Terras: 204 — Antarctic Ocean.
Procellaria gularis Peale, 1848, Proc. U.S. Explor. Exped., Birds, 8: 299 — 68°S, 95°W Pacific Ocean.
Procellaria affinis Buller, 1875, Trans. Proc. NZ Inst. (1874) 7: 216 — Potts River, South Island.
Oestrelata fisheri Ridgway, 1883, Proc. U.S. Nat. Mus. 5: 656 — Kodiak Island, Alaska.
Aestrelata scalaris Brewster, 1886, Auk 3: 390 — Mount Morris, New York State.
Pterodroma inexpectata thompsoni Mathews, 1915, Austral Avian Rec. 2: 125 — Tasmania.
Pterodroma neglus Mathews, 1928, Bull. Br. Ornith. Club 49: 51 — new name for *Procellaria lugens* Mathews, 1912.

Breeds in southern New Zealand: Fiordland (Shag and Front Islands in Dusky Sound, Lake Hauroko islet), Solander Islands, numerous islands around Stewart Island (notably Codfish, Big South Cape), and The Snares. Formerly bred in a few lesser ranges of the North and South Islands (e.g. Banks Peninsula). Reaches the pack-ice between 90°E and 75°W, but mainly frequents subantarctic seas. Migrates to the North Pacific, mainly to the subarctic convergence zone but reaching the Bering Sea and Alaska. Common in subfossil and midden deposits in North, South, and Chatham Islands.

HARPER, P. C. 1973. The field identification and supplementary notes on the Soft-plumaged Petrel (*Pterodroma mollis* Gould, 1844). Notornis 20: 193–201.

IMBER, M.J. 1985. Origins, phylogeny and taxonomy of the gadfly petrels *Pterodroma* spp. Ibis 127: 197–229.
NAKAMURA, K.; TANAKA, Y. 1977. Distribution and migration of two species of the genus *Pterodroma* in the North Pacific. Misc. Rep. Yamashina Inst. Ornith. 9: 112–120.
WARHAM, J.; KEELEY, B.R.; WILSON, G.J. 1977. Breeding of the Mottled Petrel. Auk 94: 1–17.

69   **Pterodroma cervicalis** (Salvin)

White-naped Petrel

Breeds on Kermadec Islands and possibly in Vanuatu (Banks Islands?). Migrates mainly to the northwest Pacific Ocean. Two subspecies, one unnamed (Falla 1976).

Pterodroma cervicalis cervicalis (Salvin)

White-naped Petrel

Oestrelata cervicalis Salvin, 1891, Ibis (1891): 192 — Kermadec Islands.
Breeds on Macauley and formerly bred on Raoul, Kermadec Islands. Ranges in adjacent seas and straggles to the east coast of Australia and to northern New Zealand (Mamaku Range 1968, Gisborne 1977, Hokianga Harbour 1982, Karikari Bay 1986). Migrates to the North Pacific Ocean, mainly to southeast of Japan.
FALLA, R.A. 1976. Notes on the gadfly petrels *Pterodroma externa* and *P. e. cervicalis*. Notornis 23: 320–322.
IMBER, M.J. 1985. Origins, phylogeny and taxonomy of the gadfly petrels *Pterodroma* spp. Ibis 127: 197–229.
OLIVER, W.R.B. 1955. New Zealand Birds. 2nd ed. Wellington: Reed.
TANAKA, Y.; INABA, F. 1981. The distribution and migration of White-necked Petrel, *Pterodroma externa cervicalis*, in the west area of North Pacific Ocean and the Japanese waters. J. Yamashina Inst. Ornith. 13: 207–214.

Subgenus **Hallstroma**

70   **Pterodroma externa** (Salvin)

Juan Fernandez Petrel

Oestrelata externa Salvin, 1875, Ibis (1875): 373 — islands of Mas-a-fuera and Juan Fernandez.
Pterodroma externa tristani Mathews, 1931, Bull. Br. Ornith. Club 52: 63 — Tristan da Cunha.
Breeds on Mas-a-fuera, Juan Fernandez Islands (c. 1 million pairs). Migrates to the North Pacific Ocean between the Hawaiian Islands, the equator and Mexico. Vagrant to the southwest Pacific Ocean: one blown inland, Waikato 1971; one prospecting at South East Island, Chatham Islands in 1984 and 1986, at least 2 in early 1989 and 1989–90 (one specimen); at Mangere Island in 1988.
BROOKE, M.L. 1987. Population estimates and breeding biology of the petrels

Pterodroma externa and *P. longirostris* on Isla Alejandro Selkirk, Juan Fernandez Archipelago. Condor 89: 581–586.
IMBER, M. J. 1985. Origins, phylogeny and taxonomy of the gadfly petrels *Pterodroma* spp. Ibis 127: 197–229.
MURPHY, R. C. 1936. Oceanic Birds of South America. Vol. II. New York: Am. Mus. Nat. Hist.
REED, S. M. 1976. Correction to short note on Black-capped Petrel in the Waikato. Notornis 23: 355.

71   Pterodroma alba (Gmelin)

Phoenix Petrel

Procellaria alba Gmelin, 1789, Syst. Nat. 1: 565 (based on "White-breasted Petrel" of Latham, 1785, General Synop. Birds 3: 400) — Turtle and Christmas Islands; restricted to the latter by Murphy and Pennoyer (1952).
Procellaria parvirostris Peale, 1848, U.S. Explor. Exped. 8: 298 — near Pukapuka Island, Tuamotu Archipelago.
Oestrelata wortheni Rothschild, 1902, Bull. Br. Ornith. Club 12: 62 — 3°S, 118°45′W in the Pacific Ocean.
Aestrelata oliveri Mathews and Iredale, 1914, Austral Avian Rec. 2: 113 — Raoul Island, Kermadec Islands.
Pterodroma alba cantonia Mathews, 1942, Emu 42: 123 — Canton Island, Phoenix Islands.

Breeds on Pacific Ocean islands: Phoenix, Line, Marquesas, Oeno, Henderson, Ducie, possibly Tonga, and probably formerly Raoul Island (Kermadecs), where four seen ashore in 1913. One over Curtis Island (Kermadecs) on 21 May 1982. Non-migratory but ranges widely in the central Pacific Ocean.

ASHMOLE, N. P.; ASHMOLE, M. J. 1967. Comparative feeding ecology of seabirds of a tropical oceanic island. Bull. Peabody Mus. Nat. Hist. 24: 1–131.
MURPHY, R. C.; PENNOYER, J. M. 1952. Larger petrels of the genus *Pterodroma*. Am. Mus. Novit. 1580.

72   Pterodroma neglecta (Schlegel)

Kermadec Petrel

Breeds on islands across the subtropical South Pacific and migrates into low latitudes of the North Pacific Ocean. Two subspecies; one in the east, the other central and western.

Pterodroma neglecta neglecta (Schlegel)

Kermadec Petrel

Procellaria neglecta Schlegel, 1863, Mus. Hist. Nat. Pays-Bas, Rev. Méthod. Crit. Coll., livr. 4, Procellariae: 10 — Raoul Island, Kermadec Islands.
Oestrelata leucophrys Hutton, 1893, Proc. Zool. Soc. Lond.: 752, pl. 63 — Sunday (= Raoul) Island, Kermadec Islands.
Rhantistes raoulensis Salvin, 1896, Cat. Birds Br. Mus. 25: 412 — synonym of *Procellaria neglecta* Schlegel.
Pterodroma neglecta quintali Mathews, 1916, Austral Avian Rec. 3: 68 — Lord Howe Island.

Breeds on Ball's Pyramid (Lord Howe Island), at Kermadec Islands (formerly large numbers on Raoul I.), Austral Islands

(Rapa, Raivavae), Oeno, Henderson and Ducie Islands, and possibly in the Tuamotu Archipelago. One prospecting at Cuvier Island, 1973–1981. Ranges mainly in the subtropical South Pacific, 20°S–35°S. Straggler to the northern North Island: 4 beach-wrecked specimens. One off the Chatham Islands (1975). Some migration to the North Pacific between Mexico and the Philippine Islands.

MERTON, D. V. 1970. Kermadec Islands Expedition reports: a general account of birdlife. Notornis 17: 147–199.
MURPHY, R. C.; PENNOYER, J. M. 1952. Larger petrels of the genus *Pterodroma*. Am. Mus. Novit. 1580.
OLIVER, W. R. B. 1955. New Zealand Birds. 2nd. ed. Wellington: Reed.

Subgenus **Pterodroma**

73   **Pterodroma solandri** (Gould)

Providence Petrel

Procellaria Solandri Gould, 1844, Proc. Zool. Soc. Lond. 1844: 57 — no locality = Bass Strait, *fide* Gould, 1844, Ann. Mag. Nat. Hist. 13: 363.
Procellaria phillipii G. R. Gray, 1862, Ibis (1862): 246 — Norfolk Island.
Oestrelata montana Hull, 1911, Proc. Linn. Soc. NSW 35: 785 — Lord Howe Island.

Breeds on Lord Howe Island and at Norfolk Island (Philip Island, formerly in large numbers on Norfolk itself). Ranges mainly in the western Tasman Sea to seas off Tasmania. Pre-breeders migrate to the North Pacific Ocean, Japan to North America but more abundant in the west. Straggler to the west coast of the northern North Island: Muriwai Beach 1921, Omamari (Dargaville coast) 1984.

HINDWOOD, K. A. 1940. The birds of Lord Howe Island. Emu 40: 1–86.
MILLER, P. 1986. Second New Zealand record of the Bird of Providence. Notornis 33: 76.
TANAKA, Y. 1986. Distribution and migration of the Solander's Petrel *Pterodroma solandri* in the North Pacific in relation to sea surface water temperatures. J. Yamashina Inst. Ornith. 18: 1–8.

74   **Pterodroma macroptera** (Smith)

Great-winged Petrel

Procellaria macroptera A. Smith, 1840, Illus. Zool. South Africa, Aves: pl.52 — seas off Cape of Good Hope.

Breeds on subtropical and subantarctic islands in the South Atlantic, Indian and southwest Pacific Oceans. Relatively sedentary. Two or three subspecies.

Pterodroma macroptera gouldi (Hutton)

Grey-faced Petrel (Oi)

Aestrelata gouldi Hutton, 1869, Ibis (1869): 351 — New Zealand seas.

Breeds on many islands, islets, headlands and cliff-tops from Three Kings Islands south to near New Plymouth on the west coast and near Gisborne on the east coast. Ranges throughout the Tasman Sea and in the South Pacific to about 130°W between 30°S and 48°S. Sedentary. Subfossil and midden deposits, North Island; subfossil from Chatham Island dunes.

IMBER, M.J. 1973. The food of Grey-faced Petrels (*Pterodroma macroptera gouldi* (Hutton), with special reference to diurnal vertical migration of their prey. J. Anim. Ecol. 42: 645–662.

IMBER, M.J. 1976. Breeding biology of the Grey-faced Petrel *Pterodroma macroptera gouldi*. Ibis 118: 51–64.

IMBER, M.J. 1985. Origins phylogeny and taxonomy of the gadfly petrels *Pterodroma* spp. Ibis 127: 197–229.

75 **Pterodroma magentae** (Giglioli & Salvadori)
Magenta Petrel (Chatham Island Taiko)

Aestrelata Magentae Giglioli and Salvadori, 1869, Atti Soc. Ital. Sci. Nat., Milan 11 (1868): 451 — 39°38'S, 125°58'W Pacific Ocean.

Chatham Islands, breeding in widely scattered burrows in bush of the southwest of Chatham Island; formerly abundant (Moriori midden and subfossil bones). Surviving number possibly 45–55. Ranges southwards while breeding and to the central South Pacific afterwards.

BOURNE, W.R.P. 1964. The relationship between the Magenta Petrel and the Chatham Island Taiko. Notornis 11: 139–144.

CROCKETT, D.E. 1985. Chatham Island Taiko. Page 78 *in* Complete Book of New Zealand Birds. Sydney: Reader's Digest.

SUTTON, D.G.; MARSHALL, Y.M. 1977. Archaeological bird bone assemblages from Chatham Island: an interpretation. Working Papers in Chatham Islands Archaeology 12. Dunedin: Otago Univ.

76 **Pterodroma lessonii** (Garnot)

White-headed Petrel

Procellaria Lessonii Garnot, 1826, Ann. Sci. Nat., Paris 7: 54, pl.4 — seas near Cape Horn and in the South Pacific at 52°S, 85°W.

Procellaria leucocephala J.R. Forster, 1844, Descr. Animal. Itinere Maris Australis Terras: 206 — South Pacific Ocean.

Aestrelata lessonii australis Mathews, 1916, Austral Avian Rec. 3: 54 — Sydney, New South Wales.

Breeds on Possession Island (Crozet group), Kerguelen, Macquarie, Auckland and Antipodes Islands. More or less circumpolar, ranging between 33°S and the pack-ice but mainly in the subantarctic zone. Regular winter-spring beach-wreck on the west coast of the North Island. Subfossil records from North Island and Chathams, subfossil and midden from South Island.

MURPHY, R.C.; PENNOYER, J.M. 1952. Larger petrels of the genus *Pterodroma*. Am. Mus. Novit. 1580.

WARHAM, J. 1967. The White-headed Petrel, *Pterodroma lessoni*, at Macquarie Island. Emu 67: 1–22.

WARHAM, J.; BELL, B.D. 1979. The birds of Antipodes Island, New Zealand. Notornis 26: 121–169.

77   **Pterodroma mollis** (Gould)

Soft-plumaged Petrel

Procellaria mollis Gould, 1844, Ann. Mag. Nat. Hist. 13: 363 — south Atlantic Ocean, 20°S to 40°S.

Pterodroma dubius Mathews, 1924, Bull. Br. Ornith. Club 44: 70; new name for bird described in Mathews, 1912, Birds Aust. 2: 157, pl.86 — ? north-west coast of Australia.

Pterodroma deceptornis Mathews, 1932, Novit. Zool. 38: 34 — at sea, 36°08′S, 88°55′E.

Pterodroma mollis fusca Imber, 1985, Ibis 127: 224 (new name for birds described by Clancey, Brooke and Sinclair, 1981, Durban Mus. Novit. 12: 211–212, Fig. 2, 3) — Marion and Prince Edward Islands.

Breeds on Tristan da Cunha, Inaccessible, Nightingale and Gough Islands; on Marion, Prince Edward and Crozet (Possession, East, Penguin, Apostles) Islands, at Kerguelen and formerly on Amsterdam and St Paul Islands; on Antipodes Island and possibly (or prospecting) on Macquarie Island (4 records).

Ranges mainly between 25°S and 50°S, reaching about 60°S, extensively east and west of colonies but rare in the South Pacific. Straggles mainly to east coast of New Zealand: about 9 records since 1971 (first recorded at Antipodes Island in 1969). Recorded once (1980) on Chatham Island.

No subspecies; related forms in the North Atlantic are here considered to be allopatric species.

HARPER, P. C. 1973. The field identification and supplementary notes on the Soft-plumaged Petrel (*Pterodroma mollis* Gould, 1844). Notornis 20: 193–201.

IMBER, M. J. 1983. The lesser petrels of Antipodes Islands, with notes from Prince Edward and Gough Islands. Notornis 30: 283–298.

JOUVENTIN, P.; MOUGIN, J.-L.; STAHL, J.-C.; WEIMERSKIRCH, H. 1985. Comparative biology of the burrowing petrels of the Crozet Islands. Notornis 32: 157–220.

SCHRAMM, M. 1983. The breeding biologies of the petrels *Pterodroma macroptera*, *P. brevirostris* and *P. mollis* at Marion Island. Emu 83: 75–81.

SCHRAMM, M. 1986. The diet of chicks of Greatwinged, Kerguelen and Soft-plumaged Petrels at the Prince Edward Islands. Ostrich 57: 9–15.

WARHAM, J.; BELL, B. D. 1979. The birds of Antipodes Island, New Zealand. Notornis 26: 121–169.

Family **OCEANITIDAE**: Storm Petrels*

Subfamily HYDROBATINAE: Northern Storm Petrels

Genus **Oceanodroma** Reichenbach

Oceanodroma Reichenbach, 1853, Avium Syst. Nat. (1852): 4 — type (by original designation) *Procellaria furcata* Gmelin.

* For family name see Olson, S. L. 1987, Comment on the family name for the storm petrels (Aves), Bull. Zool. Nomencl. 44(1): 44–45. See also Olson, S. L., 1985, Ann. S. Afr. Mus. 95(3): 123–145, who points out that "Both on osteological and myological grounds the storm petrels fall into two very distinct groups that are best ranked as subfamilies.... The more specialized of these...is the Oceanitinae."

Cymochorea Coues, 1864, Proc. Acad. Nat. Sci. Philad.: 75 — type (by original designation) *Procellaria leucorhoa* Vieillot.
Pacificodroma Bianchi, 1913, Faune Russie, Oiseaux 1, pt.2: 516, 559 — type (by original designation) *Thalassidroma monorhis* Swinhoe.
Bannermania Mathews and Iredale, 1915, Ibis 1915: 578 — type (by monotypy) *Thalassidroma hornbyi* G. R. Gray.
Tethysia Mathews, 1933, Bull. Br. Ornith. Club 53: 154 — type (by original designation) *Procellaria tethys* Bonaparte.
Loomelania Mathews, 1934, Bull. Br. Ornith. Club 54: 119 — type (by original designation) *Procellaria melania* Bonaparte.
Thalobata Mathews, 1943, in Mathews & Hallstrom, Notes Order Procellariiformes: 27 — type (by original designation) *Thalassidroma castro* Harcourt.
Bianchoma Mathews, 1943, in Mathews & Hallstrom, Notes Order Procellariiformes: 29 — type (by original designation) *Oceanodroma melania matsudairae* Kuroda.

78 **Oceanodroma leucorhoa** (Vieillot)

Leach's Storm Petrel

Breeds on islands in the North Pacific and North Atlantic Oceans, and migrates to the tropics after breeding. Up to four subspecies.

Oceanodroma leucorhoa leucorhoa (Vieillot)

Leach's Storm Petrel

Procellaria leucorhoa Vieillot, 1818, Nouv. Dict. Hist. Nat., nouv. ed. (1817), 25: 422 — maritime parts of Picardy, France.

Breeds on islands between 42 and 68°N in the North Pacific and North Atlantic Oceans. After breeding, migrates mainly to the tropics, where non-breeders are present all year. Straggler to New Zealand: Muriwai Beach, August 1922; Hauraki Plains, April 1978; Dargaville Beach, August 1978; Rabbit I., Chatham Islands, November 1980 (two prospecting for nest sites); off Chatham Island, December 1983.

GROSS, W. A. O. 1935. The life history cycle of Leach's Petrel (*Oceanodroma leucorhoa leucorhoa*) on the outer sea islands of the Bay of Fundy. Auk 52: 382–399.
IMBER, M. J.; LOVEGROVE, T. G. 1982. Leach's Storm Petrels (*Oceanodroma l. leucorhoa*) prospecting for nest sites on the Chatham Islands. Notornis 29: 101–108.
WATANUKI, Y. 1985. Food of breeding Leach's Storm Petrels (*Oceanodroma leucorhoa*). Auk 102: 884–886.
WILBUR, K. 1969. The breeding biology of Leach's Petrel, *Oceanodroma leucorhoa*. Auk 86: 433–442.

Subfamily OCEANITINAE: Southern Storm Petrels
Genus **Oceanites** Keyserling and Blasius

Oceanites Keyserling and J. H. Blasius, 1840, Wirbelthiere Europa's: xciii, 131, 238 — type (by subsequent designation, G. R. Gray, 1841, List Gen. Birds, ed. 2: 99) *Procellaria wilsonii* Bonaparte = *Procellaria oceanica* Kuhl.
Garrodia Forbes, 1881, Coll. Sci. Papers Garrod: 521 footnote — type (by original designation and monotypy) *Thalassidroma nereis* Gould.
Procellata Bianchi, 1913, Faune Russie, Oiseaux 1, pt 2: 805 — type (by original designation) *Procellaria oceanica* Kuhl.

Pealeornis Mathews, 1932, Bull. Br. Ornith. Club 52: 132 — type (by original designation) *Pealeornis maoriana* Mathews = *Procellaria oceanica* Kuhl.

Subgenus **Oceanites**

79   **Oceanites oceanicus** (Kuhl)

Wilson's Storm Petrel

Procellaria oceanica Kuhl, 1820, Beitr. Zool. vergl. Anat., Abth. 1: 136, pl.10, fig.
1 — no locality; South Georgia designated by Murphy, 1918, Bull. Am. Mus. Nat.
Hist. 38: 128.

Breeds on coasts and islands of Antarctica and the Antarctic
Peninsula, and on antarctic and subantarctic archipelagoes as
far north as Crozet Islands (46°S). Migrates to the North Atlantic,
north Indian and North Pacific Oceans after breeding, reaching
about 55°N in the Atlantic. Two subspecies.

Oceanites oceanicus exasperatus Mathews

Wilson's Storm Petrel

Oceanites oceanicus exasperatus Mathews, 1912, Birds Aust. 2: 11, pl.68 — New Zealand
seas.
Pealeornis maoriana Mathews, 1932, Bull. Br. Ornith. Club 52: 132 — Banks Peninsula.

Breeds on coasts and islands of Antarctica, its Peninsula and
several archipelagoes and islands in the antarctic zone; including
many Ross Sea localities, Balleny and Scott Islands. Migrates to
northern oceans but uncommon on passage past New Zealand,
mainly November-December and March-May; over 40 records.
Subfossil from one South Island cave (Punakaiki).

COPESTAKE, P.G.; CROXALL, J.P. 1985. Aspects of the breeding biology of
Wilson's Storm Petrel *Oceanites oceanicus* at Bird Island, South Georgia. Br. Antarct.
Surv. Bull. 66: 7–17.
NAKAMURA, K.; TANAKA, Y.; HASEGAWA, M. 1983. Distribution status of
the Wilson's Storm-Petrel *Oceanites oceanicus* in Japanese waters. Bull. Biogeogr. Soc.
Japan 38: 125–127.
ROBERTS, B. 1940. The life cycle of the Wilson's Storm-Petrel *Oceanites oceanicus*
(Kuhl). Sci. Rep. Br. Graham Land Exp. 1: 141–194.

Subgenus **Garrodia**

80   **Oceanites nereis** (Gould)

Grey-backed Storm Petrel

Thalassidroma Nereis Gould, 1841, Proc. Zool. Soc. Lond. 1840: 178 — Bass Strait.
Procellaria saltatrix Mathews, 1912, Birds Aust. 2: 16 — 110 km southeast of Kai-
koura, New Zealand; *ex* Solander MS.
Procellaria longipes Mathews, 1912, Birds Aust. 2: 17 — off New Zealand; *ex* Solander
MS.
Oceanites nereis chubbi Mathews, 1912, Birds Aust. 2: 18 — Falkland Islands.
Oceanites nereis couesi Mathews, 1912, Birds Aust. 2: 18 — Kerguelen Island.

A circumpolar, predominantly subantarctic, species breeding on
Falkland Islands, South Georgia, Gough, Prince Edward, Crozet

(East, ? Penguin, ? Apostles), Kerguelen, Auckland, Antipodes and Chatham Islands, and possibly on islets off Macquarie and Campbell Islands. Sedentary but ranges to about 30°S in New Zealand seas. Recorded, subfossil, on Chatham Island (and, tentatively, from one North Island cave).

FLEMING, C. A. 1939. Birds of the Chatham Islands. Part I. Emu 38: 380–413.
IMBER, M. J. 1981. Diets of stormpetrels *Pelagodroma* and *Garrodia* and of prions *Pachyptila* (Procellariiformes): ecological segregation and bill morphology. Pages 63–88 *in* Proc. Symp. Birds Sea Shore, 1979. Cape Town: African Seabird Group.
PLANT, A. R. 1989. Incubation and early chick-rearing in the Grey-backed Storm Petrel (*Garrodia nereis*). Notornis 36: 141–147.

Genus **Pelagodroma** Reichenbach

Pelagodroma Reichenbach, 1853, Avium Syst. Nat. (1852): 4 — type (by original designation) *Procellaria marina* Latham.

81 **Pelagodroma marina** (Latham)
White-faced Storm Petrel

Procellaria marina Latham, 1790, Index Ornith.: 826 — based on "Frigate Petrel" of Latham, 1785, General Synop. Birds 3: 410 — southern oceans = off the mouth of the Rio de la Plata, 35–37°S, *fide* Murphy, 1924, Bull. Am. Mus. Nat. Hist. 50: 233.

Widespread in temperate and subtropical parts of Atlantic, Indian and western South Pacific Oceans, reaching subantarctic seas at Gough and Auckland Islands and migrating to lower latitudes after breeding, including the eastern tropical Pacific Ocean. About 6 subspecies.

Pelagodroma marina dulciae Mathews
Australian White-faced Storm Petrel

Pelagodroma marina dulciae Mathews, 1912, Birds Aust. 2: 20 (in key), 21 — Breaksea Island, off Albany, Western Australia.
Pelagodroma marina howei Mathews, 1912, Birds Aust. 2: 26 — Mud Island, Port Phillip Bay, Victoria.

Breeds on Australian islands from Houtman Abrolhos, Western Australia, to Bass Strait and to Broughton Islands, New South Wales. Migrates to the tropics of the Indian Ocean particularly, and probably to the southwest Pacific Ocean. Straggles to northern New Zealand (Muriwai Beach, May 1983); probably occurs more frequently than recognised, April–September.

IMBER, M. J. 1984. Migration of White-faced Storm-Petrels *Pelagodroma marina* in the South Pacific and the status of the Kermadec subspecies. Emu 84: 32–35.
SERVENTY, D. L.; SERVENTY, V.; WARHAM, J. 1971. The Handbook of Australian Sea-birds. Sydney: Reed.

Pelagodroma marina maoriana Mathews
New Zealand White-faced Storm Petrel (Takahikare-moana)

Pelagodroma marina maoriana Mathews, 1912, Birds Aust. 2: 24 — Chatham Islands (type) and Auckland Islands.

Procellaria passerina Mathews, 1912, Birds Aust. 2: 24—29° 10'S, 159° 20'W, Pacific Ocean (*ex* Solander MS).

Breeds on many islands of northern New Zealand: Three Kings ?, Moturoa, Cavalli, Poor Knights, Mokohinau, Mercury, Noises, Cow, Motuokino, Aldermen and Motunau (Bay of Plenty); Motumahunga (off New Plymouth); Sentinel Rock (Cook Strait); Motunau (Canterbury); several islands around Stewart Island; Chatham Islands (most islands around Pitt I.); Auckland Islands (Port Ross area, scarce). Migrates to the eastern tropical Pacific Ocean, particularly the Peru Current off Peru and Ecuador and west of the Galapagos Islands. Subfossil and midden records from North and South Islands, and Chatham Island (where it is particularly abundant in dune deposits).

IMBER, M.J. 1981. Diets of storm petrels *Pelagodroma* and *Garrodia* and of prions *Pachyptila* (Procellariiformes): ecological segregation and bill morphology. Pages 63–88 *in* Proc. Symp. Birds Sea Shore, 1979. Cape Town: African Seabird Group.
IMBER, M.J. 1984. Migration of White-faced Storm-petrels *Pelagodroma marina* in the South Pacific and the status of the Kermadec subspecies. Emu 84: 32–35.
PITMAN, R. L. 1986. Atlas of Seabird Distribution and Relative Abundance in the Eastern Tropical Pacific. U.S. National Marine Fisheries Service, SW Center, Admin. Rep. LJ-86-02C.
RICHDALE, L. E. 1943. The White-faced Storm Petrel or Takahi-kare-moana (*Pelagodroma marina maoriana* Mathews). Trans. Proc. Roy. Soc. NZ 73: 97–115, 217–232, 335–350.

Pelagodroma marina albiclunis Murphy and Irving
Kermadec Storm Petrel

Pelagodroma marina albiclunis Murphy and Irving, 1951, Am. Mus. Novit. 1506: 15— Sunday (= Raoul) Island, Kermadec Islands.

Breeding grounds unknown. About 30 records from around Kermadec Islands but only once ashore (December 1988). Once seen off eastern Australia (4 birds). Perhaps formerly bred in the Norfolk Island group (subfossil bones not identifiable to subspecies).

IMBER, M.J. 1984. Migration of White-faced Storm-petrels *Pelagodroma marina* in the South Pacific and the status of the Kermadec subspecies. Emu 84: 32–35.
MEREDITH, C. A. 1985. The vertebrate fossil fauna of Norfolk Island, and the phylogeny of the genus *Pterodroma*. PhD thesis, Monash University, Victoria.
MURPHY, R. C.; IRVING, S. 1951. A review of the frigate-petrels (*Pelagodroma*). Am. Mus. Novit. 1506: 1–17.

Genus Fregetta Bonaparte

Fregetta Bonaparte, 1855, C. R. Acad. Sci., Paris 41: 1113—type (by original designation) *Thalassidroma leucogaster* Gould.
Cymodroma Ridgway, 1884, Mem. Mus. comp. Zool., Harvard 13: 363, 418—type (by monotypy) *Procellaria grallaria* Vieillot.

Pealea Ridgway, 1886, Auk 3: 334—type (by original designation) *Thalassidroma lineata* Peale.

Fregettornis Mathews, 1912, Birds Aust. 2: 31—type (by original designation) *Procellaria grallaria* Vieillot.

Fregodroma Mathews, 1937, Bull. Br. Ornith. Club 57: 145—type (by original designation) *Thalassidroma tropica* Gould.

Fregolla Mathews, 1937, Emu 37: 142—type (by original designation) *Fregetta melanoleuca* Salvadori = *Procellaria grallaria* Vieillot.

Fregandria Mathews, 1938, Bull. Br. Ornith. Club 59: 10—new name for *Fregolla* Mathews.

82   **Fregetta tropica** (Gould)
                                        Black-bellied Storm Petrel

Thalassidroma tropica Gould, 1844, Ann. Mag. Nat. Hist. 13: 366—equatorial regions of Atlantic Ocean = 6° 33'N, 18° 6'W.

Thalassidroma melanogaster Gould, 1844, Ann. Mag. Nat. Hist. 13: 367—off St Paul and Amsterdam Islands, Indian Ocean.

Thalassidroma lineata Peale, 1848, Proc. U.S. Explor. Exped., Birds 8: 293—Upolu, Samoa (error ? = ? Drake Strait or Bellingshausen Sea, Antarctica).

Fregetta tropica australis Mathews, 1914, Austral Avian Rec. 2: 86—New Zealand.

Breeds on South Shetland and South Orkney Islands, South Georgia (Bird I.), Bouvet ?, Prince Edward, Crozet group (East, Penguin, Apostles), Kerguelen, Auckland and Antipodes Islands. Range possibly circumpolar in subantarctic seas, and mainly south of New Zealand. Migrates to the tropics in all oceans, including the southwest Pacific Ocean north of New Zealand. On passage mainly east of New Zealand and past Chatham Islands (from which it has been recorded subfossil).

BECK, J.R.; BROWN, D.W. 1971. The breeding biology of the Black-bellied Storm-petrel *Fregetta tropica*. Ibis 113: 73–90.

IMBER, M.J. 1983. The lesser petrels of Antipodes Islands, with notes from Prince Edward and Gough Islands. Notornis 30: 283–298.

LOVEGROVE, T.G. 1978. Seabird observations between New Zealand and Fiji. Notornis 25: 291–298.

MURPHY, R.C.; SNYDER, J.P. 1952. The "Pealea" phenomenon and other notes on storm petrels. Am. Mus. Novit. 1596: 1–16.

83   **Fregetta grallaria** (Vieillot)
                                        White-bellied Storm Petrel

A widespread, but uncommon, subtropical species breeding on Nightingale, Middle, Inaccessible and Gough Islands in the South Atlantic, St Paul Island (Roche Quille) in the Indian Ocean, and on Lord Howe (Roach I.), Kermadec (Macaulcy, Curtis Is), Tubuai (Rapa) and Juan Fernandez (Santa Clara) Islands in the South Pacific. Apparently disperses northwards into the tropics after breeding. About four subspecies.

Fregetta grallaria grallaria (Vieillot)

White-bellied Storm Petrel

Procellaria grallaria Vieillot, 1817, Nouv. Dict. Hist. Nat., nouv. ed., 25: 418—
"Nouvelle–Hollande" = Australia.
Fregetta tubulata Mathews, 1912, Birds Aust. 2: 42; based on Gould, 1844, Ann. Mag.
Nat. Hist. 13: 367–368—near the coast of Australia.
Fregettornis royanus Mathews, 1914, Austral Avian Rec. 2: 86—Lord Howe Island.
Fregettornis alisteri Mathews, 1915, Austral Avian Rec. 2: 124—Lord Howe Island.
Fregettornis innominatus Mathews, 1915, Austral Avian Rec. 2: 124—Lord Howe
Island.
Fregettornis insularis Mathews, 1915, Austral Avian Rec. 2: 124—Lord Howe Island.
Cymodroma howensis Mathews, 1928, Birds Norfolk Lord Howe Islands: 11—Lord
Howe Island.
Fregettornis guttata Mathews, 1933, Novit. Zool. 39: 44 (in key), 46—Ua Pu Island,
Marquesas Islands.

Breeds on Lord Howe Islands (Roach I.) and on Kermadec
Islands (Macauley, Curtis, ? Haszard and Cheeseman). Eight
records from New Zealand: "off New Zealand"; off Farewell Spit
(2), November 1969; off Poor Knights Islands, December 1969;
Waikawa Beach, July 1975; Ninety Mile Beach, April 1978; Piha
Beach, May 1985; Hampden Beach, June 1987.

JENKINS, J. A. F.; CROXALL, J. P. 1970. Sightings of White-bellied Storm-
Petrels in coastal waters. Notornis 17: 75–76.
LOVEGROVE, T. G. 1978. Seabird observations between New Zealand and Fiji.
Notornis 25: 291–298.

Order **SPHENISCIFORMES**: Penguins
Family **SPHENISCIDAE**: Penguins

Note: As many as five subfamilies have been used in the past for fossil penguins (Palaeospheniscinae, Paraptenodytinae, Anthropornithinae, Palaeeudyptinae, Spheniscinae). Currently most authors use one family, Spheniscidae, without subfamilies. Reappraisals of penguin systematics could lead to the renewed use of some subfamilies.

Genus **Palaeeudyptes** Huxley

Palaeeudyptes Huxley 1859, Quart. J. Geol. Soc. Lond. 15: 675 — type (by monotypy) *Palaeeudyptes antarcticus* Huxley.

Note: One or more indeterminate species were referred to the genus by Hector (1872), Marples (1952, 1962) and Simpson (1971). Nominally congeneric species have been reported from Australia and Seymour Island (Antarctic Peninsula).

84   Palaeeudyptes antarcticus Huxley

Palaeeudyptes antarcticus Huxley, 1859, Quart. J. Geol. Soc. Lond. 15: 675

Age uncertain within the range Runangan Stage (Late Eocene) to Waitakian Stage (Early Miocene), but probably either lower Whaingaroan Stage (Early Oligocene) or Waitakian Stage (Early Miocene); Kakanui, South Island only.

Records from Australia are not accepted.

FORDYCE, R. E.; JONES, C. M. 1990. The history of penguins, and new fossil penguin material from New Zealand. Accepted for publication in L. S. Davis and J. T. Darby (eds), Penguin Biology. Academic Press.

HECTOR, J. 1872. On the remains of a gigantic penguin (*Palaeeudyptes antarcticus*, Huxley) from the Tertiary rocks on the west coast of Nelson. Trans. Proc. NZ Inst. 4: 341–346.

MARPLES, B. J. 1952. Early Tertiary penguins of New Zealand. NZ Geol. Surv. Pal. Bull. 20: 66.

MARPLES, B. J. 1962. Observations on the history of penguins. Pages 408–416 *in* The Evolution of Living Organisms. G. W. Leeper (ed.). Melbourne: Melbourne University Press.

SIMPSON, G. G. 1971. A review of the pre-Pliocene penguins of New Zealand. Bull. Am. Mus. Nat. Hist. 144: 321–376.

85   Palaeeudyptes marplesi Brodkorb

Palaeeudyptes antarcticus Huxley, 1859: Marples, 1952, NZ Geol. Surv. Pal. Bull 20: 31.

Palaeeudyptes marplesi Brodkorb, 1963, Bull. Florida State Mus., Biol. Sci. 7: 231.

Probably Kaiatan Stage (Late Eocene) but possibly Runangan Stage (Late Eocene); Burnside, South Island, only.

Genus **Pachydyptes** Oliver

Pachydyptes Oliver, 1930, New Zealand Birds: 85—type (by original designation) *Pachydyptes ponderosus* Oliver, 1930, New Zealand Birds: 86.
Note: A nominally congeneric species has been reported from Australia.

86   **Pachydyptes ponderosus** Oliver

Palaeeudyptes antarcticus Huxley, 1859: Hector 1873, Trans. Proc. NZ Inst. 5: 438–439.
Pachydyptes ponderosus Oliver, 1930, New Zealand Birds: 86.
Pachydyptes ponderosa Lowe, 1939, Ibis, series 14, 3: 282.
Anthropornis ponderosus (Oliver, 1930): Lowe, 1939, Ibis, series 14, 3: 291.
Anthropornis ponderosa (Lowe, 1939): Lowe, 1939, Ibis, series 14, 3: 291.
Anthropornis (Pachydyptes) ponderosus (Oliver, 1930): Lowe, 1939, Ibis, series 14, 3: 292.
Anthropornis nordenskjoeldi Wiman, 1905: Lowe, 1939, Ibis, series 14, 3: 293.

Runangan Stage (Late Eocene); Oamaru, South Island, only.

Genus **Platydyptes** Marples

Platydyptes Marples, 1952, NZ Geol. Surv. Pal. Bull. 20: 37—type (by original designation) *Pachydyptes novaezealandiae* Oliver, 1930.

87   **Platydyptes novaezealandiae** (Oliver)

Pachydyptes novaezealandiae Oliver, 1930, New Zealand Birds: 86.
Pachydyptes novae-zelandiae Lowe, 1939, Ibis, series 14, 3: 282.
Platydyptes novaezealandiae (Oliver, 1930): Marples, 1952, NZ Geol. Surv. Pal. Bull. 20: 38.

Duntroonian Stage (Late Oligocene) or Waitakian Stage (Early Miocene); Oamaru, South Island, only.

FORDYCE, R. E.; JONES, C. M. 1990. The history of penguins, and new fossil penguin material from New Zealand. Accepted for publication in L. S. Davis and J. T. Darby (eds), Penguin Biology. Academic Press.
MARPLES, B. J. 1962. Observations on the history of penguins. Pages 408–416 *in* The Evolution of Living Organisms. G. W. Leeper (ed.). Melbourne: Melbourne University Press.

88   **Platydyptes amiesi** Marples

Platydyptes amiesi Marples, 1952, NZ. Geol. Surv. Pal. Bull. 20: 39.

Duntroonian Stage (Late Oligocene), possibly Waitakian Stage (Early Miocene); Hakataramea and Duntroon, South Island, only.

89   **"Platydyptes" marplesi** Simpson

Platydyptes novaezealandiae (Oliver, 1930): Marples, 1952, NZ. Geol. Surv. Pal. Bull. 20: 36, in part.
"Platydyptes" marplesi Simpson, 1971, Bull. Am. Mus. Nat. Hist. 144: 354.
?Platydyptes marplesigi Simpson, 1975, The Biology of Penguins: 31.

Duntroonian Stage (Late Oligocene); probably Wharekuri, South Island, only.

Genus **Archaeospheniscus** Marples

Archaeospheniscus Marples, 1952, NZ Geol. Surv. Pal. Bull. 20: 40 — type (by original designation) *Archaeospheniscus lowei* Marples, 1952, NZ Geol. Surv. Pal. Bull. 20: 41.

0 **Archaeospheniscus lowei** Marples

Archaeospheniscus lowei Marples, 1952, NZ Geol. Surv. Pal. Bull. 20: 41.
Duntroonian Stage (Late Oligocene); Duntroon, South Island, only.

1 **Archaeospheniscus lopdelli** Marples

Archaeospheniscus lopdelli Marples, 1952, NZ Geol. Surv. Pal. Bull. 20: 41.
Duntroonian Stage (Late Oligocene); Duntroon, South Island, only.

Genus **Duntroonornis** Marples

Duntroonornis Marples, 1952, NZ Geol. Surv. Pal. Bull. 20: 42 — type (by original designation) *Duntroonornis parvus* Marples, 1952, NZ Geol. Surv. Pal. Bull. 20: 42.

92 **Duntroonornis parvus** Marples

Duntroonornis parvus Marples, 1952, NZ Geol. Surv. Pal. Bull. 20: 42.
Duntroonian Stage (Late Oligocene); Duntroon, South Island, only.

Genus **Korora** Marples

Korora Marples, 1952, NZ Geol. Surv. Pal. Bull. 20: 43 — type (by original designation) *Korora oliveri* Marples, 1952, NZ Geol. Surv. Pal. Bull. 20: 43.

93 **Korora oliveri** Marples

Korora oliveri Marples, 1952, NZ Geol. Surv. Pal. Bull. 20: 43.
Waitakian Stage (Early Miocene); Hakataramea Valley, South Island, only.

Genus **Marplesornis** Simpson

Marplesornis Simpson, 1972, Rec. Cant. Mus. 9: 162 — type (by original designation) *Palaeospheniscus novaezealandiae* Marples, 1960, Rec. Cant. Mus. 7: 194.

94 **Marplesornis novaezealandiae** (Marples)

Palaeospheniscus novaezealandiae Marples, 1960, Rec. Cant. Mus. 7: 194.
Marplesornis novaezealandiae (Marples, 1960): Simpson, 1972, Rec. Cant. Mus. 9: 162.
Age uncertain within the range Otaian–Altonian Stages (Early Miocene) to Waiauan–Tongaporutuan Stages (Middle–Late

Miocene) to Waipipian Stage (Pliocene); Motunau, South Island, only.

FORDYCE, R. E. 1982. The fossil vertebrate record of New Zealand. Pages 629–698 *in* The fossil vertebrate record of Australasia. P. V. Rich & E. M. Thompson (eds): Clayton: Monash University Offset Printing Unit.
MARPLES, B. J. 1962. Observations on the history of penguins. Pages 408–416 *in* The Evolution of Living Organisms. G. W. Leeper (ed.). Melbourne: Melbourne University Press.
SIMPSON, G. G. 1972. Pliocene penguins from North Canterbury, New Zealand. Rec. Cant. Mus. 9: 159–182.

Genus **Tereingaornis** Scarlett

Tereingaornis Scarlett, 1984, NZ J. Geol. Geophys. 26: 419—type (by monotypy) *Tereingaornis moisleyi* Scarlett, 1984. NZ J. Geol. Geophys. 26: 419.

95   **Tereingaornis moisleyi** Scarlett

Tereingaornis moisleyi Scarlett, 1984, NZ J. Geol Geophys. 26: 419.

Waipipian Stage (Pliocene), Hawke's Bay and Hawera, North Island, only.

McKEE, J. W. A. 1987. The occurrence of the Pliocene penguin *Tereingaornis moisleyi* (Sphenisciformes: Spheniscidae) at Hawera, Taranaki, New Zealand. NZ J. Zool. 14: 557–561.

Genus **Aptenodytes** Miller

Aptenodytes J. F. Miller, 1778, Icones Animalium, part 4, pl.23—type (by monotypy) *Aptenodytes patagonicus* Miller.

96   **Aptenodytes forsteri** Gray

Emperor Penguin

Aptenodytes Forsteri G. R. Gray, 1844, Ann. Mag. Nat. Hist. 13: 315—no locality; antarctic seas, G. R. Gray, 1844, List Birds Br. Mus. 3: 156.
Aptenodytes excelsior Mathews and Iredale, 1935, Bull. Br. Ornith. Club 55: 101—Cape Royds, McMurdo Bay, Antarctica.

Circumpolar winter breeder around the coast and islands of Antarctica, mainly on sea ice. At least six colonies known in the Ross Sea area containing about 36 000 pairs. Seldom ranges north of the Antarctic Circle. One record in New Zealand: Oreti Beach, Southland, April 1967.

BUDD, G. M. 1961. The biotopes of Emperor Penguin rookeries. Emu 61: 171–189.
BUDD, G. M. 1962. Population studies in rookeries of the Emperor Penguin *Aptenodytes forsteri*. Proc. Zool. Soc. Lond. 139: 365–388.
HENDERSON, L. E. 1968. First record of the Emperor Penguin in New Zealand. Notornis 15: 34–35.
ISENMANN, P. 1971. Contribution à l'éthologie et à l'écologie du Manchot Empereur (*Aptenodytes forsteri*, Gray) à la colonie de Pointe Géologie (Terre Adélie). Oiseau Rev. fr. Ornith. 41, No Spéc. 9–64.
JOUVENTIN, P. 1971. Comportement et structure sociale chez le manchot empereur. Terre Vie 25: 510–586.

WILSON, G. J.; TAYLOR, R. H. 1984. Distribution and abundance of penguins in the Ross Sea sector of Antarctica. NZ Antarct. Rec. 6(1): 1–7.

97 **Aptenodytes patagonicus** Miller

King Penguin

Aptenodytes patagonica J. F. Miller, 1778, Icones Animalium, pt.4, pl.23 — no locality; South Georgia designated by Mathews, 1911, Birds Aust. 1: 274.
Aptenodytes patagonicus halli Mathews, Birds Aust. 1: 272 — Macquarie Island.

Circumpolar, mainly in the subantarctic zone, breeding on many islands, including Macquarie and Heard Islands. Straggles south to the antarctic islands and Antarctica and north to Campbell Island (regularly), southern Australia, and occasionally to the Auckland, Snares and Antipodes Islands. Two New Zealand mainland records: Auckland Harbour; Moeraki, Otago. Recorded from middens, Chatham Island.

BARRAT, A. 1976. Quelques aspects de la biologie et de l'écologie du manchot royal (*Aptenodytes patagonicus*) des Iles Crozet. Com. Nat. fr. Rech. Antarct. 40: 9–52.
CONROY, J. W. H.; WHITE, M. G. 1973. The breeding status of the King Penguin (*Aptenodytes patagonicus*). Br. Antarct. Surv. Bull. 32: 31–40.
SCARLETT, R. J. 1976. King Penguins at Chatham Islands. Notornis 23: 355.
STONEHOUSE, B. 1960. The King Penguin *Aptenodytes patagonica* of South Georgia. I. Breeding behaviour and development. Falkland Islands Dependencies Survey, Sci. Rep. No. 23.

98 **Aptenodytes ridgeni** Simpson

Aptenodytes ridgeni Simpson, 1972, Rec. Cant. Mus. 9: 167.

Age uncertain within the range Otaian-Altonian Stages (Early Miocene) to Waiauan-Tongaporutuan Stages (Middle-Late Miocene) to Waipipian Stage (Pliocene); Motunau, South Island, only.

Genus **Megadyptes** Milne-Edwards

Megadyptes Milne-Edwards, 1880, Ann. Sci. Nat. Zool. Paris, Ser. 6, 9, art.9, p.56 — type (by monotypy) *Catarrhactes antipodes* Hombron and Jacquinot.

99 **Megadyptes antipodes** (Hombron and Jacquinot)

Yellow-eyed Penguin (Hoiho)

Catarrhactes antipodes Hombron and Jacquinot, 1841. Ann. Sci. Nat. Zool. Paris, Ser. 2, 16, p.320 — Auckland Islands.

Endemic to New Zealand, breeding at Campbell, Auckland, Stewart and Codfish Islands and Southland, Otago and Canterbury coasts (including Banks Peninsula). Straggles to Cook Strait, western Foveaux Strait, and the Chatham Islands. Fossil: Okehuan (Early Pleistocene). Subfossil and midden records from South Island; one subfossil record from Chatham Island.

FALLA, R. A. 1935. Notes on penguins of the genera *Megadyptes* and *Eudyptes* in southern New Zealand. Rec. Auck. Inst. Mus. 1. 319–326.

HARROW, G. 1971. Yellow-eyed Penguins breeding on Banks Peninsula. Notornis 18(3): 199–201.
RICHDALE, L. E. 1951. Sexual Behavior in Penguins. Lawrence: Univ. Kansas Press.
RICHDALE, L. E. 1957. A Population Study of Penguins. Oxford: Clarendon Press.

Genus **Pygoscelis** Wagler

Pygoscelis Wagler, 1832, Isis von Oken, col. 281 — type (by monotypy) *Aptenodytes papua* Forster.

100   **Pygoscelis papua** (Forster)

Gentoo Penguin

Two subspecies are generally recognised, a large form *papua* breeding mainly on subantarctic islands, and a smaller one *ellsworthi* with a more southerly distribution. Presumably all those that have straggled to New Zealand shores have been of the northern subspecies.

Pygoscelis papua papua (Forster)

Northern Gentoo Penguin

Aptenodytes papua J. R. Forster, 1781, Comment. Phys. Soc. Reg. Sci. Goettingensis, 3 (1780), pp.134, 140, pl.3 — Falkland Is.

Circumpolar in subantarctic surface waters, breeding at the Falkland Islands, at Staten, Marion and Prince Edward Islands, and at the Crozet, Kerguelen and Macquarie Islands. South of the Antarctic Convergence also nests at South Georgia and Heard Island. Straggles north: Campbell Island (December 1964 — March 1965, August 1965); Otago (September 1970, October 1974); Bluff (November 1970); Banks Peninsula (February 1976). Most of these birds were apparently immatures.

DARBY, J.; WRIGHT, A. W. 1973. First New Zealand record of the Gentoo Penguin (*Pygoscelis papua*). Notornis 20(1): 28–30.
EDGAR, A. T. 1972. Classified Summarised Notes. Notornis 19: 339–364.
HINDELL, M. A. 1989. The diet of Gentoo Penguins *Pygoscelis papua* at Macquarie Island: winter and early breeding season. Emu 89: 71–78.
JACKSON, T. 1975. Another Gentoo Penguin. Notornis 22(1): 82.
KINSKY, F. C. 1969. New and rare birds on Campbell Island. Notornis 16(4): 225–236.
STONEHOUSE, B. 1970. Geographic variation in Gentoo Penguins *Pygoscelis papua*. Ibis 112: 52–57.

101   **Pygoscelis adeliae** (Hombron and Jacquinot)

Adélie Penguin

Catarrhactes Adeliae Hombron and Jacquinot, 1841, Ann. Sci. Nat. Zool., Paris, ser. 2, 16, p.320 — Adélie Land.

Circumpolar, breeding on ice-free coasts and islands of Antarctica and on South Shetland, South Orkney, South Sandwich and

Bouvet Islands. About 750 000 pairs, or about one-third of the world population, breed in the Ross Sea region, in 34 colonies. Rarely straggles north to reach Heard and Macquarie Islands, once as far as the Marlborough coast (December 1962).

KENNINGTON, S. R. 1963. Adelie Penguin from Marlborough coast. Notornis 10: 234.

SPURR, E. B. 1975. Breeding of the Adelie Penguin *Pygoscelis adeliae* at Cape Bird. Ibis 117: 324–338.

WILSON, G. J.; TAYLOR, R. H. 1984. Distribution and abundance of penguins in the Ross Sea sector of Antarctica. NZ Antarct. Rec. 6(1): 1–7.

102 **Pygoscelis antarctica** (Forster)

Chinstrap (Ringed) Penguin

Aptenodytes antarctica J. R. Forster, 1781, Comment. Phys. Soc. Reg. Sci. Goettingen-sis, 3(1780), pp.134, 141, pl.4—South Shetland Is.

Circumpolar, breeding on the Antarctic Peninsula, on islands off Antarctica, at the South Shetland, South Orkney, South Sandwich Islands, at South Georgia, and on Bouvet Island. Has nested on Heard Island and straggled to Macquarie Island. Only known colony in New Zealand zone is on an islet off Sabrina Island, Balleny Islands (about 10 pairs). One at Campbell Island, March 1984.

CONROY, J. W. H.; WHITE, M. G.; FURSE, J. R.; BRUCE, G. 1975. Observations on the breeding biology of the Chinstrap Penguin, *Pygoscelis antarctica*, at Elephant Island, South Shetland Islands. Br. Antarct. Surv. Bull. 40: 23–32.

ROBERTSON, C. J. R.; GILBERT, J. R.; ERICKSON, A. W. 1980. Birds and seals of the Balleny Islands, Antarctica. Rec. Nat. Mus. NZ 1: 271–279.

103 **Pygoscelis tyreei** Simpson

Pygoscelis tyreei Simpson, 1972, Rec. Cant. Mus. 9: 166.

Age uncertain within the range Otaian-Altonian Stages (Early Miocene) to Waiauan-Tongaporutuan Stages (Middle-Late Miocene) to Waipipian Stage (Pliocene); Motunau, South Island, only.

Genus **Eudyptula** Bonaparte

Eudyptula Bonaparte, 1856, Compt. Rend. hebd. Seanc. Acad. Sci., Paris, 42, p.775—type (by monotypy) *Aptenodytes minor* Forster.

104 **Eudyptula minor** (Forster)

Blue Penguin (Korora)

Aptenodytes minor J. R. Forster, 1781, Comment. Phys. Soc. Reg. Sci. Goettingensis, 3(1780), pp.135–147—Dusky Sound, S. I. New Zealand.

Eudyptula albosignata Finsch, 1874, Proc. Zool. Soc. Lond., p.207—Akaroa, South Island, New Zealand.

Eudyptula minor iredalei Mathews, 1911, Birds Aust. 1, p.286, pl.67—Chatham Islands (error – Motuora Island, North Island, New Zealand: Kinsky and Falla 1976).

Eudyptula minor chathamensis Kinsky and Falla, 1976, Rec. Nat. Mus. NZ 1: 115—
Star Keys, Chatham Islands.
Eudyptula minor variabilis Kinsky and Falla, 1976, Rec. Nat. Mus. NZ 1: 116—
Wellington Harbour, New Zealand.

Southern Australia and Tasmania; New Zealand. In the New Zealand region, throughout on coastal North and South Islands; also Stewart and the Chatham Islands. Young birds banded at Motunau Island have been recovered as far north as Wellington but most tend to disperse southwards. Vagrants have reached The Snares. A distinctive population of 'White-flippered Penguins' breeds around Banks Peninsula and on Motunau Island. On Motunau, some 'Little Blue' penguins interbreed with white-flippered morphs, producing viable offspring. Fossil: Pleistocene. Subfossil and midden deposits, often abundant, throughout North, South and Chatham Islands.

[*Note*: Meredith and Sin 1988a re-analysed the mensural data of Kinsky and Falla 1976 and found that the differences between their figures for the various populations were not statistically significant and did not support their proposal to divide the New Zealand birds into five subspecies as followed in the 1980 amendments to the 1970 *Checklist*. Meredith and Sin also compared populations from the North Island, Cook Strait, Motunau Island and Banks Peninsula, using a range of morphological, biochemical and statistical techniques. The results showed clinal variations and so much intra- and inter-population variability that they considered none of the populations to be discrete entities. Comparable data for the southern South Island, Chatham Island and Australian populations are not available. In view of this uncertainty about the taxonomic status of these various populations, we have placed all the New Zealand birds in one taxon, *E. minor*, including the white-flippered birds often classified as *E. albosignata* or *E. m. albosignata*. Jacob and Hoerschelmann (1981) found that the preen gland waxes of 'Little Blue' and 'White-flippered' Penguins were chemically indistinguishable, whereas the waxes of all the other nine penguin species they analysed were clearly separable on their fatty acid compositions. For an analysis of the genetics of the same four populations, see Meredith and Sin 1988b.]

GALES, R. P. 1987. Growth strategies in Blue Penguins *Eudyptula minor*. Emu 87: 212–219.
JACOB, J.; HOERSCHELMANN, H. 1981. Verwandtschaftbeziehungen bei Pinguinen (Sphenisciformes). J. Orn. Lpz. 122(1): 78–88.
KINSKY, F. C. 1960. The yearly cycle of the Northern Blue Penguin (*Eudyptula minor novaehollandiae*) in the Wellington Harbour area. Rec. Dom. Mus. 3(3): 145–218.
KINSKY, F. C.; FALLA, R. A. 1976. A subspecific revision of the Australasian

Blue Penguin (*Eudyptula minor*) in the New Zealand area. Rec. Nat. Mus. NZ 1: 105–126.
MEREDITH, M. A. M.; SIN, F. Y. T. 1988a. Morphometrical analysis of four populations of the Little Blue Penguin, *Eudyptula minor*. J. Nat. Hist. 22: 801–809.
MEREDITH, M. A. M.; SIN, F. Y. T. 1988b. Genetic variation of four populations of the Little Blue Penguin, *Eudyptula minor*. Heredity 60: 69–76.

Genus **Eudyptes** Vieillot: Crested Penguins

Eudyptes Vieillot, 1816. Analyse d'une nouvelle ornithologie élémentaire, pp.67, 70 — type (by subsequent designation) (G. R. Gray, 1840, List Genera of Birds, p.77), *Aptenodytes chrysocome* Forster.
Catadyptes Mathews, 1934, Bull. Br. Ornith. Club, 55: 74 — type (by original designation) *Catarhactes chrysolophus* Brandt.

WARHAM, J. 1975. The Crested Penguins. Pages 189–269 *in* Stonehouse, B. (ed.), The Biology of Penguins.

105 **Eudyptes chrysocome** (Forster)
Rockhopper Penguin

The most widespread crested penguin, circumpolar, breeding on subantarctic and antarctic islands but only straggling to mainland New Zealand. Different populations show slight differences in morphology and a number of subspecies have been proposed, but precise delineation and evaluation await comprehensive comparisons of all populations.

Eudyptes chrysocome chrysocome (Forster)
Western Rockhopper Penguin

Aptenodytes chrysocome J. R. Forster, 1781, Comment. Soc. Reg. Sci. Goettingensis, 3, pp.133, pl.1 — Tasmania and Falkland Islands (= Falkland Islands). [For use of *chrysocome* Forster instead of *crestatus* Miller, 1784, see Serventy and Whittell, Emu, 52: 63–64 (1952).]

Breeds on islands off Cape Horn and the Falkland Islands. Two records at the Snares Islands, 1985–87.

TENNYSON, A. J. D.; MISKELLY, C. M. 1989. "Dark-faced" Rockhopper Penguins at the Snares Islands. Notornis 36: 183–189.

Eudyptes chrysocome filholi Hutton
Eastern Rockhopper Penguin

Eudyptes filholi Hutton, 1879, Proc. Linn. Soc. NSW. 3 (1878), 334 — Campbell Island.

Breeds abundantly on Heard, Macquarie, Campbell, Auckland and Antipodes Islands, but has declined seriously at Campbell Island in recent decades. Breeds also at Kerguelen, Marion and Prince Edward Islands and at the Crozets. Straggler to The Snares and as far north as Cook Strait.

HINDELL, M. A. 1988. The diet of the Rockhopper Penguin *Eudyptes chrysocome* at Macquarie Island. Emu 88: 227–233.

WARHAM, J. 1963. The Rockhopper Penguin, *Eudyptes chrysocome*, at Macquarie Island. Auk 80: 229–256.
WARHAM, J. 1972. Breeding seasons and sexual dimorphism in Rockhopper Penguins. Auk 89: 86–105.
WARHAM, J. 1975. Pages 189–269 *in* Stonehouse, B. (ed.), The Biology of Penguins.

Eudyptes chrysocome moseleyi Mathews and Iredale
Moseley's Rockhopper Penguin

Eudyptes serresianus moseleyi Mathews and Iredale, 1921, Manual Birds Aust., 1, p.11 — Inaccessible Island, Tristan da Cunha Group.

Breeds in the subtropical and low subantarctic zones at Tristan da Cunha Group (Inaccessible and Nightingale Islands) and Gough Island in the South Atlantic Ocean and on St Paul and Amsterdam Islands in the Indian Ocean. Ranges to southern and particularly southwestern Australia. One bird recorded on South East Island, Chatham Islands, from 1968 to 1970, and one on Wellington coast, January 1984.

MOORS, P.J.; MERTON, D.V. 1984. First records for New Zealand of Moseley's Rockhopper Penguin (*Eudyptes chrysocome moseleyi*). Notornis 31: 262–265.

106 **Eudyptes chrysolophus** (Brandt)
Macaroni Penguin

Breeds on islands of both antarctic and subantarctic zones.

Eudyptes chrysolophus chrysolophus (Brandt)
Macaroni Penguin

Catarhactes chrysolophus Brandt, 1837, Bull. Scient. Acad. Imp. Sci. St. Peterburg., Col. 2, 315 — Falkland Islands.

Breeds on South Shetland, South Orkney and South Sandwich Islands, on Elephant Island, and at South Georgia and Heard Island. Also in warmer subantarctic seas at Falkland, Bouvet, Prince Edward, Marion, Crozet and Kerguelen Islands. Birds, evidently of this form, straggle to Antarctica, including Cape Hallett and the Balleny Islands in the New Zealand sector. Occasionally reaches Campbell Island and, three times, The Snares (but see *Note* below).

Eudyptes chrysolophus schlegeli Finsch
Royal Penguin

Eudyptes schlegeli Finsch, 1876, Trans. NZ Inst. 8: 204 — Macquarie Island.
Eudyptes albigularis Milne-Edwards, 1880, Annals Sci. Nat. (6), 9: 55 — Macquarie Island.
Catadyptes chrysolophus redimitis Mathews and Iredale, 1935, Bull Br. Ornith. Club 55: 102 — Macquarie Island.

Breeds only at Macquarie Island, straggling north to Tasmania and (rarely) to South Australia. Birds evidently of this subspecies have reached Cook Strait, Hawke's Bay, and Dunedin and a few pairs moult at Campbell Island among the Rockhopper Penguins.

[*Note*: Among the vast colonies of Macaroni Penguins at Marion, Crozet, Kerguelen and Heard Islands a very few white-faced birds may be found. These look like typical Royal Penguins and they may breed with partners that are typical dark-faced Macaroni Penguins. Likewise, among the Royal Penguins at Macquarie Island a very few dark-faced birds are found and these may interbreed with typical Royal Penguins. Whether these 'Macaroni' and 'Royal' types are true immigrants of those subspecies or are just rare morphs of Macaroni and Royal Penguins respectively, or whether both immigrants and morphs are involved, is not known. In addition, birds of the two subspecies can seldom be separated on size and external characters because, although Royals tend to be bigger than Macaronis, female Royal Penguins are of similar size to male Macaroni Penguins. In consequence, unbanded stragglers cannot be precisely identified.]

CARRICK, R. 1972. Population ecology of the Australian Black-backed Magpie, Royal Penguin and Silver Gull. Pages 41–99 *in* Population Ecology of Migratory Birds, U.S. Bureau Sport Fish. Wildl. Washington D.C. 278 pp.

HINDELL, M. A. 1988. The diet of the Royal Penguin *Eudyptes schlegeli* at Macquarie Island. Emu 88: 219–226.

WARHAM, J. 1971. Aspects of breeding behaviour in the Royal Penguin *Eudyptes chrysolophus schlegeli* Notornis 18: 91–115.

107 **Eudyptes pachyrhynchus** Gray
Fiordland Crested Penguin (Pokotiwha)

Eudyptes pachyrhynchus Gray, 1845, in Richardson and J. E. Gray (eds). Zool. Voyage Erebus and Terror, 1, Birds, p.17 — Waikowaiti, South Island.

Endemic, breeding mainly in South Westland and Fiordland and on Codfish Island. Nests under forest or in caves, mainly on headlands, islets and around the entrances to fiords, from near Bruce Bay southwards, including Open Bay Islands and Green Islets (166°40'E). A few nest on Stewart Island, large numbers on Codfish Island, and fewer on Big South Cape, Solomon, Stage, Ernest, and Solander Islands. Attempted breeding on islet in Palliser Bay, Wellington, 1953 and 1954, and near Abut Head, Westland, but no recent reports. Stragglers are found around all South Island coasts and as far north as the Bay of Islands, mostly in summer. Straggles to Campbell and Auckland Islands; southern Australia; and even to the Falkland Islands (specimen in the British Museum). Yearlings and occasionally older birds are common on The Snares in summer but there is no evidence of interbreeding with *E. robustus*. Subfossil and midden, North and South Islands.

van HEEZIK, Y. M. 1989. Diet of the Fiordland Crested Penguin during the post-guard phase of chick growth. Notornis 36: 151–156.
WARHAM, J. 1974. The Fiordland Crested Penguin *Eudyptes pachyrhynchus*. Ibis 116: 1-23.

108   **Eudyptes robustus** Oliver

Snares Crested Penguin

Eudyptes robustus Oliver, Emu 53, p.187 — Snares Island.
Eudyptes pachyrhynchus atratus 'Hutton', Falla, 1935, Rec. Auck. Inst. Mus. 1: 324.
   Int. Comm. Zool. Nomencl. 1976, Opinion No. 1056, Bull. Zool. Nomencl. 33: 16–18.

Endemic, breeding on The Snares (Main and Broughton Islands and in small numbers on Toru and Rima islets of the Western Reefs). The total population may be 20 000 breeding pairs. A rare straggler to the Antipodes, Macquarie, Solander and Chatham Islands; to southern Australia and Tasmania; and more commonly to Stewart Island and South Island beaches — as far north as Hokitika and Akaroa.

WARHAM, J. 1974. The breeding biology and behaviour of the Snares Crested Penguin. J. Roy. Soc. NZ 4: 63–108.

109   **Eudyptes sclateri** Buller

Erect-crested Penguin

Eudyptes sclateri Buller, 1888, Hist. Birds NZ, 2nd ed., 2, p.289 — Auckland Islands.
Eudyptes atrata Finsch, 1875, *ex* Hutton MS Ibis 5(3): 112 — Snares Island. Melanistic specimen, species indeterminable.
Eudyptes vittata Finsch, 1875, Ibis 5(3): 112 — Dunedin, species indeterminable — see Ogilvie-Grant, 1905, Ibis, 8(5): 552–553.
   Int. Comm. Zool. Nomencl. 1976, Opinion No. 1056., Bull. Zool. Nomencl. 33: 16–18.

Endemic, breeding in large numbers on the Antipodes and Bounty Islands and in small numbers at Campbell Island and on Disappointment Island (Auckland Group). Has attempted to breed on Otago Peninsula. Straggles commonly to eastern coasts of the North and South Islands and Cook Strait, reaching Taranaki once. A few birds visit The Snares in summer and rarely Macquarie and Chatham Islands. Occasionally reaches Tasmania and southern Australia. One that reached the Falkland Islands was present for four seasons and for two of these tended eggs with a Rockhopper Penguin, but no chicks were raised. The abundant Chatham Island subfossil and midden *Eudyptes* material is currently referred (R.J. Scarlett) to this species.

RICHDALE, L. E. 1941. The Erect-crested Penguin (*Eudyptes sclateri* Buller). Emu 41: 25–53.
RICHDALE, L. E. 1950. Further notes on the Erect-crested Penguin. Emu 49: 153–166.

ROBERTSON, C.J.R.; VAN TETS, G.F. 1982. The status of birds at the Bounty Islands. Notornis 29: 311–336.
WARHAM, J. 1972. Aspects of the biology of the Erect-crested Penguin *Eudyptes sclateri*. Ardea 60: 145–184.

[**Note:** The Opinion of the International Commission on Zoological Nomenclature quoted above placed the specific name *sclateri*, as published in the binomen *Eudyptes sclateri* Buller 1888, and the specific name *robustus*, as published in the binomen *Eudyptes robustus* Oliver 1953, in the Official List of Specific Names in Zoology with the Name Nos. 2571 and 2572 respectively. It also placed the specific name *atratus*, as published in the binomen *Eudyptes atratus* Finsch 1875 *ex* Hutton MS, on the Official List of Rejected and Invalid Specific Names in Zoology with the Name No. 1009.]

Genus **Spheniscus** Brisson

Spheniscus Brisson, 1760, Ornithologie, 1, p.52; 6, p.96 — type (by monotypy) *Diomedea demersa* Linnaeus.

110 **Spheniscus magellanicus** (Forster)
Magellanic Penguin

Aptenodytes magellanicus J.R. Forster, 1781, Comment. Phys. Soc. Reg. Sci. Goettingensis, 3(1780), pp.134, 143, pl.5 — Straits of Magellan.

Breeds on the Pacific coast of South America south of about lat. 32°S and on the Atlantic coast south of about lat. 43°S to Tierra del Fuego and Cape Horn and their islets and outliers. Breeds also on Juan Fernandez and the Falkland Islands. At least part of these populations winters to the north, on the Pacific coast as far as Coquimbo, Chile, and on the Atlantic coast as far as Rio de Janeiro. Stragglers have reached South Georgia; Phillip Island, Victoria, Australia; and Waimarama Beach, Hawke's Bay (March 1972). The possibility of an assisted passage by a ship for the Victorian and Hawke's Bay birds cannot be ruled out; as the latter bird took its first fish without the usual need for forced feeding, it may have been fed like this before arrival in New Zealand.

BOSWALL, J.; MacIVER, D. 1975. The Magellanic Penguin *Spheniscus magellanicus*. Pages 271–305 *in* Stonehouse, B. (ed.), The Biology of Penguins, Macmillan.
ROBERTSON, C.J.R.; ABEL, R.S.; KINSKY, F.C. 1972. First New Zealand record of Magellanic Penguin (*Spheniscus magellanicus*). Notornis 19: 111–113.

Order **PELECANIFORMES**: Pelicans, Gannets, Cormorants and Allies
Suborder PHAETHONTES: Tropicbirds
Family **PHAETHONTIDAE**: Tropicbirds
Genus **Phaethon** Linnaeus

Phaethon Linnaeus, 1758, Syst. Nat., ed. 10, 1: 134—type (by subsequent designation) *Phaethon aethereus* Linnaeus (Gray, List Gen. Bds., 1840, p. 80).
Scaeophaethon (*sic*) Mathews, 1913, Austral Avian Rec. 2: 56—type (by original designation) *Phaethon rubricauda westralis* Mathews (new name for *Phoenicurus* Bonaparte, not Forster).
Leptophaethon (*sic*) Mathews, 1913, Austral Avian Rec. 2: 56—type (by original designation) *Phaethon lepturus dorotheae* Mathews (new name for *Lepturus* Reichenbach, not Brisson).

111   **Phaethon rubricauda** Boddaert

Red-tailed Tropicbird

Phaethon rubricauda Boddaert, 1783, Tabl. Pl. enlum.: 57—Mauritius.
Breeds on islands of the tropical Indian and Pacific Oceans including Lord Howe, Norfolk, and Kermadec Islands. Straggles south to the Tasman Sea and northern New Zealand (once reported regularly), but few recent records: Taupo, February 1936; Muriwai, May 1942; off Taranaki, February 1951; Toreparu Beach, October 1963; a red tail feather, Karekare, c. April 1986.

TARBURTON, M. K. 1989. Subspeciation in the Red-tailed Tropicbird. Notornis 36: 39–49.

112   **Phaethon lepturus** Daudin

White-tailed Tropicbird

Phaethon lepturus Daudin, 1802, Buffon, Hist. Nat., ed. Didot, Quadr. 14: 319.
Breeds on islands in the tropical Indian, Pacific and Atlantic Oceans and the Caribbean Sea.

Phaethon lepturus dorotheae Mathews

White-tailed Tropicbird

Phaethon lepturus dorotheae Mathews, 1913, Austral Avian Rec. 2: 7—Queensland.
Breeds on islands in the southwest Pacific. Straggles to northern New Zealand: Bay of Plenty, January 1973; Oakura Beach, February 1979; Dargaville, February 1979; Muriwai, June 1979; Ninety Mile Beach, March and May 1983; Omamari Beach, April 1983; Ruakaka, January 1989.

BROWN, S. R. 1973. First record of White-tailed Tropic Bird in New Zealand. Notornis 20: 380–381.
MEDWAY, D. G.; MEDWAY, J. C. 1979. Second record of White-tailed Tropic Bird in New Zealand. Notornis 26: 170.

Suborder PELECANI: Pelicans, Gannets, Cormorants, Darters
Superfamily PELECANOIDEA: Pelicans and Allies
Family **PELECANIDAE**: Pelicans
Genus **Pelecanus** Linnaeus

Pelecanus Linnaeus, 1758, Syst. Nat., ed. 10, 1: 132—type (by subsequent designation) *Pelecanus onocrotalus* Linnaeus (Gray, List Gen. Bds., 1840, p. 80).
Catoptropelecanus Reichenbach, 1852 (1853), Vollst. Naturgesch., 2 Vogel, 1 Avium Syst. Nat.: 7—type (by original designation) *C. perspicillatus* = *P. conspicillatus* Temminck.

113 **Pelecanus conspicillatus** Temminck
Australian Pelican
Australia (including fossil), Tasmania, southern New Guinea, and New Zealand (accidental).

Pelecanus conspicillatus conspicillatus Temminck
Australian Pelican
Pelecanus conspicillatus Temminck, 1824, pl. col., livr. 47, pl.276—Australia = Swan River, Western Australia, *apud* Stresemann.
Breeds Australia and Tasmania; straggles north to New Guinea and east to New Zealand.
New Zealand records: Wanganui River (1890); near Dargaville (August 1976); Southland (November 1977); South Canterbury (at least 3 additional birds, December 1977–June 1978).

EDGAR, A. T. 1978. Australian Pelican (*Pelecanus conspicillatus*) in Kaipara Harbour. Notornis 25: 89–90.
SAGAR, P. M. 1978. Australian Pelicans in Canterbury. Notornis 25: 353–354.

114 **Pelecanus novaezealandiae** Scarlett
New Zealand Pelican
Pelecanus conspicillatus novaezealandiae Scarlett, 1966, Notornis 13: 209—Poukawa, Hawke's Bay.
Subfossil, in the North Island, from Karikari Peninsula, Waikaremoana and Poukawa; possibly midden from Motutapu Island and (South Island) Lake Grassmere.

RICH, P. V.; VAN TETS, G. F. 1981. The fossil pelicans of Australasia. Rec. S Aust. Mus. 18: 235–264.
SCARLETT, R. J. 1966. A pelican in New Zealand. Notornis 13: 204–217.

Family **PELAGORNITHIDAE**: Bony-toothed Pelicans
Genus **Pelagornis** Lartet

Pelagornis Lartet, 1857, C.r.hebd. Seanc. Acad. Sci., Paris 44: 736–741—type (by monotypy) *Polagornis miocaenus* Lartet.

115 Pelagornis miocaenus Lartet

Pelagornis miocaenus Lartet, 1857, C.r.hebd. Seanc. Acad. Sci., Paris 44: 736–741.

Fossil: near mouth of Waipara River, North Canterbury; Late Miocene. Also from France; Middle Miocene.

HARRISON, C.J.; WALKER, C.A. 1976. A review of the bony-toothed birds (Odontopterygiformes) with descriptions of some new species. Tertiary Res. Spec. Pap. 2: 1–62.

SCARLETT, R.J. 1972. Bones of a presumed odontopterygian bird from the Miocene of New Zealand. NZ J. Geol. Geophysics 15: 269–274.

Genus **Pseudodontornis** Lambrecht

Pseudodontornis Lambrecht, 1930, Geol. Hungarica ser. Palaeontologica 7: 1–17—type.

Neodontornis Harrison and Walker, 1976, Tertiary Res. Spec. Pap. 1976, 2: 22—type (by original designation) *Neodontornis stirtoni* (Howard and Warter, 1969).

116 Pseudodontornis stirtoni Howard and Warter

Pseudodontornis stirtoni Howard and Warter, 1969, Rec. Cant. Mus. 8: 348— Motunau Beach, North Canterbury, New Zealand.

Fossil: Motunau Beach, North Canterbury; uncertain age within the range of Early Miocene to Late Pliocene.

Bones from Hawera of middle Pliocene age may belong to the genus *Pseudodontornis*.

HARRISON, C.J.; WALKER, C.A. 1976. A review of the bony-toothed birds (Odontopterygiformes) with descriptions of some new species. Tertiary Res. Spec. Pap. 2: 1–62.

HOWARD, H.; WARTER, S.L. 1969. A new species of bony-toothed bird (Family *Pseudodontornithidae*) from the Tertiary of New Zealand. Rec. Cant. Mus. 8: 345–357.

McKEE, J.W.A. 1985. A pseudodontorn (Pelecaniformes: Pelagornithidae) from the middle Pliocene of Hawera, Taranaki, New Zealand. NZ J. Zool. 12: 181–184.

OLSON, S.L. 1985. The fossil record of birds. In Avian Biology 8, D.S. Farner, J.R. King and K.C. Parkes (eds). New York: Academic Press.

STEADMAN, D.W. 1981. Review (of Harrison and Walker 1977, Birds of the British Upper Eocene). Auk 98: 205–207.

Superfamily SULOIDEA: Gannets, Cormorants, Darters

Family **SULIDAE**: Gannets and Boobies

Genus **Morus** Vieillot

Morus Vieillot, 1816, Analyse: 63—type (by monotypy) "Fou de Bassan" Buffon = *Pelecanus bassanus* Linnaeus.

Sulita Mathews, 1915, Austr. Av. Rec. 2: 123—type (by original designation) *Pelecanus bassanus* Linnaeus (new name for *Morus* Vieillot on grounds of preoccupation by *Morum* Bolten).

VAN TETS, G. F.; MEREDITH, C. W.; FULLAGAR, P. J.; DAVIDSON, P. M. 1988. Osteological differences between *Sula* and *Morus*, and a description of an extinct species of *Sula* from Lord Howe and Norfolk Islands, Tasman Sea. Notornis 35: 35–57.

117 **Morus serrator** (G. R. Gray)

Australasian Gannet (Takapu)

Pelecanus serrator G. R. Gray, 1843, *in* Dieffenbach, Travels in New Zealand, 2: 200 — Tasmania; substitute name for *Sula australis* Gould, not Stephens.
Sula serrator dyotti Mathews, 1913, Austral Avian Rec. 2: 63 — Tasmania.
Sula serrator rex Mathews and Iredale, 1921, Manual Birds Aust.: 77 — New Zealand.

Australia (breeding on islets off Tasmania and southeastern Australia), Philip Island (Norfolk Group), and New Zealand. In New Zealand, breeds on outlying islands from Three Kings to Hauraki Gulf, Bay of Plenty and Poverty Bay on the east coast of the North Island; Oaia, Motutara, and Gannet Islands on the west coast, North Island. Cape Kidnappers (south end of Hawke Bay) and two subsidiary colonies at Muriwai, recently formed opposite Motutara Island, are the only North Island mainland colonies. In the South Island, a small colony established c.1975 at Waimaru Bay (Pelorus Sound) and another larger colony more recently on shellbanks at the end of Farewell Spit; also two breeding colonies at The Nuggets and on Little Solander Island. Adult birds range widely in New Zealand seas during the winter; juveniles and some adults disperse to coastal waters of Australia, as far west as the Indian Ocean. Stragglers reach Chathams, Auckland Islands and Campbell Island (January 1968). Sub-fossil and midden deposits in North Island, and middens in South Island.

FLEMING, C. A.; WODZICKI, K. A. 1952. A census of the Gannet (*Sula serrator*) in New Zealand. Notornis 5: 39–78.
HAWKINS, J. M. 1988. The Farewell Spit gannetry—a new sea level colony. Notornis 35: 249–260.
NELSON, B. 1978. The Gannet. Berkhamsted: Poyser.
REED, S. M. 1979. Establishment of a new gannetry. Notornis 26: 89–93.
WINGHAM, E. J. 1985. Food and feeding range of the Australasian Gannet *Morus serrator* (Gray). Emu 85: 231–239.
WODZICKI, K. 1967. The Gannets at Cape Kidnappers. Trans. Roy. Soc. NZ 8: 149–162; 9: 17–31.
WODZICKI, K.; STEIN, P. 1958. Migration and dispersal of New Zealand Gannets. Emu 58: 289–312.
WODZICKI, K.; ROBERTSON, C. J. R.; THOMPSON, H. R.; ALDERTON, C. J. T. 1984. The distribution and numbers of Gannets (*Sula serrator*) in New Zealand. Notornis 31: 232–261.

Genus **Sula** Brisson

Sula Brisson, 1760, Orn., 1: 60; 6: 494 — type (by tautonymy) "Sula" = *Sula leucogaster* Boddaert.

Hemisula Mathews, 1913, Austral Avian Rec. 2: 55 — type (by original designation)
Sula leucogaster rogersi Mathews.
Parasula Mathews, 1913, Austral Avian Rec. 2: 55 — type (by original designation)
Sula dactylatra bedouti Mathews.

118   **Sula leucogaster** (Boddaert)

Brown Booby

Pelecanus Leucogaster Boddaert, 1783, Table Pl. enlum.: 57, pl.973 — no locality =
Cayenne.
Breeds on tropical islands of the Indian, Pacific and Atlantic
Oceans and the Caribbean Sea.

Sula leucogaster plotus (Forster)

Brown Booby

Pelecanus plotus Forster, 1844, Descr. Anim., ed. Licht.: 278 — near New Caledonia.
Tropical western and central Pacific Ocean, reaching New
Zealand waters probably every summer, occasionally to about
45°S; in New Zealand normally associating with Gannets.
GAZE, P. D. 1975. Brown Booby in Wellington Harbour. Notornis 22: 253–255.
HEATHER, B. D. 1956. Brown Booby off Cavallis. Notornis 6: 247.
PIERCE, R. J. 1969. Brown Booby on South Canterbury coast. Notornis 16: 125.
STEIN, P. A. S. 1952. Brown Booby in the Hauraki Gulf. Notornis 4: 213.

119   **Sula dactylatra** Lesson

Masked (Blue-faced) Booby

Sula dactylatra Lesson, 1831, Traité d'Orn. 8: 601 — Ascension Island.
Breeds on tropical islands in the Indian, Pacific and Atlantic
Oceans and the Caribbean Sea.

Sula dactylatra personata Gould

Masked (Blue-faced) Booby

Sula personata Gould, 1846, Proc. Zool. Soc. Lond.: 21 — north and northeast coasts
of Australia = Raine Island, North Queensland.
Breeds on islands in the Indian Ocean and Banda Sea; islands
off Queensland and Western Australia; Lord Howe Island;
Norfolk Island (large numbers on Philip and Nepean Islands);
and Kermadec Islands (Herald, Macauley, Curtis). Straggles
south to northern New Zealand: Gannet Island, 1883 (Reischek);
west of North Cape, 1964; two, Firth of Thames, October 1977;
one beach-wrecked near Dargaville, 1988. Subfossil on Norfolk
Island and the Chathams.
BROWN, B.; LAURIE, D. A. 1979. Masked (Blue-faced) Boobies in the Firth of
Thames. Notornis 26: 304–320.
SCHODDE, R.; FULLAGAR, P.; HERMES, N. 1983. A Review of Norfolk Island
Birds: past and present. Canberra: Australian National Parks and Wildlife Service.

Family **PHALACROCORACIDAE**: Cormorants and Shags

Genus **Phalacrocorax** Brisson

Phalacrocorax Brisson, 1760, Orn. 1: 60—type (by tautonymy) *Phalacrocorax* = *Pelecanus carbo* Linnaeus.
Hypoleucus Reichenbach, 1852 (1853), Vollst. Naturgesch., 2 Vogel, 1 Avium Syst. Nat.: 7—type (by original designation) *Pelecanus varius* Gmelin.
Microcarbo Bonaparte, 1856, C. r. hebd. Seanc. Acad. Sci., Paris, 43: 577—type (by original designation) *Pelecanus pygmaeus* Pallas.

SIEGEL-CAUSEY, D. 1988. Phylogeny of the Phalacrocoracidae. Condor 90: 885–905.
VAN TETS, G. F. 1976. Australasia and the origin of shags and cormorants. Proc. 16th Int. Orn. Congr.: 161–174. Canberra: Australian Academy of Science.
VOISIN, J.-F. 1973. Notes on the Blue-eyed Shags (Genus *Leucocarbo* Bonaparte). Notornis 20: 262–271.

120 **Phalacrocorax carbo** (Linnaeus)
            Black Shag (Black Cormorant, Great Cormorant)

Pelecanus carbo Linnaeus, 1758, Syst. Nat., ed. 10, 1: 133—Sweden.

Widespread in the Palaearctic Region, also in Iceland, Greenland and the eastern coast of temperate North America; Malay Archipelago to New Guinea, Australia and New Zealand. At least three subspecies.

Phalacrocorax carbo novaehollandiae Stephens
            Black Shag (Black Cormorant, Kawau)

Phalacrocorax Novae Hollandiae Stephens, 1826, Shaw's Gen. Zool., 13: 93—New South Wales.
Carbo carbo steadi Mathews and Iredale, 1913, Ibis—New Zealand.

Breeds throughout the main islands of New Zealand and on the Chatham Islands; straggling to Norfolk, Campbell and Macquarie Islands. Breeds also in Australia, Tasmania, and western and southern New Guinea. Common in subfossil and midden deposits, North and South Islands; a few subfossil records from Chatham Island.

121 **Phalacrocorax varius** (Gmelin)
            Pied Shag (Pied Cormorant)

Coastal Australia, visiting inland lakes on the east (extinct in Tasmania); New Zealand. Two subspecies.

Phalacrocorax varius varius (Gmelin)
            Pied Shag (Pied Cormorant, Karuhiruhi)

Pelecanus varius Gmelin, 1789, Syst. Nat. 1: 576—Queen Charlotte Sound, New Zealand.

New Zealand. Breeds on coasts, harbours, estuaries and offshore islands, from Three Kings to Stewart Island, rarely on inland waters (freshwater lakes in northern North Island and near Kaikoura). Straggles to The Snares. Subfossil and midden deposits, North and South Islands.

LALAS, C. 1979. Double breeding season in Pied Shags on Stewart Island, from records by Roy Traill. Notornis 26: 94–95.

MILLENER, P.R. 1972. The biology of the New Zealand Pied Cormorant. Unpubl. MSc thesis (Zoology). University of Auckland, 303 pp.

SIBSON, R.B.; DAVENPORT, J.C. 1956 A freshwater colony of Pied Shags (*P. varius*) at Takapuna. Notornis 7: 20–25.

STONEHOUSE, B. 1967. Feeding behaviour and diving rhythms of some New Zealand shags, Phalacrocoracidae. Ibis 109: 600–605

122 **Phalacrocorax sulcirostris** (Brandt)
Little Black Shag (Little Black Cormorant)

Carbo sulcirostris Brandt, 1837, Bull. Scient. Acad. Imp. Sci., St Petersb., 3: col. 56 — Terrae australes = New South Wales.

Borneo, Java, Moluccas, Aru Is, New Guinea and New Caledonia; western, northern and eastern Australia and Tasmania. In New Zealand, widely distributed on lakes and estuaries of the North Island south to Taupo and Hawke's Bay, on west coast as far south as Wellington; South Island, rare (Southland, 1963; Nelson 1966). Breeds regularly in Lower Waikato, Rotorua, Lake Taupo, Hawke's Bay, probably elsewhere also (e.g. southern Wairarapa); disperses in autumn, especially northwards to tidal estuaries. No subfossil or midden records.

123 **Phalacrocorax melanoleucos** (Vieillot)
Little Shag (Little Pied Cormorant)

Hydrocorax melanoleucos Vieillot, 1817, Nouv. Dict. Hist. nat. 8: 88 — 'Australasie' = New South Wales *apud* Mathews.

Lesser Sunda, Molucca and Aru Islands, New Guinea, Palau, Solomon Islands, Australia (recent and fossil), Tasmania and New Zealand.

Phalacrocorax melanoleucos brevirostris Gould
Little Shag (Kawaupaka)

Phalacrocorax brevirostris Gould, 1837, Proc. Zool. Soc. Lond.: 26 — no locality = New Zealand.

New Zealand. Breeds from North Cape to Stewart Island, and on nearby offshore islands. Straggles to The Snares and the Auckland Islands (sight records), and has bred on Campbell Island since 1967. Subfossil and midden deposits, North and South Islands.

Note: A dimorphic subspecies with some intermediate variants;

the relative scarcity of the latter suggests that the white-breasted phase may be maintained by occasional immigration from Australia.

DOWDING, J.E.; TAYLOR, M.J. 1987. Genetics of polymorphism in the Little Shag. Notornis 34: 51–57.
KINSKY, F.C. 1969. New and rare birds on Campbell Island. Notornis 16: 225–236.
MATTHEWS, C.W.; FORDHAM, R.A. 1986. Behaviour of the Little Pied Cormorant *Phalacrocorax melanoleucos*. Emu 86: 118–121.
STONEHOUSE, B. 1967. Feeding behaviour and diving rhythms of some New Zealand shags, Phalacrocoracidae. Ibis 109: 600–607.
TAYLOR, M.J. 1987. A colony of the Little Shag and the Pied Shag in which the plumage forms of the Little Shag freely interbreed. Notornis 34: 41–50.

Genus **Leucocarbo** Bonaparte

Leucocarbo Bonaparte, 1855, Consp. Gen. Avium 2: 176 — type (by subsequent designation) *Carbo bougainvillii* Lesson.

124 **Leucocarbo carunculatus** (Gmelin)

New Zealand King Shag

Pelecanus carunculatus Gmelin, 1789, Syst. Nat. 1: 576 — Queen Charlotte Sound, South Island, New Zealand.

Endemic. Breeds on islands on the south side of Cook Strait — White Rocks, Sentinel Rock, Duffer's Reef, North Trio and Stewart Island (French Pass). Subfossil and midden deposits in the northern South Island.

NELSON, A. 1971. King Shags in the Marlborough Sounds. Notornis 18: 30–37.

125 **Leucocarbo chalconotus** (Gray)

Stewart Island Shag, Bronze Shag

Graculus chalconotus Gray, 1845, Zool. Voy. 'Erebus' and 'Terror', Birds, 20 — Otago, South Island.

Endemic. Inhabits, coastal waters and breeds from Otago Peninsula to Foveaux Strait and Stewart Island. A dimorphic species, of which the dark phase is commonly called the Bronze Shag.

Subfossil and midden deposits, South and Stewart Islands.

SANSOM, M.L. 1956. Two nesting colonies of Stewart Island Shags. Notornis 7: 16–20.

126 **Leucocarbo onslowi** (Forbes)

Chatham Island Shag

Phalacrocorax onslowi Forbes, 1893, Ibis 1893: 533 — Chatham Islands.

Endemic. Breeds on main islands and outliers of Chatham Islands. Recorded from both subfossil and midden deposits.

FLEMING, C.A. 1939. Birds of the Chatham Islands. Emu 38: 380–509.

127   **Leucocarbo ranfurlyi** (Ogilvie-Grant)

Bounty Island Shag

Phalacrocorax ranfurlyi Ogilvie-Grant, 1901, Bull. Br. Ornith. Club 11: 66 — Bounty Island.

Endemic. Breeds on Bounty Islands and (?) Antipodes Islands.

ROBERTSON, C.J.R.; VAN TETS, G.F. 1982. The status of birds at the Bounty Islands. Notornis 29: 311–336.

WARHAM, J.; BELL, B.D. 1979. The birds of Antipodes Island, New Zealand. Notornis 26: 121–169.

128   **Leucocarbo colensoi** (Buller)

Auckland Island Shag

Phalacrocorax colensoi Buller, 1888, Birds New Zealand, 2nd ed., p.161 — Auckland Islands.

Endemic. Breeds on Auckland Islands. A variable species with a black-necked phase approaching *L. campbelli.*

129   **Leucocarbo campbelli** (Filhol)

Campbell Island Shag

Urile campbelli Filhol, 1878, Bull. Soc. Philom. 2: 132 — Campbell Island.

Endemic. Breeds on Campbell Island.

130   **Leucocarbo atriceps** (King)

Imperial/Blue-eyed/King Shag

Phalacrocorax atriceps King, 1828, Zool. J. 4: 102 — Straits of Magellan.

Southern South America, Falkland Islands, South Georgia, South Orkney, South Shetland, South Sandwich and islands of Antarctic Peninsula to about 66°S, Heard, Crozet, Prince Edward, Kerguelen, and Macquarie Islands. Eight subspecies.

Leucocarbo atriceps purpurascens (Brandt)

Macquarie Island Shag

Carbo purpurascens Brandt, 1837, Bull. Sci. Acad. Imp. St Petersb. 3: 56 — locality unknown = Macquarie Island.

Phalacrocorax traversi Rothschild, 1903, Bull. Br. Ornith. Club 2: 81 — Macquarie Island.

Macquarie Island.

BROTHERS, N.P. 1985. Breeding biology, diet and morphometrics of the King Shag, *Phalacrocorax albiventer purpurascens*, at Macquarie Island. Aust. Wldl. Res. 12: 81–94.

Genus **Stictocarbo** Bonaparte

Stictocarbo Bonaparte, 1855, Compt. Rend. Acad. Sci. Paris, 41: 115 — type (by subsequent designation) *Pelecanus punctatus* Sparrman.

131 **Stictocarbo punctatus** (Sparrman)

Spotted Shag

Endemic. Breeds on offshore islands and some mainland cliffs of the North and South Islands.

Stictocarbo punctatus punctatus (Sparrman)

Spotted Shag (Parekareka)

Pelecanus punctatus Sparrman, 1786, Mus. Carlson, fasc. 1, no. x — Queen Charlotte Sound, South Island, New Zealand.

In the North Island, breeds on islands of the inner Hauraki Gulf (e.g. Noises, Waiheke, Tarahiki, North Kahu), Auckland west coast (Oaia Island, Te Henga and Girdwood Point) and Somes Island, Wellington Harbour. In the South Island, breeds in Marlborough Sounds, including D'Urville Island, and on Banks Peninsula, Otago Peninsula and coastal cliffs east of Palmerston (Otago). Ranging short distances from breeding colonies. Common in subfossil and midden deposits of North and South Islands.

TURBOTT, E. G. 1956. Notes on the plumages and breeding cycle of the Spotted Shag, *Phalacrocorax (Stictocarbo) punctatus punctatus* (Sparrman, 1786). Rec. Auck. Inst. Mus. 4: 343–363.

Stictocarbo punctatus steadi Oliver

Blue Shag

Stictocarbo steadi Oliver, 1930, Trans. NZ Inst. 61: 138 — Otago.

Breeds on Stewart and its inshore islands, on Codfish and Centre Islands, and along the South Island west coast, where three breeding colonies are known (Steeples, Perpendicular Point and Open Bay Islands). Recorded, as this subspecies, from subfossil and midden deposits on Stewart Island.

KINSKY, F. C. 1970. "Spotted" Shags in Westland. Notornis 17: 102–104.

132 **Stictocarbo featherstoni** (Buller)

Pitt Island Shag

Phalacrocorax featherstoni Buller, 1873, Ibis: 90 — Chatham Islands.

Endemic. Breeds throughout the Chatham Islands but greatest numbers south of Pitt Strait. Recorded from subfossil dune and midden deposits.

FLEMING, C. A. 1939. Birds of the Chatham Islands. Emu 38: 380–509.

Family **ANHINGIDAE**: Darters
Genus **Anhinga** Brisson

Anhinga Brisson, 1760, Orn. 1: 60; 6: 47 — type (by tautonymy and monotypy) *Anhinga (anhinga)* Brisson = *Plotus anhinga* Linnaeus.

133   **Anhinga melanogaster** Pennant

Darter

Anhinga melanogaster Pennant, 1769, Indian Zool. 13, pl.12 — Sri Lanka and Java.
India, Sri Lanka and Indonesia to Philippines; Iraq and Syria to
Senegal, Sudan and Cape of Good Hope; Madagascar; New
Guinea and Australia. About five subspecies.

Anhinga melanogaster rufa (Daudin)

Darter

Plotus rufus Daudin, 1802, Buffon Hist. Nat., ed. Didot, Quadr. 14: 319 — Senegal.
Plotus Novae-hollandiae Gould, 1847, Proc. Zool. Soc. Lond.: 34 — southern coast of
Australia = New South Wales *apud* Mathews.
Africa, Asia Minor and Australia, straggling to New Zealand
(one record, Hokitika, 1874.)

OLIVER, W. R. B. 1930. New Zealand Birds, 1st ed., p.201. Wellington: Fine Arts.
VAN TETS, G. F.; SCARLETT, R. J. 1972. Sex and age of the only specimen of the
Darter *Anhinga rufa* (Daudin) recorded from New Zealand. Notornis 19: 85–86.

Suborder FREGATAE: Frigatebirds
Family **FREGATIDAE**: Frigatebirds
Genus **Fregata** Lacépède

Fregata Lacépède, 1799, Tabl. Oiseaux: 15 — type (by subsequent designation) *Pele-
canus Aquilus* Linnaeus.
Tachypetes Vieillot, 1816, Analyse: 63 — (by monotypy) '*Fregate* Buff' = *Pelecanus minor*
Gmelin.
Atagen Gray, 1841, List Gen. Birds, ed. 2: 101 — type (by original designation) '*A.
aquilla*' = *P. minor* Gmelin.
Parvifregata Mathews, 1920, Birds Aust. Suppl. 1, Checkl. 1: 64 — type (by original
designation) *Atagen ariel* G. R. Gray.

134   **Fregata minor** (Gmelin)

Greater Frigatebird

Pelecanus minor Gmelin, 1789, Syst. Nat. 1: 572 — no locality = Christmas Island,
Indian Ocean, *apud* Mathews.
Pacific, Indian and South Atlantic Oceans. About six subspecies.

Fregata minor peninsulae Mathews

Greater Frigatebird

Fregata minor peninsulae Mathews, 1923, Bull. Br. Ornith. Club 44: 15 — Raine I.,
northern Queensland.
Fregata minor mathewsi Lowe, 1924, Novit. Zool. 31: 309 — Raine I.
Twelve New Zealand records since 1861, the most southerly
being Westport. Attribution to subspecies follows Condon, 1975,
Checklist of the Birds of Australia, Part 1.

135   **Fregata ariel** (Gray)

Lesser Frigatebird

Atagen ariel G. R. Gray, 1845, Genera Birds 3: 669, pl.183 (or 185) — Raine Island, northern Queensland *apud* Mathews 1914.

Breeds on islands off Queensland, New Caledonia, Fiji and elsewhere in tropical Pacific Ocean; straggles to New Zealand, about 20 records since 1907, mostly in the north, but once to Cook Strait and once to Chatham Islands. Three subspecies.

EDGAR, A. T. 1971. Field study course, Far North, 11–18 January, 1971. Notornis 18: 118–130.

TURBOTT, E. G. 1952. Some stray tropical and sub-tropical sea birds in New Zealand. Rec. Auck. Inst. Must. 4: 187–192.

Order **CICONIIFORMES**: Herons, Ibises, Storks and Allies
Suborder ARDEAE: Herons, Bitterns and Allies
Family **ARDEIDAE**: Herons and Bitterns
Subfamily ARDEINAE: Herons, Egrets
Genus **Ardea** Linnaeus

Ardea Linnaeus, 1758, Syst. Nat., ed. 10, 1: 141 — type (by subsequent designation) *Ardea cinerea* Linnaeus (Gray, List. Gen. Bds., 1840, p.60).

Notophoyx Sharpe, 1895, Bull. Br. Ornith. Club 5: 13 — type (by original designation) *Ardea novaehollandiae* Latham.

136   **Ardea novaehollandiae** Latham

White-faced Heron

Celebes, Lesser Sunda Islands (Lombok to Timor), southern and southeastern New Guinea, New Caledonia, Australia, and New Zealand. Two subspecies, *nana* in New Caledonia and Loyalty Islands, *novaehollandiae* in the remaining regions.

Ardea novaehollandiae novaehollandiae Latham

White-faced Heron

Ardea novae Hollandiae Latham, 1790, Index Orn. 2: 701 — New South Wales.
Eastern Indonesia, southern and southeastern New Guinea, Australia and New Zeland.

In New Zealand, sporadically reported from c. 1865. Now widely distributed. Breeding suspected in 1939 in Westland (Okarito) and Otago (Bushey Park); confirmed in 1941 at Shag River. It spread rapidly northwards, especially in the 1950s; the expansion continuing to Kermadec and Norfolk Islands. It has bred at Chatham Islands since the 1970s, perhaps earlier. Straggler to subantarctic islands (Campbell, Macquarie).

CARROLL, A. L. K. 1970. The White-faced Heron in New Zealand. Notornis 17: 3–24.

HEATHER, B. D. 1983. Albinistic White-faced Herons. Notornis 30: 341–343.

HEMMINGS, A. D.; CHAPPELL, R. G. 1988. Nesting of White-faced Herons at the Chatham Islands. Notornis 35: 245–247.

MOORE, P. J. 1984. Foraging and social behaviour of the White-faced Heron at Pauatahanui Inlet. Notornis 31: 285–299.

137   **Ardea pacifica** Latham

White-necked Heron

Ardea pacifica Latham, 1801, Index Orn. Suppl.: 45 — New South Wales.
Australia and Tasmania.

In New Zealand a scarce vagrant. Only three acceptable records: Methven (1952); Onepu (1981); Waipu (1984). Because of confusion with albinistic ("white-necked") *A. novaehollandiae* several sightings have to be rejected.

HEATHER, B. D. 1983. Albinistic White-faced Herons. Notornis 30: 341–343.
HENSLEY, V. H. 1982. A White-necked Heron in the Far North. Notornis 29: 207–208.
STIDOLPH, R. H. D. 1952. Occurrence of White-necked Heron in New Zealand. Notornis 5: 38.

Genus **Egretta** T. Forster

Egretta T. Forster, 1817, Synopt. Cat. Brit. Bds: 59—type (by monotypy) *Ardea garzetta* Linnaeus.
Casmerodius Gloger, 1842 (1841), Gemein. Handb. Hilfsb. Naturgesch.: 412—type (by subsequent designation) *Ardea egretta* Gmelin.
Demigretta Blyth, 1846, J. Asiat. Soc. Bengal 15: 372—type (by monotypy) *Demigretta concolor* Blyth.

138   **Egretta alba** (Linnaeus)
                              Great White Heron (Great Egret)
Ardea alba Linnaeus, 1758, Syst. Nat., ed. 10, 1: 144—Sweden.
Worldwide in temperate and tropical regions. Four or more subspecies.

Egretta alba modesta (J. E. Gray)
                              White Heron (White Egret, Kotuku)
Ardea modesta J. E. Gray, 1831, Zool. Misc.: 19—India.
India, China and Japan to Australia and New Zealand. In New Zealand, the only known breeding place is at Okarito, Westland (15–25 pairs). Immature birds disperse widely, mainly northwards, but some even reach the subantarctic islands. Winter numbers are sometimes boosted, as in 1957, by vagrants from Australia.

Subfossil dune deposits in the Far North (particularly Tom Bowling Bay and Waikuku Beach) include bones of immature birds, and are numerous enough to suggest an early (1000–6000 yrs BP) breeding colony in this area. Otherwise only records are Hawke's Bay (subfossil); Whangamata (midden); Marfell Beach, Lake Grassmere (dune/?midden).

ANDREW, I. G. 1963. White Heron invasion, 1957. Notornis 10: 311–315.
HEATHER, B. D. 1978. The Cattle Egret in New Zealand in 1977. Notornis 25: 218–234.
WARBURTON, H. G. 1957. The White Heron (*Egretta alba*) in New Zealand. Notornis 7: 98–101.

139   **Egretta garzetta** Linnaeus

Little Egret

Egretta Garzetta Linnaeus, 1766, Syst. Nat., ed. 12, 1: 237 — "in Oriente" = Reno, north-eastern Italy, *apud* Grant and Mackworth-Praed, 1933.

Southern Europe, Africa, east to India, South-East Asia, China, Japan, Indonesia and Australia.

Egretta garzetta nigripes (Temminck)

Little Egret

Ardea nigripes Temminck, 1840, Man. Orn., ed. 2, 4: 376 — "L'Archipel des Indes".
Herodias immaculata Gould, 1846, Birds Aust. 6: pl.58 — "northern portion of Australia" = Port Essington, Northern Territory, *apud* Mathews.

Indonesia (Sunda Islands), New Guinea, Australia (mainly northern and eastern) and Tasmania; straggler to New Zealand. A scarce annual autumn vagrant; records include birds banded in Australia. Recorded from many localities, mainly coastal, throughout North and South Islands. Three the most reported together.

BRATHWAITE, D. H. 1952. Occurrence of Little Egret in Hawke's Bay. Notornis 5: 78–79.
FALLA, R. A. 1958. Some records of Australian birds in New Zealand. Notornis 8: 29–32.
GRANT, P. 1964. Little Egrets at Greymouth. Notornis 11: 135.
HEATHER, B. D. 1978. The Cattle Egret in New Zealand in 1977. Notornis 25: 218–234.

140   **Egretta intermedia** (Wagler)

Intermediate Egret (Plumed Egret)

Ardea intermedia Wagler, 1829, Isis 6: col. 659 — Java.

Southern and eastern Africa, India, South-East Asia, Japan, Sunda Islands, New Guinea and Australia; straggling to New Zealand. Three subspecies.

The first New Zealand record was of an adult in breeding plumage shot in the Manawatu River estuary near Foxton in May/June during the period 1970–73 (now in National Museum). Subsequently several sightings of single birds, which may have accompanied Cattle Egrets across the Tasman Sea: Lower Waikato (1979, 1981, 1985), Kaikohe (1986), Avon-Heathcote Estuary (1986).

SEDDON, J. H.; SEDDON, B. H. 1979. Sight record of *Egretta intermedia* in New Zealand. Notornis 26: 330.

141   **Egretta sacra** (Gmelin)

Reef Heron

Asia to Australia, Tasmania, and New Zealand and eastward through the tropical Pacific to the Marquesas, Tuamotu and

Austral Islands. Two subspecies, of which *albolineata* is in New Caledonia and Loyalty Islands only

Egretta sacra sacra (Gmelin)
Reef Heron (Blue Heron, Matuku-moana)

Ardea sacra Gmelin, 1789, Syst. Nat. 1: 640 — Tahiti.
Ardea matook Vieillot, 1817, Nouv. Dict. Hist. nat. 14: 416 — Queen Charlotte Sound, New Zealand.

Distribution as above, but not New Caledonia and Loyalty Islands.

Breeds in the North and South Islands, mainly along rocky shores; especially numerous in Northland; thinly distributed south of Marlborough Sounds; scarce on Stewart Island. Chatham Islands: rare (one at Owenga, c.1985). One South Island midden record (Kaikoura). The white phase common on many tropical Pacific islands has been identified in New Zealand only once: Avon-Heathcote Estuary, June 1987.

EDGAR, A. T. 1978. The Reef Heron (*Egretta sacra*) in New Zealand. Notornis 25: 25–58.
WODZICKI, K. A.; EYLES, J. R. 1945. White phase of the Reef Heron or Matuku-moana *Demigretta sacra* (Gmelin) at Wairau Bar. NZ Bird Notes 1: 115–117. (Subsequently reidentified as *E. garzetta*.)

Genus Bubulcus Bonaparte

Bubulcus Bonaparte, 1855, Consp. Gen. Avium 2: 124 — type (by tautonymy) *Ardea ibis* Linnaeus = *Ardea bubulcus* Audouin.

142 Bubulcus ibis (Linnaeus)
Cattle Egret

Ardea Ibis Linnaeus, 1758, Syst. Nat., ed. 10, 1: 144 — Egypt.
Southern Europe, Africa, and Asia, recently colonising widely: now also northern South America, North America, Australia and New Zealand. Two subspecies.

Bubulcus ibis coromandus (Boddaert)
Cattle Egret

Cancroma Coromanda Boddaert, 1783, Tabl. Planches enlum: 54 — Coromandel, *ex* Daubenton, Pl.190.

Throughout southern Asia including south China and Japan, and south to Australia since about 1948. First recognised as a straggler to New Zealand in the early 1960s (Canterbury and Otago, 1963; West Coast, Wairarapa and Manawatu, 1964); however, a small flock is credibly reported to have consorted with cattle in Moutere, Nelson, in 1956. Since then there has been a spectacular increase in the number of winterers, sizable flocks reappearing annually in many favoured localities from Northland to Southland; by the mid-1980s winter counts showed several thousands of birds present. Regular also on Chatham Island.

BROWN, B. 1980. Possible early record of Cattle Egrets in New Zealand. Notornis 27: 400.

HEATHER, B. D. 1978. The Cattle Egret in New Zealand in 1977. Notornis 25: 218–234.

HEATHER, B. D. 1982. The Cattle Egret in New Zealand 1978–1980. Notornis 29: 241–268.

HEATHER, B. D. 1986. Cattle Egret numbers in New Zealand in 1984. Notornis 33: 185–188.

JACKSON, W. R.; OLSEN, M. 1988. A study of Cattle Egret numbers in the Horowhenua. Notornis 35: 83–85.

PRATT, E. 1979. The growth of a Cattle Egret colony. Notornis 26: 353–356.

TURBOTT, E. G. 1964. Cattle Egret: a second Canterbury record. Notornis 10: 383–385.

TURBOTT, E. G.; BRATHWAITE, D. H.; WILKIN, F. W. 1963. Cattle Egret: a new bird for New Zealand. Notornis 10: 316.

Subfamily NYCTICORACINAE: Night Herons
Genus **Nycticorax** T. Forster

Nycticorax T. Forster, 1817, Synopt. Cat. Br. Birds: 59 — type (by monotypy) *Nycticorax infaustus* Forster = *Ardea nycticorax* Linnaeus.

143   **Nycticorax caledonicus** (Gmelin)

Nankeen Night Heron

Ardea caledonicus Gmelin, 1789, Syst. Nat. 1: 626 — New Caledonia.

Philippines, Indonesia, New Guinea, Solomon Islands, New Caledonia, Australia. Five subspecies; New Zealand records not subspecifically identified. Straggler to New Zealand; also unsuccessfully liberated (Wellington, 1852); a specimen shot near Wellington in 1856 may have been one of the liberated birds. Birds breeding at Wellington Zoo were released in 1982, all with leg bands; after a year most disappeared; several reported subsequently: Collingwood 1983, Lower Hutt 1984, Warkworth 1984. Probably an occasional vagrant from Australia; recent records of unbanded single birds: adult, Wellington, January 1972; adult, southern Wairarapa, 1977; immature, near Owaka, Otago, June–September 1980; immature, near Whangamomona, Taranaki, August 1983; upper Taieri River, 1988. May have bred near Blenheim, where two immatures were seen in 1958.

BELL, B. D. 1958. Nankeen Night-herons at Blenheim. Notornis 8: 52.

JACKSON, T. 1981. Immature night heron in Otago. Notornis 28: 217–218.

LAMBERT, R. 1981. Another Nankeen Night Heron. Notornis 28: 254.

Subfamily BOTAURINAE: Bitterns
Genus **Botaurus** Stephens

Botaurus Stephens, 1819, Shaw's Gen. Zool. 11: 592—type (by subsequent designation) *Ardea stellaris* Linnaeus.

144 **Botaurus poiciloptilus** (Wagler)
Australasian Bittern (Matuku)

Ardea poiciloptila Wagler, 1827, Syst. Avium Ardea, sp. 28, note—New South Wales.
Botaurus melanotus Gray, 1843, Dieff. Travels in NZ, Append.: 196—New Zealand.
Botaurus poiciloptilus maorianus Iredale and Mathews, 1926, Bull. Br. Ornith. Club 46: 76—new name for *B. melanotus* Gray.

New Caledonia, Australia (all coastal areas except the tropical north), Tasmania and New Zealand. Sometimes treated as a subspecies of the Eurasian *stellaris*.

In New Zealand still widely distributed, but numbers have declined through drainage of wetlands and loss of breeding cover. No acceptable records for Chatham Islands. Two "subfossil" records (Ngaroto and Poukawa) but at neither site is it likely that the bones are more than a few hundred years old.

MOON, G.J.H. 1967. Refocus on New Zealand Birds. Wellington: Reed.
OGLE, C.; CHEYNE, J. 1983. Wildlife of the Whangamarino Wetlands, Lower Waikato River basin. Wildlife: A Review 12: 27–32. NZ Wildlife Service, Dept of Internal Affairs.
SOPER, M.F. 1972. New Zealand Birds. Christchurch: Whitcoulls.
WHITESIDE, A.J. 1989. The behaviour of Bitterns and their use of habitat. Notornis 36: 89–95.

Genus **Ixobrychus** Billberg

Ixobrychus Billberg, 1828, Syn. Faun. scand. 1: 166—type (by subsequent designation) *Ardea minuta* Linneaus.

145 **Ixobrychus novaezelandiae** (Potts)
New Zealand Little Bittern

Ardeola Novae Zelandiae Potts, 1871, Trans. NZ Inst. 3: 99—Lake Wakatipu, New Zealand.

New Zealand. Allegedly first obtained at Tauranga, the sole North Island record; but no longer traceable. Fewer than 10 specimens from the South Island, the first from Lake Kaniere (1868), and all from Westland, except one from Lake Wakatipu (1870?).

Five subfossil bones of a small bittern from swamp deposits at Lake Poukawa, Hawke's Bay, referred by Horn (1980) to the Black Bittern *Dupetor flavicollis*, are now believed to be of the present species (P.R. Millener, pers. comm.). Also identified from a midden site at Paekakariki.

FALLA, R. A. 1963. Note on the Little Bittern. Notornis 10: 412–413.
HORN, P. L. 1980. Probable occurrence of the Black Bittern *Dupetor flavicollis* (Linnaeus) in New Zealand. Notornis 27: 401–403.
O'DONNELL, C.; DILKS, P. 1988. First record of the Australian Little Bittern (*Ixobrychus minutus*) in New Zealand. Notornis 35: 153–157.
OLIVER, W. R. B. 1955. New Zealand Birds, 2nd ed. Wellington: Reed.
POTTS, T. H. 1871. On the birds of New Zealand, Part II. Trans. NZ Inst. 3: 59–109.

146   **Ixobrychus minutus** (Linnaeus)
Little Bittern

Ardea minuta Linnaeus, 1766, Syst. Nat., ed. 12, 1: 240 — "Helvetia Aleppo"; restricted to Switzerland.

Europe, Asia, Africa (except north), southern New Guinea and Australia. About four subspecies.

Ixobrychus minutus dubius Mathews
Australian Little Bittern

Ixobrychus minutus dubius Mathews, 1912, Novit. Zool. 18: 234 — south-western Australia.

Southern New Guinea and Australia. One New Zealand record: Westport, February 1987, caught and later released.

O'DONNELL, C.; DILKS, P. 1988. First record of the Australian Little Bittern (*Ixobrychus minutus*) in New Zealand. Notornis 35: 153–157.

Suborder THRESKIORNITHES: Ibises and Spoonbills
Family **THRESKIORNITHIDAE**: Ibises and Spoonbills
Subfamily THRESKIORNITHINAE: Ibises
Genus **Plegadis** Kaup

Plegadis Kaup, 1829, Skizz. Entw.-Gesch. eur. Theirw: 82 — type (by monotypy) *Tantalus Falcinellus* Linnaeus.

147   **Plegadis falcinellus** (Linnaeus)
Glossy Ibis

Tantalus Falcinellus Linnaeus, 1766, Syst. Nat., ed. 12, 1: 241 — "Austria, Italia" = Austria.

Southern N. America and Europe, Africa, central Asia, India, Malaysia, Indonesia, New Guinea, Australia.

Vagrant to New Zealand, sometimes irrupting in small flocks as in 1953, 1968, 1975, 1988. First recorded at Washdyke, Timaru, in 1902; now expected almost annually, wandering from one wetland to another; no indication of staying to breed.

Chatham Islands: one, December 1984.

HEATHER, B.D. 1978. The Cattle Egret in New Zealand in 1977. Notornis 25: 218–234.
POWLESLAND, R.; CROCKETT, D. 1986. A Glossy Ibis in the Chatham Islands. Notornis 33: 132.
SANSOM, O.; BELL, B.D.; ANDREWS, T.; WILSON, R.A. 1954. Visitation of Glossy Ibis. Notornis 6: 18–19.

Genus **Threskiornis** G. R. Gray

Threskiornis G. R. Gray, 1842, Append. List Gen. Birds: 13 — type (by original designation) *Tantalus aethiopicus* Latham.

148 Threskiornis molucca (Cuvier)

White Ibis

Ibis molucca Cuvier, 1829, Regne anim., ed. 2, 1: 520 (note) — Moluccas.
Moluccas to New Guinea, Solomon Islands and Australia. Three subspecies.

Threskiornis molucca strictipennis (Gould)

Australian White Ibis

Ibis strictipennis Gould, 1838, Syn. Birds Aust., 4 Append.: 7 — Australia = New South Wales *apud* Mathews.
Southern New Guinea and Australia. Straggler to Tasmania and New Zealand.

First recorded at Appleby, near Nelson (1925). Minor irruptions in 1957 and 1975, probably of young (subadult) birds which, during their stay, apparently drifted northwards.

Sometimes treated as a subspecies of the widespread *T. aethiopica* (Sacred Ibis).

FALLA, R.A. 1958. Some records of Australian birds in New Zealand, 1957. Notornis 8: 29–32.
HEATHER, B.D. 1978. The Cattle Egret in New Zealand in 1977. Notornis 25: 218–234.
MONCRIEFF, P. 1925. Occurrence of the Australian White Ibis in New Zealand. NZ J. Sci. Tech. 7: 371–372.

Subfamily PLATALEINAE: Spoonbills
Genus **Platalea** Linnaeus

Platalea Linnaeus, 1758, Syst. Nat., ed. 10, 1: 139 — type (by subsequent designation) *Platalea leucorodia* Linnaeus (Gray, 1840).

149 Platalea regia Gould

Royal Spoonbill (Kotuku-ngutupapa)

Platalea regia Gould, 1838. Syn. Birds Aust. 4 append.: 7 — eastern coast of New South Wales.
Australia, except southwest; has wandered to Indonesia, New Guinea and islands of the southwest Pacific.

After a century of vagrant records, it has successfully colonised New Zealand. First reported at Castle Point, Wairarapa (1861). Breeding in South Westland suspected by mid-1940s; confirmed at Okarito (1949). Now breeds at Wairau River estuary, Marlborough (since 1978), on Maukiekie Island, Moeraki, North Otago (since 1984), and on Green Island, Dunedin (since 1988). Disperses in autumn, mainly northwards to several coastal areas, especially Nelson-Golden Bay and Manawatu River estuary, where it settles into winter quarters. Vagrants probably continue to arrive from Australia.

No valid subfossil records, bones from Tom Bowling and Waikuku Beaches, reported by Scarlett (1979), having been reidentified as those of *Egretta alba* (Millener 1981).

Sometimes treated as a subspecies of the widespread *leucorodia*.

HEATHER, B.D. 1978. The Cattle Egret in New Zealand in 1977. Notornis 25: 218–234.
HOLDAWAY, R.N. 1980. Royal Spoonbills nesting near Blenheim. Notornis 27: 169.
MILLENER, P.R. 1981. The Quaternary avifauna of the North Island, New Zealand. Unpubl. PhD thesis (Geology), Univ. of Auckland.
SCARLETT, R.J. 1979. Avifauna and man. Pages 75–90 *in* Anderson, A. (ed.). Birds of a Feather. NZAA Monograph 2. BAR Int. Series 62.
STIDOLPH, R.H.D. 1948. Royal Spoonbill in New Zealand. NZ Bird Notes 2: 195–196.

150   **Platalea flavipes** Gould

Yellow-billed Spoonbill

Platalea flavipes Gould, 1838, Syn. Birds Aust. 4 Append.: 7 — New South Wales.

Australia. Straggler to New Zealand: one, first recorded in August 1976 in Rangaunu Harbour, Northland, apparently stayed for at least two years; one, Te Whiti, Wairarapa, December 1981.

BILLING, A.E. 1977. The first occurrence of the Yellow-billed Spoonbill (*Platalea flavipes*) in New Zealand. Notornis 24: 192.
BOOTH, D.F. 1984 Classified Summarised Notes. Notornis 31: 40–85.

Order **ANSERIFORMES**: Duck-like Birds
Suborder ANSERES: Swans, Geese, Ducks
Family **ANATIDAE**: Swans, Geese, Ducks
Subfamily DENDROCYGNINAE: Whistling Ducks
Genus **Dendrocygna** Swainson

Dendrocygna Swainson, 1837, Nat. Hist. Class. Birds 2: 365 — type (by monotypy) *Anas arcuata* Horsfield.
Leptotarsis Eyton, 1838, Monogr. Anatidae: 29, 111 — type (by monotypy) *Leptotarsis eytoni* Eyton.
Ctenanas Mathews, 1914, Austral Avian Rec. 2: 90 — type (by monotypy) *Leptotarsis eytoni*; new name for *Leptotarsis* Eyton.

51 **Dendrocygna eytoni** (Eyton)
Grass (Plumed) Whistling Duck

Leptotarsis eytoni Eyton, 1838, Monogr. Anatidae: 111 — north-western Australia.
Breeds throughout tropical Australia, with scattered colonies in New South Wales river systems. Straggler to New Zealand: five records (Thames, 1871; Kaitangata, 1871, flock of 14; Ashburton, 1894–6; Little Wanganui, N.W. Nelson, 1975, flock of 12; Elbow landing, Lower Waikato River, April 1982, flock of 9–11).

FRITH, H.J. 1967. Waterfowl in Australia. Sydney: Angus and Robertson.
HUTTON, F.W. 1871. Catalogue of the Birds of New Zealand, p.77. Wellington: Govt Printer.

Subfamily ANSERINAE: Swans and Geese
Genus **Cygnus** Bechstein

Cygnus Bechstein, 1803, Ornith. Taschenbuch Deutschland, 2: 404 (footnote) — type (by monotypy) *Anas olor* Gmelin.
Chenopis Wagler, 1832, Isis von Oken: col. 1234 — type (by monotypy) *Chenopis atrata* = *Anas atrata* Latham.

*152 **Cygnus olor** (Gmelin)
Mute (White) Swan

Anas Olor Gmelin, 1789, Syst. Nat. 1: 502 — Russia.
Northern Eurasia; introduced from Great Britain as an ornamental bird. Feral population, now less than 50 birds, at Lake Ellesmere, some small wetlands north of Christchurch, and Lake Poukawa, Hawke's Bay.

CRAMP, S; SIMMONS, K.E.L. (eds). 1977. The Birds of the Western Palearctic, Vol. 1: pp.372–379. Oxford: Univ. Press.
HUTTON, F.W. 1871. Catalogue of the Birds of New Zealand, p. 68. Wellington: Govt Printer.

(*)153 **Cygnus atratus** (Latham)

Black Swan

Anas atrata Latham, 1790, Index Orn. 2: 834—New South Wales.

Australia, Tasmania; in New Zealand, widespread and abundant throughout main islands and on Chatham Island. The New Zealand stocks are probably to be regarded as both introduced and self-introduced (see below).

(*)A recent reassessment of the history of this species in New Zealand by M.J. Williams (Williams, 1982 and pers. comm.) suggests that its wide distribution and marked abundance in the 1864–68 period are inexplicable without spontaneous immigration: a major increase occurred at or slightly after the period of liberation (liberations were made in 1864–68 by the Nelson, Canterbury, Southland and Otago Acclimatisation Societies: about 100 liberated in all) (see Kirk, 1895). Introduced also to the Chatham Islands, but the population there is possibly also derived partly by self-introduction from Australia or the New Zealand mainland.

KIRK, T. 1896. The displacement of species in New Zealand. Trans. NZ Inst. 28: 1–27.

MIERS, K. H.; WILLIAMS, M. 1969. Nesting of the Black Swan at Lake Ellesmere, New Zealand. Wildfowl 20: 23–32.

WILLIAMS, M. 1981. The demography of New Zealand's *Cygnus atratus* population. Pages 147–161 *in* Proceedings of the 2nd International Swan Symposium, Sapporo, Japan. International Waterfowl Research Bureau, Slimbridge.

WILLIAMS, M. 1982. The Duckshooter's Bag. Wellington: The Wetland Press.

154 **Cygnus sumnerensis** (Forbes)

Chenopis sumnerensis Forbes, 1892, Ibis: 264—Sumner.
Cygnus chathamicus Oliver, 1955, New Zealand Birds: 603—Chatham Islands.

Subfossil and midden deposits throughout the North and South Islands; subfossil Chatham Islands and Stewart Island.

Genus **Branta** Scopoli

Branta Scopoli, 1769, Annus I Hist.–Nat.: 67—type (by subsequent designation —J. A. Allen, 1907) *Anas bernicla* Linnaeus.

*155 **Branta canadensis** (Linnaeus)

Canada Goose

Anas canadensis Linnaeus, 1758, Syst. Nat., ed. 10: 123—Canada.

North America and north-eastern Asia (Kamchatka to Japan).

Branta canadensis maxima Delacour

Canada Goose

Branta canadensis maxima Delacour, 1951, Am. Mus. Novit. 1537: 5—Round Lake, Grant County, Minnesota.

Northern and central states of the U.S.A. (North Dakota to

Arkansas). First successfully introduced to New Zealand in 1905; in the South Island abundant from Marlborough to North Otago and Fiordland, North Canterbury birds regularly migrating from hill country breeding areas to Lake Ellesmere. North Island numbers and distribution expanding as result of recent liberations at Wairoa and in the Wairarapa and Waikato.

Note: Possibly more than one race was introduced, but Imber (1971) has shown that the population belongs predominantly to *B.c.maxima*.

HANSON, H.C. 1965. The Giant Canada Goose. Southern Illinois University Press.
IMBER, M.J. 1971. The identity of New Zealand's Canada Geese. Notornis 18: 253–261.

Genus **Cereopsis** Latham

Cereopsis Latham, 1801, Index Orn. Suppl.: 67 — type (by monotypy) *Cereopsis novaehollandiae* Latham.

*156 **Cereopsis novaehollandiae** Latham

Cape Barren Goose

Cereopsis N. Hollandiae Latham, 1801, Index Orn. Suppl.: 65 — New South Wales.

Breeds on islands off southern Australia (Bass Strait and Great Australian Bight); liberated at Lake Hawea in 1914; survived as a small population in the Hawea, Wanaka, Hunter River area until about 1946. Reports from Fiordland (1947, 1967), Waitaki-Benmore (1966), South Auckland (1986) considered stragglers from Australia. Recent records in Manawatu are of birds released from captivity. Contrary to Forbes' (1892) and Oliver's (1955) indications there is no evidence for the former existence of an endemic species of *Cereopsis* ("*novaezealandiae*") (see Dawson 1958) nor are there any subfossil records of *C. novaehollandiae*.

DAWSON, E.W. 1958. Re-discoveries of the New Zealand subfossil birds named by H.O. Forbes. Ibis 100: 232–237.
FORBES, H.O. 1892. Preliminary notice of additions to the extinct avifauna of New Zealand. Trans. NZ Inst. 24: 185–189.
OLIVER, W.R.B. 1955. New Zealand Birds. 2nd. ed. Wellington: Reed.
WILLIAMS, G.R. 1968. The Cape Barren Goose (*Cereopsis novaehollandiae* Latham) in New Zealand. Notornis 15: 66–69.

Genus **Cnemiornis** Owen

Cnemiornis Owen, 1865, Trans. Zool. Soc. Lond. 5: 396 — type (by monotypy) *Cnemiornis calcitrans* Owen.

157 **Cnemiornis calcitrans** Owen

Cnemiornis calcitrans Owen, 1865, Trans. Zool. Soc. Lond. 5: 396 — Timaru.
Cnemiornis minor Forbes, 1892, Trans. NZ Inst. 24: 187.
Cereopsis novae-zealandiae Forbes, 1892, Trans. NZ Inst. 24: 188.

Subfossil, particularly in caves and swamps of the eastern South Island (Marlborough to Southland), but also from northern west coast caves (Karamea, Charleston); only one probable midden record (Ototara, N. Otago).

158 Cnemiornis gracilis Forbes

Cnemiornis gracilis Forbes, 1892, Trans. NZ Inst. 24: 187—Te Aute.
Cnemiornis septentrionalis Oliver, 1955, New Zealand Birds: 602—Hunterville.

Fossil (Early Pleistocene), Kaiiwi; subfossil elsewhere in the North Island from Waitomo and Mahoenui to Hunterville, and in Hawke's Bay; only one probable midden record (Paremata, Wellington).

DAWSON, E. W. 1958. Re-discoveries of the New Zealand subfossil birds named by H. O. Forbes. Ibis 100: 232–237.

Subfamily TADORNINAE: Shelducks
Genus **Tadorna** Lorenz von Oken

Tadorna Lorenz von Oken, 1817, Isis von Oken 1: 1183—type (by tautonymy) *Anas tadorna* Linnaeus.
Casarca Bonaparte, 1828, Geogr. Comp. List. Birds Europe North Amer.: 56—type (by monotypy) *Anas rutila* Pallas = *Anas ferruginea* Pallas.

159 **Tadorna variegata** (Gmelin)
Paradise Shelduck (Putangitangi)

Anas variegata Gmelin, 1789, Syst. Nat. 1: 505—Dusky Sound.

New Zealand. In the North Island, largest concentrations in the Gisborne-East Cape area, Tongariro National Park, and Northland, increasing elsewhere. In the South Island, widely distributed throughout with greatest numbers along the eastern foothills of the Southern Alps. Stewart Island, and most major offshore islands including Great Barrier, Little Barrier and Kapiti. Chatham Islands, one recorded South East Island, January 1984. Subfossil and midden from widely distributed sites throughout North and South Islands, and in the Chathams.

FENNELL, J.; MERTON, D. 1984. A Paradise Shelduck in the Chatham Islands. Notornis 31: 311.
WILLIAMS, M. J. 1971. The distribution and abundance of the Paradise Shelduck (*Tadorna variegata* Gmelin) in New Zealand from pre-European times to the present day. Notornis 18: 71–86.
WILLIAMS, M. J. 1979. The social structure, breeding and population dynamics of Paradise Shelduck in the Gisborne-East Coast district. Notornis 26: 213–272.
WILLIAMS, M. J. 1979. The moult gatherings of Paradise Shelduck in the Gisborne-East Coast district. Notornis 26: 369–390.

60   Tadorna tadornoides (Jardine and Selby)
Chestnut-breasted Shelduck (Australian Shelduck)

Anas tadornoides Jardine and Selby, 1828, Illus. Orn. 4: Pl.62 and text—New South Wales.

Southwestern and southeastern Australia, Tasmania. First records: two, Hokitika River, January 1973; next, Lake Ellesmere, December 1982. In 1983–86 recorded widely throughout New Zealand (including Snares, Auckland and Campbell Islands) in January–May: highest number recorded was in 1983 (56), only 8 in 1984, but rising to 33 in 1985. A pair with half-grown young near Lake Tekapo in January 1985 the only confirmed breeding record. Few recorded since, mainly in Marlborough (Lakes Elterwater and Grassmere).

FENNELL, J.; FENNELL, J.; SAGAR, P.; HARRISON, K. 1983. First sighting of Chestnut-breasted Shelduck in New Zealand. Notornis 30: 85–86.
GRANT, P. 1989. A 1973 record of Chestnut-breasted Shelduck. Notornis 36: 284.
HEATHER, B.D. 1987. The Chestnut-breasted Shelduck in New Zealand 1983–1986. Notornis 34: 71–77.
RIGGERT, T.L. 1977. The biology of the Mountain Duck on Rottnest Island, Western Australia. Wildlife Monograph No. 52, the Wildlife Society.

Subfamily ANATINAE: Ducks
Genus **Chenonetta** Brandt

Chenonetta Brandt, 1836, Descr. Icones Animalium Rossicorum Novorum, Aves 1: 5—type (by monotypy) *Anas jubata* Latham.

61   Chenonetta jubata (Latham)
Australian Wood Duck (Maned Goose)

Anas jubata Latham, 1801, Index Orn. Suppl.: 69—New South Wales.
Australia and Tasmania. Straggler to New Zealand: four records (Glendhu, Wanaka, 1910; Orawia, Southland, 1944; Wairau River, near mouth of the Waikakaho R., Marlborough, 1980; Snares Islands, 1983, 1985–86).

FRITH, H.J. 1967. Waterfowl in Australia. Sydney: Angus and Robertson.
JENKINS, P. 1982. Wood Duck in Marlborough. Notornis 29: 22.
OLIVER, W.R.B. 1955. New Zealand Birds, 2nd ed. Wellington: Reed.

Genus **Hymenolaimus** Gray

Hymenolaimus G.R. Gray, 1843, Ann. Mag. Nat. Hist. 11: 370   type (by monotypy) *Anas malacorhynchos* Gmelin.

162   **Hymenolaimus malacorhynchos** (Gmelin)

Blue Duck (Whio)

Anas malacorhynchos Gmelin, 1789, Syst. Nat. 1: 526—Dusky Sound.

New Zealand. North Island: restricted mostly to headwaters of some Bay of Plenty rivers and rivers draining from central mountains and eastern ranges. South Island: widespread in headwaters of rivers on western side of the Southern Alps and in Fiordland and the Catlins. Subfossil and midden: a few records, from both North and South Islands.

KEAR, J.; STEEL, T.H. 1971. Aspects of the social behaviour of Blue Duck. Notornis 18: 187–198.

KEAR, J. 1972. The Blue Duck of New Zealand. Living Bird 11: 175–192.

Genus **Anas** Linnaeus

Anas Linnaeus, 1758, Syst. Nat., ed. 10, 1: 122—type (by subsequent designation) *Anas Boschas* Linnaeus = *Anas platyrhynchos* Linnaeus.

Spatula Boie, 1822, Isis von Oken 10: col. 564—type (by monotypy) *Anas clypeata* Linnaeus.

Querquedula Stephens, 1824, Shaw's Gen. Zool. 12: 142—type (by tautonymy) *Anas querquedula* Linnaeus.

Nesonetta G.R. Gray, 1844, Gen. Birds 3: 627—type (by original designation) *Nesonetta aucklandica* G.R. Gray.

Elasmonetta Salvadori, 1895, Cat. Birds Br. Mus. 27: 287—type (by monotypy) *Anas chlorotis* G.R. Gray.

Xenonetta J.H. Fleming, 1935, Occas. Papers Roy. Ontario Mus. Zool. 1: 1—type (by original designation) *Xenonetta nesiotis* = *Anas aucklandica* G.R. Gray.

*163   **Anas platyrhynchos** Linnaeus

Mallard

Northern Hemisphere from North America, North Africa, and Europe to Asia, Hawaiian Islands and Laysan Island. Seven subspecies.

Anas platyrhynchos platyrhynchos Linnaeus

Mallard

Anas platyrhynchos Linnaeus, 1758, Syst. Nat., ed. 10, 1: 125—Sweden.

Breeds in arctic and temperate regions of North America, North Africa, Europe and Asia, wintering in southern North and Central America, North Africa and southern Asia. Introduced to New Zealand from North America and the United Kingdom. Now the most numerous and most widespread waterfowl in New Zealand. Established on Chatham, Snares, Auckland, Campbell, Antipodes Islands and most offshore islands.

BALHAM, R.W. 1952. Grey and Mallard Ducks in the Manawatu district, New Zealand. Emu 52: 163–191.

BALHAM, R.W.; MIERS, K.H. 1959. Mortality and survival of Grey and Mallard Ducks banded in New Zealand. NZ Dept. Int. Affairs Wildlife Publ. No. 5.

WILLIAMS, M. 1982. The Duckshooter's Bag. Wellington: The Wetland Press.

54 **Anas superciliosa** Gmelin

Grey Duck

South Pacific (Palau to Austral Islands), Indonesia, Australia, New Zealand. Three subspecies (*pelewensis, rogersi, superciliosa*).

Anas superciliosa superciliosa Gmelin

Grey Duck (Parera)

Anas superciliosa Gmelin, 1789, Syst. Nat. 1: 537 — Dusky Sound.

New Zealand and outlying islands (Kermadec, Chatham, Snares, Auckland, Antipodes, Campbell and Macquarie Islands). A declining subspecies, suffering from loss of wild habitats and from competition from Mallard in modified wetlands. Most numerous in Northland and Westland. Widespread in subfossil and midden deposits in North, South and Chatham Islands; however, except in a site at Poukawa, represented even in middens by small numbers of individuals, suggesting that it may formerly not have been abundant.

BALHAM, R.W. 1952. Grey and Mallard Ducks in the Manawatu district, New Zealand. Emu 52: 163–191.

BALHAM, R.W.; MIERS, K.H. 1959. Mortality and survival of Grey and Mallard Ducks banded in New Zealand. NZ Dept. Int. Affairs Wildlife Pub. No.5.

WILLIAMS, M. 1982. The Duckshooter's Bag. Wellington: The Wetland Press.

65 **Anas gracilis** Buller

Grey Teal (Tete)

Anas gracilis Buller, 1869, Ibis (2) 5: 41 — Manawatu River area.

New Guinea, Australia, Tasmania and New Zealand. Previously rare and local in New Zealand, but now established in several districts and spreading; frequent irruptions from Australia. Only tentatively identified from a few subfossil and midden sites (North and South Islands and Chathams).

MILLS, J.A. 1976. Status, mortality and movements of Grey Teal (*Anas gibberifrons*) in New Zealand. NZ J. Zool. 3: 261–267.

66 **Anas aucklandica** (Gray)

Brown Teal

New Zealand, Auckland Islands, Campbell Island.

Anas aucklandica chlorotis Gray

Brown Teal (Patcke)

Anas chlorotis G.R. Gray, 1845, *in* Richardson and J.E. Gray (eds), Voyage Erebus and Terror, Birds: 15, pl.20 — New Zealand.

Elasmonetta chlorotis peculiaris Mathews, 1937, Emu 37: 31 — South Island, New Zealand.

New Zealand. Originally widely distributed in lowland swamps and swamp forests of both main islands and Stewart Island; now rare and declining. Persists on Great Barrier Island; Little

Barrier Island; locally as small groups in Northland (Whananaki, Helena Bay, Whangaruru Harbour and south side of Bay of Islands); also occasional sightings in Waikato area and Fiordland. Recently extinct on Stewart Island. Successfully introduced to Kapiti and Tiritiri Islands; additional releases now in progress in Northland. Subfossil and midden from the North and South Islands, and Chathams.

HAYES, F.N.; WILLIAMS, M.J. 1982. The status, aviculture and re-establishment of Brown Teal in New Zealand. Wildfowl 33: 73–80.
WELLER, M.J. 1974. Habitat selection and feeding patterns of Brown Teal (*Anas castanea chlorotis*) on Great Barrier Island. Notornis 21: 25–35.
WILLIAMS, M.J. 1978. Rehabilitation of Brown Teal. Wildlife—A Review (NZ Wildlife Service) 9: 43–45.

Anas aucklandica aucklandica (Gray)
Auckland Island Teal (Flightless Duck)

Nesonetta aucklandica G.R. Gray, 1844, Gen. Birds, 3: 627, pl. 169—Auckland Islands.

Auckland Islands (now Enderby, Rose, Ocean, Ewing, Dundas, Adams and Disappointment Islands).

Anas aucklandica nesiotis (Fleming)
Campbell Island Teal

Xenonetta nesiotis J.H. Fleming, 1935, Occas. Papers. Roy. Ontario Mus. Zool. 1: 1—Campbell Island.

Campbell Island (now only on a closely adjacent islet, Dent Island, where it was rediscovered in 1975; total population probably less than 30).

ROBERTSON, C.J.R. 1976. The Campbell Island Teal. Wildlife—A Review (NZ Wildlife Service) 7: 45–46.

167   Anas rhynchotis Latham
Australasian Shoveler

Anas rhynchotis Latham, 1801, Index Orn. Suppl.: 70—New South Wales.

Australia and New Zealand. Two subspecies.

Anas rhynchotis variegata (Gould)
New Zealand Shoveler (Kuruwhengi)

Spatula variegata Gould, 1856, Proc. Zool. Soc. Lond.: 95—New Zealand.

New Zealand. Throughout both main islands; formerly Chatham Islands (last record 1925); straggler to Stewart Island and Auckland Islands. Subfossil and midden from scattered North Island sites, and from two South Island middens; also Chathams.

CAITHNESS, T.A. 1975. The New Zealand Shoveler. Wildlife—A Review (NZ Wildlife Service) 6: 14–18.
SIBSON, R.B. 1967. Speculating about Shovelers near Auckland. Notornis 14: 22–26.

168 Anas clypeata Linnaeus

Northern Shoveler

Anas clypeata Linnaeus, 1758, Syst. Nat., ed. 10, 1: 124—Sweden.

Europe, Asia and North America; migrating south to Africa, southern and south-east Asia, Hawaii and Central and South America. Regularly straggles to Micronesia and rarely to Polynesia and Australia (one record). Four records in New Zealand (Mangatawhiri swamp, lower Waikato, 6 May 1968; Lake Ngakawau, near Lake Horowhenua, 4 May 1969; Lake Horowhenua, 7 August 1971; Pauri Lake, Wanganui, 19–23 August 1989).

CRAMP, S; SIMMONS, K. E. L. 1977. The Birds of the Western Palearctic. Vol. 1, pp. 539–548. Oxford: University Press.

HOWARD, P. J. 1968. A New Zealand record of the Northern Shoveler. Notornis 15: 253.

KINSKY, F. C.; JONES, E. B. 1972. Northern Shovelers (*Anas clypeata*) in New Zealand. Notornis 19: 105–110.

STIDOLPH, R. H. D. 1974. Northern Shovelers in New Zealand. Notornis 21: 270.

Genus **Pachyanas** Oliver

Pachyanas Oliver, 1955, New Zealand Birds, 2nd ed.: 599—type (by original designation) *Pachyanas chathamica* Oliver.

169 Pachyanas chathamica Oliver

Pachyanas chathamica Oliver, 1955, New Zealand Birds, 2nd ed.: 599—Chatham Islands.

Subfossil at Chatham Islands.

Genus **Euryanas** Oliver

Euryanas Oliver, 1930, New Zealand Birds, 1st ed.: 220—type (by original designation) *Anas finschi* Van Beneden.

170 Euryanas finschi (Van Beneden)

Anas finschi Van Beneden, 1875, Journ. Zool. 4: 267—Earnscleugh.

Of wide distribution in subfossil and midden deposits throughout North and South Islands; most commonly subfossil in caves.

Genus **Malacorhynchus** Swainson

Malacorhynchus Swainson, 1831, J. Roy. Inst. Gt. Br. 2: 18—type (by monotypy) *Anas membranacea* Latham.

171 Malacorhynchus scarletti Olson

Malacorhynchus scarletti Olson, 1977, Emu 77: 132—Pyramid Valley, North Canterbury.

Subfossil; to date only from Pyramid Valley swamp. A larger representative of the Australian Pink-eared Duck *Malacorhynchus membranaceus*. Olson (p. 133) said: "*M. scarletti* may have been largely restricted to the open areas and swamps in and around the Canterbury Plains, to which certain other species, such as the quail *Coturnix novaezealandiae*, were mainly confined."

OLSON, S. L. 1977. Notes on subfossil Anatidae from New Zealand, including a new species of Pink-eared Duck *Malacorhynchus*. Emu 77: 132–135.

Genus **Aythya** Boie

Aythya Boie, 1822, Tageb. Reise Norw.: 308, 351 — type (by monotypy) *Anas marila* Linnaeus.
Nyroca Fleming, 1822, Phil. Zool.: 260 — type (by tautonymy) *Anas nyroca* Gülden-städt.
Fuligula Stephens, 1824, Shaw's Gen. Zool. 12: 187 — type (by tautonymy) *Anas fuligula* Linnaeus.
Zeafulix Mathews, 1937, Emu 37: 32 — type (by original designation) *Anas novaeseelandiae* Gmelin.

172   **Aythya australis** (Eyton)

White-eyed Duck (Hardhead)

Nyroca australis Eyton, 1838, Monogr. Anatidae: 160 — New South Wales.

Australia (mainly south-eastern) and Tasmania; nomadic, ranging as far as eastern Java, Celebes, New Guinea; a possibly distinct subspecies (*extima*) on Banks Islands, Vanuatu, and New Caledonia, but these populations may not be resident but represent part of this species' nomadic range. Temporarily established for about 30 years from 1867 to 1895 in New Zealand. Since 1895 the only records are: Hamurana, 1934 (a single bird seen); Runanga Lake, Hawke's Bay, one of a flock of eight shot, May 1973; Western Springs, Auckland, 30 April 1980 (one seen, probably a female).

ANON, 1973. A duck returns. Notornis 20: 185.
FLEMING, C. A. 1982. George Edward Lodge: the Unpublished New Zealand Bird Paintings. Wellington: Nova Pacifica.
FRITH, H. J. 1967. Waterfowl in Australia. Sydney: Angus & Robertson.
HUTTON, F. W. 1870. Descriptions of two birds new to the fauna of New Zealand. Trans. NZ Inst. 2: 78–80.
JOWETT, C. 1980. White-eyed Duck at Western Springs. Notornis 27: 392.

173   **Aythya novaeseelandiae** (Gmelin)

New Zealand Scaup (Papango)

Anas novaeseelandiae Gmelin, 1789, Syst. Nat. 1: 541 — Dusky Sound.
Zeafulix novaeseelandiae maui Mathews, 1937, Emu 37: 32 — North Island, New Zealand.

New Zealand. Lagoons and lakes, including mountain lakes and numerous small coastal ponds and sand-dune lakes, in both

North and South Islands; numbers reduced following settlement, but colonising hydro lakes in both islands and has been successfully reintroduced to small lakes within its former range. Subfossil and midden from widely distributed sites in both main islands and the Chathams.

SOPER, M. F. 1976. New Zealand Birds, 2nd ed. Christchurch: Whitcoulls.

Subfamily MERGINAE: Sea Ducks
Genus **Mergus** Linnaeus

Mergus Linnaeus, 1758, Syst. Nat., ed. 10: 129—type (by subsequent designation) *Mergus castor* Linnaeus = *Mergus serrator* Linnaeus.

174 **Mergus australis** Hombron and Jacquinot
Auckland Island Merganser

Mergus australis Hombron and Jacquinot, 1841, Ann. Sci. Nat. Zool. Paris, sér. 2, 16: 320—Auckland Islands.

The only historical records are from Auckland and Adams Islands of the Auckland group; the last specimens were apparently a pair shot on 9 January 1902, and the species is now almost certainly extinct. Subfossil and midden from widely scattered localities in both main islands; also Stewart Island and the Chathams; its presence in a number of midden deposits indicates that Polynesian occupation probably brought about its extinction on the mainland and the Chathams.

KEAR, J.; SCARLETT, R.J. 1970. The Auckland Islands Merganser. Wildfowl 21: 78–86.

OLSON, S. L. 1977. Notes on subfossil Anatidae from New Zealand, including a new species of Pink-eared Duck *Malacorhynchus*. Emu 77: 132–135.

Subfamily OXYURINAE: Stifftailed Ducks
Genus **Oxyura** Bonaparte

Oxyura Bonaparte, 1828, Ann. Lyceum Nat. Hist. New York 2: 390—type (by monotypy) *Anas rubidus* Wilson.

175 **Oxyura australis** Gould

Blue-billed Duck

Oxyura australis Gould, 1836, Proc. Zool. Soc. Lond. 85—Swan River, Western Australia.

Australia (mainly southwestern and southeastern) and Tasmania. Subfossil material representing at least nine individuals has been identified from swamp deposits at Poukawa, Hawke's Bay.

HORN, P.L. 1983. Subfossil avian deposits from Poukawa, Hawkes Bay, and the first record of *Oxyura australis* (Blue-billed Duck) from New Zealand. J. Roy. Soc. NZ 13: 67–78.

Genus **Biziura** Stephens

Biziura Stephens, 1824, Shaw's Gen. Zool. 12: 221 — type (by monotypy) *Anas lobata* Shaw.

176   **Biziura delautouri** Forbes

Biziura delautouri Forbes, 1892, Nature 45 (1166): 416 — Enfield Swamp, Oamaru.

Subfossil from five North Island (Far North, Waitomo, Poukawa) and three South Island (Marlborough, Oamaru) sites. Olson (p. 134) suggests that, pending the discovery of further material, this form should be regarded as specifically or at least subspecifically distinct from the living Australian Musk Duck *Biziura lobata*.

OLSON, S. L. 1977. Notes on subfossil Anatidae from New Zealand, including a new species of Pink-eared Duck *Malacorhynchus*. Emu 77: 132–135.

SCARLETT, R. J. 1969. The occurrence of the Musk Duck *Biziura lobata* (Shaw) in New Zealand. Notornis 16: 57–59.

Order **FALCONIFORMES**: Diurnal Birds of Prey
Suborder ACCIPITRES: Secretarybird, Kites, Eagles, Hawks and Allies
Family **ACCIPITRIDAE**: Kites, Eagles, Hawks and Allies
Subfamily ACCIPITRINAE: Kites, Eagles, Hawks and Allies
Genus **Circus** Lacépède

Circus Lacépède, 1799, Tabl. Oiseaux: 4—type (by subsequent designation) *Falco aeruginosus* Linnaeus.

177 Circus approximans Peale

Australasian Harrier (Kahu)

Circus approximans Peale, 1848, U.S. Expl. Exp. 8: 64—Mathuata, Vanua Levu, Fiji Islands.
Circus gouldi Bonaparte, 1850, Consp. Av. 1: 34—Australia (restricted type locality New South Wales *apud* Mathews).
Circus approximans drummondi Mathews and Iredale, 1913, Ibis (10) 1: 419—North Island, New Zealand.

Southeastern New Guinea; Australia (mainly northern, eastern and southwestern); Tasmania; New Caledonia; New Zealand and offshore islands, straggling to the subantarctic islands; Chatham Islands; Vanuatu, Society (introduced), Tonga, Fiji, and Loyalty Islands; Wallis (Ueu) Island. A regular visitor to the Kermadec Islands, Norfolk Island and Lord Howe Island, and a straggler to Samoa.

Widely distributed on the New Zealand mainland, its range having extended greatly with human settlement. A few subfossil and more numerous midden records from widely distributed sites in both North and South Islands; also Chathams.

BAKER-GABB, D.J. 1979. Remarks on the taxonomy of the Australasian Harrier (*Circus approximans*). Notornis 26: 325–329.
BAKER-GABB, D.J. 1981. Breeding behaviour and ecology of the Australasian Harrier (*Circus approximans*) in the Manawatu-Rangitikei sand country. Notornis 28: 103–119.
BAKER-GABB, D.J. 1986. Ecological release and behavioural and ecological flexibility in Marsh Harriers on islands. Emu 86: 71–81.
CARROLL, A.L.K. 1968. Foods of the Harrier. Notornis 15: 23–24.
DOUGLAS, M.J.W. 1970. Foods of Harriers in a high country habitat. Notornis 17: 92–95.
FOX, N.C. 1977. Some morphological data on the Australasian Harrier (*Circus approximans gouldi*) in New Zealand. Notornis 24: 9–19.
PIERCE, R.J.; MALONEY, R.F. 1989. Responses of Harriers in the MacKenzie Basin to the abundance of rabbits. Notornis 36: 1–12.
REDHEAD, R.E. 1969. Some aspects of the feeding of the Harrier. Notornis 16: 262–284.

178   Circus eylesi Scarlett*

Extinct Harrier

Circus eylesi Scarlett, 1953, Rec. Cant. Mus. 6: 245–252—Pyramid Valley, South Island, New Zealand.

Subfossil and midden from widely scattered sites in both North and South Islands.

Forbes in 1892 named two subfossil harriers, *Circus hamiltoni* and *Circus teauteensis*, but without adequate descriptions. These names are accordingly regarded as *nomina nuda*.

Genus **Haliaeetus** Savigny

Haliaeetus Savigny, 1809, Descr. Egypt. Hist. Nat. 68: 85—type (by monotypy) *Haliaeetus nisus* Savigny = *Falco albicilla* Linnaeus.

179   Haliaeetus australis (Harrison and Walker)

Extinct Chatham Island Sea Eagle

Ichthyophaga australis Harrison and Walker, 1973, Ibis 115: 274–277—Chatham Island, New Zealand.

Described from subfossil material obtained on Chatham Island by H. O. Forbes and presented to the British Museum in 1892.

DAWSON, E. W. 1961. An extinct sea eagle in the Chatham Islands. Notornis 9: 171–172.

OLSON, S. L. 1984. The relationships of the extinct Chatham Island eagle. Notornis 31: 272–277.

Genus **Harpagornis** Haast

Harpagornis Haast, 1872, Trans. NZ Inst. 4: 193—type (by monotypy) *Harpagornis moorei* Haast.

180   Harpagornis moorei Haast

Extinct New Zealand Eagle

Harpagornis moorei Haast, 1872, Trans. NZ Inst. 4: 193—Glenmark, Canterbury.
Harpagornis assimilis Haast, 1874, Trans. NZ Inst. 6: 64—Glenmark, Canterbury.

Subfossil and possibly midden from widely scattered sites in the southern North Island and the South Island; found more often in the South Island, but nowhere common. Unequivocal evidence of association with human sites is still required.

Note: H. assimilis, described by Haast in 1874, is simply the smaller male of *H. moorei*.

---

* Pending publication of the results of re-examination by R. J. Scarlett and R. N. Holdaway of material of this species, it is retained under *Circus*. However, it is likely that it will be transferred to *Accipiter* and the vernacular changed to "Extinct Goshawk".

Suborder FALCONES: Falcons and Allies
Family **FALCONIDAE**: Falcons
Genus **Falco** Linnaeus

Falco Linnaeus, 1758, Syst. Nat. ed. 10, 1: 88—type (by subsequent designation)
Falco subbuteo Linnaeus.

181 **Falco novaeseelandiae** Gmelin
New Zealand Falcon (Karearea)

Falco novae-Seelandiae Gmelin, 1788, Syst. Nat. 1: 268—Queen Charlotte Sound,·
South Island, New Zealand, *ex* Latham.
Nesierax pottsi Mathews and Iredale, 1913, Ibis (10) 1: 420—Paroah Bay, North
Island, New Zealand.

New Zealand. Probably originally throughout both main islands,
but now mainly in hilly and mountain districts; rare in the North
Island, especially north of the Volcanic Plateau. Distribution
includes offshore islands; present only at low densities on Stewart
Island and its outliers. Breeds also on the Auckland Islands.
Known from the Chathams only from subfossil bones.

Subfossil and midden records from widely distributed sites in
the North and South Islands.

FOX, N.C. 1977. Guano deposits in New Zealand hill cavities. NZ J. Zool.
4: 97–98.
FOX, N.C. 1978. Territorial spacing of the New Zealand Falcon (*Falco novaeseelandiae*). Notornis 25: 203–212.
FOX, N.C. 1978. The distribution and numbers of New Zealand Falcons (*Falco
novaeseelandiae*). Notornis 25: 317–331.
FOX, N.C. 1988. A taxonomic redescription of the New Zealand Falcon, *Falco
novaeseelandiae* Gmelin, 1788. Notornis 35: 270–272.

182 **Falco cenchroides** Vigors and Horsfield
Nankeen Kestrel

Australia, Tasmania, and New Guinea (subspecies *baru* Rand).

Falco cenchroides cenchroides Vigors and Horsfield
Nankeen Kestrel

Falco cenchroides Vigors and Horsfield, 1827, Trans. Linn. Soc. Lond. 15: 183—New
South Wales.

Throughout Australia and Tasmania, migrating to Indonesia in
winter; breeding on Lord Howe and (since about 1971) Norfolk
Island. A frequent straggler to New Zealand; the numerous
records since 1889 include a small irruption in 1969, when there
were sightings in nine localities in North and South Islands.

EDGAR, A.T.; GRANT, P. 1969. Nankeen Kestrels in New Zealand. Notornis
16: 288–298.
MOORE, J.L. 1985. Norfolk Island notes 1968 to 1984. Notornis 32: 311–318.
POWELL, W.J. 1978. An analysis of Nankeen Kestrel pellets. Notornis 25: 44–45

183   **Falco subniger** Gray

Black Falcon

Falco subniger Gray, 1843, Ann. Mag. nat. Hist. 11: 371 — Australia = Victoria *apud* Mathews.

Australia, mostly inland but reaching the coast in South Australia and adjacent areas of Victoria. One New Zealand record: Gisborne, 21 November 1983.

BLACKBURN, A. 1984. A record of the Australian Black Falcon. Notornis 31: 6.

Order **GALLIFORMES**: Game Birds and Allies
Family **PHASIANIDAE**: Partridges, Quails, Pheasants, Turkeys
Subfamily ODONTOPHORINAE: American Quails
Genus **Callipepla** Wagler

Callipepla Wagler, 1832, Isis von Oken, col. 277—type (by monotypy) *Callipepla strenua* Wagler = *Ortyx squamata* Vigors.
Lophortyx Bonaparte, 1838, Geogr. Comp. List., p.42—type (by subsequent designation) *Tetrao californicus* Shaw.
Note: The *A.O.U. Check-list* 1983 transferred Gambel's and California Quail to *Callipepla*: previously separated as *Lophortyx*.

*184 **Callipepla californica** (Shaw)
California Quail

Tetrao californicus Shaw, 1798, *in* Shaw and Nodder, Naturalists' Misc. 9, text to pl.345—California = Monterey.
Western North America from southern British Columbia to Baja California. Introduced to Hawaii, Chile, Australia and New Zealand.

Callipepla californica brunnescens (Ridgway)
California Quail

Lophortyx californicus brunnescens Ridgway, 1884, Proc. Biol. Soc. Wash. 2: 94—Santa Barbara, California, error = San Francisco.
Southwest Oregon and California. Introduced to New Zealand in 1860–1870 (both North and South Islands) with subsequent liberations of New Zealand-bred stock. Now widely distributed in both main islands, including some settled offshore islands; in small numbers on the Chathams.
WILLIAMS, G.R. 1963. A four-year population cycle in California Quail...in New Zealand. J. Anim. Ecol. 32: 441–459.
WILLIAMS, G.R. 1967. The breeding biology of California Quail in New Zealand. Proc. NZ Ecol. Soc. 14: 88–99.

Genus **Colinus** Goldfuss

Colinus Goldfuss, 1820, Handb. Zool. 2: 220—type (by monotypy) *Perdix mexicanus*, Caille de la Louisiane, Planches enlum. 149 = *Tetrao virginianus* Linnaeus.

*185 **Colinus virginianus** (Linnaeus)
Bobwhite Quail

Tetrao virginianus Linnaeus, 1758, Syst. Nat., ed. 10, 1: 161— America = Virginia.
Eastern North America, Mexico, Central America and Cuba: widely introduced in the western U.S.A. and the West Indies. Extensive introductions to New Zealand in 1898–99 were mainly

unsuccessful, but still present at Waingaro, South Auckland, in 1922 and at Wairoa, Hawke's Bay, in 1952; unconfirmed sightings at Wairoa up to 1970.

Subfamily PHASIANINAE: Partridges, Quails, Pheasants

Genus **Alectoris** Kaup

Alectoris Kaup, 1829, Skizz. Entw.-Ges. Eur. Thierw., pp.180, 193 — type (by monotypy) *Perdix petrosa* auct. (not Gmelin) = *Perdix barbara* Bonnaterre.

*186 **Alectoris rufa** (Linnaeus)

Red-legged Partridge

Tetrao rufus Linnaeus, 1758, Syst. Nat., ed. 10, 1: 160 — southern Europe, restricted type locality, northern Italy, *fide* Hartert.

Western Europe, Corsica, Canary Islands. Since 1984 a programme of introduction by acclimatisation societies with stock obtained from Britain has been in progress, the greatest activity having been in the Auckland and North Canterbury districts.

*187 **Alectoris chukar** (J. E. Gray)

Chukor

Perdix Chukar J. E. Gray, 1830, *in* Hardwicke, Illus. Indian Zool. 1(2), pl.54 — India = Srinagar, Kumaon.

Eurasia from southeastern Europe and Asia Minor east through central Asia to outer Mongolia.

Two subspecies, *A.c.chukar* and *A.c.koroviakovi* (Zarudny, 1914), were introduced to New Zealand and have probably interbred widely. Now well established on the dry, rocky country of the eastern South Island from Marlborough to Central Otago. Most liberations in the North Island unsuccessful, but some birds persist in horticultural land about Tauranga.

WILLIAMS, G. R. 1950. Chukar in New Zealand. NZ Science Review 8: 2–6.
WILLIAMS, G. R. 1951. Further notes on the Chukar. Notornis 4: 151–157.

Genus **Perdix** Brisson

Perdix Brisson, 1760, Orn. 1: 26, 219 — type (by tautonymy) *Perdix cinerea* Brisson = *Tetrao perdix* Linnaeus.

*188 **Perdix perdix** (Linnaeus)

Grey Partridge

Europe, western Asia.

Perdix perdix perdix (Linnaeus)

Grey Partridge

Tetrao Perdix Linnaeus, 1758, Syst. Nat., ed. 10, 1: 160 — Europe, restricted type locality Sweden.

British Isles and Europe from southern Sweden to France, Italy, Macedonia and eastern Russia.

Extensively introduced to New Zealand without success in the late 19th century and early 20th century, and again widely introduced from Denmark in 1961–68; the last introductions have apparently also had no success, although the birds persisted in Southland until recently.

WILLIAMS, G. R. 1969. "Introduced birds" *in* The Natural History of Canterbury, ed. G. A. Knox. Wellington: Reed.

Genus **Coturnix** Bonnaterre

Coturnix Bonnaterre, 1791, Tabl. Encyc. Meth. Orn. 1: 87 — type (by tautonymy) "Caille", *Coturnix communis* Bonnaterre = *Tetrao coturnix* Linnaeus.

189 **Coturnix novaezelandiae** Quoy and Gaimard

New Zealand Quail/Stubble Quail

Throughout Australia and Tasmania (Stubble Quail, *C.n. pectoralis* Gould, 1837) and, formerly, New Zealand (New Zealand Quail, *C.n. novaezelandiae*).

Coturnix novaezelandiae novaezelandiae Quoy and Gaimard

New Zealand Quail (Koreke)

Coturnix Novae-Zelandiae Quoy and Gaimard, 1830, Voyage de l'Astrolabe, Zool., 1: 242 — Baie Chouraki = Hauraki Gulf, North Island, New Zealand.

New Zealand: North, South and Great Barrier Islands. Extinct since about 1870; although the use of fire for clearing has been commonly regarded as the main cause of extinction, the cause of the sudden disappearance of the quail, especially in the eastern South Island where it was especially abundant, remains uncertain (Fleming, 1982). Subfossil and midden from numerous, but scattered, sites in both main islands; one of the more abundant species from subfossil and midden sites in the Far North of the North Island.

FLEMING, C. A. 1982. George Lodge: the Unpublished New Zealand Bird Paintings. Wellington: Nova Pacifica.

Genus **Synoicus** Gould

Synoicus Gould, 1843, Birds Aust. 5: pl.89 — type (by monotypy) *Perdix australis* Latham.

Ypsilophorus Mathews, 1912, Austral Avian Rec. 1: 112; new name for *Synoicus* Gould on grounds of preoccupation by *Synoicum* Phipps 1774.

***190 Synoicus ypsilophorus** (Bosc)

Brown Quail

Coturnix ypsilophorus Bosc, 1792, J. Hist. Nat. 2: 297, pl. 39—no locality = Tasmania *apud* Mathews.

Indonesia, New Guinea, Australia (northern, southwestern and eastern) and Tasmania.

Introduced to New Zealand and widely liberated in the 1860s and 1870s in both North and South Islands. Now apparently surviving only in the North Island: common in Northland, and of scattered occurrence elsewhere; also on northern offshore islands (Three Kings, Poor Knights, Great and Little Barrier, Tiritiri, Mayor, Mercury, Aldermen, Whale). (Note: Introductions from Australia came from both the Australian mainland and Tasmania and probably included at least two subspecies; the taxonomy of Australian Brown Quail is still under review.)

Note: This species was recorded on the Three Kings Islands as early as 1887 and Turbott and Buddle (1948) discussed the possibility that it reached northern New Zealand by self-introduction before the 1860–70 liberations.

TURBOTT, E. G.; BUDDLE, G. A. 1948. Birds of the Three Kings Islands. Rec. Auck. Inst. Mus. 3: 319–336.
TURBOTT, E. G. 1961. "Birds" *in* Little Barrier Island (Hauturu). NZ Dept. Sci. Ind. Res. Bulletin 137.

Genus **Phasianus** Linnaeus

Phasianus Linnaeus, 1758, Syst. Nat., ed. 10, 1:158—type (by tautonymy) *Phasianus* = *Phasianis colchicus* Linnaeus.

***191 Phasianus colchicus** Linnaeus

Ring-necked Pheasant

Phasianus colchicus Linnaeus, 1758, Syst. Nat., ed. 10, 1: 158—Africa, Asia = valley of Rioni River, western Transcaucasia.

Central temperate Asia from Asia Minor to Japan; widely introduced and established.

In New Zealand repeatedly introduced from 1842 onwards; local populations are still being reinforced by releases of New Zealand-bred stock. Most common in the northern and western North Island; of scattered distribution elsewhere in the North Island, and very sparse in South Island, except about Nelson.

The New Zealand stock is derived from several interbreeding subspecies.

WESTERSKOV, K. A. 1955. The Pheasant in New Zealand. NZ Dept. of Internal Affairs Wildlife Publication No. 40.

Genus **Pavo** Linnaeus

Pavo Linnaeus, 1758, Syst. Nat., ed. 10, 1: 156—type (by tautonymy) *Pavo* = *Pavo cristatus* Linnaeus.

192 **Pavo cristatus** Linnaeus

Peafowl

Pavo cristatus Linnaeus, 1758, Syst. Nat., ed. 10, 1: 156—"India orientali, Zeylona" = India.

India and Sri Lanka. Introduced to New Zealand for ornamental purposes; now wild in various localities in Northland, Miranda, Rotorua district, Opotiki, Wanganui district, Gisborne and Napier districts, Mahia, northwest Nelson.

Subfamily MELEAGRIDINAE: Turkeys
Genus **Meleagris** Linnaeus

Meleagris Linnaeus, 1758, Syst. Nat., ed. 10, 1: 156—type (by tautonymy) *Meleagris* = *Meleagris gallopavo* Linnaeus.

193 **Meleagris gallopavo** Linnaeus

Wild Turkey

Meleagris Gallopavo Linnaeus, 1758, Syst. Nat., ed. 10, 1: 156—North America = Mexico.

North America, from northeastern and central U.S.A. to Mexico. Established in the wild in rough farmland in many North Island and a few South Island localities.

Subfamily NUMIDINAE: Guineafowl
Genus **Numida** Linnaeus

Numida Linnaeus, 1766, Syst. Nat., ed. 12, 1: 273—type (by monotypy) *Numida meleagris* Linnaeus = *Phasianus meleagris* Linnaeus.

*194 **Numida meleagris** (Linnaeus)

Tufted Guineafowl

Phasianus Meleagris Linnaeus, 1758, Syst. Nat., ed. 10, 1: 158—Africa = Nubia, upper Nile.

Africa, south of the Sahara. Wild populations in rough farmland in a few New Zealand localities: inland from Wanganui, Waikato.

OLIVER, W. R. B. 1955. New Zealand Birds, 2nd ed. Wellington: Reed.

Order **GRUIFORMES**: Rails, Cranes and Allies
Family **RALLIDAE**: Rails, Gallinules and Coots

Note: This classification and nomenclature of rails largely follows Ripley (1977, Rails of the World. A Monograph of the Family Rallidae. Boston: Godine).

Subfamily RALLINAE: Rails, Gallinules, Coots and Allies
Genus **Rallus** Linnaeus

Rallus Linnaeus, 1758, Syst. Nat., ed. 10, 1: 153 — type (by subsequent designation) *Rallus aquaticus* Linnaeus.
Hypotaenidia Reichenbach, 1852 (1853), Vollst. Naturgesch., 2 Voegel, 1 Avium Syst. nat.: 23 — type (by original designation) *Rallus pectoralis* Gould (not Temminck) = *Hypotaenidia australis* von Pelzeln.
Lewinia Gray, 1855, Cat. Genera Subgen. Birds Br. Mus.: 120 — type (by monotypy) *Rallus lewinii* Swainson = *Rallus pectoralis* Temminck.
Cabalus Hutton, 1874, Trans. NZ Inst. 6: 108 — type (by monotypy) *Rallus modestus* Hutton.
Nesolimnas Andrews, 1896, Novit. Zool. 3: 260, 266 — type (by monotypy) *Rallus Dieffenbachii* G. R. Gray.
Hyporallus Iredale and Mathews, 1926, Bull. Br. Ornith. Club 46: 76 — type (by original designation) *Rallus muelleri* Rothschild.
Huttonena Mathews, 1929, Bull. Br. Ornith, Club 50: 19 — new name for *Cabalus* Hutton.

195   **Rallus philippensis** Linnaeus

Banded Rail

Rallus philippensis Linnaeus, 1766, Syst. Nat., ed. 12, 1: 263 — Philippines.
Indonesia, Philippines, Melanesia, Australia, Tasmania, Western Polynesia, New Zealand, Chatham and subantarctic islands.

SCHODDE, R.; de NAUROIS, R. 1982. Patterns of variation and dispersal in the Buff-banded Rail (*Gallirallus philippensis*) in the South-west Pacific, with description of a new subspecies. Notornis 29: 131–142.

Rallus philippensis assimilis G. R. Gray

Banded Rail (Moho-pereru)

Rallus assimilis G. R. Gray, 1843, *in* E. Dieffenbach, Travels in New Zealand, 2: 197 — New Zealand.
Main islands of New Zealand. North Island: Northland including Three Kings, Poor Knights and Great Barrier Islands; Auckland, Waikato, Coromandel and Bay of Plenty; rare south of 39°S. South Island: coastal northwest Nelson, Golden Bay and Pelorus Sound; rare elsewhere. Stewart Island and outliers. Rarely found subfossil or midden associated.

ELLIOTT, G. 1989. The distribution of Banded Rails and Marsh Crakes in coastal Nelson and the Marlborough Sounds. Notornis 36: 117–123.

Rallus philippensis macquariensis Hutton
Macquarie Island Banded Rail

Rallus macquariensis Hutton, 1879, Ibis (ser. 4) 3: 455 — Macquarie Island.

Macquarie Island. Extinct since about 1880.

FALLA, R. A. 1937. BANZARE Report (B), 2: 20.
RIPLEY, S. D. 1977. Rails of the World. A Monograph of the Family Rallidae.
Boston: Godine.

Rallus philippensis dieffenbachii G. R. Gray
Dieffenbach's Rail

Rallus Dieffenbachii G. R. Gray, 1843, *in* E. Dieffenbach, Travels in New Zealand,
2: 197 — Chatham Islands.

Extinct. Known from one skin collected on Chatham Island in
1840. Common in subfossil and some probable midden deposits
on Chatham and Pitt Islands. This rail, being much larger and
less modified than *R. modestus*, is likely to have been the more
recent arrival in the Chatham group.

OLSON, S. L. 1975. A review of the extinct rails of the New Zealand region (Aves:
Rallidae). Nat. Mus. NZ Rec. 1: 63–79.

196 **Rallus modestus** Hutton
Chatham Island Rail

Rallus modestus Hutton, 1872, Ibis (ser. 3) 2: 247 — Mangere Island, Chatham
group.

Chatham, Mangere and Pitt Islands, Chatham group. Extinct
since about 1900. Common in subfossil and some probable
midden deposits.

OLSON, S. L. 1975. A review of the extinct rails of the New Zealand region (Aves:
Rallidae). Nat. Mus. NZ Rec. 1: 63–79.
RIPLEY, S. D. 1977. Rails of the World. A Monograph of the Family Rallidae.
Boston: Godine.

197 **Rallus pectoralis** Temminck
Lewin's Rail

Rallus pectoralis Temminck, 1831, Nouveau Recueil de Planches Coloriees d'Oiseaux,
livr. 88: text to pl.523 (part) — New South Wales.

Philippines, Flores, New Guinea, Australia, Tasmania, Auckland Islands.

Rallus pectoralis muelleri Rothschild
Auckland Island Rail

Rallus muelleri Rothschild, 1893, Bull. Br. Ornith. Club 1(8): 40 — Auckland Island.

Known until recently only from the type specimen (now missing,
presumed destroyed) and a live bird collected on Adams Island
in 1966. In 1989 rediscovered on Adams Island in good numbers.

FALLA, R. A. 1967. An Auckland Island rail. Notornis 14: 107–113.

Genus **Gallirallus** Lafresnaye

Galli-rallus Lafresnaye, 1841, Rev. Zool. 1841: 234 — type (by monotypy) *Gallirallus brachypterus* Lafresnaye = *Rallus troglodytes* Gmelin.

Note: *Gallirallus minor* Hamilton, 1893 (Trans. NZ Inst. 25: 88–106), based on subfossil bones from Castle Rock, Southland, is doubtfully distinct from *G. australis* — see Olson (1975. Nat. Mus. NZ Rec. 1: 63–79). *Ocydromus* (=*Gallirallus*) *insignis* Forbes, 1892 (Trans. NZ Inst. 24: 185–189), based on a large subfossil tibiotarsus from New Zealand, is dubious — see Ripley (1977. Rails of the World).

198   **Gallirallus australis** (Sparrman)

Weka

New Zealand. Found widely in subfossil and midden deposits in North, South and Stewart Islands, but the bones cannot be determined to subspecies.

Gallirallus australis greyi (Buller)

North Island Weka

Ocydromus greyi Buller, 1888, Birds of New Zealand, ed. 2, 2: 105, pl.34 — North Island, New Zealand.

North Island. Formerly throughout but now confined mainly to the Poverty Bay area. Successfully reintroduced to Kapiti Island, Mokoia Island (Lake Rotorua), Kawau Island and the Bay of Islands.

BEAUCHAMP, A.J. 1988. Status of the Weka on Cape Brett, Bay of Islands. Notornis 35: 282–284.

CARROLL, A.L.K. 1963. Food habits of the North Island Weka. Notornis 10: 289–300.

Gallirallus australis australis (Sparrman)

Western Weka

Rallus australis Sparrman, 1786, Mus. Carls., fasc. 1: no. xiv, pl.14 — Dusky Sound New Zealand.

Rallus troglodytes Gmelin, 1789, Syst. Nat., 1(2); 713 — Dusky Sound, New Zealand.

Ocydromus assimilis Buller, 1888, Guide New Zealand Birds, Silver col.: 44 — southernmost part of South Island.

Gallirallus townsoni Mathews and Iredale, 1914, Ibis for 1914: 295, pl.11 — Westport, Westland.

South Island. Widespread in northern Marlborough, Nelson, north Westland and Fiordland; local from Hokitika to Milford Sound. Introduced to D'Urville and Chetwode Islands. This subspecies is dimorphic in Fiordland.

Gallirallus australis hectori (Hutton)

Buff Weka

Ocydromus hectori Hutton, 1874, Trans. NZ Inst. 6: 110 — Lake Te Anau.
Gallirallus hectori reischeki Iredale, 1913, Austral Avian Rec. 2: 15 — Canterbury.

South Island. Formerly widespread in eastern low-rainfall areas from Marlborough to Southland. It apparently died out on the mainland, but remains abundant on the Chatham Islands (Chatham and Pitt) where it was introduced in 1905. Successfully reintroduced from the Chathams to Arthur's Pass National Park in 1962.

Gallirallus australis scotti (Ogilvie-Grant)

Stewart Island Weka

Ocydromus scotti Ogilvie-Grant, 1905, Bull. Br. Ornith. Club 15: 78 — Port Pegasus, Stewart Island.

Stewart Island. Introduced to numerous outlying islands including Solander and Codfish Islands (but removed from Codfish by 1987). Also introduced successfully to Kapiti Island (c. 1895) and Macquarie Island (1872 and later).

Genus **Capellirallus** Falla

Capellirallus Falla, 1954, Rec. Auck. Inst. Mus. 4: 242 — type (by original designation) *Capellirallus karamu* Falla.

199 **Capellirallus karamu** Falla

New Zealand Snipe-rail

Capellirallus karamu Falla, 1954, Rec. Auck. Inst. Mus. 4: 242, pl.40–42 — Karamu Cave, near Hamilton, North Island.

New Zealand. Subfossil. Known from numerous North Island sites, including caves, dunes, swamps and middens. Very distinctive with perhaps the longest bill and smallest wings (relative to body size) of any rail. Flightless.

Genus **Diaphorapteryx** Forbes

Diaphorapteryx Forbes, 1892, Bull. Br. Ornith. Club 1: 21 — type (by monotypy) *Aphanapteryx hawkinsi* Forbes.

200 **Diaphorapteryx hawkingi** (Forbes)

Giant Chatham Island Rail

Aphanapteryx hawkinsi Forbes, 1892, Nature 45: 416 — Chatham Island.
Diaphorapteryx hawkinsi Forbes, 1892, Bull. Br. Ornith. Club 1: 21 — Chatham Island.

Chatham Island. Subfossil. A large, ponderous, flightless rail known from middens and abundant dune deposits.

Genus **Porzana** Vieillot

Porzana Vieillot, 1816, Analyse d'une Nouvelle Ornithologie Elementaire: 61 — type (by monotypy and tautonymy) "Marouette" of Buffon = *Rallus porzana* Linnaeus.

201   **Porzana tabuensis** (Gmelin)

Spotless Crake

Rallus tabuensis Gmelin, 1789, Syst. Nat. 1(2): 717 — Tongatapu, Tahiti and neighbouring islands.

Philippines and Moluccas, New Guinea, Melanesia, Australia and Tasmania, southwest Polynesia including New Zealand.

Porzana tabuensis plumbea (J. E. Gray)

Spotless Crake (Puweto)

Crex plumbea J. E. Gray, 1829, *in* E. Griffith, Animal Kingdom 8 (Aves, 3): 410 — no locality; New Zealand designated by Mathews, 1911, Birds Aust. 1: 217.

Australia, Tasmania and New Zealand. In New Zealand, widespread, including Kermadec, Three Kings and Chatham Islands. Known from a very few subfossil and midden sites on the mainland and Chathams.

According to Onley (1982a) this race is doubtfully valid.

HADDEN, D. 1970. Notes on the Spotless Crake in the Waingaro district. Notornis 17: 200–213.

HADDEN, D. 1972. Further notes on the Spotless Crake. Notornis 19: 323–329.

KAUFMANN, G. 1987. Swamp habitat used by Spotless Crakes and Marsh Crakes at Pukepuke Lagoon. Notornis 34: 207–216.

KAUFMANN, G.; LAVERS, R. 1987. Observations of breeding behaviour of Spotless Crake (*Porzana tabuensis*) and Marsh Crake (*P. pusilla*) at Pukepuke Lagoon. Notornis 34: 193–205.

ONLEY, D. 1982a. The nomenclature of the Spotless Crake (*Porzana tabuensis*). Notornis 29: 75–79.

ONLEY, D. 1982b. The Spotless Crake (*Porzana tabuensis*) on Aorangi, Poor Knights Islands. Notornis 29: 9–21.

202   **Porzana pusilla** (Pallas)

Marsh Crake

Rallus pusillus Pallas, 1776, Reise durch verschiedene Provinzen des Russischen Reichs 3: 700 — Dauria, Siberia.

Throughout the Old World, including New Guinea, Australia, Tasmania and New Zealand. Migratory in the Palaearctic.

Porzana pusilla affinis (J. E. Gray)

Marsh Crake (Koitareke)

Ortygometra affinis J. E. Gray, 1845, Voyage Erebus and Terror, Birds: 14 — Wanganui River, North Island.

New Zealand and Chatham Islands. Widespread. Very rare as a subfossil or in middens; recorded from only four sites, two in the North Island and two on Chatham Island.

ELLIOTT, G. 1989. The distribution of Banded Rails and Marsh Crakes in coastal Nelson and the Marlborough Sounds. Notornis 36: 117–123.
KAUFMANN, G. 1987. Swamp habitat used by Spotless Crakes and Marsh Crakes at Pukepuke Lagoon. Notornis 34: 207–216.
KAUFMANN, G.; LAVERS, R. 1987. Observations of breeding behaviour of Spotless Crake (*Porzana tabuensis*) and Marsh Crake (*P. pusilla*) at Pukepuke Lagoon. Notornis 34: 193–205.

Genus **Gallinula** Brisson

Gallinula Brisson, 1760, Orn. 1: 50, 6: 2 — type (by tautonymy) Gallinula of Brisson = *Fulica chloropus* Linnaeus.
Tribonyx DuBus, 1840, Bull. Acad. Roy. Sci. Bruxelles 7(1): 212 — type (by monotypy) *Tribonyx mortierii* DuBus.
Pyramida Oliver, 1955, New Zealand Birds, 2nd ed.: 595 — type (by monotypy) *Rallus hodgeni* Scarlett.

203 **Gallinula ventralis** Gould

Black-tailed Native-hen

Gallinula ventralis Gould, 1837, Proc. Zool. Soc. Lond. 1836: 85 — Swan River, Western Australia.

Australia. Straggler to New Zealand. At least four records: Oraki, Colac Bay, Southland (1923); Tukituki River, Hawke's Bay (May 1957); Kongahu Swamp, Karamea (August–November 1985); Opuatia Swamp, Waikato (May 1986).

BRATHWAITE, D. H. 1963. Another record of the Black-tailed Waterhen in New Zealand. Notornis 10: 233.

204 **Gallinula tenebrosa** Gould

Dusky Moorhen

Gallinula tenebrosa Gould, 1846, Birds Aust. 6: pl.73 (of bound volume) — South Australia.

Australia, New Guinea and East Indies. Straggler to New Zealand. One record: Lake Hayes, Otago (August–October 1968).

BARLOW, M. 1969. Dusky Moorhen on Lake Hayes. Notornis 16: 81–84.

205 **Gallinula hodgeni** (Scarlett)

Hodgen's Rail

Rallus hodgeni Scarlett, 1955, Rec. Cant. Mus. 6: 265 — Pyramid Valley swamp, South Island.
Gallirallus hartreei Scarlett, 1970, Notornis 17: 70 — near Napier, North Island.
Capellirallus hodgeni (new combination), Scarlett, 1970, Notornis 17: 71.
Gallinula (Tribonyx) hodgeni (new combination), Olson, 1975, Nat. Mus. NZ Rec. 1: 68.

New Zealand. Subfossil. Known from several North and South Island sites, including middens. Flightless.

Genus **Porphyrio** Brisson

Porphyrio Brisson, 1760, Orn. 1: 48, 5: 522—type (by tautonymy) *Porphyrio* Brisson = *Fulica porphyrio* Linnaeus.
Notornis Owen, 1848, Proc. Zool. Soc. Lond. 1848: 2—type (by diagnosis) *Notornis mantelli* Owen.
Mantellornis Mathews, 1911, Birds Aust. 1: 249—type (by original designation) *Notornis hochstetteri* A. B. Meyer.

206   **Porphyrio porphyrio** (Linnaeus)
Purple Gallinule/Purple Swamphen

Fulica Porphyrio Linnaeus, 1758, Syst. Nat., ed. 10, 1: 152—lands bordering western Mediterranean.

Southern Europe, Africa, India, southeast Asia, New Guinea, Melanesia, western Polynesia, Australia, Tasmania, New Zealand and Chatham Islands.

Porphyrio porphyrio melanotus Temminck
Pukeko (Swamphen— Australia)

Porphyrio melanotus Temminck, 1820, Manuel d'Orn., ed. 2, 2: 701—New South Wales.
Porphyrio stanleyi Rowley, 1875, Orn. Miscellany 1: 37—New Zealand (based on an albino).
Porphyrio chathamensis Sharpe, 1893, Ibis 1893: 531—Chatham Islands.

Australia, Tasmania and New Zealand. In New Zealand, North, South and Stewart Islands and many offshore islands, including Great Barrier, Great Mercury, Waiheke, and Kapiti Islands; also Kermadec and Chatham Islands. Straggler to Three Kings Islands and Campbell Island. Known from only a few "subfossil" and midden sites on the mainland (none likely to be more than a few hundred years old).

CARROLL, A. L. K. 1969. The Pukeko (*Porphyrio melanotus*) in New Zealand. Notornis 16: 101–120.

207   **Porphyrio mantelli** (Owen)
Takahe (Notornis)

New Zealand.

Porphyrio mantelli mantelli (Owen)
North Island Takahe

Notornis Mantelli Owen, 1848, Trans. Zool. Soc. Lond. 3: 347, pl.56 fig. 7–13—Waingongoro R., Taranaki, North Island (based on a skull from volcanic sand deposits).

North Island. Extinct. Known as a Pleistocene fossil from Scinde Island, Napier. Bones widespread in subfossil and midden sites. Larger than the South Island race.

Porphyrio mantelli hochstetteri (A. B. Meyer)
South Island Takahe

Notornis Hochstetteri A. B. Meyer, 1883, Abbildungen von Voegel-Skeletten, Lief. 4, 5: 28, pls. 34–37—Bare-patch Plains, east of Lake Te Anau, South Island.

South Island. Four specimens were seen or taken in the south-western corner of the South Island between 1849 and 1898. Then assumed to be extinct until rediscovered by G. B. Orbell (November 1948) west of Lake Te Anau, and subsequently found to be widespread in the Murchison Mountains. Wild population currently c. 120 birds. Bones widespread in subfossil and midden sites, more often at lowland than subalpine altitudes.

LAVERS, R.; MILLS, J. 1984. Takahe. Dunedin: John McIndoe.
MILLS, J. A.; MARK, A. F. 1977. Food preferences of Takahe in Fiordland National Park, New Zealand, and the effect of competition from introduced red deer. J. Anim. Ecol. 46: 939–958.
MILLS, J. A.; LAVERS, R. B.; LEE, W. G. 1984. The Takahe—a relict of the Pleistocene grassland avifauna of New Zealand. NZ J. Ecol. 7: 57–70.
WILLIAMS, G. R. 1960. The Takahe (*Notornis mantelli* Owen, 1848): a general survey. Trans. Roy. Soc. NZ 88: 235–258.

Genus **Fulica** Linnaeus

Fulica Linnaeus, 1758, Syst. Nat., ed. 10, 1: 152—type (by tautonymy) *Fulica atra* Linnaeus.
Palaeolimnas Forbes, 1893, Ibis (ser. 6) 5: 521–546—type (by monotypy) *Fulica newtoni* Milne-Edwards.
Nesophalaris Brodkorb & Dawson, 1962, Auk 79: 268—type (by monotypy) *Fulica chathamensis* Forbes.

208 **Fulica atra** Linnaeus

Eurasian Coot

Fulica atra Linnaeus, 1758, Syst. Nat., ed. 10, 1: 152—Sweden.

Europe, north Africa, Asia, New Guinea, Australia, Tasmania. Recent arrival in New Zealand.

Fulica atra australis Gould

Australian Coot

Fulica australis Gould, 1845, Proc. Zool. Soc. Lond. 1845: 2—Western Australia.

Australia and Tasmania; straggler to Macquarie Island. New Zealand: eight records (all in South Island) between 1875 and 1953. Recorded Lake Tutira (Hawke's Bay) 1954. An invasion from Australia apparently occurred c. 1957. First proved breeding Lake Hayes (Otago) 1958; now widespread and increasing.

JACKSON, R.; LYALL, H. 1964. An account of the establishment of the Australian Coot in the Rotorua district with some notes on its nesting habits. Notornis 11: 82–86.
MacDONALD, R. 1968. The Australian Coot established on Virginia Lake, Wanganui. Notornis 15: 234–237.
SMALL, M. M.; SOPER, M. F. 1959. Australian Coots nesting in Otago. Notornis 8: 93.

209   Fulica chathamensis Forbes

Chatham Island Coot

Fulica chathamensis Forbes, 1892, Nature 46: 252—Chatham Island.

Chatham Island. Known from subfossil and midden sites. Flightless and very large.

210   Fulica prisca Hamilton

New Zealand Coot

Fulica prisca Hamilton, 1893, Trans. NZ Inst. 25: 98—Castle Rock, Southland, South Island.

New Zealand. Subfossil. Known from numerous North and South Island sites, including middens. Slightly smaller than the Chatham Island form. Flightless. Both this and *F. chathamensis* were probably derived from an early colonisation of New Zealand by *F. atra* stock from Australia.

MILLENER, P.R. 1980. The taxonomic status of extinct New Zealand coots, *Fulica chathamensis* subspp. (Aves: Rallidae). Notornis 27: 363–367.

MILLENER, P.R. 1981. The subfossil distribution of extinct New Zealand Coots *Fulica chathamensis* subspp. (Aves: Rallidae). Notornis 28: 1–9.

Family **APTORNITHIDAE**: The Aptornis

Note: The recognition of this family follows Bonaparte (1856. C.R. Acad. Sci. Paris 43(18): 841), Oliver (1955, New Zealand Birds. 2nd ed.) and Olson (1985. The fossil record of birds, *in* Farner, King & Parkes. Avian Biology, Vol. 8: 162).

Olson stated that these large, flightless birds, which display a unique jaw mechanism, have a few suggestive resemblances to the Rhynochetidae (the Kagu) of New Caledonia, but are distinct from that and other living gruiform families. *Apterornis* Owen, 1848 may have priority over *Aptornis* Owen, 1848, but the point has not been settled.

Genus **Aptornis** Owen

Aptornis Owen, 1848, Trans. Zool. Soc. Lond. 3: 347—type (by monotypy) *Dinornis otidiformis* Owen.

211   Aptornis otidiformis (Owen)

North Island Aptornis

Dinornis otidiformis Owen, 1844, Trans. Zool. Soc. Lond. 3: 247—Poverty Bay.

North Island. Subfossil from numerous sites, but rare in middens.

212   Aptornis defossor Owen

South Island Aptornis

Aptornis defossor Owen, 1871, Trans. Zool. Soc. Lond. 7: 354, pl.40–44—Oamaru, South Island.

South Island. Subfossil and midden-associated from numerous sites.

Family **GRUIDAE**: Cranes
Subfamily GRUINAE: Cranes
Genus **Grus** Brisson

Grus Brisson, 1760, Orn. 5: 375 — type (by tautonymy) *Ardea grus* Linnaeus.
Grus Pallas, 1766, Misc. Zool.: 66 — type (by tautonymy) *Ardea grus* Linnaeus.

213 **Grus rubicundus** (Perry)

Brolga

Ardea rubicunda Perry, 1810, Arcana 6: pl.22 — Botany Bay, NSW.

New Guinea and Australia. Straggler to New Zealand; two records: Clevedon (1947, doubtful) and Punakaiki (1968).

McKENZIE, H.R.; CUNNINGHAM, J.M. 1952. Occurrence of the Brolga (*Megalornis rubicundus*) in New Zealand. Notornis 4: 198.

WESTERSKOV, K.E. 1968. Australian Brolga (*Grus rubicunda*) recorded in New Zealand. Notornis 15: 248–253.

Order **CHARADRIIFORMES**: Waders, Gulls and Terns, Auks
Suborder CHARADRII: Waders and Allies
Family **ROSTRATULIDAE**: Painted Snipe
Genus **Rostratula** Vieillot

Rostratula Vieillot, 1816, Analyse: 56—type (by monotypy) "Becassine de Madagascar" of Buffon = *Rallus benghalensis* Linnaeus.

214   **Rostratula benghalensis** (Linnaeus)
Painted Snipe

Rallus benghalensis Linnaeus, 1758, Syst. Nat., ed. 10, 1: 153—Asia.
Africa; southern Asia north to Manchuria and Japan; Australia, especially the southeast. An Australian subspecies *R.b. australis* (Gould, 1838) has been defined on the basis of slight differences in size and coloration.
One New Zealand record: Lake Ellesmere, August 1986.
HARRISON, K.C.; MULLIGAN, S. 1987. Painted Snipe at Lake Ellesmere. Notornis 34: 78–79.

Family **HAEMATOPODIDAE**: Oystercatchers
Genus **Haematopus** Linnaeus

Haematopus Linnaeus, 1758, Syst. Nat., ed. 10, 1: 152—type (by monotypy) *Haematopus ostralegus* Linnaeus.

215   **Haematopus ostralegus** Linnaeus
Pied Oystercatcher

Haematopus ostralegus Linnaeus, 1758, Syst. Nat., ed. 10, 1: 152—Sweden.
Almost cosmopolitan; numerous subspecies.

Haematopus ostralegus finschi Martens
South Island Pied Oystercatcher (Torea)

Haematopus finschi Martens, 1897, Orn. Monatsb. 5: 190—Saltwater Creek, South Island, New Zealand.
Breeds inland in the South Island, mainly east of the Southern Alps, on shingle riverbeds, shores of mountain lakes, in pastures and on ploughed lands, on fellfields and "tundra" up to 2000 m. Since 1980, several pairs have attempted to breed in Hawke's Bay; in 1988, a pair attempted to breed in southern Wairarapa. Migratory, tens of thousands wintering north of 38°S but many remaining on coasts and estuaries of the South Island. Straggling to the Chatham Islands, one record 1968. Subfossil from North Island, subfossil and midden from South Island.

BAKER, A. J. 1974. Ecological and behavioural evidence for the systematic status of the New Zealand Oystercatchers (Charadriiformes: Haematopodidae). Rec. Ontario Mus. Life Sci. Contribn. 34pp.
FALLA, R. A. 1939. New Zealand oystercatchers. Rec. Cant. Mus. 4: 259–266.
SIBSON, R. B. 1966. Increasing numbers of South Island Pied Oystercatchers visiting northern New Zealand. Notornis 13: 94–97.
TWYDLE, M.; TWYDLE, W. 1983. South Island Pied Oystercatchers nesting in Hawkes Bay. Notornis 30: 197–198.

216 **Haematopus unicolor** J. R. Forster
  Variable Oystercatcher (Torea; dark phase, Toreapango)

Haematopus unicolor J. R. Forster, 1844, Descr. Anim., ed. Licht., p.112—Dusky Sound, New Zealand.
Haematopus reischeki Rothschild, 1899, Bull. Br. Ornith. Club 10: 4—Kaipara, New Zealand.

Coasts of North, South and Stewart Islands (not Chathams) and on many offshore islands where there are sandy or pebble beaches. There is some flocking and local movement in autumn, but no pronounced migration. Subfossil and midden from North, South and Stewart Islands.

H. unicolor is polymorphic with three plumage phases: black, pied and an intermediate colouring that is a hybrid of the other two. (Pied birds are probably homozygous dominant (WW) for a major gene (W). Black birds appear to be homozygous recessive (ww) and intermediate-plumaged birds heterozygous (Ww)). In southern New Zealand there are few pied and hybrid birds, and only black birds occur in Stewart Island; however, immature pied or intermediate birds occasionally wander to the far south.

BAKER, A. J. 1973. Distribution and numbers of New Zealand oystercatchers. Notornis 20: 128–144.
BAKER, A. J. 1973. Genetics of plumage variability in the Variable Oystercatcher (*Haematopus unicolor*). Notornis 20: 330–345.
BAKER, A. J. 1974. Ecological and behavioural evidence for the systematic status of the New Zealand Oystercatchers (Charadriiformes: Haematopodidae). Rec. Ontario Mus. Life Sci. Contribn. 34pp.
BAKER, A. J. 1975. Morphological variation, hybridization and systematics of New Zealand oystercatchers (Charadriiformes: Haematopodidae). J. Zool. Lond. 175: 357–390.
FALLA, R. A. 1939. New Zealand oystercatchers. Rec. Cant. Mus. 4: 259–266.

217 **Haematopus chathamensis** Hartert
  Chatham Island Pied Oystercatcher

Haematopus ostralegus chathamensis Hartert, 1927, Nov. Zool. 34: 17—Chatham Islands.

Chatham Islands: throughout the group but mainly on Mangere and South East Islands. A small (fewer than 50) sedentary population, just holding its own. Subfossil and midden, Chatham Island.

FLEMING, C. A. 1939. Birds of the Chatham Islands, II. Emu 38: 492–509.

Family **RECURVIROSTRIDAE**: Stilts and Avocets
Subfamily RECURVIROSTRINAE: Stilts and Avocets
Genus **Himantopus** Brisson

Himantopus Brisson, 1760, Orn. 1: 46 — type (by tautonymy) *Himantopus* Brisson = *Charadrius Himantopus* Linnaeus.
Hypsibates Nitzsch, 1827, Ersch and Grube's Allg. Encycl. 1(16): 150 (new name for *Himantopus* Bonnaterre = Brisson).

218   **Himantopus himantopus** (Linnaeus)

Pied Stilt

Charadrius Himantopus Linnaeus, 1758, Syst. Nat., ed. 10, 1: 151 — southern Europe.
Almost cosmopolitan; about five subspecies. Also called Black-winged or White-headed Stilt.

Himantopus himantopus leucocephalus Gould

Australasian Pied Stilt (Poaka)

Himantopus leucocephalus Gould, 1837, Proc. Zool. Soc. Lond. 1837: 26 — Australia = New South Wales.
Himantopus albus Ellman, 1861, Zoologist, p.7470 — New Zealand.
Philippines, Borneo, Java, Lesser Sunda Islands, Celebes, Moluccas, Bismarck Archipelago, Australia and New Zealand. Winter visitor from Australia to New Guinea.

Throughout New Zealand; partly migratory. Also on suitably large and open offshore islands with shallow ponds or lagoons e.g. Great Barrier, Waiheke, Kapiti, Ruapuke. Rare on Stewart Island and the Chathams. Range has greatly increased with the spread of farmland.

In the New Zealand population birds are variably marked, particularly in the pattern and extent of black and white on the head, neck and throat; they far outnumber those of the Australian type i.e. with unbroken white band around the lower neck or across the upper shoulders. These New Zealand birds evidently show the result of hybridisation with the once common Black Stilt (*H. novaezelandiae*).

PIERCE, R.J. 1984. The changed distribution of stilts in New Zealand. Notornis 31: 7–18.
PIERCE, R.J. 1984. Plumage, morphology and hybridisation of New Zealand stilts *Himantopus* spp. Notornis 31: 106–130.
PIERCE, R.J. 1985. Feeding methods of stilts (*Himantopus* spp.) NZ J. Zool. 12: 467–472.
PIERCE, R.J. 1986. Differences in susceptibility to predation during nesting between Pied and Black Stilts (*Himantopus* spp.) Auk 103: 273–280.
SCOTT WOOD, D. 1985. A note on the nomenclature of the New Zealand stilts (*Himantopus*). Notornis 32: 152–155.

219   **Himantopus novaezelandiae** Gould

Black Stilt (Kaki)

Himantopus novaezelandiae Gould, 1841, Proc. Zool. Soc. Lond. 1841: 8 — Port Nicholson, North Island, New Zealand.
Himantopus melas Hombron and Jacquinot, 1841, Ann. Sci. Nat. 16: 320 — Otago.

Formerly the dominant and probably the only stilt in New Zealand, breeding along many braided shingle riverbeds in the South Island and in the southern part of the North Island and dispersing widely in autumn. Now much reduced and breeding apparently only within the Waitaki river-system. Adults rather sedentary; but a few subadults annually move to winter on the intertidal flats of the big inlets north of 38°S. The few subfossil and midden records of *Himantopus* sp. from the North and South Islands are probably of this species, but this and the previous species cannot be reliably distinguished osteologically.

PIERCE, R.J. 1984. The changed distribution of stilts in New Zealand, Notornis 31: 7–18.
PIERCE, R.J. 1984. Plumage, morphology and hybridisation of New Zealand stilts *Himantopus* spp. Notornis 31: 106–130.
PIERCE, R.J. 1985. Feeding methods of stilts (*Himantopus* spp.), NZ J. Zool. 12: 467–472.
PIERCE, R.J. 1986. Differences in susceptibility to predation during nesting between Pied and Black Stilts (*Himantopus* spp.). Auk 103: 273–280.
SCOTT WOOD, D. 1985. A note on the nomenclature of the New Zealand stilts (*Himantopus*). Notornis 32: 152–155.

Genus **Recurvirostra** Linnaeus

Recurvirostra Linnaeus, 1758, Syst. Nat., ed. 10, 1:151 — type (by monotypy) *Recurvirostra avosetta* Linnaeus.

220   **Recurvirostra novaehollandiae** Vieillot

Australian Red-necked Avocet

Recurvirostra Novae-Hollandiae Vieillot, 1816, Nouv. Dict. Hist. Nat. 3: 103 — New Holland = Victoria *apud* Mathews = probably Van Diemen's Land *apud* Stresemann.

Breeds in Australia, mainly in southern parts. In the latter half of the 19th century, New Zealand received a minor irruption, during which (1859–1892) Avocets were reported widely from Whangarei to Invercargill, and a straggler reached Norfolk Island (1859). In the South Island breeding was attempted at several estuarine localities in Canterbury. Only two 20th century records: Lake Ellesmere (1912) and Orowaiti Lagoon, Westport (1968–1970).

BULLER, W.L. 1888. A History of the Birds of New Zealand, 2nd ed. London: the author.
KAIGLER, C.G. 1968. Red-necked Avocet in Westland. Notornis 15: 123.

Family **GLAREOLIDAE**: Pratincoles and Coursers
Subfamily GLAREOLINAE: Pratincoles
Genus **Glareola** Brisson

Glareola Brisson, 1760, Orn. 1: 48; 5: 141 — type (by tautonymy) *Glareola* Brisson = *Hirundo pratincola* Linnaeus.

221   **Glareola maldivarum** J. R. Forster
Oriental Pratincole

Glareola (Pratincola) Maldivarum J. R. Forster, 1795, Faunula Indica, ed. 2, p.11 — open sea near Maldive Islands, northern Indian Ocean.

Breeding continental Asia from Pakistan eastwards; partially migratory, many reaching northern Australia and a few straggling to islands of Indian Ocean and south-west Pacific, including New Zealand (south to Stewart Island).

Westport (1898); Appleby (1959); Port Adventure (1963); Raoul Island (1976); Lake Wainono (1977); South Turnbull (1977); Jordans, Kaipara (1985); Ruapuke Island (1988).

BULLER, W. L. 1898. On the ornithology of New Zealand. Trans. NZ Inst. 31: 23.
FALLA, R. A. 1959. Pratincole records in New Zealand. Notornis 8: 126–127.
FALLA, R. A. 1963. The Oriental Pratincole, another record. Notornis 10: 355.
PIERCE, R. J. 1978. Feeding methods of an Oriental Pratincole. Notornis 25: 290.

Family **CHARADRIIDAE**: Dotterels, Plovers, Lapwings
Subfamily CHARADRIINAE: Plovers
Genus **Charadrius** Linnaeus

Charadrius Linnaeus, 1758, Syst. Nat., ed. 10, 1: 150 — type (by tautonymy) *Charadrius hiaticula* Linnaeus.
Ochthodromus Reichenbach, 1852 (1853), Av. syst. Nat., p.xviii — type (by original designation) *Charadrius wilsonia* Ord.
Pluviorhynchus Bonaparte, 1856, Compt. Rend. Acad. Sci. Paris 43: 417 — type (by subsequent designation) *Charadrius obscurus* Gmelin.

222   **Charadrius obscurus** Gmelin
New Zealand Dotterel (Tuturiwhatu)

Charadrius obscurus Gmelin, 1789, Syst. Nat. 1: 686 — New Zealand i.e. Dusky Sound *ex* Latham.

New Zealand only; in the North Island breeds on beaches from Spirits Bay to Kawhia and the eastern Bay of Plenty; also on some offshore islands, including Cavalli, Great Barrier, Great Mercury, Waiheke, Browns Island (Motukorea), Rurima Rocks, Whale Island. A scarce visitor, not found breeding, to beaches of central New Zealand, on either side of Cook Strait, and especially

Farewell Spit. Breeds on Stewart Island, mainly on hilltops above the bush line, descending to beaches in autumn, some crossing Foveaux Strait to the coast of Southland.

Subfossil and midden records from the North Island.

EDGAR, A. T. 1959. Estimated population of the Red-breasted Dotterel. Notornis 16: 85–100.

McKENZIE, H. R. 1952. Nesting of New Zealand Dotterel, 1950. Notornis 5: 15–17.

223 **Charadrius bicinctus** Jardine and Selby

Banded Dotterel

New Zealand, breeding North, South and some offshore and outlying islands; partially migratory, many reaching Australia.

Charadrius bicinctus bicinctus Jardine and Selby

Banded Dotterel (Tuturiwhatu)

Charadrius bicinctus Jardine and Selby, 1827, Illus. Orn. 1: pl.28 and text—"New Holland" = New South Wales *apud* Mathews.

New Zealand, breeding North and South Islands from Spirits Bay to Bluff, some coastally, some far inland; also on some offshore and outlying islands, including Great Barrier, Great Mercury, Kapiti, Ruapuke, Stewart, Chatham. Partially migratory, many moving to Australia to winter, but substantial flocks remaining in New Zealand. Passing migrants visit Lord Howe and Norfolk Islands, apparently with some regularity. Also recorded from Fiji, New Caledonia, Vanuatu, and Auckland Islands (Enderby). Subfossil from North and South Islands.

BOMFORD, M. 1986. Breeding displays and calls of the Banded Dotterel (*Charadrius bicinctus*). Notornis 33: 219–232.

BOMFORD, M. 1988. Breeding of the Banded Dotterel on the Cass River delta, Canterbury. Notornis 35: 9–14.

PIERCE, R. J. 1989. Breeding and social patterns of Banded Dotterels (*Charadrius bicinctus*) at Cass River. Notornis 36: 13–23.

STIDOLPH, R. H. D. 1944. Breeding of Double-banded Dotterel. Emu 44: 85–86.

THOMAS, D. G. 1972. Moult of the Banded Dotterel (*Charadrius bicinctus*) in winter quarters. Notornis 19: 33–35.

Charadrius bicinctus exilis Falla

Auckland Island Banded Dotterel

Charadrius bicinctus exilis Falla, 1978, Notornis 25: 101–108—Adams Island, Auckland Islands.

Auckland Islands only. Apparently sedentary; breeding on high tops of Auckland and Adams Islands, and descending to sea-level to winter, especially on Enderby Island where c. 155 were counted, April 1980.

PIERCE, R. J. 1980. Habitats and feeding of the Auckland Island Banded Dotterel (*Charadrius bicinctus exilis* Falla 1978) in autumn. Notornis 27: 309–324.

224   **Charadrius ruficapillus** Temminck

Red-capped Dotterel

Charadrius ruficapillus Temminck, 1821, Planches col. Oiseaux 1: pl.47; 5: pl.68—
"Oceanie" = New South Wales.
Charadrius alexandrinus ruficapillus Temminck, 1945, C. A. Fleming *et al.*, Checklist of
New Zealand Birds. Wellington: OSNZ.

Breeds in Australia and Tasmania. A straggler to New Zealand.
First record, near Waikanae (1878); next, 1947–1950, a female
bred with a Banded Dotterel, Ashley River, Canterbury. In
1960s and 1970s, records of breeding on North Canterbury rivers
and several records of single birds Manukau Harbour and Lake
Tuakitoto (Otago). Last breeding record 1979–80 and last sighting Lake Ellesmere 1981, despite intensive searches made of
breeding rivers in 1986–1987. Closely related to the widespread
Kentish or Snowy Plover *C. alexandrinus* Linnaeus, but best
regarded as a full species.

DAVIS, M. M. 1980. Red-capped Dotterel in North Canterbury. Notornis 27:
367–368.
FALLA, R. A. 1948. Breeding of Red-capped Dotterel in New Zealand. NZ Bird
Notes 2: 194.
HUGHEY, K. F. D. 1989. The status of the Red-capped Dotterel in New Zealand.
Notornis 36: 24–26.
KIRK, T. 1880. On the occurrence of the Red-capped Dotterel (*Hiaticula ruficapilla*)
in New Zealand. Trans NZ Inst. 12: 246–247.
McKENZIE, H. R. 1980. Red-capped Dotterel in North Canterbury. Notornis
27: 291–292.

225   **Charadrius melanops** Vieillot

Black-fronted Dotterel

Charadrius melanops Vieillot, 1818, Nouv. Dict. Hist. nat. 27: 139—"aux Terres
Australes Baudin Exp." = New South Wales *apud* Mathews.

Australia, both coastal and inland; nomadic but rather rare in
the southeast. Began to colonise New Zealand c. 1954. Now
strongly established on the shingle rivers of Hawke's Bay (north
to Mohaka River), Wairarapa and Manawatu; vagrants have
appeared north to Parengarenga; a few winter regularly in the
Bay of Plenty. In the South Island, breeds in Marlborough
(Wairau and Awatere Rivers), Canterbury (Ashburton, Orari,
Opihi Rivers), Otago (Taieri, Manuherikia Rivers), and Southland (mainly Aparima River).

BARLOW, M. 1989. Establishment of the Black-fronted Dotterel in Southland.
Notornis 36: 76–78.
BRATHWAITE, D. H. 1955. Waders on Ahuriri Lagoon, Napier. Notornis 6:
145–150.
CHILD, P.; CHILD, M. 1984. The Alexandra Black-fronted Dotterels: 1982/83
season. Notornis 31: 31–39.
HEATHER, B. D. 1973. The Black-fronted Dotterel (*Charadrius melanops*) in the
Wairarapa. Notornis 20: 251–261.

MACKENZIE, N.B. 1962. A new breeding bird for New Zealand: Black-fronted Dotterel in Hawke's Bay. Notornis 9: 269–270.
MACKENZIE, N.B. 1963. The Black-fronted Dotterel in Hawke's Bay. Notornis 10: 202–206.
TARBURTON, M.K. 1989. Feeding behaviour of the Black-fronted Dotterel. Notornis 36: 249–259.

226 **Charadrius hiaticula** Linnaeus

Ringed Plover

Charadrius Hiaticula Linnaeus, 1758, Syst. Nat., ed. 10, 1: 150 — Europe and America = Sweden.

Almost circumpolar, if the North American Semipalmated Plover *Charadrius semipalmatus* Bonaparte is merely a subspecies. Siberian Ringed Plovers, subspecies *tundrae* (Lowe), migrate great distances, mainly southwestwards towards Africa; rarely to Australasia. Two New Zealand records: Firth of Thames, 1970–71 and 1983–84.

An Australian specimen has been assigned to *tundrae* (Lowe).

BROWN, J.; BROWN, B.; McKENZIE, H.R.; SIBSON, R.B. 1971. Ringed Plover in the Firth of Thames. Notornis 18: 262–266.

227 **Charadrius leschenaultii** Lesson

Large Sand Dotterel

Charadrius Leschenaultii Lesson, 1826, Levrault's Dict. Sci. nat. 42: 36 — Pondicherry, India.

Breeds across northern Asia from Armenia to Mongolia; winters commonly from Africa to northern Australia, straggling to islands of the southwest Pacific. First recognised in New Zealand in 1943; now accepted as a rare but annual summer visitor, sometimes overwintering. Most frequently reported from the intertidal flats of the Auckland isthmus. Reaches the South Island, especially Farewell Spit (four in 1974); others from Canterbury estuaries.

SIBSON, R.B.; BULL, P.C. 1946. The occurrence of Geoffroy's Sand-plover in New Zealand. Emu 45: 223–224.
SIBSON, R.B. 1953. Further notes on *Charadrius leschenaulti*. Notornis 5: 179–181.

228 **Charadrius mongolus** Pallas

Mongolian Dotterel

Charadrius mongolus Pallas, 1776, Reise Prov. russ. Reichs. 3: 700 — "salt lakes towards Mongolian border"

Breeds in northeastern Asia; winters from southeast China to coastal Australia, straggling to islands of the southwest Pacific. First recognised in New Zealand at Farewell Spit in 1961; now accepted as a rare but probably regular summer visitor especially to the Auckland isthmus (four at Karaka in 1981). South Island sightings include three at Farewell Spit in 1967, one from Southland lagoons (1964) and others from Canterbury estuaries.

The subspecies seen in New Zealand has not been ascertained. Four subspecies are recognised, two of which, *mongolus* Pallas and *stegmanni* Portenko from far-eastern Siberia, are known from Australia.

HEATHER, B. D.; ROBERTSON, H. A. 1981. A Mongolian Dotterel in breeding plumage. Notornis 28: 82–83.

HOGG, M. J. 1961. "Mongolian Dotterel" *in* Bell, B. D., McKenzie, H. R. and Sibson, R. B., Field Study Course at Farewell Spit. Notornis 9: 145–156.

SIBSON, R. B. 1975. Some thoughts on a difficult dotterel, *Charadrius mongolus*. Notornis 22: 347–349.

URQUHART, J. 1963. Mongolian Dotterel at Karaka. Notornis 10: 234–235.

229   **Charadrius veredus** Gould

Oriental Dotterel

Charadrius veredus Gould, 1848, Proc. Zool. Soc. Lond.: 38 — northern Australia.

Breeds in northern China, Mongolia and Manchuria; migrates to winter in Indonesia and Australia, straggling to islands of the southwest Pacific and to New Zealand: Raoul Island (1908); Firth of Thames, flock of 10 (1954–55); Parengarenga (1955, 1968–69); Manukau (1975); Lake Wainono (1977); Greymouth airfield (1982); Invercargill estuary (1988); Waituna (1988); Lake Ellesmere (1989).

EDGAR, A. T. Oriental Dotterel in Northland. Notornis 15: 211–212.

OLIVER, W. R. B. 1930. New Zealand Birds, 1st ed., pp.286–287. Wellington: Fine Arts.

Genus **Erythrogonys** Gould

Erythrogonys Gould, 1838, Syn. Birds Aust. 4: pl.73 — type (by monotypy) *Erythrogonys cinctus* Gould.

230   **Erythrogonys cinctus** Gould

Red-kneed Dotterel

Erythrogonys cinctus Gould, 1838, Syn. Birds Aust. 4: pl.73 — New South Wales.

Australia only, mainly inland. Nomadic. One sighting for New Zealand, Manawatu estuary (1976).

An aberrant monotypic genus closely related to *Charadrius*.

BOCK, W. J. 1958. A generic review of the plovers. Bull. Mus. Comp. Zool., Harv. 118: 29–97.

ROBERTSON, H. A.; DENNISON, M. D. 1977. Red-kneed Dotterel (*Charadrius cinctus*) — first record for New Zealand. Notornis 24: 193–194.

Genus **Thinornis** G. R. Gray

Thinornis G. R. Gray, 1845, Voyage Erebus and Terror, Birds, p.12 — type (by monotypy) *Thinornis rossii* G. R. Gray = *Charadrius novaeseelandiae* (Gmelin).

231 **Thinornis novaeseelandiae** (Gmelin)
Shore Plover (Tuturuatu)

Charadrius novae-Seelandiae Gmelin, 1789, Syst. Nat. 1: 684 — New Zealand, i.e. Queen Charlotte Sound *ex* Latham.

New Zealand only. North Island, former alleged distribution and movements cannot be verified and are in some doubt; South Island, recorded at Dusky Sound and Queen Charlotte Sound in 1773, but quickly exterminated after arrival of European carnivores. Now restricted to the Chatham Islands; total population 100–150 breeding South East Island; rarely straggling to other islands in the group. Subfossil and midden on Chatham Island. *Thinornis rossii* G. R. Gray, 1845 (G. R. Gray, Voy. Erebus and Terror, Birds, p.12, pl.11, "Auckland Island"), known from only a single specimen, has long been believed to be a young *T. novaeseelandiae*, strayed or wrongly labelled. In Gray's illustration the head is mainly dark, but as pointed out by Fleming (1982), a later illustration by G. E. Lodge based on the holotype differs from Gray's plate and is more like a normal Shore Plover.

FLEMING, C. A. 1939. Birds of the Chatham Islands, Part III. Emu 39: 1–15.
FLEMING, C. A. 1982. George Edward Lodge: the Unpublished New Zealand Bird Paintings. Wellington: Nova Pacifica.
PHILLIPS, R. E. 1980. Behaviour and systematics of New Zealand plovers. Emu 80: 117–197.

Genus **Anarhynchus** Quoy and Gaimard

Anarhynchus Quoy and Gaimard, 1830, Voyage de l'Astrolabe, Zool. 1: 252 — type (by monotypy) *Anarhynchus frontalis* Quoy and Gaimard.

232 **Anarhynchus frontalis** Quoy and Gaimard
Wrybill (Ngutuparore)

Anarhynchus frontalis Quoy and Gaimard, 1830, Voyage de l'Astrolabe, Zool. 1: 252 — Baie Chouraki i.e. Hauraki Gulf, New Zealand.
Anarhynchus albifrons Schlegel, 1857, Handl. Dierk. 1: 435.

New Zealand only. Breeds on the riverbeds of Canterbury and Otago; migrates to the North Island, although a few wander to Southland, and winters mainly north of 38°S. Subfossil (dune) and midden records from the North Island.

BOCK, W. J. 1958. A generic review of the plovers. Bull. Mus. Comp. Zool. Harv. 118: 29–97.
HUGHEY, K. F. D. 1985. The relationship between riverbed flooding and non-breeding Wrybills on northern feeding grounds in summer. Notornis 32: 42–50.
PHILLIPS, R. E. 1980. Behaviour and systematics of New Zealand plovers. Emu 80: 117–197.
PIERCE, R. J. 1979. Foods and feeding of the Wrybill (*Anarhynchus frontalis*) on its riverbed breeding grounds. Notornis 26: 1–21.
SIBSON, R. B. 1943. Observations on the distribution of the Wrybill in the North Island, New Zealand. Emu 43: 49–62.

SIBSON, R. B. 1963. A population study of the Wry-billed Plover (*Anarhynchus frontalis*). Notornis 10: 146–153.

URQUHART, D. A.; SIBSON, R. B. 1952. Observations on Wrybilled Plover at Karaka. Notornis 4: 170–172.

Genus **Pluvialis** Brisson

Pluvialis Brisson, 1760, Orn.1: 46; 5: 42 — type (by tautonymy) *Pluvialis aurea* Brisson = *Charadrius apricarius* Linnaeus.
Squatarola Cuvier, 1817 (1816), Regne anim. 1: 467 — type (by tautonomy) *Tringa squatarola* Linnaeus.

233   **Pluvialis fulva** (Gmelin)

Pacific Golden Plover

Charadrius fulvus Gmelin, 1789, Syst. Nat. 1: 687 — Tahiti.

Breeds on the tundras of Siberia and western Alaska; migrates on a broad front to India, Malaysia, Australasia and most Pacific islands. Regularly returns to summer in certain favoured areas from Norfolk and Kermadec Islands to Chatham Island and the Southland lagoons, straggling to the Auckland Islands. Very few overwinter in New Zealand.

CONNORS, P. G. 1983. Taxonomy, distribution, and evolution of golden plovers (*Pluvialis dominica* and *Pluvialis fulva*). Auk 100: 607–620.

KNOX, A. 1987. Taxonomic status of 'Lesser Golden Plovers'. Br. Birds 80: 482–487.

McKENZIE, H. R. 1967. Census records of Pacific Golden Plover for Firth of Thames and Manukau Harbour. Notornis 14: 214–217.

SIBSON, R. B. 1946. Notes on two migrant waders near Auckland. NZ Bird Notes 2: 4–7.

STEAD, E. F. 1923. Notes on the migratory plovers of New Zealand, with records of some additional species. Trans. NZ Inst. 54: 490–495.

234   **Pluvialis squatarola** (Linnaeus)

Grey Plover

Tringa squatarola Linnaeus, 1758, Syst. Nat., ed. 10, 1: 149 — Sweden.

Almost circumpolar, breeding on arctic tundras; strongly migratory, some reaching the tips of the southern continents and many isolated islands. First recorded in New Zealand in 1948; now known to be a scarce but probably annual visitor. Numerous occurrences from the Far North (7 at Houhora in 1982), Auckland isthmus, and Farewell Spit (4 in 1977–1978, 5 in 1983). Recorded also at Grassmere (1961), Macquarie Island (1964), Kermadec Islands (1966), Chatham Island (1968), Southland lagoons (1969 and 1980).

SIBSON, R. B. 1949. New Arctic wader for New Zealand list. NZ Bird Notes 3: 82.

Genus **Vanellus** Brisson

Vanellus Brisson, 1760, Orn. 1: 48; 5: 94 — type (by tautonymy) *Vanellus* Brisson = *Tringa vanellus* Linnaeus.

Lobibyx Heine, 1890, Nom. Mus. Hein. Orn.: 334 — type (by original designation) *Tringa lobata* Latham = *Vanellus novaehollandiae* Stephens.

35 **Vanellus miles** (Boddaert)

Masked Plover

Tringa miles Boddaert, 1783, Tabl. Planches enlum.: 51 — Timor-laut; designated Mathews, 1912.

Australia and Tasmania; southern New Guinea, Aru Islands to Moluccas. Three subspecies.

Vanellus miles novaehollandiae Stephens

Spur-winged Plover

Vanellus Novae-Hollandiae Stephens, 1819, Shaw's Gen. Zool. 11: 516 — New South Wales.

Australia mainly south of tropics; abundant in Tasmania. Only twice recorded in New Zealand in 19th century (Kaiiwi, 1886; Hokitika, 1892); breeding began near Invercargill c. 1932 and spread northwards. Now abundant in the South Island; widespread in the North Island as far as North Cape; abundant north to Taranaki and Hawke's Bay; well established on Chatham Islands (Chatham and Pitt Islands). Has straggled to Stewart and Campbell Islands. Also Norfolk Island (subspecies?), 1980.

BARLOW, M. 1972. The establishment, dispersal and distribution of the Spur-winged Plover in New Zealand. Notornis 19: 201–211.
BOCK, W.J. 1958. A generic review of the plovers. Bull. Mus. comp. Zool. Harv. 118: 29–97.
SANSOM, O. 1951. Spur-winged Plover in New Zealand. Notornis 4: 138–139.
WARHAM, J. 1960. The Spur-winged Plover in North Queensland. Emu 60: 61–63.

Subfamily ARENARIINAE: Turnstones and Surfbird
Genus **Arenaria** Brisson

Arenaria Brisson, 1760, Orn. 1: 48; 5: 132 — type (by tautonymy) *"Arenaria"* = *Tringa interpres* Linnaeus.

36 **Arenaria interpres** (Linnaeus)

Turnstone

Tringa Interpres Linnaeus, 1758, Syst. Nat., ed. 10, 1: 148 — Gotland, Sweden.

Almost holarctic, breeding along northern coasts of Eurasia and America and on many subarctic islands. Strongly migratory and one of the most cosmopolitan waders. Thousands reach New Zealand annually and tend to concentrate in certain favoured localities, including Chatham Island; probably regularly visits Antipodes and Auckland Islands. Regular at Norfolk Island and a straggler to Campbell Island. Many overwinter. Of the three weakly defined subspecies, *A.i.cinclus* (Pallas) and *A.i.morinella* (Linnaeus) have been recognised in Australia and are likely to be

the forms which occur in New Zealand. One midden record
(Kaikoura, South Island); also subfossil in Chatham Island
dunes.

BULLER, W. L. 1888. A History of the Birds of New Zealand, 2nd ed. London: the
author.
FALLA, R. A. 1936. Arctic birds as migrants in New Zealand. Rec. Auck. Inst.
Mus. 2: 3–14.
McKENZIE, H. R. 1968. Census records of Turnstone for Firth of Thames and
Manukau Harbour. Notornis 15: 238–241.
SIBSON, R. B. 1946. Notes on two migrant waders near Auckland. NZ Bird Notes
2: 4–7.

Family **SCOLOPACIDAE**: Snipe, Sandpipers,
Godwits, Curlews
Subfamily SCOLOPACINAE: Snipe
Genus **Coenocorypha** G. R. Gray

Coenocorypha G. R. Gray, 1855, Cat. Gen. Subgen. Birds, p.119—type (by original
designation) *Gallinago aucklandicus* G. R. Gray.

237   **Coenocorypha aucklandica** (G. R. Gray)

New Zealand Snipe

New Zealand (except Chatham Islands): mainland (including
Little Barrier Island), extinct; islands off Stewart Island,
recently extinct; still present on subantarctic islands.

Coenocorypha aucklandica aucklandica (G. R. Gray)

Auckland Island Snipe

Gallinago aucklandica G. R. Gray, 1845, Voyage Erebus and Terror, Birds, p.13,
pl.13—Auckland Islands.
Gallinago tristrami Rothschild, 1893, Bull. Br. Ornith. Club 3: 12—Antipodes Island,
error = Auckland Islands.

Auckland Islands; present on Ewing, Adams and probably Disappointment Island. Believed exterminated on main island by
introduced carnivores.

FALLA, R. A. 1965. Birds and mammals of the subantarctic islands. Proc. NZ Ecol.
Soc. 12: 63–68.

Coenocorypha aucklandica huegeli (Tristram)

Snares Island Snipe

Gallinago huegeli Tristram, 1893, Bull. Br. Ornith. Club 1: 47—Snares Islands.

Snares Islands; discovered in 1873 but first described in 1893.

ANDERSON, R. A. 1968. Notes on the Snares Island snipe. Notornis 15: 223–227.
RICHDALE, L. E. 1948. Wildlife on an island outpost. Dunedin: the author.
STEAD, E. F. 1948. Bird life on the Snares. NZ Bird Notes 3: 70–80.
WARHAM, J. 1967. Snares Islands birds. Notornis 14: 122–139.

Coenocorypha aucklandica iredalei Rothschild
Stewart Island Snipe (Tutukiwi)

Coenocorypha aucklandica iredalei Rothschild, 1921, Bull. Br. Ornith. Club 41: 63—
Jack Lees Island, New Zealand.

Big South Cape Island till 1964; also formerly Jacky Lee Island
and other outliers of Stewart Island. Apparently now extinct.

BLACKBURN, A. 1965. Muttonbird Islands diary. Notornis 12: 191–207.
GUTHRIE-SMITH, H. 1936. Sorrows and Joys of a New Zealand Naturalist.
Dunedin and Wellington: Reed.
MISKELLY, C. M. 1987. The identity of the Hakawai. Notornis 34: 95–116.

Coenocorypha aucklandica meinertzhagenae Rothschild
Antipodes Island Snipe

Coenocorypha aucklandica meinertzhagenae Rothschild, 1927, Nov. Zool. 34: 15—
Antipodes Island.

Antipodes Island; discovered in 1887 but not recognised as
distinct till 1927.

WARHAM, J.; BELL, B. D. 1979. The birds of Antipodes Island, New Zealand.
Notornis 26: 121–169.

Coenocorypha aucklandica barrierensis Oliver
Little Barrier Snipe

Coenocorypha aucklandica barrierensis Oliver, 1955, New Zealand Birds, 2nd ed., p. 275.
Wellington: Reed.

An indigenous form of snipe seems to have survived on Little
Barrier Island till c.1870, when two were seen and one became a
specimen, now in the Auckland Museum; as it differs from any
of the known surviving snipe of the subantarctic islands, Oliver
named it *barrierensis*.

It is now clear from subfossil bones, especially from limestone
caves, that a form of *Coenocorypha* was once widespread in the
North and South Islands; midden records are not known, imply-
ing that it was probably rare, if not extinct, on the mainland by
the time of Polynesian settlement. (Note that R. J. Scarlett had
originally intended to give the name *Coenocorypha aucklandica
medwayi* to bones from caves in the Awakino-Mahoenui district,
but the name is merely listed by Medway (1971) and is hence a
nomen nudum.)

HUTTON, F. W. 1871. Comments on a snipe from Little Barrier Island. Proc. NZ
Inst. 3: 86.
MEDWAY, D. G. 1971. Sub-fossil avian remains from the Awakino-Mahoenui
area. Notornis 18: 218–219.
MISKELLY, C. M. 1987. The identity of the Hakawai. Notornis 34: 95–116.
MISKELLY, C. M. 1988. The Little Barrier Snipe. Notornis 35: 273–281.
SCARLETT, R. J. 1979. Avifauna and man. *In* Birds of a Feather, NZ Archaeol.
Assn. Monograph II; BAR (Brit. Archaeol. Repts) International Series 62.
TURBOTT, E. G. 1961. Birds. *In* Little Barrier Island (Hauturu), compiled by
W. M. Hamilton. NZ Dept. Sci. Ind. Res. Bull. 137.

238   **Coenocorypha pusilla** (Buller)
Chatham Island Snipe

Gallinago pusilla Buller, 1869, Ibis 1869, p.41 — small rocky islet off Chatham Island.
Chatham Islands, where it became restricted to thriving populations on South East Island and Star Keys. Now successfully re-established on Mangere Island.
Abundant in subfossil and midden deposits.

FLEMING, C. A. 1939. Birds of the Chatham Islands, II. Emu 38: 492–509.
FLEMING, C. A. 1982. George Edward Lodge: the Unpublished New Zealand Bird Paintings. Wellington: Nova Pacifica.
FORBES, H. O. 1893. A list of the birds inhabiting the Chatham Islands. Ibis 1893: 521–546.
LOWE, P. R. 1915. Studies on the Charadriiformes. II. On the osteology of the Chatham Island Snipe (*Coenocorypha pusilla* Buller). Ibis 1915: 690–716.
OLIVER, W. R. B. 1955. New Zealand Birds, 2nd. ed. Wellington: Reed.

239   **Coenocorypha chathamica** (Forbes)
Extinct Chatham Island Snipe

Gallinago chathamica Forbes, 1893, Ibis 1893, p.545 — Chatham Islands.
Chatham Island: subfossil and midden. *Coenocorypha* bones, tentatively assigned to this species, are known from Pitt Island (subfossil) and Mangere Island (midden).

DAWSON, E. W. 1958. Re-discoveries of the New Zealand subfossil birds named by H. O. Forbes. Ibis 100: 232–237.
LOWE, P. R. 1915. Studies on the Charadriiformes. II. On the osteology of the Chatham Island Snipe (*Coenocorypha pusilla* Buller). Ibis 1915: 690–716.

Genus **Gallinago** Brisson

Gallinago Brisson, 1760, Orn. 5: 298–310 — type (by tautonymy) *Scolopax Gallinago* Linnaeus.
Capella Frenzel, 1801, Beschr. Vog. Eyer Wittenb.: 58 — type (by monotypy) *Capella coelestis* Frenzel = *Scolopax gallinago* Linnaeus.

240   **Gallinago hardwickii** (J. E. Gray)
Japanese Snipe

Scolopax Hardwickii J. E. Gray, 1831, Zool. Misc.: 16 — Tasmania.
Breeds in Japan; strongly migratory, apparently on a narrow front, to northern and eastern Australia, south to Tasmania; rarely straggling to New Zealand. Two specimens: Arch Hill, Auckland (1898) and Castlecliff (1914). Occasional sightings: Taieri (1941 and 1942), Ahuriri, Napier (1952), Otaki (1972), Lake Ellesmere (1973), Lake Tekapo (1983, 1984, 1988), Colac Bay (1984, 1985), Mangere, Manukau Harbour (1985). Also Norfolk Island; probable sightings on Macquarie Island.

BAKER, D. G.; CHILD, R. J.; TAYLOR, M. J. 1986. A Japanese Snipe at Mangere. Notornis 33: 149–150.
CHEESEMAN, T. F. 1899. Notice of the occurrence of the Australian Snipe

(*Gallinago australis*) in New Zealand. Trans. NZ Inst. 31: 105–106.
FUJIMAKI, Y.; SKIRA, I.J. 1984. Notes on Latham's Snipe *Gallinago hardwickii* in Japan. Emu 84: 49–51.
MISKELLY, C.M.; COOPER, W.J.; MORRISON, K; MORRISON, J.V. 1985. Snipe in Southland. Notornis 32: 327–328.
WARHAM, J. 1969. Notes on some Macquarie Island birds. Notornis 16: 190–197.

Subfamily CALIDRINAE: Sandpipers, Stints
Genus **Calidris** Merrem

Calidris Anonymous = Merrem, 1804, Allg. Lit.-Ztg: 2 (168), col. 542 — type (by tautonymy) *Tringa calidris* Gmelin = *Tringa Canutus* Linnaeus.
Erolia Vieillot, 1816, Analyse: 55 — type (by monotypy) *Erolia variegata* Vieillot = *Scolopax testacea* Pallas.
Crocethia Billberg, 1828, Syn. Faun. scand. 1: 132 — type (by monotypy) *Charadrius calidris* Linnaeus = *Trynga alba* Pallas.

41 **Calidris canutus** (Linnaeus)

Lesser Knot

A holarctic breeder; winters in western Europe, South America, Africa and Australasia. Two subspecies.

Calidris canutus canutus (Linnaeus)

Lesser Knot (Huahou)

Tringa Canutus Linnaeus, 1758, Syst. Nat., ed. 10, 1: 149 — Sweden.
Canutus canutus rogersi Mathews, 1913, Birds Aust. 3: 270 — Japan.

A holarctic breeder; the Siberian *rogersi* is doubtfully distinct from typical *canutus*, except in its migratory behaviour, in which the bulk of the population overflies the tropics to winter in New Zealand and Australia.

In summer unevenly distributed around the coast with large concentrations in northern harbours and at Farewell Spit; smaller flocks at Chatham Island, Southland lagoons and Paterson Inlet; small numbers on passage in the Bay of Plenty and along the coasts of the North and South Islands. A straggler to Auckland, Campbell and Macquarie Islands. Many often overwinter, mainly north of 38°S. Identified from one North Island midden, and subfossil in Chatham Island dunes.

If the subspecies *rufa* (Wilson, 1813), which breeds in the high arctic of America and winters mainly in South America, straggled to New Zealand it is unlikely that it would be recognised in the field.

FALLA, R.A. 1936. Arctic birds as migrants in New Zealand. Rec. Auck. Inst. Mus. 2: 3–14.
HUTTON, F.W. 1871. Catalogue of the Birds of New Zealand, p. 77.
McKENZIE, H.R. 1967. Census records of Knot for Firth of Thames and Manukau Harbour. Notornis 14: 154–157.

242   **Calidris tenuirostris** (Horsfield)

Great Knot

Totanus tenuirostris Horsfield, 1821, Trans. Linn. Soc. Lond. 13: 192—Java.
Breeds on the Siberian tundra; range not fully known; migratory
through eastern Asia, especially to the coast of northern Australia, where large flocks have recently been discovered. Rare in
southern Australia. First New Zealand record three at Manawatu
estuary (1967). Two at Miranda (1970) and singles (1971, 1972,
1973 and 1981); Karaka, Manukau Harbour, singles (1972,
1979); Manawatu River estuary (1980, 1983); Wanganui River
estuary (1986); Farewell Spit (1981).

ANDREW, I.G. 1968. Occurrence of Great Knot in New Zealand. Notornis
15: 207–210.
BROUN, M. 1970. Another occurrence of Great Knots in New Zealand. Notornis
17: 299.
BROWN, B. 1980. A Great Knot in Manukau Harbour. Notornis 27: 91.

243   **Calidris alba** (Pallas)

Sanderling

Tringa alba Pallas, 1764, Vroeg's Cat. Oiseaux Adumbr.: 7—coast of North Sea.
A holarctic breeder; migratory, many wintering in the Northern
Hemisphere, others reaching the tips of the southern continents.
First recorded in New Zealand at Lake Ellesmere in 1917.

A scarce but probably regular visitor, preferring smooth sandy
shores; sometimes in small flocks, e.g. five at Parengarenga
(1950); five Waituna Lagoon, Southland (1966), five Kaituna,
Bay of Plenty (1967); six Farewell Spit (1983). Has straggled to
Chatham Island (1977).

FALLA, R.A. 1936. Arctic birds as migrants in New Zealand. Rec. Auck. Inst.
Mus. 2: 3–14.
JACKSON, R. 1968. Sanderlings in the Bay of Plenty. Notornis 15: 122.
STEAD, E.F. 1923. Notes on the migratory plovers of New Zealand, with records
of some additional species. Trans. NZ Inst. 54: 490–495.
SUTTON, R.R. 1967. Sanderlings at Lake Waituna (Southland). Notornis 14: 83.
TURBOTT, E.G. 1951. Notes on Parengarenga Harbour waders. Notornis 4:
122–134.

244   **Calidris alpina** (Linnaeus)

Dunlin

Tringa alpina Linnaeus, 1758, Syst. Nat., ed. 10, 1: 149—Lappland.
A holarctic breeder; migratory but wintering mainly north of the
tropics. A rare vagrant to Australasia. Sight records in New
Zealand: Manukau (1969); Kaipara (1974); Miranda (1977);
Karaka, Manukau (1979) where one in breeding plumage over-
wintered.

Of the several accepted subspecies, *sakhalina* (Vieillot, 1816) from northeastern Asia and *pacifica* (Coues, 1861) from northern America may stray to New Zealand.

BROWN, B. 1975. Sight record of a Dunlin in New Zealand. Notornis 22: 241–255.
BROWN, B. 1979. Dunlin in the Firth of Thames. Notornis 26: 202–203.
HABRAKEN, A. 1980. A Dunlin at Karaka shellbank. Notornis 27: 300–301.

245 **Calidris ferruginea** (Pontoppidan)

Curlew Sandpiper

Tringa Ferrugineus Pontoppidan, 1763, Danske Atlas 1: 624 — no locality = Christiano I., off Bornholm, Denmark.
Scolopax testacea Pallas, 1764, Vroeg's Cat. Oiseaux Adumbr.: 5 — Holland.

Breeds in arctic Asia; migrates dispersively to Europe, Africa, southern Asia and Australia. Not recognised in New Zealand till 1903; few recorded before mid-1950s; then apparently slowly increased. Now a regular visitor, casual at many coastal estuaries and wetlands from Parengarenga to Southland lagoons, some scores especially favouring the Firth of Thames and Lake Ellesmere; rarely inland. Casual at Kermadec Islands. A few may overwinter in New Zealand.

FALLA, R.A. 1936. Arctic birds as migrants in New Zealand. Rec. Auck. Inst. Mus. 2: 3–14.
SIBSON, R.B. 1943. Additions to the avifauna of the North Island, New Zealand. Emu 43: 136–139.
SIBSON, R.B. 1970. Curlew Sandpipers in New Zealand 1969–70. Notornis 17: 291–296.
STEAD, E.F. 1923. Notes on the migratory plovers of New Zealand, with records of some additional species. Trans. NZ Inst. 54: 490–495.

246 **Calidris acuminata** (Horsfield)

Sharp-tailed Sandpiper

Totanus acuminatus Horsfield, 1821, Trans. Linn. Soc. Lond.13: 192 — Java.

Breeding range in arctic Siberia ill-defined and apparently rather restricted; strongly migratory southwards, mainly to Australasia. First obtained in New Zealand in 1871, four at Lake Ellesmere. Now an annual visitor, sometimes in small flocks, especially on Auckland isthmus, Lake Wairarapa, Lake Ellesmere and Southland lagoons. A casual transient at Norfolk and Kermadec Islands; has straggled to the Snares (1968) and Chatham Islands (1977, 1983). Rarely overwinters in New Zealand.

FALLA, R.A. 1946. Arctic birds as migrants in New Zealand. Rec. Auck Inst. Mus.2: 3 14.
POTTS, T.H. 1873. On the birds of New Zealand, pt.3. Trans. NZ Inst.5: 198.
STEAD, E.F. 1923. Notes on the migratory plovers of New Zealand, with records of some additional species. Trans. NZ Inst.54: 490–495.

247   **Calidris melanotos** (Vieillot)

Pectoral Sandpiper

Tringa melanotos Vieillot, 1819, Nouv. Dict. Hist. nat.34: 462 — Paraguay *ex* Azara, No. 401.
Tringa maculata Vieillot, 1819, Nouv. Dict. Hist. nat.34: 465 — Antilles.
Pelidna pectoralis Say, 1823, Long's Acc. Exped. Rocky Mts.1: 171 — N. America.

Breeds across arctic America and westward as far as the Taimyr Peninsula in Siberia; migrates mainly to South America; but some, presumably from the western population, regularly winter in Australasia. First obtained in New Zealand in 1903, Lake Ellesmere. Apparently favours eastern and inland places, south to Bluff, sometimes in small flocks, e.g. 10 at Lake Wainono (1984).

FALLA, R. A. 1936. Arctic birds as migrants in New Zealand. Rec. Auck. Inst. Mus.2: 3–14.
SIBSON, R. B. 1943. Additions to the avifauna of the North Island, New Zealand. Emu 43: 136–139.
STEAD, E. F. 1923. Notes on the migratory plovers of New Zealand, with records of some additional species. Trans. NZ Inst. 54: 490–495.

248   **Calidris bairdii** (Coues)

Baird's Sandpiper

Actodromas Bairdii Coues, 1861, Proc. Acad. nat. Sci. Philad.13: 194 — Fort Resolution, Mackenzie District, Canada.

Breeds in extreme northeastern Siberia and eastward across arctic America to Greenland. Strongly migratory, mainly by the mid-continental (Mississippi) flyway to South America. A rare straggler to Australasia, first recorded in New Zealand, 1970, in March at Karaka and in December at Miranda. Further sight records of single birds, Firth of Thames (October, 1972), Manukau (April 1976), Manawatu estuary (October 1976).

BROWN, J.; BROWN, B.; McKENZIE, H. R.; SIBSON, R. B. 1971. Ringed Plover in the Firth of Thames. Notornis 18: 262–266.
McKENZIE, H. R.; McKENZIE, M. E.; BURCH, B. J.; FOGARTY, S. M. 1971. A sighting of Baird's Sandpiper in New Zealand. Notornis 18: 58–60.

249   **Calidris fusicollis** (Vieillot)

White-rumped Sandpiper

Tringa fusicollis Vieillot, 1819, Nouv. Dict. Hist. nat.34: 461 — Paraguay *ex* Azara, No. 404.

Breeds mainly in subarctic Canada; strongly migratory, generally along the Atlantic coast to southern South America, returning by the mid-continental flyway. In New Zealand, two at Karaka (1969); one at Paua, Parengarenga (1971).

EDGAR, A. T. 1971. Sightings of rare waders in the Far North. Notornis 18: 116–117.
McKENZIE, H. R. 1970. A new arctic wader for New Zealand: two White-rumped (Bonaparte's) Sandpipers at Karaka. Notornis 17: 236–237.

250   Calidris ruficollis (Pallas)

Red-necked Stint

Trynga ruficollis Pallas, 1776, Reise Prov. russ. Reichs 3: 700—"circa lacus salsos Dauriae campestris" = "Kulusutay, Transbaikalia" (Ridgway, 1919) or "Siberia" *apud* Mathews.

Breeds in northern Siberia eastwards from Taimyr Peninsula to Bering Sea and coast of Alaska; strongly migratory southwards to Australasia. An annual visitor to New Zealand, flocks assembling in a few favoured coastal wetlands, south to Southland lagoons. Biggest flocks have been reported from the South Island, especially Lake Ellesmere, where the species was first collected in New Zealand and was confused with the Little Stint *Calidris minutus* (Leisler, 1812), the two species in winter plumage being almost indistinguishable. A transient visitor at Norfolk Island. Has straggled (1963) to the Auckland Islands. A few usually overwinter in northern New Zealand.

BARLOW, M. 1968. Record stint count, and American Pectoral Sandpipers in Southland. Notornis 15: 219.

SIBSON, R. B. 1968. Red-necked Stints in northern New Zealand. Notornis 15: 241–243.

SIBSON, R. B. 1979. Early record of a stint in New Zealand. Notornis 26: 120.

STEAD, E. F. 1923. Notes on the migratory plovers of New Zealand, with records of some additional species. Trans NZ Inst. 54: 490–495.

251   Calidris mauri (Cabanis)

Western Sandpiper

Ereunetes Mauri Cabanis, 1856 (1857), J. Orn., Lpz. 4: 419—South Carolina.

Breeds mainly in Alaska; also in extreme northeastern Siberia. Strongly migratory, especially along the west coast of America. A rare vagrant to Australasia. New Zealand records: Rangiputa Bank, Rangaunu (1970); Parengarenga (1979); Firth of Thames (1970–71, 1984); Farewell Spit (1964).

BLACKBURN, A.; BELL, B. D. 1965. A record of the Western Sandpiper on Farewell Spit. Notornis 12: 109–110.

EDGAR, A. T. 1971. Sightings of rare waders in the Far North. Notornis 18: 116–117.

Genus **Limicola** Koch

Limicola Koch, 1816, Syst. baier. Zool.: 316—type (by monotypy) *Numenius pygmaeus* Bechstein = *Scolopax Falcinellus* Pontoppidan; not *Limicula* Vieillot, 1816 = *Limosa* Brisson.

252   Limicola falcinellus (Pontoppidan)

Broad-billed Sandpiper

Scolopax Falcinellus Pontoppidan, 1763, Danske Atlas 1: 623—no locality = Denmark.

Breeds in arctic Europe and Asia; winters in southern Europe, India, China, Sunda Islands, New Guinea and Australasia.

Limicola falcinellus sibiricus Dresser
Eastern Broad-billed Sandpiper

Limicola sibirica Dresser, 1876, Proc. Zool. Soc. Lond.: 674 — Siberia and China.

Breeds in eastern Siberia; migrates to southeast Asia and more sparingly to Australasia. First recorded in New Zealand in Firth of Thames (1960), and subsequently (1964, 1966, 1968–two, 1969–two); Manukau Harbour (1963); Parengarenga (1970). Has overwintered.

The eastern subspecies *sibiricus* is more richly rufous than the nominate western form in breeding dress and is said to be greyer in non-breeding plumage.

McKENZIE, H. R.; SIBSON, R. B. 1965. Broad-billed Sandpiper in the Firth of Thames in winter. Notornis 12: 55.

SIBSON R. B. 1963. Broad-billed Sandpiper in Manukau Harbour. Notornis 10: 411–412.

SIBSON, R. B.; McKENZIE, H. R. 1960. Broad-billed Sandpiper in the Firth of Thames: a new bird for New Zealand. Notornis 8: 233–235.

Genus **Philomachus** Merrem

Philomachus Anonymous (= Merrem), 1804, Allg. Lit.-Ztg.2: col. 542 — type (by monotypy) *Tringa pugnax* Linnaeus.

253   **Philomachus pugnax** (Linnaeus)
Ruff

Tringa Pugnax Linnaeus, 1758, Syst. Nat. ed. 10, 1: 148 — Sweden.

Breeds across temperate and subarctic zones of the Palaearctic from western Europe to northeastern Siberia; strongly migratory mainly in a southwesterly direction towards Africa and India; an occasional vagrant to Australasia. Four, possibly five, sight records in New Zealand: Karaka, Manukau Harbour (one possibly, 1964); Colac Bay, Southland (one, December 1984 to March 1985); Lake Ellesmere (two, December 1984 to January 1985); Lake Poukawa, Hawke's Bay (one, November 1985); Lake Wainono (one, November 1987).

HARRISON, K. C.; FENNELL, J.; FENNELL, J. 1985. Ruff (*Philomachus pugnax*) at Lake Ellesmere. Notornis 32: 332–333.

MACKENZIE, N. B.; McKENZIE, H. R. 1965. Probable sighting of a Ruff. Notornis 12: 108–109.

MALONEY, R. 1988. A Ruff at Lake Wainono. Notornis 35: 328.

MISKELLY, C. M.; COOPER, W. J. 1985. A Ruff in Southland. Notornis 32: 329–330.

Genus **Limnodromus** Wied

Limnodromus Wied, 1833, Beitr. Naturg. Brasil. 4: 716 — type (by monotypy) *Scolopax novaeboracensis* Gmelin = *Scolopax grisea* Gmelin.

254   **Limnodromus semipalmatus** (Blyth)

Asiatic Dowitcher

Macrorhamphus semipalmatus Blyth, 1848, J. Asiat. Soc. Bengal 17: 252 — Calcutta.

Breeds discontinuously in northern Asia, from western Siberia through Transbaikalia and Mongolia to Manchuria. In winter thinly distributed from coastal Arabia, across southern Asia to northern Australia.

Two New Zealand records: Heathcote-Avon estuary (August–September 1985); Firth of Thames (February–May 1987); both with Bar-tailed Godwits.

CRAWFORD, D. N. 1972. First Australian record of the Asiatic Dowitcher. Emu 72: 112–113.

FENNELL, J.; FENNELL, J.; CROSSLAND, A.; LANGLANDS, P. 1985. Asiatic Dowitcher at the Heathcote-Avon Estuary, Christchurch. Notornis 32: 322–323.

PAIGE, J. P. 1965. Field identification and winter range of the Asiatic Dowitcher *Limnodromus semipalmatus*. Ibis 107: 95–97.

Subfamily TRINGINAE: Curlews, Godwits, Shanks
Genus **Numenius** Brisson

Numenius Brisson, 1760, Orn. 1: 48 — type (by tautonymy) *"Numenius"* = *Scolopax arquata* Linnaeus.

255   **Numenius madagascariensis** (Linnaeus)

Eastern Curlew

Scolopax madagascariensis Linnaeus, 1766, Syst. Nat., ed. 12, 1: 242 — "Madagascar"; error = "Macassar, Celebes"; error, Neumann, 1932, Anz. Orn. Ges. Bayern, p. 150 = Philippines *apud* Stresemann 1941.

Numenius cyanopus Vieillot, 1817, Nouv. Dict. Hist. nat. 8: 306 — New Holland.

Breeds in northeastern Asia; range ill-defined; migrates mainly to eastern Australia. First obtained in New Zealand at Wairau River mouth, Marlborough (1874); not recognised as a regular visitor in small numbers till c.1952, small flocks assembling in the larger mudflat harbours and estuaries from Parengarenga to Southland.

Immature non-breeders may overwinter. An occasional transient at Norfolk Island.

BULLER, W. L. 1875. On some additions to the collection of birds in the Colonial Museum. Trans. NZ Inst. 7: 224–225.

CLOSE, D.; NEWMAN, O. M. G. 1984. The decline of the Eastern Curlew in south-eastern Australia. Emu 84: 38–40.

256   **Numenius phaeopus** (Linnaeus)

Whimbrel

Scolopax Phaeopus Linnaeus, 1758, Syst. Nat., ed. 10, 1: 146 — Europe = Sweden.

Breeds from Alaska and arctic Canada to arctic Europe and Asia; migrates as far as South America, Africa and Australasia. Three or four subspecies.

Numenius phaeopus variegatus (Scopoli)
Asiatic Whimbrel

Tantalus variegatus Scopoli, 1786, Delic. Flor. Faun. insubr. 2: 92 — no locality = Luzon, Philippines, *ex* Sonnerat.
Numenius uropygialis Gould, 1840 (1841), Proc. Zool. Soc. Lond.: 175 — southern coast Australia.

Breeds in northeastern Asia; migrates mainly to southeast Asia and disperses widely among islands of the southwest Pacific. First obtained in New Zealand near New Brighton in 1879, but seldom recorded before c.1950. Now known to be a regular summer visitor, often in small flocks, from Norfolk and Kermadec Islands to the Southland lagoons. A few overwinter.

BULL, P. C. 1948. Field notes on waders in the South-west Pacific with special reference to the Russell Islands. Emu 47: 165–176.
BULLER, W. L. 1882. Manual of the Birds of New Zealand, p. 56. Wellington: Colonial Museum and Geological Survey Dept.

Numenius phaeopus hudsonicus Latham
American Whimbrel (Hudsonian Curlew)

Numenius hudsonicus Latham, 1790, Ind. Orn. 2: 712 — Hudson Bay.

Breeds in northern Canada and Alaska; strongly migratory mainly to Central and South America; a few dispersing south westwards across the Pacific. First obtained in New Zealand in 1874 at Wairau River mouth, Marlborough. Since 1949, numerous sight records, especially from Parengarenga, Manukau Harbour, Firth of Thames, Farewell Spit and Southland lagoons. Some may overwinter.

The sole subfossil specimen (Marlborough) cannot be identified to subspecies.

BULLER, W. L. 1875. On some additions to the collection of birds in the Colonial Museum. Trans. NZ Inst. 7: 224–225.
HOGG, M. J.; BROWN, B. 1966. American Whimbrel (Hudsonian Curlew) in Firth of Thames. Notornis 13: 67–68.
McKENZIE, H. R. 1950. Records of Hudsonian Curlew in N.Z. Notornis 4: 18–21.

257   Numenius minutus Gould
Little Whimbrel

Numenius minutus Gould, 1840 (1841), Proc. Zool. Soc. Lond.: 176 — New South Wales.

Breeds in central and northeastern Siberia, range not well known; migrates to eastern Indonesia and Australia, straggling to islands of the southwest Pacific. First New Zealand record, two at Lake Ellesmere in 1900; now recognised as an almost annual vagrant, sometimes in small parties, which has summered or even overwintered at numerous estuarine habitats from Parengarenga to Lake Ellesmere.

HEATHER, B.D.; MACKENZIE, N.B. 1973. Little Whimbrels at Napier. Notornis 20: 167.
HUTTON, F.W. 1901. Our migratory birds. Trans. NZ Inst. 33: 251–264.
McGILL, A.R. 1960. The Little Whimbrel. Emu 60: 89–94.
STEAD, E.F. 1923. Notes on the migratory plovers of New Zealand, with records of some additional species. Trans. NZ Inst. 54: 490–495.

258 Numenius tahitiensis (Gmelin)

Bristle-thighed Curlew

Scolopax tahitiensis Gmelin, 1789, Syst. Nat. 1, pt.2: 656 — Tahiti, Society Islands, based on the Otaheite Curlew of Latham, Gen. Syn. 3, pt.1, p. 122, no.4.

Breeds in western Alaska; migrates mainly southwestwards dispersing widely over islands of the central and south Pacific, as far as the Kermadec Islands (Macauley, 1966; North Meyer, 1972; Raoul, 1972) and Norfolk Island (1968).

VEITCH, C.R. 1974. Bristle-thighed Curlew records from the Kermadec Islands. Notornis 21: 83–84.

Genus Limosa Brisson

Limosa Brisson, 1760, Orn. 1: 48 — type (by tautonymy) *"Limosa"* = *Scolopax Limosa* Linnaeus.

259 Limosa lapponica (Linnaeus)

Bar-tailed Godwit

Scolopax lapponica Linnaeus, 1758, Syst. Nat., ed. 10, 1: 147 — Swedish Lappland.
Breeds from Lappland eastward, mostly north of Arctic Circle, to Alaska. Winters as far south as tropical Africa, western India, Sunda Islands, New Guinea, western Polynesia, Australia and New Zealand. Two or three subspecies.

Limosa lapponica baueri Naumann

Eastern Bar-tailed Godwit (Kuaka)

Limosa Baueri Naumann, 1836, Naturgesch. Vog. Dtl. 8: 29 — New Holland = Victoria.
Limosa lapponica menzbieri Portenko, 1936, Auk 53: 195 — north-eastern Siberia.

Breeds in Siberia east of the Lena River and across the Bering Sea into northern Alaska at least as far east as Point Barrow; strongly migratory to southeast Asia and Australasia; some on passage visit many islands of the southwest Pacific. In summer, is on all New Zealand coasts, concentrating in inlets and estuaries with broad intertidal flats; south to Chatham and Stewart Islands; seldom inland. Has straggled to most subantarctic islands. Substantial flocks of immature non-breeders, with perhaps a few ageing adults, overwinter mainly north of 38°S. Recorded from subfossil and midden deposits on the mainland.

Portenko attempted, on rather slight morphological differences, to distinguish two forms of the Eastern Bar-tailed Godwit, *menzbieri* on its Siberian breeding grounds filling the gap between nominate *lapponica* and the far-eastern *baueri*. Even if the two forms are valid, they are doubtfully recognisable in the field, particularly in non-breeding plumage. Most of the Bar-tailed Godwits which winter in New Zealand are likely to come from the eastern region of the species' broad arctic breeding range.

HAWKINS, J. M. 1980. Seasonal fluctuations in the numbers of Bar-tailed Godwits on Nelson Haven. Notornis 27: 88–90.
McKENZIE, H. R. 1967. Census records of Godwit for Firth of Thames and Manukau Harbour. Notornis 14: 18–21.
STIDOLPH, R. H. D. 1954. Status of Godwit in New Zealand. Notornis 6: 31–39.
TURBOTT, E. G. 1951. Notes on Parengarenga Harbour waders. Notornis 4: 122–134.

260   **Limosa limosa** (Linnaeus)

Black-tailed Godwit

Scolopax Limosa Linnaeus, 1758, Syst. Nat., ed. 10, 1: 147 — Europe = Sweden.

Breeds in Iceland, Europe, Asia; migrates south to the Mediterranean, tropical and southern Africa, India, South-east Asia and Australasia. Three subspecies.

Limosa limosa melanuroides Gould

Asiatic Black-tailed Godwit

Limosa Melanuroides Gould, 1846, Proc. Zool. Soc. Lond.: 84 — Port Essington, Northern Territory.

Breeds in northern Asia from Mongolia and the upper Yenesei River eastwards, migrating to winter in a wide arc from eastern India to Australasia. First recognised in New Zealand in 1952 at Miranda; has now been recorded from many harbours and estuaries between Parengarenga and Bluff; straying to Enderby Island (1963 and 1976). Occasionally in small flocks e.g. six at Miranda (1959). Immature non-breeders may overwinter.

ARNOLD, G. N. L. 1976. Black-tailed Godwit in the Bay of Plenty. Notornis 23: 257.
SIBSON, R. B. 1956. Abnormal Black-tailed Godwit (*L. limosa*) in the Firth of Thames. Notornis 6: 241–242.
SIBSON, R. B. 1956. Asiatic Black-tailed Godwits in the Firth of Thames. Notornis 7: 58–59.

261   **Limosa haemastica** (Linnaeus)

Hudsonian Godwit

Scolopax Haemastica Linnaeus, 1758, Syst. Nat., ed. 10, 1: 147 — North America = Hudson Bay *ex* Edwards, pl.138.

Breeds in North America apparently in two disjunct regions, one along the south side of Hudson Bay, the other in northwest Canada and Alaska, whence presumably come the few Hudsonian

Godwits seen in the southwest Pacific. Strongly and rigidly migratory, the bulk of the rather small population flying to South America.

First recognised in New Zealand in 1902 at Lake Ellesmere. Now perhaps an annual vagrant; sight records from at least 15 estuaries between Parengarenga and Bluff; usually single birds. Immature non-breeders may overwinter. Norfolk Island (one, November 1980).

SIBSON, R. B. 1943. Additions to the avifauna of the North Island, New Zealand. Emu 43: 136–139.

STEAD, E. F. 1923. Notes on the migratory plovers of New Zealand, with records of some additional species. Trans. NZ Inst. 54: 490–495.

Genus **Bartramia** Lesson

Bartramia Lesson, 1831, Traité Orn. 7: 553—type (by monotypy) *Bartramia laticauda* Lesson = *Tringa longicauda* Bechstein.

262 **Bartramia longicauda** (Bechstein)

Upland Sandpiper

Tringa longicauda Bechstein, 1812, Latham's Allg. Ubers. Vog. 4: 453—North America.

Breeds in North America, locally in southern Alaska but mainly on grasslands east of the Rockies; migrates to South America, usually by the inland continental flyway. A very rare straggler to the southwest Pacific. One sight record in New Zealand: Karaka, Manukau Harbour (1967). There is also one Australian record, Sydney (1848).

McKENZIE, H. R. 1968. Suspected Upland Plover (*Bartramia longicauda*) in Manukau Harbour. Notornis 15: 216–218.

Genus **Tringa** Linnaeus

Tringa Linnaeus, 1758, Syst. Nat., ed. 10, 1: 148—type (by tautonymy) *Tringa Ochropus* Linnaeus.

Actitis Illiger, 1811, Prodromus: 263—type (by subsequent designation) *Tringa hypoleucos* Linnaeus.

Xenus Kaup. 1829, Skizz. Entw.-Gesch. eur. Thierw.: 115—type (by monotypy) *Scolopax cinerea* Guldenstadt.

Heteroscelus Baird, 1858, Rep. Explor. Surv. Railrd. Pacif. 9: 734—type (by monotypy) *Totanus brevipes* Vieillot.

263 **Tringa incana** (Gmelin)

Wandering (Alaskan) Tattler

Scolopax incana Gmelin, 1789, Syst. Nat. 1: 658—Moorea Island, Society Group and Palmerston Island, Pacific Ocean.

Breeds in Alaska; disperses widely to winter especially among the islands of the central and south Pacific. Normally not gregarious. A scarce but perhaps annual straggler to New Zealand at the southwest limits of its range.

First recorded in New Zealand in 1883 at Portland Island. Now numerous sight records from Norfolk and Kermadec Islands to South East Island (Chathams) and Kaikoura Peninsula; mostly on the east coast, e.g. Kawakawa Bay, Cuvier Island, Cape Colville, Cape Kidnappers; seldom on the west coast e.g. Farewell Spit.

BULLER, W. L. 1888. A History of the Birds of New Zealand, 2nd ed. London: the author.
McKENZIE, H. R. 1949. A Wandering Tattler. NZ Bird Notes 3: 178–180.
SIBSON, R. B. 1965. A note on Wandering Tattlers in Fiji. Notornis 12: 248–250.

264   **Tringa brevipes** (Vieillot)

Siberian (Grey-tailed) Tattler

Totanus brevipes Vieillot, 1816, Nouv. Dict. Hist. nat. 6: 410 — Timor.

Breeds across northern Asia, perhaps from the upper Yenesei River and Lake Baikal to the mountains of eastern Siberia and to Kamchatka; migrates to the East Indies and Australasia, but is often a vagrant.

A scarce annual visitor to New Zealand, first recognised at Parengarenga (1950); now numerous sight records especially from northern New Zealand and Farewell Spit; a casual visitor to several South Island estuaries; straggling to the Snares (1968) and Enderby Island (three, 1980). Immature non-breeders may overwinter. Marginally outnumbers *T. incana* in New Zealand.

DAWSON, D. G. 1968. New Zealand tattler records. Notornis 15: 39–42.
SIBSON, R. B. 1956. Tattler (*Heteroscelus incanus*) in Manukau. Notornis 6: 243–244.
TURBOTT, E. G. 1951. Notes on Parengarenga Harbour waders. Notornis 4: 122–134.
TURBOTT, E. G.; SIBSON, R. B.; IMBER, M. J. 1961. Tattler and Hudsonian Godwit in the Heathcote-Avon estuary. Notornis 9: 135–136.

265   **Tringa hypoleucos** Linnaeus

Common Sandpiper

Tringa Hypoleucos Linnaeus, 1758, Syst. Nat., ed. 10, 1: 149 — Sweden.

Breeds across temperate and subarctic Eurasia; migrates to winter in Africa, southern Asia and Australasia. Seldom truly gregarious.

First recognised in New Zealand in 1964 in Taranaki. Now from North Island tidal estuaries more than a dozen sight records; but only two South Island records: West Wanganui Inlet (1981–1983) and Lake Wainono (1980). Has overwintered.

BELL, B. D. 1981. Common Sandpiper in South Island. Notornis 28: 160.
BELLINGHAM, M.; DAVIS, A. 1982. Common Sandpipers in Far North. Notornis 29: 149.

BROWN, B. 1974. Common Sandpiper in the Kaipara Harbour. Notornis 21: 267–268.
EDGAR, A.T. 1969. Common Sandpiper in Northland. Notornis 16: 202–203.
MEDWAY, D.G. 1974. A Common Sandpiper near New Plymouth—the third New Zealand record. Notornis 21: 387–389.
PENGELLY, W.J.; MacDONALD, R.W.; MERTON, D.V. 1965. Suspected Common Sandpiper near New Plymouth. Notornis 12: 107–108.

266 **Tringa nebularia** (Gunnerus)

Greenshank

Scolopax nebularia Gunnerus, 1767, Leem's Beskr. Finm. Lapp.: 251—Norway.

Breeds across subarctic Eurasia; migrates to Africa, southern Asia and Australasia.

First recognised in New Zealand in 1874 near Dunedin; next recorded at Gisborne (1952); now expected as an annual vagrant with a wide scatter of sight records from Norfolk Island (1911) southwards, straggling to Macquarie (1962), the Snares (1968) and the Chatham Islands (1978). May overwinter.

HUTTON, F.W. 1901. Our migratory birds. Trans. NZ Inst. 33: 251–264.
SIBSON, R.B. 1965. The Greenshank in Manukau Harbour. Notornis 12: 44–46.
STIDOLPH, R.H.D. 1953. Greenshank in New Zealand. Notornis 5: 123.

267 **Tringa stagnatilis** (Bechstein)

Marsh Sandpiper

Totanus stagnatilis Bechstein, 1803, Orn. Taschenb. Dtl.: 292, Pl.29—Germany; on migration.

Breeds locally from eastern Europe across Asia to Mongolia; migrates to winter in Africa, southern Asia and sparingly in Australasia.

First recognised in New Zealand in 1959 in Manukau Harbour; has now been recorded at several estuaries of the North Island and a lake close to the coast at Hawera (1963); also from two South Island saltmarshes (Westport, 1968; Lake Ellesmere, 1981–82). Occasionally in small flocks e.g. four at Kaituna, Bay of Plenty (1970); three at Lake Ellesmere (1981–82). Has overwintered.

SEDDON, J.H. 1971. Marsh Sandpipers in the Bay of Plenty. Notornis 18: 132.
SIBSON, R.B. 1959. Marsh Sandpipers in Manukau—a new bird for New Zealand. Notornis 8: 125–126.

268 **Tringa flavipes** (Gmelin)

Lesser Yellowlegs

Scolopax flavipes Gmelin, 1789, Syst. Nat. 1, pt.2: 659—New York.

Breeds across subarctic America from Alaska to Hudson Bay; migrates on a broad front to Central and South America; is often a vagrant.

First acceptably recognised in New Zealand in 1963 at Ahuriri

Lagoon, Napier, where again recorded in 1973 and 1983. Other sight records mostly from coastal marshes, but two inland (Pukepuke, 1974; Boggy Pond, adjacent to Lake Wairarapa, 1983); five in the South Island (Farewell Spit, 1974, 1977; Ellesmere, 1964; Washdyke, 1971; Wainono, 1972); Chatham Island (1985).

In November 1962 a Yellowlegs visited a roadside pond near Porirua where, after long and critical study by several well-known ornithologists, it was accepted as a Greater Yellowlegs *Tringa melanoleuca* (Gmelin, 1789). Subsequently this identification was challenged. But some hold that the original identification was correct. Despite photographs the problem remains un-resolved. There seems to be little difference between a small male Greater and a large female Lesser.

BROWN, B. 1977. Two Lesser Yellowlegs in New Zealand in summer 1973/74. Notornis 24: 198–200.
FALLA, R.A. 1964. The Porirua Yellowlegs. Notornis 11: 104–106.
FLEMING, C.A. 1963. The Greater Yellowlegs: a New Zealand sight record. Notornis 10: 258–262.
MACKENZIE, N. 1964. Lesser Yellowlegs at Napier. Notornis 11: 100–103.
PIERCE, R. 1971. Lesser Yellowlegs at Timaru. Notornis 18: 366.
TUNNICLIFFE, G.A. 1964. A Lesser Yellowlegs at Lake Ellesmere. Notornis 11: 103–104.

269 **Tringa terek** (Latham)

Terek Sandpiper

Scolopax terek Latham, 1790, Index Orn. 2: 724 — shores of Caspian Sea about mouth of Terek River, USSR.
Scolopax cinerea Güldenstädt, 1774, Nov. Comment. Acad. scient. imp. Petropol. 19: 473, Pl.19 — shores of Caspian Sea; not *Tringa cinerea* Brunnich, 1764 = *Calidris canutus* Linnaeus.

Breeds across the Palaearctic from the Gulf of Bothnia to the Sea of Okhotsk; migrates to Africa, especially the east coast south to the Cape, and to southern Asia and Australasia.

First recognised in New Zealand in 1951 (Firth of Thames). Now expected as a scarce annual visitor, especially to northern New Zealand, but sometimes south to the Southland lagoons. Non-breeders may overwinter.

McKENZIE, H.R. 1952. Terek Sandpiper at Miranda. Notornis 4: 212.
SIBSON, R.B. 1968. A good summer for Terek Sandpipers. Notornis 15: 123–125.

Family **PHALAROPODIDAE:** Phalaropes
Genus **Phalaropus** Brisson

Phalaropus Brisson, 1760, Orn. 1: 50; 6: 12 — type (by tautonymy) *"Phalaropus"* Brisson = *Tringa fulicaria* Linnaeus.

70 Phalaropus fulicarius (Linnaeus)

Grey (Red) Phalarope

Tringa fulicaria Linnaeus, 1758, Syst. Nat., ed. 10, 1: 148—Hudson Bay *ex* Edwards, pl.142.

Almost circumpolar in the Northern Hemisphere; strongly migratory, wintering at sea mainly off the west coast of Africa and of South America.

A rare straggler to New Zealand. Five records: Lake Wainono (June 1883, June 1987); Lake Ellesmere (1925); Hastings (July 1934); Kaituna, Bay of Plenty (1977). All five were found near the middle of the southern winter.

BROWN, B.; LATHAM, P.C.M. 1978. Grey Phalarope in the Bay of Plenty. Notornis 25: 198–202.
FALLA, R.A. 1936. Arctic birds as migrants in New Zealand. Rec. Auck. Inst. Mus. 2: 3–14.
MALONEY, R.; WATOLA, G. 1989. A second Grey Phalarope at Lake Wainono. Notornis 36: 88.

71 Phalaropus lobatus (Linnaeus)

Red-necked Phalarope

Tringa tobata (*sic*) Linnaeus, 1758, Syst. Nat., ed. 10, 1: 148—Hudson Bay *ex* Edwards, pl.143; *Tringa lobata* in Emendanda, p.824.

Almost circumpolar, breeding in the subarctic zone; strongly migratory, wintering at sea mainly in four large concentrations: (a) off tropical West Africa; (b) off the west coast of South America; (c) in the Arabian Sea; (d) at sea to the north and west of New Guinea.

A rare straggler to New Zealand. Three records: Lake Ellesmere (1929); Wanganui estuary (1935); and Washdyke Lagoon (1961).

CROCKETT, D.E. 1961. Red-necked Phalarope at Washdyke Lagoon. Notornis 9: 266.
FALLA, R.A. 1936. Arctic birds as migrants in New Zealand. Rec. Auck. Inst. Mus. 2: 3–14.
JENKINS, J.A.F.; LOVEGROVE, T.G.; SIBSON, R.B. 1986. Red-necked Phalarope at Mangere, Manukau Harbour. Notornis 33: 191–192.
OLIVER, W.R.B. 1930. New Zealand Birds. Wellington: Fine Arts.

72 Phalaropus tricolor (Vieillot)

Wilson's Phalarope

Steganopus tricolor Vieillot, 1819, Nouv. Dict. Hist. nat. 32: 136—Paraguay; *ex* Azara (107).

Breeds typically near sloughs on the prairies of central North America roughly between 35°N and 55°N; migrates to southern South America; is often a vagrant.

First recognised in New Zealand in 1983 at Manawatu River estuary and Lake Ellesmere; two at Lake Ellesmere (1984).

MOORE, J. L.; MOORE M. 1984. Wilson's Phalarope at Manawatu River estuary
—a new bird for New Zealand. Notornis 31: 330–333.
SAGAR, P. M.; HARRISON K. C. 1984. Wilson's Phalaropes at Lake Ellesmere.
Notornis 31: 333–334.

Suborder LARI: Skuas, Gulls, Terns, Skimmers
Family **STERCORARIIDAE**: Greater Skuas
(Bonxies), Lesser Skuas (Jaegers)

FURNESS, R. W. 1987. The Skuas. Calton: T. & A. D. Poyser.

Genus **Catharacta** Brünnich

Catharacta Brünnich, 1764, Orn. Boreal.: 32—type (by subsequent designation)
Catharacta skua Brünnich.
Megalestris Bonaparte, 1856, C.r.hebd. Séanc. Acad. Sci. Paris 43: 643—type (by
monotypy) *Stercorarius catarrhactes* = *C. skua* Brünnich.

273   **Catharacta skua** Brünnich
Great Skua

Catharacta Skua Brünnich, 1764, Orn. Boreal, p. 33—Faeroes and Iceland.

Distribution bipolar, breeding in the North Atlantic (the nominate race *C. skua skua*) and in the subantarctic and antarctic
zones (three subspecies).

Catharacta skua lonnbergi Mathews
Brown (Subantarctic) Skua (Hakoakoa)

Catharacta antarctica lonnbergi Mathews, 1912, Novit. Zool. 18: 212—New Zealand
seas.

Circumpolar on subantarctic islands; also on northern parts of
the Antarctic Peninsula and the Balleny Islands, where breeding
distribution overlaps with that of *C. maccormicki*. In the New
Zealand region, breeds on Macquarie, Campbell, Auckland,
Antipodes, Snares, Chatham, Stewart, Solander Islands and
their outliers. A mainland nest and eggs reported at Puysegur
Point (November 1962). Straggles to Ross Sea in summer.
Disperses northwards in autumn, especially to southern Australia
and occasionally to 33°S. Both subfossil and midden from the
mainland of North and South Islands and Chatham Island.

MOORS, P. J. 1980. Southern Great Skuas on Antipodes Island, New Zealand:
observations on foods, breeding, and growth of chicks. Notornis 27: 133–146.
YOUNG, E. C. 1977. Egg-laying in relation to latitude in southern hemisphere
skuas. Ibis 119: 191–195.
YOUNG, E. C. 1978. Behavioural ecology of *lönnbergi* skuas in relation to environ-
ment on the Chatham Islands, New Zealand. NZ J. Zool. 3: 401–416.
YOUNG, E. C. 1988. Nocturnal foraging by Chatham Island skuas. NZ J.
Ecol. 11: 113–117.

274 Catharacta maccormicki (Saunders)

South Polar Skua

Stercorarius maccormicki Saunders, 1893, Bull. Br. Ornith. Club 3: 12—Possession I., Victoria Land, Antarctica.
Catharacta maccormicki wilsoni Mathews, 1913, Birds Aust. 2: 495—Weddell Sea.

Breeds on shores and offshore islands of Antarctica, mainly near penguin and petrel colonies; winters at sea, some ranging to the North Pacific, northern Indian and North Atlantic Oceans; rarely seen on New Zealand coasts. Occasionally storm-wrecked on passage. One banded at Cape Hallett (1964) was recovered in Japan (1966). Tentatively identified subfossil on Chatham Island.

AINLEY, D.G.; MORRELL, S.H.; WOOD, R.C. 1986. South Polar Skua breeding colonies in the Ross Sea region, Antarctica. Notornis 33: 155–163.
PASCOE, J.G. 1984. A census of the South Polar Skua at Cape Hallett, Antarctica. Notornis 31: 312–319.
YOUNG, E.C. 1963. The breeding behaviour of the South Polar Skua *Catharacta maccormicki*. Ibis 105: 205–233.
YOUNG, E.C. 1963. Feeding habits of the South Polar Skua *Catharacta maccormicki*. Ibis 105: 301–318.
YOUNG, E.C. 1977. Egg-laying in relation to latitude in Southern Hemisphere skuas. Ibis 119: 191–195.

Genus **Stercorarius** Brisson

Stercorarius Brisson, 1760, Orn. 1: 56—type (by tautonymy) *Stercorarius* Brisson = *Larus parasiticus* Linnaeus.

275 Stercorarius parasiticus (Linnaeus)

Arctic Skua

Larus parasiticus Linnaeus, 1758, Syst. Nat., ed. 10, 1: 136—within Tropic of Cancer of Europe, America and Asia; restricted type locality, coast of Sweden.
Stercorarius parasiticus visitori Mathews, 1915, Austral Avian Rec. 2: 126—Sydney, NSW.

Breeds in arctic and subarctic regions; migrates to the Southern Hemisphere. Summer visitor to New Zealand south to Foveaux Strait and east to the Chatham Islands; sometimes in large gatherings e.g. c.50 at Kaipara Heads, December 1955. Non-breeders may overwinter.

FALLA, R.A. 1936. Arctic birds as migrants in New Zealand. Rec. Auck. Inst. Mus. 2: 3–14.

276 Stercorarius pomarinus (Temminck)

Pomarine Skua

Lestris pomarinus Temminck, 1815, Man. Orn.: 514—arctic regions of Europe.
Coprotheres pomarinus nutcheri Mathews, 1917, Austral Avian Rec. 3: 72—Broken Bay, NSW.

Breeds in arctic regions, migrating to the Southern Hemisphere; an uncommon though regular visitor to New Zealand south to

Foveaux Strait; more pelagic than *parasiticus*. An unusual assemblage of 38 counted, 56 nautical miles west of Waikato River mouth, in February 1984 (J. A. F. Jenkins).

FALLA, R. A. 1936. Arctic birds as migrants in New Zealand. Rec. Auck. Inst. Mus. 2: 3–14.

277   **Stercorarius longicaudus** Vieillot
Long-tailed Skua

Stercorarius longicaudus Vieillot, 1819, Nouv. Dict. Hist. nat. 21: 157—northern Europe, Asia and America; restricted type locality, northern Europe.

Breeds in arctic and subarctic regions, migrating to the Southern Hemisphere; generally rare in the southwest Pacific. Only once recorded in New Zealand (specimen from Muriwai, January 1964) until summer of 1981–82 (three from northern beaches and one inland alive at Lake Taupo); again 1982–83 (?16 found wrecked south to Wellington); one dead on Otaki Beach, 1988. Tentatively identified subfossil on Chatham Island.

MELVILLE, D. S. 1985. Long-tailed Skuas *Stercorarius longicaudus* in New Zealand. Notornis 32: 51–73.
SIBSON, R. B. 1967. Long-tailed Skua ashore at Muriwai. Notornis 14: 79–81.
SIBSON, R. B. 1985. Small skua at Taupo. Notornis 32: 108.

Family **LARIDAE**: Gulls and Terns
Subfamily LARINAE: Gulls
Genus **Larus** Linnaeus

Larus Linnaeus, 1758, Syst. Nat., ed. 10, 1: 136—type (by subsequent designation, Selby, 1840) *Larus marinus* Linnaeus.
Bruchigavia Bonaparte, 1857, Consp. Gen. Avium 2: 228—type (by monotypy) *Larus novaehollandiae*.

278   **Larus dominicanus** Lichtenstein
Southern Black-backed Gull (Kelp Gull, Dominican Gull)

Coasts and offshore islands of South America, South Africa, Australia, New Zealand, subantarctic oceanic islands and coasts of Antarctica. Two subspecies, South African birds being separated as *vetula* (Bruch, 1853).

BROOKE, R. K.; COOPER, J. 1979. The distinctiveness of Southern African *Larus dominicanus* (Aves: Laridae). Durban Mus. Novit. 12: 27–37.

Larus dominicanus dominicanus Lichtenstein
Southern Black-backed Gull (Karoro)

Larus dominicanus Lichtenstein, 1823, Verz. Doublett. Zool. Mus. Univ. Berl.: 82—coasts of Brazil.

Breeds throughout coastal districts of New Zealand and on most offshore islands; also inland on riverbeds and high into the mountains. Not at the Three Kings or the Snares; straggles to the Ross Sea and north to the Kermadec Islands. Also in Australia (believed to be a mid-20th century colonist and now breeding) and South America (Kelp Gull). Both subfossil and midden from North, South, Stewart and Chatham Islands.

FORDHAM, R. A. 1964. Breeding biology of the Southern Black-backed Gull. I. Pre-egg and egg stage. Notornis 11: 3–34.
FORDHAM, R. A. 1964. Breeding biology of the Southern Black-backed Gull. II. Incubation and the chick stage. Notornis 11: 110–126.
KINSKY, F. C. 1963. The Southern Black-backed Gull (*Larus dominicanus* Lichtenstein). Rec. Dom. Mus. 4: 149–219.

279 **Larus novaehollandiae** Stephens

Red-billed Gull

Larus Novae-Hollandiae Stephens, 1826, Shaw's Gen. Zool. 13: 196 — New South Wales.

Australia (*novaehollandiae*, Silver Gull); New Caledonia and southwest Pacific west to Torres Strait (*forsteri*); South Africa (*hartlaubii*); New Zealand (*scopulinus*); straggling to Norfolk Island, where may have bred (subspecies unknown).

Larus novaehollandiae scopulinus J. R. Forster

Red-billed Gull (Tarapunga)

Larus scopulinus J. R. Forster, 1844, Descr. Anim., ed. Licht., p.106 — Dusky Sound, New Zealand.

New Zealand, breeding on coasts and islets from the Three Kings to Stewart, Chatham, Snares, Auckland and Campbell Islands. Also breeds inland at Lake Rotorua. Straggler to the Kermadecs. Mathews' alleged subspecies *coincidens* for Red-billed Gulls from the New Zealand subantarctic islands still lacks confirmation.

Both subfossil and midden from North, South, Stewart and Chatham Islands.

GURR, L.; KINSKY, F. C. 1965. The distribution of breeding colonies and status of the Red-billed Gull in New Zealand and its outlying islands. Notornis 12: 223–240.
MILLS, J. A. 1979. Factors affecting the egg size of Red-billed Gulls *Larus novaehollandiae scopulinus*. Ibis 121: 53–67.
TASKER, C. R.; MILLS, J. A. 1981. A functional analysis of courtship feeding in the Red-billed Gull *Larus novaehollandiae scopulinus*. Behaviour 77: 222–241.

280 **Larus bulleri** Hutton

Black-billed Gull

Larus bulleri Hutton, 1871, Cat. Birds New Zealand, p.41 — New Zealand.
Larus bulleri Potts, 1872, Ibis 1872, p.38.

New Zealand only, breeding mainly on South Island riverbeds; some northward movement in autumn, including to Manawatu coast. A few go south to Stewart Island or straggle to the Snares. Breeds also on North Island coasts (Firth of Thames, Ohiwa Harbour, Gisborne, Wairoa, Clive, Porangahau) and inland (Lake Rotorua, upper Manawatu River, sometimes northern Wairarapa).

Subfossil and midden records from the South Island; midden only from the North Island.

DRAKE, J. R. 1980. Inland breeding of Black-billed Gulls in southern Hawke's Bay and northern Wairarapa. Notornis 27: 86–88.
GLEESON, N. M.; FOGARTY, S. M.; PLAYER, J. L.; McKENZIE, H. R. 1972. Black-billed Gulls extend breeding range north. Notornis 19: 330–334.
REID, D.; REID, B. 1965. The Sulphur Point (Lake Rotorua) gull colony. Notornis 12: 138–157.

Subfamily STERNINAE: Terns
Genus **Chlidonias** Rafinesque

Chlidonias Rafinesque, 1822, Kentucky Gaz., new ser. 1 (8): 3, col. 5—type (by monotypy) *Sterna melanops* Raf. = *Sterna surinamensis* Gmelin.
Hydrochelidon Boie, 1822, Isis 5: col. 563—type (by subsequent designation) *Sterna nigra* Linnaeus.

281   **Chlidonias hybrida** (Pallas)

Whiskered Tern

Sterna hybrida Pallas, 1811, Zoogr. ross. asiat. 2: 338—Southern Russia.

Breeds in marshes across southern Eurasia, Africa and Australia. A casual vagrant to New Zealand, probably from Australia, where the subspecies *javanicus* breeds mainly in the southeast. Five sight records: Lake Horowhenua, August-October 1977, May—September 1978; lower Waikato River, August—September 1978; Pukekohe, March 1980; Lake Rotorua, May 1987.

BROWN, B.; HABRAKEN, A. 1979. Whiskered Tern on lower Waikato River. Notornis 26: 195–197.
HABRAKEN, A.; FIELD, M. S. 1982. Whiskered Tern in breeding plumage Notornis 29: 337.
HEATHER, B. D.; JONES, E. B. 1979. The Whiskered Tern in New Zealand— first records. Notornis 26: 185–195.

282   **Chlidonias leucopterus** (Temminck)

White-winged Black Tern

Sterna leucoptera Temminck, 1815, Man. Orn.: 483—Mediterranean coasts.

Breeds in marshes across Eurasia, north to Siberia, and probably in East Africa; migrates to the Southern Hemisphere and prone to wander, especially birds in their first year. Almost a regular casual in New Zealand from the harbours of Northland to the Southland lagoons; generally singles, but sometimes in small flocks (4 at Norfolk Island in 1967; 13 at Ahuriri Lagoons, Napier, in 1972).

Stead suspected breeding in Canterbury as long ago as 1927; Pierce (1974) proved it in 1973. The true picture is obscured because White-winged Black Terns may be seen in breeding plumage in New Zealand in any month of the year.

BULLER, W. L. 1888. Manual of the Birds of New Zealand, pp.81–82. Wellington: Govt. Printer.

PIERCE, R. J. 1974. Presumed attempted breeding of the White-winged Black Tern in New Zealand. Notornis 21: 129–134. See also KINSKY, F. C. 1977. AGM 1977: a later report, Rare Birds Committee. Notornis 24: 294.

SIBSON, R. B. 1954. White-winged Black Terns near Auckland. Notornis 6: 43–47.

SIBSON, R. B. 1955. Further notes on White-winged Black Tern (*C. leucopterus*) in Manukau. Notornis 6: 159–160.

TODD, K.; LLOYD, J. 1980. White-winged Black Terns, Napier 1972. Notornis 27: 91–92.

Genus **Gelochelidon** Brehm

Gelochelidon Brehm, 1830, Isis 23: col. 994 — type (by monotypy) *G. meridionalis* Brehm = *Sterna nilotica* Gmelin.

283 **Gelochelidon nilotica** (Gmelin)

Gull-billed Tern

Sterna nilotica Gmelin, 1789, Syst. Nat. 1: 606 — Egypt.

Almost cosmopolitan, breeding across the temperate Northern Hemisphere and in Australia; migratory and nomadic. First recorded in New Zealand near Invercargill, where two overwintered in 1955. Now numerous sight records from coastal estuaries and marshes, occasionally in small flocks e.g. Manukau, south shore, 8 in 1976, 6 in 1977. Subspecies not ascertained, but probably Australian *macrotarsa*. Of several named races *affinis* from southeastern Asia might also stray to New Zealand.

BARLOW, M. L. 1965. Another record of the Gull-billed Tern near Invercargill. Notornis 12: 54.

McKENZIE, H. R. 1955. A new bird for New Zealand: Gull-billed Terns (*Gelochelidon nilotica*) near Invercargill. Notornis 6: 163–164.

Genus **Sterna** Linnaeus

Sterna Linnaeus, 1758, Syst. Nat. ed.10, 1. 137 — type (by tautonymy) *Sterna Hirundo* Linnaeus.

Thalasseus Boie, 1822, Isis 5: col. 563 — type (by subsequent designation) *S. cantiaca* Gmelin.

Sternula Boie, 1822, Isis 5: col.563 — type (by monotypy) *Sternula minuta* Linnaeus = *S. albifrons* Vroeg.

Hydroprogne Kaup, 1829, Skizz. Entw.-Gesch. eur. Thierw.: 91 — type (by subsequent designation) *Sterna caspia* Pallas = *Sterna Tschegrava* Lepechin (Gray, 1846).

284   **Sterna albostriata** (G. R. Gray)

Black-fronted Tern (Tarapiroe)

Sterna antarctica J. R. Forster, 1844, Descr. Anim., p.107 — New Zealand. (Pre-occupied by *Sterna antarctica* Lesson, 1831. Traité d'Orn. 8: 621 — Mauritius and Calcutta.)
Hydrochelidon albostriatus G. R. Gray, 1845, Voyage Erebus and Terror, Birds, p.19, pl.21 — New Zealand.
Sterna cinerea Ellman, 1861, Zoologist, p.7473 — New Zealand.

New Zealand. Breeds on the riverbeds of the eastern South Island from Marlborough to Southland, rarely in Westland; ranges south to Stewart Island. In winter, most feed at sea off the east South Island coast and in Cook Strait, in harbours, and over coastal fields; small numbers winter annually in the Bay of Plenty and Hawke Bay, also feeding at sea and over coastal fields. On the west, ranging to the southern Manawatu coast; a few rarely as far north as Kaipara Harbour. Formerly may have bred high on the Volcanic Plateau.

LALAS, C.; HEATHER, B. D. 1980. The morphology, moult and taxonomic status of the Black-fronted Tern. Notornis 27: 45–68.
LATHAM, P. C. M. 1981. Black-fronted Terns wintering in the Bay of Plenty. Notornis 28: 221–239.
MEES, G. F. 1977. The subspecies of *Chlidonias hybridus* (Pallas), their breeding distribution and migrations (Aves, Laridae, Sterninae). Zool. Verh., Leiden 157: 1–64.
POTTS, T. H. 1882. Out in the Open. Christchurch: Lyttelton Times Co.
SIBSON, R. B. 1948. Black-fronted Terns in the north. NZ Bird Notes 3: 10–12.
STEAD, E. F. 1932. The Life Histories of New Zealand Birds. London: Search Pub. Co.

285   **Sterna caspia** Pallas

Caspian Tern (Taranui)

Sterna caspia Pallas, 1770, Novi Comment. Acad. Scient. imp. Petropol. 14: 582, pl.22, fig. 2 — Caspian Sea.
Sterna Tschegrava Lepechin, 1770, Novi Comment. Acad. Scient. imp. Petropol. 14: 500, pl.13, fig. 2 — Caspian Sea.
Hydroprogne tschegrava oliveri Mathews and Iredale, 1913, Ibis (10) 1: 242 — New Zealand.

Almost cosmopolitan; breeding locally across temperate zones of Eurasia, Africa, and North America, and in Australia and New Zealand. Partially migratory. Various geographical races have been named, but the distinctions between them are doubtful.

Both main islands, breeding in small colonies or singly, fewer in the South Island. Mainly coastal; pairs sometimes breed inland e.g. on Volcanic Plateau and on Canterbury rivers. Some northward movement from southern colonies in autumn, proved by banding.

A very rare subfossil in the North and South Islands; a single (South Island) midden record.

BUDDLE, G. A. 1951. Bird Secrets. Wellington: Reed.
GUTHRIE-SMITH, H. 1925. Bird Life on Island and Shore. Edinburgh and London: Blackwood.
PIERCE, R. J. 1984. Breeding success of isolated pairs of Caspian Terns in Canterbury. Notornis 31: 185–190.

286 **Sterna striata** Gmelin

White-fronted Tern (Tara)

Sterna striata Gmelin, 1789, Syst. Nat. 1: 609 — New Zealand.
Sterna frontalis G. R. Gray, 1845, Voyage Erebus and Terror, Birds, p.19, pl.20 — New Zealand.
Sterna bethunei Buller, 1896, Trans. NZ Inst. 28: 349 — Auckland Islands. (Not *Sterna bethunei* Buller, Id., p.348).
Sterna striata aucklandorna Mathews, 1929, Bull. Br. Ornith. Club 50: 19. (New name for *Sterna bethunei* Buller, Id., p.349, preoccupied.)

Breeds abundantly from Northland (not Three Kings Islands) to Stewart Island and at Chatham and Auckland Islands; a casual visitor to Snares, Campbell and Macquarie Islands. Part of the population, apparently chiefly first-year birds, migrates to south-eastern Australia. Formerly believed to breed only in New Zealand; now confirmed as breeding on some islands in Bass Strait.

Both subfossil and midden from the North and South Islands and Chatham Island.

CLARK, W. C.; DAWSON, E. W. 1957. The trans-Tasman dispersal of the White-fronted Tern (*Sterna striata* Gm.). Notornis 7: 65–69.
HINDWOOD, K. A. 1946. The White-fronted Tern (*Sterna striata*) in Australia. Emu 45: 179–200.
SERVENTY, D. L.; SERVENTY, V.; WARHAM, J. 1971. The Handbook of Australian Sea-birds, pp.215–217. Sydney: Reed.

287 **Sterna fuscata** Linnaeus

Sooty Tern

Sterna fuscata Linnaeus, 1766, Syst. Nat. ed. 12, 1: 228 — Santo Domingo.

Circumtropical, ranging widely over subtropical seas and sometimes under stress into temperate waters.

Numerous races have been described on rather slight morphological grounds.

Sterna fuscata serrata Wagler

Sooty Tern

Sterna serrata Wagler, 1830, Nat. Syst. Amphib.: 89, note — New Caledonia.
Onychoprion fuscatus kermadeci Mathews, 1916, Austral Avian Rec. 3: 55 — Kermadec I. = Sydney, N.S.W., *apud* Mathews, 1927.

Breeds abundantly in the southwest Pacific, especially at Norfolk and Kermadec Islands. Strays occasionally to the North Island, where usually found after autumn or winter gales, south to Cook Strait.

JENKINS, J. A. F. 1962. Sooty Tern off Cape Reinga. Notornis 9: 295.
MERTON, D. V. 1970. Kermadec Islands Expedition reports: a general account of birdlife. Notornis 17: 147–199.
SIBSON, R. B. 1961. Tropical terns ashore on the Auckland west coast. Notornis 9: 137.
TURBOTT, E. G. 1952. Some stray tropical and sub-tropical sea birds in New Zealand. Rec. Auck. Inst. Mus. 4: 187–192.

288 **Sterna vittata** Gmelin

Antarctic Tern

Sterna vittata bollonsi Mathews and Iredale 1913, Ibis 1913: 244 — Subantarctic Islands of New Zealand.

Circumpolar, the typical subspecies breeding at subantarctic islands of the Indian and Atlantic Oceans.

Sterna vittata bethunei Buller

New Zealand Antarctic Tern

Sterna bethunei "Travers" Buller, 1896, Trans NZ Inst. 28: 348 — Bounty Islands.
Sterna vittata bollonsi Mathews and Iredale 1913, Ibis 1913: 244 — Subantarctic Islands of New Zealand.

Breeds at Stewart Island (Port Pegasus) and its outliers (including Stage, Solomon and Moggy Islands); and subantarctic islands (Snares, Antipodes, Bounty, Auckland, Campbell and Macquarie Islands). May straggle to the Chatham Islands, but verification needed. Subfossil bones, which may be of this species and/or *S. paradisaea*, are not uncommon in Chatham Island dunes.

BLACKBURN, A. 1965. Muttonbird Islands diary. Notornis 12: 191–207.
KINSKY, F. C. 1969. New and rare birds on Campbell Island. Notornis 16: 225–236.
SADLEIR, R. M. F. S.; TAYLOR, R. H.; TAYLOR, G. A. 1986. Breeding of Antarctic Terns. Notornis 33: 264–265.
SAGAR, P. M. 1978. Breeding of Antarctic Terns at the Snares Islands, New Zealand. Notornis 25: 59–70.
SAGAR, P. M.; SAGAR, J. L. 1989. The effects of wind and sea on the feeding of Antarctic Terns at the Snares Islands, New Zealand. Notornis 36: 171–182.
STEAD, E. F. 1948. Bird life on the Snares. NZ Bird Notes 3: 70–80.

289 **Sterna nereis** (Gould)

Fairy Tern

Sternula nereis Gould, 1843, Proc. Zool. Soc. Lond.: 140 — Bass Straits.

Predominantly an Australian species of the southern and western coasts, replaced in eastern Australia by *S. albifrons*; but rather anomalously with isolated populations in New Caledonia (*exsul*) and New Zealand (*davisae*).

Sterna nereis davisae (Mathews and Iredale)

New Zealand Fairy Tern

Sternula nereis davisae Mathews and Iredale, 1913, Ibis 1913: 245 — New Zealand.

Rare; known to breed only on the coasts of Northland; formerly said to have bred on some Canterbury riverbeds.

Apparently moves locally, but not wholly migratory. Subfossil (dune) from the North Island and midden associated on Chatham Island.

CHAMBERLIN, S.; DOWDING, J. 1985. Fairy Terns at Tapora, Kaipara Harbour. Notornis 32: 324–325.
GOFFIN, R. B. 1978. Unusual flock of Fairy Terns. Notornis 25: 331.
HITCHCOCK, W. B. 1959. A review of "Least" Terns in Australian waters. S. Aust. Orn. 22: 87–106.
MacDONALD, N. 1953. Inquiry into the status of Fairy Tern in New Zealand: interim report. Notornis 5: 84.
MOON, G. J. H. 1979. The Birds Around Us. Auckland: Heinemann.

290 **Sterna albifrons** Pallas

Little Tern

Sterna albifrons Pallas, 1764, Vroeg's Cat. Oiseaux Adumbr.: 6 — Maasland, Netherlands.

Almost worldwide outside the polar regions, with several subspecies.

Sterna albifrons sinensis Gmelin

Eastern Little Tern

Sterna sinensis Gmelin, 1789, Syst. Nat. 1: 608 — China *ex* Latham.

Breeds in eastern Asia; also northern and eastern Australia south to Tasmania. Not recognised in New Zealand till the mid-1940s. Now known to be a regular non-breeding summer visitor, probably from eastern Asia; sometimes in substantial flocks, especially at the big shallow inlets of northern New Zealand; also casually visits estuarine habitats south to Stewart Island. Immature non-breeders may overwinter.

ECKERT, J. 1970. An extension of the geographic and breeding range of the Little Tern. S. Aust. Orn. 25: 142–144.
HITCHCOCK, W. B. 1959. A review of "Least" Terns in Australian waters. S. Aust. Orn. 22: 87–106.
McKENZIE, H. R.; SIBSON, R. B. 1957. Does the Little Tern (*Sterna albifrons*) reach New Zealand? Notornis 7: 174–182.
SIBSON, R. B.; EDGAR, A. T. 1962. Little Terns in the Firth of Thames. Notornis 10: 91–92.

291 **Sterna paradisaea** Pontoppidan

Arctic Tern

Sterna Paradisaea Pontoppidan, 1763, Danske Atlas 1: 622 — no locality = Christiansoë I., off Burnholm, Denmark.
Sterna macrura Naumann, 1819, Isis: 1847 — Nordstrand I., Schleswig.

Circumpolar, breeding in arctic and subarctic regions; strongly migratory, using two main routes to Antarctica by the eastern

Atlantic and eastern Pacific Oceans; return routes less clearly defined. No subspecies.

First obtained in New Zealand at Waikanae in 1929. Probably an annual visitor, found more particularly after gales. Subadults may overwinter. Records include Chatham (? subfossil also) Auckland and Campbell Islands.

EDGAR, A. T. 1961. Arctic Terns near Manukau Heads. Notornis 9: 173.
KINSKY, F. C. 1969. New and rare birds on Campbell Island. Notornis 16: 225–236.
LATHAM, P. C. M. 1979. An Arctic Tern at the Tarawera River mouth. Notornis 26: 63–67.
SIBSON, R. B. 1982. Arctic Tern in Manukau Harbour. Notornis 29: 47–48.
STORR, G. M. 1958. Migration routes of the Arctic Tern. Emu 58: 59–62.

292   **Sterna bergii** Lichtenstein

Crested Tern

Sterna bergii Lichtenstein, 1823, Verz. Doublett. Zool. Mus. Univ. Berl.: 80—Cape of Good Hope.

Breeds in South Africa, the Indian Ocean, Australia, and the tropical southwest Pacific east to the Society Islands (Tahiti). A curiously scarce vagrant to New Zealand, first recorded at the Kermadec Islands (1910). One dead, Spirits Bay (1951). Other records: Farewell Spit (1960), Firth of Thames (1974), Napier (1981), Wellington Harbour and west coast (1981–88), and Kaikoura (1985).

The subspecific identity of Crested Terns observed in New Zealand has not been determined. Of several subspecies, three from Australia (*pelecanoides, poliocerca* and *gwendolenae*) and one from Fiji (*cristata*) may stray to New Zealand.

BELL, B. D. 1960. Rare birds at Farewell Spit—Crested Tern. Notornis 8: 261–262.
HABRAKEN, A. M. 1975. A Crested Tern in the Firth of Thames. Notornis 22: 69.
TURBOTT, E. G. 1952. Some stray tropical and sub-tropical sea birds in New Zealand. Rec. Auck. Inst. Mus. 4: 187–192.

293   **Sterna hirundo** Linnaeus

Common Tern

Sterna Hirundo Linnaeus, 1758, Syst. Nat., ed. 10, 1: 137—Sweden.

Breeds in eastern North America and across temperate Eurasia, both on the coast and inland; strongly migratory on a broad front.

Sterna hirundo longipennis Nordmann

Eastern Common Tern

Sterna longipennis Nordmann, 1835, Erman's Verz. Thier. Pfl.: 17—mouth of Kukhtuy River, Okhotsk, eastern Siberia.

Breeds in northern Asia, eastwards from Lake Baikal; winters from eastern India to Australasia. A regular migrant to the east coast of Australia, but not certainly recognised in New Zealand until 1984 (mouth of Rangitaiki River, Bay of Plenty), although suspected at Mangawhai (1981), Point Chevalier (1980), Manukau Harbour (1981), Lake Horowhenua (1977, 1980). Further records at Bowentown (1987), mouth of Tarawera River (1988), Waikanae (1984, 1985) and Pukerua Bay (1984).

BLAKERS, M.; DAVIES, S.J.J.F.; REILLY, P.N. 1984. The Atlas of Australian Birds. Melbourne University Press.

LATHAM, P.C.M. 1986. A Common Tern in the Bay of Plenty. Notornis 33: 69–76.

294 **Sterna anaethetus** Scopoli
Bridled Tern (Brown-winged Tern)

Sterna Anaethetus Scopoli, 1786, Delic. Flor. Faun. insubr. 2: 92 — "In Guinea" = Panay, Philippine Is. *ex* Sonnerat.

Breeding and widely distributed across all tropical seas, seldom straying to temperate waters; gregarious. Several subspecies have been described.

Only once reported in New Zealand: a beach-cast specimen from New Brighton, Canterbury, November 1987.

HULSMAN, K.; LANGHAM, N.P.E. 1985. Breeding biology of the Bridled Tern *Sterna anaethetus*. Emu 85: 240–249.

TUNNICLIFFE, G.A.; LANGLANDS, P.A. 1990. First record of the Bridled (Brown-winged) Tern (*Sterna anaethetus*) in New Zealand. Notornis 37: in press.

Subfamily MEGALOPTERINAE: Noddies
Genus **Anous** Stephens

Anous Stephens, 1826, Shaw's Gen. Zool. 13: 139 — type (by subsequent designation) *Anous niger* Stephens = *Sterna stolida* Linnaeus.

Megalopterus Boie, 1826, Isis 10: col. 980 — type (by monotypy) *Sterna tenuirostris* Temminck.

295 **Anous stolidus** (Linnaeus)
Common Noddy

Sterna stolida Linnaeus, 1758, Syst. Nat., ed.10, 1: 137 — West Indies.

Circumtropical, seldom ranging outside subtropical seas.

Anous stolidus pileatus (Scopoli)
Common Noddy

Sterna pileata Scopoli, 1786, Delic. Flor. Faun. insubr. 2: 92 — no locality = Philippines *ex* Sonnerat.

Breeds widely in the Indian and Pacific Oceans; modest numbers at Norfolk Island; not at the Kermadecs until c. 25 pairs found nesting on Curtis Island in 1989 (A.J.D. Tennyson and G.A. Taylor). Two early records: east coast of North Island (1885, Reischek) and "High Seas" (Buller).

SCHODDE, R.; FULLAGAR, P.; HERMES, N. 1983. A Review of Norfolk Island Birds: Past and Present Aust. Nat. Parks Wildl. Serv. Spec. Publ. 8.

296   **Anous tenuirostris** (Temminck)

Lesser Noddy

Sterna tenuirostris Temminck, 1823, Planches col. Oiseaux 2: 202 — Senegal = Seychelles *apud* Mathews.

Circumtropical, ranging over the subtropical Indian, Pacific and Atlantic Oceans.

Anous tenuirostris minutus Boie

White-capped Noddy

Anous minutus Boie, 1844, Isis 3: col. 188 — north-eastern Australia = Raine Island. *Megalopterus minutus kermadeci* Mathews, 1916, Austral Avian Rec. 3: 55 — Kermadec Island (error) = MacKay, Queensland.

Breeds widely in the southwest Pacific on small forested islands; in the New Zealand region especially at Norfolk and Kermadec Islands; sometimes strays outside subtropical waters to the North Island and twice recorded from the South Island (Farewell Spit 1961 and Taieri estuary 1977).

Some authors assign full specific status to the Lesser Noddies of the Indian Ocean (*A. tenuirostris*), but it seems preferable to accept only one circumtropical species with a number of local races.

MAYR, E. 1945. Birds of the Southwest Pacific. New York: MacMillan.
MERTON, D. V. 1970. Kermadec Islands Expedition reports: a general account of birdlife. Notornis 17: 147–199.
SCHODDE, R.; FULLAGAR, P.; HERMES, N. 1983. A Review of Norfolk Island Birds: Past and Present. Aust. Nat. Parks Wildl. Serv. Spec. Publ. 8.
SERVENTY, D. L.; SERVENTY, V.; WARHAM, J. 1971. The Handbook of Australian Sea-birds. Sydney: Reed.
SOPER, M. F. 1969. Kermadec Islands Expedition reports: the White-capped Noddy (*Anous tenuirostris minutus*). Notornis 16: 71–75.
WESTERSKOV, K. E. 1977. Southernmost occurrence of White-capped Noddy (*Anous minutus*). Notornis 24: 232–238.

Genus **Procelsterna** Lafresnaye

Procelsterna Lafresnaye, 1842, Mag. Zool.: pl.29, p.1 — type (by monotypy) *Procelsterna tereticollis* = *Sterna teretirostris* Lafresnaye; a form of *Procelsterna cerulea* (Bennett).

297   **Procelsterna cerulea** (Bennett)

Blue-grey Noddy

Sterna cerulea Bennett, 1840, Narr. Whaling Voy., 2: 248 — Christmas Island, Pacific Ocean.

Breeds on tropical and subtropical islands of the Pacific Ocean. Several subspecies.

Procelsterna cerulea albivittata Bonaparte

Grey Ternlet

Procelsterna albivittata Bonaparte, 1856, Compt. Rend. Acad. Sci. Paris, 42: 773.
(New name for *Anous cinereus* Gould, Lord Howe Island; not *Sterna cinerea* Haldeman,
which is *Sterna cerulea* Bennett.)
Procelsterna cerulea kermadeci Mathews, 1916, Austral Avian Rec. 3: 55—Kermadec
Islands.

Breeds on Lord Howe, Norfolk and Kermadec Islands. Apparently a summer visitor, sometimes in small flocks, to the outer waters of the North Island from North Cape to Bay of Plenty. First recorded in the North Island (1882) at Cape Maria van Diemen. One record for the South Island: Little River, one wrecked (1968) in the "Wahine gale". Breeding recently recorded on the Three Kings (West Island) and in the Bay of Plenty (Volkner Rocks and Sugarloaf Rock, Alderman Islands).

FALLA, R. A. 1970. Grey Ternlets in the Bay of Plenty. Notornis 17: 83–86.
MERTON, D. V. 1970. Kermadec Island Expedition reports: a general account of
birdlife. Notornis 17: 147–199.
SOPER, M. F. 1969. Kermadec Islands Expedition reports: the Grey Ternlet
(*Procelsterna cerulea albivitta*). Notornis 16: 75–80.

Genus **Gygis** Wagler

Gygis Wagler, 1832, Isis 11: col.1223—type (by monotypy) *Sterna candida* Gmelin.

?98 **Gygis alba** (Sparrman)

White Tern

Sterna alba Sparrman, 1786, Mus. Carlson.1(11)—East Indies, Cape of Good Hope,
and islands of the Pacific Ocean = Ascension Island, South Atlantic *apud* Mathews.

Circumtropical, also ranging widely over subtropical seas. Several subspecies.

Gygis alba royana Mathews

White Tern

Gygis alba royana Mathews, 1912, Birds Aust.2: 433—Kermadec Islands.

Breeds at Norfolk and Kermadec Islands; straggles occasionally to the North Island; only once recorded in the South Island (Ettrick, Otago, 1945).

CHEESEMAN, T. F. 1889. On some birds from the Kermadec Islands. Trans. NZ
Inst. 21: 121–124.
MERTON, D. V. 1970. Kermadec Island expedition reports: a general account of
birdlife. Notornis 17: 147–199.
SCHODDE, R.; FULLAGAR, P.; HERMES, N. 1983. A Review of Norfolk Island
Birds: Past and Present. Aust. Nat. Parks Wildl. Serv. Spec. Publ. 8.
SIBSON, R. B. 1961. Tropical terns ashore on the Auckland west coast. Notornis
9: 137.

Order **COLUMBIFORMES**: Pigeons and Doves
Suborder COLUMBAE: Pigeons and Doves
Family **COLUMBIDAE**: Pigeons and Doves
Subfamily PTILINOPINAE: Fruit-pigeons
Genus **Hemiphaga** Bonaparte

Hemiphaga Bonaparte, 1854, Compt. Rend. Acad. Sci. Paris 39: 1076—type (by original designation) *Columba novaeseelandiae* Gmelin.

299   **Hemiphaga novaeseelandiae** (Gmelin)
New Zealand Pigeon

New Zealand and the Chatham Islands. Three subspecies, including *spadicea* of Norfolk Island (extinct).

Hemiphaga novaeseelandiae novaeseelandiae (Gmelin)
New Zealand Pigeon (Kereru)

Columba novae Seelandiae Gmelin, 1789, Syst. Nat. 1(2): 773—Dusky Sound.

New Zealand: main islands and most larger offshore islands. Reduced with deforestation after European settlement, the decline accelerated adjacent to the new settlements by shooting. (Restriction on shooting was necessary as early as 1864, and full protection was given in 1921.) Now common and widespread in native forests and remnants throughout. Perhaps now expanding its range by adapting to feed on exotic vegetation. Subfossil and midden at numerous sites in the North and South Islands; four Stewart Island midden records.

CLOUT, M.N.; GAZE, P.D.; HAY, J.R.; KARL, B.J. 1986. Habitat use and spring movements of New Zealand Pigeons at Lake Rotoroa, Nelson Lakes National Park. Notornis 33: 37–44.
McEWEN, W.M. 1978. The food of the New Zealand Pigeon (*Hemiphaga novaeseelandiae novaeseelandiae*). NZ J Ecol. 1: 99–108.

Hemiphaga novaeseelandiae chathamensis (Rothschild)
Chatham Island Pigeon

Carpophaga chathamensis Rothschild, 1891, Proc. Zool. Soc. Lond. 1891: 312—main island, Chatham group.
Carpophaga chathamica Forbes, 1892, Nature 46: 252–3—Chatham Islands.

Chatham Islands: originally on Chatham, Mangere and Pitt. Now only on Chatham, but reintroduced to Pitt; possibly fewer than 100 remain. Common as a subfossil on Pitt and Chatham. Abundant in middens (on Chatham and Mangere).

MORRIS, R. 1979. Observations on the Chatham Island Pigeon in Cascades Gorge. Notornis 26: 390–392.

Subfamily COLUMBINAE: Typical Pigeons
Genus **Columba** Linnaeus

Columba Linnaeus, 1758, Syst. Nat., ed. 10, 1: 162—type (by subsequent designation) *Columba oenas* Linnaeus.

300 **Columba livia** Gmelin

Rock Pigeon

Columba domestica β livia Gmelin, 1789, Syst. Nat. 1(2): 769—Southern Europe.
Europe, northern Africa and western Asia. Domestic forms brought to New Zealand in the early days of European settlement have become feral; widespread, including most cities and major towns, especially in parts of Hawke's Bay, Marlborough, Canterbury and Otago.

Genus **Streptopelia** Bonaparte

Streptopelia Bonaparte, 1855, Compt. Rend. Acad. Sci. Paris 40: 17—type (by subsequent designation) *Columba risoria* Linnaeus.

301 **Streptopelia roseogrisea** (Sundevall)

Barbary Dove

Columbam roseogriseam Sundevall, 1857, Kongl. Sv. Vet.-Akad. Handl. 2(1): 54—Nubia.
Northern Africa, Arabia. The domesticated form (often wrongly called *Streptopelia risoria*) has been feral at Masterton since about 1970 and at Whakatane and in the Rotorua area since about 1978; feral also in parts of Hawke's Bay.
STIDOLPH, R.H.D. 1974. Feral Barbary Doves in Masterton. Notornis 21: 383–384.

302 **Streptopelia chinensis** (Scopoli)

Spotted Dove

Columba chinensis Scopoli, 1786, Delic. Flor. et Faun. Insubr. 2: 94—Canton.
Southeast Asia from India to southern China and Indonesia. Introduced to Australia, New Zealand, New Britain, Fiji, Hawaii, California, Mauritius.

Streptopelia chinensis tigrina (Temminck)

Spotted Dove

Columba Tigrina Temminck, 1810, Les Pigeons (Knip): 94, Pl.43—Java.
Eastern Bengal, Burma, southeast Asia. A common cage-bird introduced to New Britain, Fiji, and parts of Australia. It breeds widely in greater Auckland.

Order **PSITTACIFORMES**: Cockatoos and Parrots
Family **CACATUIDAE**: Cockatoos
Subfamily CACATUINAE: White Cockatoos and Allies
Genus **Cacatua** Vieillot

Cacatua Vieillot, 1817, Nouv. Dict. Hist. nat. 17: 6 — type (by subsequent designation) *Cacatua cristata* Vieillot.

*303   **Cacatua galerita** (Latham)
Sulphur-crested Cockatoo

Psittacus galeritus Latham, 1790, Index orn. 1: 109 — New South Wales.
Northern, eastern and southeastern Australia and Tasmania, New Guinea, and islands from the Moluccas to the Bismarck and Louisiade archipelagoes. Three subspecies. Probably introduced to New Zealand by escape from captivity, but possibly self-introduced. Established in the Turakina Valley, near Wanganui, ranging to Hunterville and Marton; in the lower Waikato-Raglan area; and in the Wellington area. New Zealand birds have not been subspecifically identified.

MARTIN, J. S.; BARTLETT, J. 1963. Sulphur-crested Cockatoos near Hunterville. Notornis 10: 241.

Family **PSITTACIDAE**: Parrots
Subfamily STRIGOPINAE: Kakapo
Genus **Strigops** Gray

Strigops G. R. Gray, 1845, Gen. Bds. 2: 426 — type (by monotypy) *Strigops habroptilus* Gray.
Stringops Finsch, 1867, Papageien. 1: 241; emendation of *Strigops*.

304   **Strigops habroptilus** Gray
Kakapo

Strigops habroptilus G. R. Gray, 1845, Gen. Bds. 2: 427 — Dusky Sound.
Strigops greyii G. R. Gray, 1862, Ibis 1862: 230 — South Island.
Strigops habroptilus innominatus Mathews and Iredale, 1913, Ibis 1913: 427 — North Island.
Strigops habroptilus parsonsi Mathews and Iredale, 1913, Ibis 1913: 427 — northwestern South Island.
New Zealand. As shown by subfossil records, formerly at all altitudes throughout North, South and Stewart Islands. Its range had shrunk considerably before European settlement, particularly in the North Island, but it was still widespread and even common in the South Island, and it remained abundant in

the southern and western South Island in certain localities until c.1900. After 1980 the only remaining populations, those in Fiordland and Stewart Island, suffered further severe decline, and in an effort to save the species some 40 birds have been transferred to two predator-free islands: Codfish Island and Little Barrier Island. Doubtfully reported as a subfossil from the Chatham Islands.

DAWSON, E. W. 1960. New evidence of the former occurrence of the Kakapo (*Strigops habroptilus*) in the Chatham Islands. Notornis 9: 65–67.
MERTON, D. V.; MORRIS, R. B.; ATKINSON, I. A. E. 1984. Lek behaviour in a parrot: the Kakapo *Strigops habroptilus* of New Zealand. Ibis 126: 277–283.
POULTON, S. 1982. Kakapo. A Bibliography. NZ Wildlife Service Occasional Pub. 1.
WILLIAMS, G. R. 1956. The Kakapo (*Strigops habroptilus* Gray). A review and re-appraisal of a near-extinct species. Notornis 7: 29–56.

Subfamily NESTORINAE: Kakas and Kea
Genus **Nestor** Lesson

Nestor Lesson, 1830, Traité d'Orn. 3: 190 — type (by monotypy and tautonymy) *Nestor novaezelandiae* Lesson = *Psittacus nestor* Latham = *Psittacus meridionalis* Gmelin.
Doreenia Mathews, 1930, Bull. Br. Ornith. Club 50: 41 — type (by original designation) *Nestor notabilis* Gould.

Apart from *Nestor productus* (Gould, 1836) of Norfolk Island (extinct), the genus is endemic to New Zealand.

305   **Nestor meridionalis** (Gmelin)

Kaka

New Zealand. Two subspecies. Subfossil bones from the Chatham Islands are of uncertain specific/subspecific status.

Nestor meridionalis septentrionalis Lorenz

North Island Kaka

Nestor septentrionalis Lorenz, 1896, Verh. zool.-bot. Ges. Wien 46: 198 — North Island.
North Island, from Mangamuka (Northland) to Rimutaka and Haurangi Ranges and on offshore islands (Hen and Chickens, Great and Little Barrier, Fanal, Arid, Mayor and Kapiti). Straggles to isolated bush patches, sometimes to towns and cities and to other islands (e.g. Poor Knights, Mokohinau). Common as a subfossil throughout the North Island; common in middens but seldom in large numbers.

Nestor meridionalis meridionalis (Gmelin)

South Island Kaka

Psittacus meridionalis Gmelin, 1788, Syst. Nat. 1(1): 333 — Dusky Sound.
Nestor esslingi Souancé, 1856, Rev. et Mag. de Zool.: 233 — ?
Nestor occidentalis Buller, 1869, Ibis 1869: 40 — South Island west coast.

South Island, Stewart Island and some offshore islands (e.g. D'Urville, Inner Chetwode, Bench, Codfish and Big South Cape). Chiefly west of the main divide and in Marlborough. Extends into Canterbury at lower mountain passes (e.g. Arthur's Pass); also throughout the southern lakes district. An occasional straggler to coastal Canterbury and Otago. Common as a sub-fossil throughout the South Island.

DAWSON, E. W. 1952. Subfossil *Nestor* (Psittacidae) from New Zealand. Emu 52: 259–72.
DAWSON, E. W. 1959. The supposed occurrence of Kakapo, Kaka and Kea in the Chatham Islands. Notornis 8: 106–15.
O'DONNELL, C. F. J.; DILKS, P. J. 1989. Sap-feeding by the Kaka (*Nestor meri-dionalis*) in South Westland, New Zealand. Notornis 36: 65–71.

306   **Nestor notabilis** Gould

Kea

Nestor notabilis Gould, 1856, Proc. Zool. Soc. Lond. 1856: 941 — Murihiku district.

South Island. High country from Fiordland to Nelson and Marlborough. Breeds chiefly above 760 m, coming down to the west coast at times of heavy snowfall on the hills. Recorded as a subfossil at only a few South Island sites. (Such apparent rarity may simply be the result of misidentification because, at certain sites where its identity has been unequivocally established, e.g. Oparara, it is abundant: see Millener 1984: 52).

CLARKE, C. M. H. 1970. Observations on population, movements and food of the Kea (*Nestor notabilis*). Notornis 17: 105–14.
JACKSON, J. R. 1963. The nesting of Keas. Notornis 10: 319–26.
MILLENER, P. R. 1984. Honeycomb Hill Cave — a survey of scientific and scenic resources. Unpubl. NZ Forest Service Report. 100pp.

Subfamily PLATYCERCINAE: Rosellas and Allies
Genus **Platycercus** Vigors

Platycercus Vigors, 1825, Zool. Jl. 1: 527 — type (by original designation) *Psittacus pennantii* Latham.

*307   **Platycercus elegans** (Gmelin)

Crimson Rosella

Psittacus elegans Gmelin, 1788, Syst. Nat. 1: 318 — New South Wales.

Eastern and southeastern Australia. Seven subspecies. Introduced to New Zealand by escape from captivity. Established since 1963 in the northwest suburbs of Wellington. Reported from the Dunedin district, but recent records are few. New Zealand birds have not been subspecifically identified.

*308 **Platycercus eximius** (Shaw)

Eastern Rosella

Psittacus eximius Shaw, 1792, Nat. Misc. 3: pl.93—New South Wales.

Southeastern Australia and Tasmania. Three subspecies. Introduced to New Zealand by escape from captivity. Well established in settled districts, native forests and forest remnants from Awanui (Northland) to Waingaro (lower Waikato) and spreading. Also (mainly at edge of forest remnants and in adjacent farmland) in Wairarapa, Waikanae, upper Hutt Valley and Otago (between Waikouaiti River and Waipori Gorge). Isolated records from Taranaki, Gisborne, Hawke's Bay, Canterbury and Stewart Island. New Zealand birds have not been subspecifically identified.

FLEMING, C. A. 1944. The Eastern Rosella (*Platycercus eximius*) in North Auckland. NZ Bird Notes 1: 59–60.

HAMEL, J. 1970. Hybridization of Eastern and Crimson Rosellas in Otago. Notornis 17: 126–129.

TURBOTT, E. G. 1950. Advance of the Rosella in North Auckland. Notornis 4: 7.

Genus **Cyanoramphus** Bonaparte

Cyanoramphus Bonaparte, 1854, Rev. et Mag. Zool. (2)6: 53—type (by subsequent designation) *Psittacus erythronotus* Kuhl.

Bulleria Iredale and Mathews, 1926, Bull. Br. Ornith. Club 46: 76—type (by original designation) *Platycercus unicolor* Lear.

For general discussion of speciation in the genus see TAYLOR, R. H. 1975. Some ideas on speciation in New Zealand parakeets. Notornis 22: 110–121.

Note: Identifications for subfossil *Cyanoramphus* must be considered tentative because most specimens (particularly isolated bones) cannot be reliably assigned.

309 **Cyanoramphus unicolor** (Lear)

Antipodes Island Parakeet

Platycercus unicolor Lear, 1831, Illustr. Psittac. pt.4 (pl.25 of bound volume)—Antipodes Island.

Pezoporus fairchildii Hector, 1895, Trans. NZ Inst. 27: 285—Antipodes Island.

Antipodes Island and its islets, including Bollons Island.

TAYLOR, R. H. 1985. Status, habits and conservation of *Cyanoramphus* parakeets in the New Zealand region. ICBP Tech. Publ. 3: 195–211.

WARHAM, J.; BELL, B. D. 1979. The birds of Antipodes Island, New Zealand. Notornis 26: 121–169.

310 **Cyanoramphus novaezelandiae** (Sparrman)

Red-crowned Parakeet

New Caledonia, Lord Howe and Norfolk Islands, New Zealand (including Kermadec, Chatham, Auckland and Antipodes

Islands) and Macquarie Island. Eight subspecies, including *saisseti* (New Caledonia), *subflavescens* (Lord Howe Island, extinct) and *cookii* (Norfolk Island).

Cyanoramphus novaezelandiae cyanurus Salvadori
Kermadec Parakeet

Cyanorhamphus cyanurus Salvadori, 1891, Ann. Mag. Nat. Hist. (6) 7: 68 — Raoul Island, Kermadec group.

Kermadec Islands. Raoul Island (visitor only); Herald Islets; Macauley Island (abundant).

TAYLOR, R. H. 1985. Status, habits and conservation of *Cyanoramphus* parakeets in the New Zealand region. ICBP Tech. Publ. 3: 195–211.

Cyanoramphus novaezelandiae novaezelandiae (Sparrman)
Red-crowned Parakeet (Kakariki)

Psittacus Novae Zelandiae Sparrman, 1787, Mus. Carls. fasc. 2, no. xxviii and pl. — Dusky Sound.
Psittacus pacificus Gmelin, 1788, Syst. Nat. 1: 329 — Dusky Sound.
Lathamus sparmanii (sic) Lesson, 1831, Traité d'Orn. 206 — ?
Platycercus forsteri Finsch, 1868, Papag. 2: 287 — ?
Platycercus rowleyi Buller, 1875, Trans. NZ Inst. 7: 220 — North Canterbury.
Cyanorhamphus novaezelandiae aucklandicus Reichenow, 1881. J. für. Ornithol. 29: 42 — Auckland Island.

New Zealand. Very rare on the mainland but common on many offshore islands. North Island: occasionally reported from remaining areas of heavy forest, but apparently absent from Mt Egmont, East Cape and the Ruahine Ranges; present on Three Kings, Poor Knights, Hen and Chickens, Mokohinau, Fanal, Little Barrier, Arid, Tiritiri Matangi, Cuvier, Mercury, Aldermen and Kapiti Islands. South Island: occasionally reported in the west. Quite widespread on Stewart Island and its outliers (Codfish, Big South Cape, Bench, Ruapuke and Green Islands). Auckland Islands (Adams, Ewing, Enderby and Rose). Common as a subfossil in caves, dunes and middens throughout the North and South Islands.

BUTLER, D. J. 1986. Hybrid parakeet on mainland. Notornis 33: 58–59.
SAGAR, P. M. 1988. Some characteristics of Red-crowned Parakeets on the Poor Knights Islands. Notornis 35: 1–8.
VEITCH, C. R. 1979. Parakeet hybridization. Notornis 26: 395.

Cyanoramphus novaezelandiae chathamensis Oliver
Chatham Island Red-crowned Parakeet

Cyanoramphus novaezelandiae chathamensis Oliver, 1930, New Zealand Birds (1st ed.) 412 — Chatham Islands.

Chatham Islands: southern portion of Chatham Island and on Pitt, Mangere and South East Islands. Common as a subfossil and in middens.

Cyanoramphus novaezelandiae hochstetteri (Reischek)
Reischek's Parakeet

Platycercus hochstetteri Reischek, 1889, Trans. NZ Inst. 21: 387 — Antipodes Island.

Antipodes Island, Bollons Island and all adjacent islets.

TAYLOR, R. H. 1985. Status, habits and conservation of *Cyanoramphus* parakeets in the New Zealand region. ICBP Tech. Publ. 3: 195–211.

WARHAM, J.: BELL, B. D. 1979. The birds of Antipodes Island, New Zealand. Notornis 26: 121–169.

Cyanoramphus novaezelandiae erythrotis (Wagler)
Macquarie Island Parakeet

Psittacus erythrotis Wagler, 1832, Abh. K. Bayer. Akad. Wiss., Math.-Phys. K., 1: 426 — Macquarie Islands.

Macquarie Island. Plentiful from the discovery of the island in 1810 to about 1880; then declined and became extinct by 1891, probably as a result of factors following from the introduction of rabbits.

TAYLOR, R. H. 1979. How the Macquarie Island Parakeet became extinct. NZ J. Ecol. 2: 42–45.

311 Cyanoramphus auriceps (Kuhl)
Yellow-crowned Parakeet

New Zealand and the Chatham Islands. Two subspecies.

Cyanoramphus auriceps auriceps (Kuhl)
Yellow-crowned Parakeet (Kakariki)

Psittacus auriceps Kuhl, 1820, Nova Acta Acad. Caes. Leop. Carol. 10: 46 — South Island.

Cyanoramphus Malherbi Souancé, 1857, Rev. et Mag. Zool. (2) 9: 98 — South Island.

Platycercus alpinus Buller, 1869, Ibis 1869: 39 — South Island high country.

Cyanorhamphus intermedia (sic) Reichenow, 1881, J. Ornithol. 1881: 44 — ?

Cyanoramphus auriceps macleani Mathews and Iredale, 1913, Ibis 1913: 246 — North Island.

Cyanoramphus auriceps novana Mathews, 1930, Bull. Br. Ornith. Club 50: 42 — Birch Ridge, "Maunghaumia" (= Maungahaumi?), North Island.

New Zealand. Now more common on the mainland than the Red-crowned Parakeet. North Island: mainly restricted to central forested areas and the Tararua Ranges; present on Three Kings, Hen and Chickens, Little Barrier, Cuvier and Kapiti Islands. South Island: widespread in western Marlborough, Nelson, Westland, inland north Canterbury, western Otago, the Catlins and Fiordland, Chetwode Islands. Present on Stewart Island and outliers (Big and Little Solander, Bench, Ulva, Jacky Lee, Codfish and Big South Cape Islands). Auckland Islands. Common as a subfossil in caves and dunes and in middens throughout the North and South Islands and on Stewart Island.

Note: The Orange-fronted Parakeet, hitherto regarded as a

distinct species (*C. malherbi* Souancé, 1857), has recently been shown by cross-breeding in captivity to be a colour morph of *C. auriceps* (Taylor *et al.* 1986).

NIXON, A.J. The external morphology and taxonomic status of the Orange-fronted Parakeet. Notornis 28: 292–300.

TAYLOR, R. H.; HEATHERBELL, E. G.; HEATHERBELL, E. M. 1986. The Orange-fronted Parakeet (*Cyanoramphus malherbi*) is a colour morph of the Yellow-crowned Parakeet (*C. auriceps*). Notornis 33: 17–22.

Cyanoramphus auriceps forbesi Rothschild
Forbes' Parakeet

Cyanorhamphus forbesi Rothschild, 1893, Proc. Zool. Soc. Lond. 1893: 529 — Chatham Islands.

Chatham Islands; resident on Little Mangere Island, ranging to Pitt and Mangere Islands. Hybridises with *C. novaezelandiae chathamensis* on Mangere. Since the early 1980s recorded in small numbers in the southern, forested part of the main island. Common as a subfossil.

GREENE, T. 1989. Forbes' Parakeet on Chatham Island. Notornis 36: 326–327.

MELVILLE, D. S. 1984. A "Yellow-crowned" Parakeet on Chatham Island. Notornis 31: 91.

Order **CUCULIFORMES**: Cuckoos and Turacos
Suborder CUCULI: Cuckoos and allies
Family **CUCULIDAE**: Cuckoos, Koels and Coucals
Subfamily CUCULINAE: Parasitic Cuckoos
Genus **Cuculus** Linnaeus

Cuculus Linnaeus, 1758, Syst. Nat., ed. 10, 1: 110—type (by tautonymy) *Cuculus canorus* Linnaeus.

312 **Cuculus saturatus** Blyth

Oriental Cuckoo

Cuculus saturatus Blyth, 1843, J. Asiat. Soc. Bengal 12: 942—Nepal.

Two subspecies are often recognised, but the status of birds in Australia and New Zealand has not been properly resolved. Breeds in central and eastern Siberia, central Asia, Himalayan region, China, Taiwan and Japan. Migratory; winters from southern India eastwards to New Guinea, the Solomon Islands and northern Australia (uncommon). Straggler to New Zealand; up to 20 records since February 1902, when a specimen was shot at Lake Te Anau (previously doubtfully recorded in Hawke's Bay in 1889). Localities range from the Far North (Te Kao) to Southland, mainly in December–February. One at Little Barrier Island in October 1971, and one on Snares Islands in December 1986.

REED, S. 1972. Oriental Cuckoo on Little Barrier Island. Notornis 19: 88.
WATT, A. H. 1953. An Oriental Cuckoo in Northland. Notornis 5: 196.

313 **Cuculus pallidus** (Latham)

Pallid Cuckoo

Columba pallida Latham, 1801, Index Orn. Suppl.: 60—New South Wales.

Breeds in coastal districts of Australia, including Tasmania. Migratory; winters in inland and northern Australia and the Moluccas. Straggler to New Zealand. Four records: Craig Flat, Otago (one bird seen between May and October in 1939, 1940 and 1941, and then found dead); Okarito (December 1941); Greymouth (March 1942) and Wairarapa (1977). No subspecies.

MARPLES, B. J. 1942. Notes on cuckoos. Bull. OSNZ 2: 10–11.

Genus **Cacomantis** Müller

Cacomantis S. Müller 1843, Verh. nat. Gesch. Ned. overz. Bez. Ld Volkk.: 177—type (by subsequent designation) *Cuculus flavus* Linnaeus.

314   **Cacomantis flabelliformis** Latham

Fan-tailed Cuckoo

Australia and Tasmania, New Guinea eastwards to New Caledonia and Fiji. About six subspecies.

Cacomantis flabelliformis flabelliformis Latham

Fan-tailed Cuckoo

Cacomantis flabelliformis Latham, 1801, Index Orn. Suppl.: 30—Sydney area, NSW.
Breeds in eastern and southwestern Australia (including Tasmania). Nomadic or partially migratory within Australia and reaches Aru and some South Pacific Islands. Straggler to New Zealand. One record—Governor's Bay, Lyttelton Harbour (June 1960).

TURBOTT, E.G.; SCARLETT, R.J. 1964. Australian stragglers in New Zealand, with first record of the Fan-tailed Cuckoo. Notornis 11: 107–109.

Genus **Chrysococcyx** Boie

Chrysococcyx Boie, 1826, Isis von Oken 2: col. 977—type (by monotypy) *Cuculus cupreus* Shaw
Chalcites Lesson, 1830, Traité d'Orn. 2: 152—type (by tautonymy) *Cuculus chalcites* Illiger = *Cuculus plagosus* Latham.
Chalcococcyx Cabanis, 1863, Mus. Hein. 4: 15—type (by original designation) *Cuculus xanthorhynchus* Horsfield.
Lamprococcyx Cabanis and Heine, 1862–63 (1863), Mus. Hein. 4: 11—type (by original designation) *Cuculus lucidus* Gmelin.

315   **Chrysococcyx lucidus** (Gmelin)

Shining Cuckoo

Breeds in southwestern and southeastern Australia (including Tasmania), New Zealand, Vanuatu, and New Caledonia. Migratory to the Lesser Sundas, New Guinea and the Solomons. Four subspecies, some doubtful.

Chrysococcyx lucidus lucidus (Gmelin)

Shining Cuckoo (Pipiwharauroa)

Cuculus lucidus Gmelin, 1788, Syst. Nat. 1: 421—Queen Charlotte Sound.
Breeds in New Zealand, including Stewart and Chatham Islands; also on Norfolk Island. One subfossil record (Chatham Island dunes). Straggles to Snares, Kermadec and Lord Howe Islands but not known to breed there. Very rare in New Zealand in May, June and July. Winters in New Britain, New Ireland, Bougainville and the Solomon Islands. Many (perhaps most) migrate via New South Wales and Queensland.

GILL, B.J. 1982. Notes on the Shining Cuckoo (*Chrysococcyx lucidus*) in New Zealand. Notornis 29: 215–27.

GILL, B.J. 1983. Brood-parasitism by the Shining Cuckoo *Chrysococcyx lucidus* at Kaikoura, New Zealand. Ibis 125: 40–55.
GILL, B.J. 1983. Morphology and migration of *Chrysococcyx lucidus*, an Australasian cuckoo. NZ J. Zool. 10: 371–81.

Genus **Eudynamys** Vigors and Horsfield

Eudynamys Vigors and Horsfield, 1826, Trans. Linn. Soc. Lond. 15: 303 — type (by subsequent designation) *Cuculus orientalis* Linnaeus.
Urodynamis Salvadori, 1880, Orn. Papua. e delle Molucc. 1: 370 — type (by original designation) *Cuculus taitensis* Sparrman.

316 **Eudynamys taitensis** (Sparrman)
Long-tailed Cuckoo (Koekoea)

Cuculus taitensis Sparrman, 1787, Mus. Carls. 2: pl.32 — Tahiti.

Breeds in New Zealand, including Stewart, Codfish, Little Barrier, Great Barrier and Kapiti Islands. Rarely overwinters. Straggles to Chatham, Snares and Auckland Islands. Migrates through Norfolk, Lord Howe and Kermadec Islands to Oceania from the Bismarck Archipelago and Micronesia to the Marquesas and Tuamotus. Chief wintering range Fiji to the Society Islands. No subspecies. Subfossil bones up to 7000–10 000 years old have been found at three North Island sites.

BOGERT, C. 1937. Birds collected during the Whitney South Sea Expedition. XXXIV. The distribution and the migration of the Long-tailed Cuckoo (*Urodynamis taitensis* Sparrman). Am. Mus. Novit. 933: 1–12.
GILL, B.J. 1980. Foods of the Long-tailed Cuckoo. Notornis 27: 96.
McLEAN, I.G. 1988. Breeding behaviour of the Long-tailed Cuckoo on Little Barrier Island. Notornis 35: 89–98.
REED, S. 1980. Food of Long-tailed Cuckoo. Notornis 27: 96.

Genus **Scythrops** Latham

Scythrops Latham, 1790, Index Orn. 1: 141 — type (by monotypy) *Scythrops novaehollandiae* Latham.

317 **Scythrops novaehollandiae** Latham
Channel-billed Cuckoo

Scythrops novae Hollandiae Latham, 1790, Index Orn. 1: 141 — New South Wales.

Eastern Indonesia, New Guinea, Bismarck Archipelago, northern and eastern Australia. Migratory. Two New Zealand records: Invercargill (December 1924) and Ngatakl, Northland (October 1986).

HOWELL, L. 1988. Classified Summarised Notes. Notornis 35: 306.
MARPLES, B.J. 1942. Notes on cuckoos. Bull. OSNZ 2: 10–11.

Order **STRIGIFORMES**: Owls
Family **STRIGIDAE**: Typical Owls
Subfamily BUBONINAE: Hawk Owls and Allies
Genus **Ninox** Hodgson

Ninox Hodgson, 1837, Madras J. Lit. Sci. 5: 23 — type (by original designation)
Ninox nipalensis Hodgson = *Ninox scutulata lugubris* (Tickell).
Spiloglaux Kaup, 1848, Isis von Oken 10: col. 768 — type (by subsequent designation) *Strix boobook* Latham = *Ninox boobook* (Latham); introduced as a subgenus.

318   **Ninox novaeseelandiae** (Gmelin)

Morepork

New Zealand, Lord Howe and Norfolk Islands. Three subspecies; *undulata* of Norfolk Island now very rare, and *albaria* of Lord Howe Island probably extinct.

Australian owls formerly considered to be subspecies of *novaeseelandiae* are now believed by some to belong to a separate species, *N. boobook* (Latham) — see SCHODDE, R.; MASON, I.J. 1980 (Nocturnal Birds of Australia. Melbourne: Lansdowne Editions). This view, however, is not accepted by MEES, G. 1982 (Emu 82: 182–184).

Ninox novaeseelandiae novaeseelandiae (Gmelin)

Morepork (Ruru)

Strix novae Seelandiae Gmelin, 1788, Syst. Nat. 1(1): 296 — Queen Charlotte Sound.
Strix fulva Latham, 1790, Index Orn. 1: 65 — New Zealand.
Strix novaeseelandiae maculata Kerr, 1792, Anim. Kingdom 1: 538 — New Zealand.
Noctua zelandica Quoy and Gaimard, 1830, Voy. Astrol. Zool. 1: 168 — Tasman Bay.
Noctua venatica Peale, 1848, U.S. Expl. Exped. 8: 75 — Bay of Islands.

New Zealand; North, South and Stewart Islands and most larger forested offshore islands from Three Kings to Codfish (not Kermadec, Chatham or subantarctic islands). Widespread, but sparingly distributed in drier eastern areas. Subfossil and midden from the North and South Islands (but not from any site demonstrably older than 1000 years). Its reported subfossil occurrence on Chatham Island (Forbes 1893) seems most unlikely.

FORBES, H.O. 1893. The Chatham Islands and their story. The Fortnightly Review 53 (117): 669–690.
IMBODEN, C. 1975. A brief radio-telemetry study on Moreporks. Notornis 22: 221–230.
LINDSAY, C.J.; ORDISH, R.G. 1964. The food of the Morepork. Notornis 11: 154–158.
SAINT-GIRONS, M.-C.; NEWMAN, D.G.; McFADDEN, I. 1986. Food of the Morepork on Lady Alice Island (Hen and Chickens Group). Notornis 33: 189–190.

Genus **Sceloglaux** Kaup

Sceloglaux Kaup, 1848, Isis von Oken 10: col. 768 — type (by monotypy) *Athene albifacies* G. R. Gray.

A monotypic genus endemic to New Zealand.

19 **Sceloglaux albifacies** (Gray)
Laughing Owl (Whekau)

Known from North, South and Stewart Islands. Its reported subfossil occurrence on Chatham Island (Dawson 1960) seems most unlikely. For a review of the species, see Williams and Harrison (1972).

DAWSON, E. W. 1960. New evidence of the former occurrence of the Kakapo (*Strigops habroptilus*) in the Chatham Islands. Notornis 9: 65–67.
WILLIAMS, G. R.; HARRISON, M. 1972. The Laughing Owl *Sceloglaux albifacies* (Gray, 1844). A general survey of a near-extinct species. Notornis 19: 4–19.

Sceloglaux albifacies rufifacies Buller
North Island Laughing Owl

Sceloglaux rufifacies Buller, 1904, Ibis 1904: 639 — Wairarapa district, North Island.
North Island only. Extinct. Only two recent specimens were taken, both now lost: near Mt Egmont (1854) and Wairarapa ("about 50 miles from Wellington", 1868–9, holotype). Only two early sight records seem reliable: Waikohu near Te Karaka (1889) and near Porirua (before 1892). Subfossil at numerous sites, including swamps, caves, dunes and a few middens.

MILLENER, P. R. 1983. *Tyto alba* (Aves: Strigidae): a deletion from the New Zealand subfossil record. Notornis 30: 15–21.

Sceloglaux albifacies albifacies (Gray)
South Island Laughing Owl (Whekau)

Athene albifacies G. R. Gray, 1844, Zool. Voy. 'Erebus' & 'Terror', Birds, p.2, pl.1 — Waikouaiti, South Island.
South Island (Nelson, Canterbury, Otago, Fiordland) and Stewart Island. Declined rapidly after about 1880; almost certainly now extinct. Last specimen obtained July 1914 (Blue Cliffs, South Canterbury). It apparently preferred rocky areas in open country or at the forest edge. Subfossil bones widespread; a few midden records, including one from Stewart Island.

Genus **Athene** Boie

Athene Boie, 1822, Isis von Oken, Bd. 1, col. 549 — type (by subsequent designation) *Athene noctua* (Scopoli).

*320 **Athene noctua** (Scopoli)

Little Owl

Strix noctua Scopoli, 1769, Annus I, Hist.-Nat., p.22 — Carniolia (= Krain).
Europe, North Africa, Middle East, Central Asia. Twelve sub-
species. Introduced to New Zealand in 1906–10. The subspecific
status of the New Zealand population has not been determined.
Widespread in all eastern parts of the South Island. Occasional
sightings in Westland and Fiordland. No recent records from
Stewart Island (present 1957, 1959) or the North Island (seen at
Rotorua 1958).

MARPLES, B.J. 1942. A study of the Little Owl, *Athene noctua*, in New Zealand.
Trans. Proc. Roy. Soc. NZ 72: 237–252.

Family **TYTONIDAE**: Barn Owls
Subfamily TYTONINAE: Barn Owls
Genus **Tyto** Billberg

Tyto Billberg, 1828, Syn. Faun. Scand. 1(2): tab. A — type (by monotypy) *Strix alba*
Scopoli.

321 **Tyto alba** (Scopoli)

Barn Owl

Strix alba Scopoli, 1769, Annus 1, Hist.-Nat., p.21 — Friuli, Italy.
Almost world-wide. More than 30 subspecies.

Tyto alba delicatula (Gould)

Australian Barn Owl

Strix delicatulus Gould, 1837, Proc. Zool. Soc. Lond. 4: 140 — New South Wales.
Throughout mainland Australia. Rare in Tasmania, where it is
probably a recent arrival (first recorded 1910). Straggler to New
Zealand. Three records based on specimens, shot or accidentally
killed, all from Westland: Barrytown 1947, Haast River mouth
1955, Runanga 1960. A fourth specimen (Papatoetoe, 1983) was
probably accidentally transported by aircraft. One seen, South
Kaipara Head, February 1986. Not known as subfossil (see
Millener 1983).

FALLA, R.A. 1948. Classified Summarised Notes. NZ Bird Notes 2: 171.
FALLA, R.A.; RINEY, T. 1958. Australian Barn Owl in Westland. Notornis
7: 208–209.
GILL, B.J.; TURBOTT, E.G. 1984. Fourth record of a Barn Owl in New Zealand,
with comments on long-distance aircraft as a possible means of dispersal. Notornis
31: 177–179.
GILL, B.J.; TURBOTT, E.G. 1985. Barn Owls transported by aircraft — a
postscript. Notornis 32: 260.
GRANT, P. 1960. Another Australian Barn-owl in Westland. Notornis 9: 110.
MILLENER, P.R. 1983. *Tyto alba* (Aves: Strigidae): a deletion from the New
Zealand subfossil record. Notornis 30: 15–21.

Order **CAPRIMULGIFORMES**: Frogmouths, Nightjars
Suborder AEGOTHELAE: Owlet-nightjars
Family **AEGOTHELIDAE**: Owlet-nightjars
Genus **Megaegotheles** Scarlett

Megaegotheles Scarlett, 1968, Notornis 15: 254—type (by monotypy) *Megaegotheles novaezealandiae* Scarlett.

22 **Megaegotheles novaezealandiae** Scarlett
New Zealand Owlet-nightjar

Megaegotheles novaezealandiae Scarlett, 1968, Notornis 15: 254—Canaan, Takaka, Nelson.

Widespread at subfossil sites (particularly caves) in the North and South Islands. Not known from middens and so may have been extinct before human occupation. Larger than *Aegotheles* of Australia and probably flightless or nearly so. Olson *et al.* (1987) have synonymised *Megaegotheles* with *Aegotheles*.

OLSON, S. L.; BALONET, J.-C.; FISHER, C. T. 1987. The Owlet-nightjar of New Caledonia, *Aegotheles savesi*, with comments on the systematics of the Aegothelidae. Le Gerfaut 77: 341–352.
RICH, P. V.; SCARLETT, R. J. 1977. Another look at *Megaegotheles*, a large owlet-nightjar from New Zealand. Emu 77: 1–8.

Order **APODIFORMES**: Swifts
Suborder APODI: Swifts
Family **APODIDAE**: Swifts
Subfamily CHAETURINAE: Spine-tailed Swifts
Genus **Hirundapus** Hodgson

Hirundapus Hodgson, 1836 (1837), J. Asiat. Soc. Bengal 5: 780 — type (by original designation and monotypy) *Cypselus (Chaetura) nudipes* Hodgson.

323   **Hirundapus caudacutus** (Latham)

Spine-tailed Swift

Breeds from western Siberia east to Japan and south to Taiwan, Burma and the Himalayas. Migratory or sedentary. Three sub-species. Sometimes placed in *Chaetura*.

Hirundapus caudacutus caudacutus (Latham)

Spine-tailed Swift

H(irundo) caudacuta Latham, 1801, Index Orn. Suppl.: 57 — New South Wales.
Breeds from western Siberia and Mongolia to Sakhalin, Kurile Islands, Manchuria and Japan. Migrates through China to winter in New Guinea, Australia and Tasmania from October to March or April. A straggler to New Zealand; many records (the earliest 1888), mainly in the North Island but as far south as the Snares Islands; all between November and April. In some years (1942–43, 1968–69) irruptions have occurred. One bird at Macquarie Island, January 1960.

McCASKILL, L. W. 1943. The invasion of New Zealand by Spine-tailed Swifts in the summer of 1942–43. NZ Bird Notes 1: 38–40.
WARHAM, J. 1961. A Spine-tailed Swift at Macquarie Island. Emu 61: 189–190.

Subfamily APODINAE: Typical Swifts
Genus **Apus** Scopoli

Apus Scopoli, 1777, Intro. Hist. Nat.: 483 — type (by tautonymy and monotypy) *Hirundo apus* Linnaeus.

324   **Apus pacificus** (Latham)

Fork-tailed Swift

Breeds in Siberia, China, Japan, Taiwan, Indochina, Malaysia and west to northern India, Tibet and the Himalayas. Migratory or sedentary. Four subspecies.

Apus pacificus pacificus (Latham)

Fork-tailed Swift

H(irundo) pacifica Latham, 1801, Index Orn. Suppl.: 58—New South Wales.

Breeds in northeastern Asia, including Japan and Korea. Migrates to winter in New Guinea, Australia and Tasmania from October to April. A straggler to New Zealand; more than a dozen records to date (the earliest 1884) from both islands. Many sightings have been between October and February, but others, surprisingly, have been in May, June, July, August and September. One at Macquarie Island, December 1958.

GIBSON, J. D. 1959. Fork-tailed Swift at Macquarie Island. Emu 59: 64.

TURBOTT, E. G.; SCARLETT, R. J. 1964. Australian stragglers in New Zealand, with first record of the Fan-tailed Cuckoo. Notornis 11: 107–109.

Order **CORACIIFORMES**: Kingfishers, Bee-eaters, Rollers and Allies
Suborder ALCEDINES: Kingfishers, Motmots and Allies
Family **ALCEDINIDAE**: Kingfishers
Subfamily DACELONINAE: Forest Kingfishers
Genus **Dacelo** Leach

Dacelo Leach, 1815, Zool. Misc. 2: 125—type (by monotypy) *Alcedo gigantea* Latham = *Alcedo novaeguineae* Hermann.

*325 **Dacelo novaeguineae** (Hermann)

Kookaburra

Eastern Australian mainland. Introduced to Western Australia, Tasmania and New Zealand. Two subspecies.

Dacelo novaeguineae novaeguineae (Hermann)

Kookaburra

Alcedo novae Guineae Hermann, 1783, Tabl. Affin. Anim.: 192—New South Wales.
Alcedo gigas Boddaert, 1783, Tabl. Planches enlum: 40—northern Queensland.

Australia. In New Zealand, a small number persists on Kawau Island and on the adjacent mainland from Cape Rodney to the Whangaparaoa Peninsula. These are assumed to be descended from Sir George Grey's introduction of Kookaburras to Kawau Island in the early 1860s. Stragglers occasionally reach other parts of New Zealand.

Genus **Halcyon** Swainson

Halcyon Swainson, 1820–21 (1821), Zool. Illustr. 1: text to Pl.27—type (by original designation) *Alcedo senegalensis* Linnaeus.

326 **Halcyon sancta** Vigors and Horsfield

Sacred Kingfisher

Halcyon sanctus Vigors and Horsfield, 1827, Trans. Linn. Soc. Lond. 15: 206—New South Wales.

Widespread in Australia (nominate subspecies); southern populations wintering in northern Australia, Philippines, Indonesia, New Guinea and Solomon Islands. Resident in New Zealand (subspecies *vagans*), Norfolk Island (*norfolkiensis*, doubtfully distinct from *vagans*), Lord Howe Island (*adamsi*, doubtfully distinct from *vagans*), the Loyalty Islands (*macmillani*) and New Caledonia (*canacorum*).

Halcyon sancta vagans (Lesson)
New Zealand Kingfisher (Kotare)

Alcedo vagans Lesson, 1826 (1830), Voy. Coquille, Zool., 1: 694—Bay of Islands.
Sauropatis sanctus forsteri Mathews and Iredale, 1913, Ibis 1913: 429—South Island.

Widespread throughout North, South and Stewart Islands and on most offshore islands; also the Kermadec group. Especially common in northern districts and least numerous inland and in southern parts of the South Island. There appears to be a movement in winter from inland high country and forest to lowland farmland and the coast. Very poorly represented in subfossil deposits, suggesting that this species may have colonised New Zealand relatively recently.

FITZGERALD, B. M.; MEADS, M. J.; WHITAKER, A. H. 1986. Food of the Kingfisher (*Halcyon sancta*) during nesting. Notornis 33: 23–32.
HAYES, L. M. 1989. Feeding behaviour of New Zealand Kingfishers at an estuary in winter. Notornis 36: 107–113.
TAYLOR, R. H. 1966. Seasonal and altitudinal distribution of Kingfishers in the Nelson district. Notornis 13: 200–203.

Suborder CORACII: Rollers and Allies
Family CORACIIDAE: Rollers
Genus Eurystomus Vicillot

Eurystomus Vieillot, 1816, Analyse: 37—type (by monotypy) *Coracias orientalis* Linnaeus.

27 Eurystomus orientalis (Linnaeus)
Eastern Broad-billed Roller

Coracias orientalis Linnaeus, 1766, Syst. Nat., ed. 12, 1: 159—Java.

Asia and Australasia. Resident, nomadic or migratory. About a dozen subspecies.

Eurystomus orientalis pacificus (Latham)
Dollarbird

Coracias pacifica Latham, 1801, Index Orn. Suppl.: 27—Australia.

Breeds in northern and eastern Australia. Migrates at the end of summer to Indonesia and New Guinea. Straggler to New Zealand; many records (the earliest 1882), mostly of young birds, singly or in small groups, between December and May (the time of the northward migration).

BARLOW, M. 1967. Broad billed Roller in Southland. Notornis 14: 82–83.
BRATHWAITE, D. H. 1956. Notes on some rare birds recently recorded in Hawke's Bay. Notornis 7: 56–58.
CLUNIE, C. D. 1971. Dollar-bird near Dargaville. Notornis 18: 261.

Order **PASSERIFORMES**: Passerine Birds
Suborder OLIGOMYODI: Suboscines
Infraorder ACANTHISITTIDES: New Zealand Wrens*
Family **ACANTHISITTIDAE**: New Zealand Wrens
Genus **Acanthisitta** Lafresnaye

Acanthisitta Lafresnaye, 1842, Mag. Zool., (Paris), ser. 2, 4, pl.27 and pp.1–2 of text — type (by monotypy) *Sitta chloris* Sparrman.
Acanthidositta Sharpe, 1901, Hand-list 3 p.186 — emendation.

328   **Acanthisitta chloris** (Sparrman)

Rifleman

New Zealand. Originally occurred widely in North, South and Stewart Islands, and outliers; reduced following settlement mainly to residual forests, although (unlike *Xenicus* spp.) capable of adapting to exotic vegetation and occurs widely in commercial pine plantations; common in *Nothofagus* forests of mountainous areas of both main islands.

Acanthisitta chloris granti Mathews and Iredale
North Island Rifleman (Titipounamu)

Acanthisitta chloris granti Mathews and Iredale, 1913, Ibis, p.432 — North Island, New Zealand.

North Island, Great and Little Barrier Islands, but no recent records on mainland north of Te Aroha. Subfossil (in caves); Waitomo, Hawke's Bay.

Acanthisitta chloris chloris (Sparrman)
South Island Rifleman (Titipounamu)

Sitta chloris Sparrman, 1787, Mus. Carlsonianum, fasc. 2, no. 33 — Cape of Good Hope; error, type probably from Queen Charlotte Sound, New Zealand, *fide* Oliver, 1955, New Zealand Birds, 2nd ed., p.449.
Motacilla citrina Gmelin, 1789, Syst. Nat., 1: 979; based on "Citrine Warbler" of Latham, 1783, Gen. Synop. Birds, 2: 464 — "Nova Seelandia" — Dusky Sound.

South Island; Stewart Island and outliers. Subfossil (in caves); northwest Nelson, Canterbury.

DAWSON, D.G.; DILKS, P.J.; GAZE, P.D.; McBURNEY, J.G.R.; WILSON, P.R. 1978. Seasonal differences in bird counts in forests near Reefton, South Island, New Zealand. Notornis 25: 257–278.
GRAY, R.S. 1969. Breeding biology of Rifleman at Dunedin. Notornis 16: 5–22.

* For separation as an Infraorder, see SIBLEY, C.G.; WILLIAMS, G.R.; AHLQUIST, J.E. 1982. The relationships of the New Zealand Wrens (Acanthisittidae) as indicated by DNA-DNA hybridization. Notornis 29: 113–130. For general biology of the group, see FITZGERALD, B.M. 1985. Wren (3) *in* Campbell, B. & Lack, E. (eds.), A Dictionary of Birds, Calton & Poyser.

Genus **Xenicus** G. R. Gray

Xenicus G. R. Gray, Cat. Genera Subgenera Birds, p.31 — type (by original designation) *Motacilla longipes* Gmelin.
Xenicornis Mathews and Iredale, 1926, Bull. Br. Ornith. Club 46: 76 — type (by original designation) *Xenicus gilviventris* Pelzeln.

329 **Xenicus longipes** (Gmelin)

Bush Wren

New Zealand. North Island, South Island, and Stewart Island and its outliers.

Xenicus longipes stokesii G. R. Gray

North Island Bush Wren

Xenicus stokesii G. R. Gray, 1862, Ibis, p.219 — Rima-Taka (= Rimutaka Range).
Until recently only two specimens were believed to be in existence (both from the Rimutaka Range, 1850); a third, collected at Taupo, has now been located in the Merseyside County Museums collections. Subfossil bones from cave and dune sites show that the species was formerly of wide distribution in the North Island; now almost certainly extinct.
EDGAR, A. T. 1949. Winter notes on New Zealand birds. NZ Bird Notes 3: 170 171.
FISHER, C. T. 1981. Specimens of extinct, endangered or rare birds in the Merseyside County Museums, Liverpool. Bull. Br. Ornith. Club 101: 276–285.

Xenicus longipes longipes (Gmelin)

South Island Bush Wren (Matuhi)

Motacilla longipes Gmelin, 1789, Syst. Nat. 1: 979; based on "Longlegged Warbler" of Latham, 1783, Gen. Synop. Birds 2: 465 — "Nova Seelandia" (Dusky Sound *fide* Oliver, 1955, New Zealand Birds, 2nd ed., p.453).
Formerly widespread, especially in forests of mountainous areas; now almost certainly extinct. Two subfossil (cave) records.

Xenicus longipes variabilis Stead

Stead's Bush Wren

Xenicus longipes variabilis Stead, 1936, Trans. Proc. Roy. Soc. NZ 66: 313 — islands southwest of Stewart Island.
Outlying islands southwest of Stewart Island; formerly on Stewart Island (presumably this subspecies). The last known population became extinct in 1965 after *Rattus rattus* reached Big South Cape Island.
BLACKBURN, A. 1965. Muttonbird Islands Diary. Notornis 12. 191–200.

330 **Xenicus gilviventris** Pelzeln

Rock Wren

Xenicus gilviventris Pelzeln, 1867, Verh. Zool.-Bot. Ges. Wien 17: 316 — New Zealand (= mountains of South Island).

Xenicus haasti Buller, 1869, Ibis p.37—Otago = Canterbury Alps, South Island.
Xenicus gilviventris rineyi Falla, 1953, Notornis 5: 142—Lake McArthur, southwestern Fiordland.

New Zealand. Now of South Island alpine and subalpine distribution (Nelson to western Southland). Still well established in subalpine fell-fields and, in Fiordland, at lower altitudes. Identified subfossil from a few caves in both North and South Islands (especially common in certain northwest Nelson caves, e.g. Honeycomb Hill, Oparara).

SOPER, M. F. 1961. Observations on Rockwrens near the Homer Tunnel. Notornis 9: 158–161.
RINEY, T. 1953. Notes on habitat and behaviour of the Rock Wren subspecies *Xenicus gilviventris rineyi* Falla. Notornis 5: 186–188.

Genus **Traversia** Rothschild

Traversia Rothschild, 1894, Bull. Br. Ornith. Club 4: 10—type (by monotypy and original designation) *Traversia lyalli* Rothschild.

331   **Traversia lyalli** Rothschild

Stephens Island Wren

Traversia lyalli Rothschild, 1894, Bull. Br. Ornith. Club 4: 10—Stephens Island, Cook Strait.
Xenicus insularis Buller, 1895, Ibis, p.237, pl.7—Stephens Island, Cook Strait.

Formerly Stephens Island, Cook Strait, New Zealand; discovered in 1894, but the small population became extinct almost immediately, more probably through collecting than, as suggested in most accounts, destruction by the lighthouse keeper's cat. Recent subfossil discoveries confirm that the Stephens Island birds were merely the last relict of the formerly more widespread species (bones obtained from caves in the King Country, North Island, and in the South Island from northwest Nelson to Fiordland).

MILLENER, P. R. 1989. The only flightless passerine: the Stephens Island Wren (*Traversia lyalli*: Acanthisittidae). Notornis 36: 280–284.

Genus **Pachyplichas** Millener

Pachyplichas Millener, 1988, J. Roy. Soc. NZ 18(4): 387—type (by original designation) *Pachyplichas yaldwyni* Millener.

332   **Pachyplichas yaldwyni** Millener

South Island Stout-legged Wren

Pachyplichas yaldwyni Millener, 1988, J. Roy. Soc. NZ 18(4): 391—Honeycomb Hill Cave, Oparara, South Island.

South Island; extinct in late Holocene, subfossil in caves in northwest Nelson, Punakaiki, North Canterbury (?midden) and Southland.

MILLENER, P.R. 1988. Contributions to New Zealand's Late Quaternary avifauna. I: *Pachyplichas*, a new genus of wren (Aves: Acanthisittidae), with two new species. J. Roy. Soc. NZ 18(4): 383–406.

333 **Pachyplichas jagmi** Millener
North Island Stout-legged Wren

Pachyplichas jagmi Millener, 1988. J. Roy. Soc. NZ 18(4): 395 — Ruakuri Cave, Waitomo, North Island.

North Island; extinct in late Holocene, subfossil in dunesands in the Far North and caves in the King Country, Hawke's Bay (?some midden), and the Wairarapa.

MILLENER, P.R. 1988. Contributions to New Zealand's Late Quaternary avifauna. I: *Pachyplichas*, a new genus of wren (Aves: Acanthisittidae), with two new species. J. Roy. Soc. NZ 18(4): 383–406.

Suborder PASSERES (or POLYMYODI): Oscines
(Songbirds)
Family **ALAUDIDAE**: Larks
Genus **Alauda** Linnaeus

Alauda Linnaeus, 1758, Syst. Nat., ed. 10, 1: 165 — type (by subsequent designation) *Alauda arvensis* Linnaeus.

*334 **Alauda arvensis** Linnaeus

Skylark

Alauda arvensis Linnaeus, 1758, Syst. Nat., ed. 10, 1: 165 — Europe = Sweden *ex* Fn. Svec., and restricted to Uppsala by Meinertzhagen, 1951: 128.

Much of Palaearctic and N.W. Africa; migratory in the northern part of range, wintering to northern Africa and India.

New Zealand: introduced on several occasions during the 1860s and now common from North Cape to Stewart Island. Breeds also at Chatham Islands (common on Chatham and Pitt Islands), and stragglers have reached Kermadecs, Snares and Auckland Islands. Occurs on open farmland, sand dunes, tussock grasslands and subalpine herb fields to an altitude of 1920m (breeding to at least 1700m); avoids forest and thick scrub.

BULL, P.C.; DAWSON, D.G. 1969. Mortality and survival of birds during an unseasonable snow-storm in South Canterbury, November 1967. Notornis 16: 172–179.

CHILD, P. 1975. Observations on altitudes reached by some birds in central and northwest Otago. Notornis 22: 143–150.

GARRICK, A.S. 1981. Diets of Pipits and Skylarks at Huiarua Station, Tokomaru Bay, North Island, New Zealand. NZ J. Ecol. 4: 106–114.

HAMEL, J. 1972. Pipits, Skylarks and rainfall. Notornis 19: 20–25.

MOEED, A. 1975. Food of Skylarks and Pipits, finches, and feral pigeons near Christchurch. Notornis 22: 135–142.

NIETHAMMER, G. 1971. Zur Taxonomie europaischer, in Neuseeland eingeburgerter Vogel. J. fur Ornithol. 112: 202–226.

Family **HIRUNDINIDAE**: Swallows and Martins
Genus **Hirundo** Linnaeus

Hirundo Linnaeus, 1758, Syst. Nat., ed. 10, 1: 191—type (by subsequent designation) *Hirundo rustica* Linnaeus (G. R. Gray, 1840, List Gen. Birds, p.8).
Cecropis Boie, 1826, Isis von Oken, 10, col. 971—type (by subsequent designation) *Hirundo capensis* Gmelin = *Hirundo cucullata* Boddaert (Salvadori, 1881, Orn. Pap. Mol. 2: 1).

335   **Hirundo tahitica** Gmelin

Welcome Swallow

Hirundo tahitica Gmelin, 1789, Syst. Nat. 1: 1016—Tahiti.
Ranges from India through Malaya and Indonesia to the western Pacific and Australia. (Known variously in different parts of range as House Swallow, Pacific Swallow and Welcome Swallow.)

Hirundo tahitica neoxena Gould

Welcome Swallow

Hirundo neoxena Gould, 1843, Proc. Zool. Soc. Lond., pt.10 (1842), p.131—"the whole of the southern coast of Australia and Van Diemen's Land" = Tasmania.
Australia except north-west, and Tasmania; a partial migrant within Australia, many staying in winter in the south. Recent colonist in New Zealand, breeding being first recorded in 1958; previously recorded only as a rare straggler (Northland, 1920; Auckland Islands, 1943; Awhitu Peninsula, 1944; Stewart Island, 1953; Farewell Spit, 1955). First recorded breeding was near Awanui, Northland, in 1958; by 1965 common throughout Northland; now common in most of North Island (except central districts), but evidently still expanding; less widespread in the South Island, but probably expanding. No evidence of migration within New Zealand. Recorded since 1958 from Kermadec and Chatham Islands.

EDGAR, A. T. 1966. Welcome Swallows in New Zealand, 1958–1965. Notornis 13: 27–60.
MICHIE, R. H. 1959. Welcome Swallows nesting in Northland—a new breeding bird for New Zealand. Notornis 8: 61–62.
TURBOTT, E. G. 1965. Welcome Swallow: first breeding records for South Island. Notornis 12: 241–244.

336   **Hirundo nigricans** Vieillot

Australian Tree Martin

Eastern and southern Australia and Tasmania (subspecies *nigricans*); west and northern Australia (subspecies *neglecta*); and Lesser Sunda Islands and Timor (subspecies *timoriensis*).

Hirundo nigricans nigricans Vieillot

Australian Tree Martin

Hirundo nigricans Vieillot, 1817, Nouv. Dict. Hist. Nat. 14: 523 — New Holland, error = Hobart, Tasmania (Mathews, 1913, Austral Avian Rec. 2: 65).

Breeds in Queensland (except northern), New South Wales, Victoria, eastern South Australia, and Tasmania. Migratory in the south, reaching N. Queensland, New Guinea area and the Solomon Islands.

New Zealand records are of vagrants, both singly and in small flocks, mainly in autumn: Hicks Bay, Mahia, Cape Campbell, Collingwood, Wakapuaka, Blenheim, Mohikinui, Christchurch, Oamaru, Featherston (May–Sept 1946), Farewell Spit (Jan 1960), Miranda (Feb 1979), Vernon Lagoons (Apr 1980), Nelson (Nov 1983), Lake Holm Farm, Taieri Plain (1981–1984), Eglinton Valley (1983), Farewell Spit (Jan 1988). Two recorded on Snares, 18–20 Feb, 1969.

NEVILL, A. 1984. Fairy and Tree Martins in New Zealand. Notornis 31: 173–175.
WARHAM, J.; KEELEY, B. R. 1969. New and rare birds at Snares Island during 1968–69. Notornis 16: 221–224.
WRIGHT, A. 1960. Rare birds at Farewell Spit: Tree Martins. Notornis 8: 260–261.

337 **Hirundo ariel** (Gould)

Fairy Martin

Collocalia Ariel Gould, 1843, Proc. Zool. Soc. Lond., pt.10 (1842), p.132 — New South Wales.

Throughout Australia, migratory in the south; only accidental in Tasmania. Straggler to New Guinea.

First recorded in New Zealand when nests believed to be of this species were found at Te Hopai, southern Wairarapa, in 1978; sight records Nov, 1982, near the base of Farewell Spit; Totaranui, Nelson, February 1983; Lake Holm Farm, Taieri Plain (sightings 1981–1984); Cape Reinga, Nov 1983; Leigh, Nov 1984; Papakura, Jan 1986.

BELL, B. D. 1984. The Fairy Martin (*Petrochelidon ariel*) in New Zealand. Notornis 31: 172–173.
NEVILL, A. 1984. Fairy and Tree Martins in Otago. Notornis 31: 173–175.
RIDDELL, D.; TAYLOR, A. 1984. Fairy Martin at Cape Reinga. Notornis 31: 224.

Family **MOTACILLIDAE**: Wagtails and Pipits
Genus **Anthus** Bechstein

Anthus Bechstein, 1805, Gemein. Nat. Deutschl. 2: 247, 302, 465 — type (by subsequent designation) *Alauda pratensis* Linnaeus (Selby, 1825, Illus. Brit. Orn., p.xxix).

338 **Anthus novaeseelandiae** (Gmelin)
Richard's/Australian/New Zealand Pipit
Of wide distribution in Africa, Eurasia (except the north), and south-eastwards through Indonesia to Australia and New Zealand (and outlying islands); winter vagrant to western Europe.

Anthus novaeseelandiae novaeseelandiae (Gmelin)
New Zealand Pipit (Pihoihoi)

Alauda novae Seelandiae Gmelin, 1789, Syst. Nat. 1(2): 799—Queen Charlotte's Sound, New Zealand.

Anthus novaezealandiae reischeki Lorenz-Liburnau, 1902, Ann. K.-K. Naturhist. Hofmus. Wien 17: 308—Little Barrier and Waikato, North Island, New Zealand.

Anthus novaeseelandiae taupoensis Mathews, 1930, Bull. Br. Ornith. Club 50: 42—Lake Taupo, New Zealand.

North, South and Stewart Islands, and offshore islands; a straggler to the Kermadecs and Snares. Originally probably restricted to mountain and lowland tussock grasslands, riverbeds and the coastal zone, but with European settlement its range increased greatly; now avoids pure pasture land, but in rougher farmland and open country generally (including alpine) still fairly common. Widely distributed subfossil and midden records from North, South and Stewart Islands.

CHILD, P. 1975. Observations on altitudes reached by some birds in central and northwest Otago. Notornis 22: 143–150.

HAMEL, J. 1972. Pipits, Skylarks and rainfall. Notornis 19:20–25.

MOEED, A. 1975. Food of Skylarks and Pipits, finches, and feral pigeons near Christchurch. Notornis 22: 135–142.

STIDOLPH, R. H. D. 1974. Decline of Pipit in Wairarapa. Notornis 21: 79–80.

Anthus novaeseelandiae chathamensis Lorenz-Liburnau
Chatham Island Pipit

Anthus novaezealandiae chathamensis Lorenz-Liburnau, 1902, Ann. K.-K. Naturhist. Hofmus. Wien 17: 309—Chatham Islands.

Chatham Islands: common throughout. Also subfossil and midden records.

FLEMING, C. A. 1939. Birds of the Chatham Islands, pt.1. Emu 38: 380–413; 492–509.

FOGGO, M. N. 1984. Some observations on the southern subspecies of the New Zealand Pipit. Notornis 31: 1–5.

Anthus novaeseelandiae aucklandicus G. R. Gray
Auckland Island Pipit

Anthus aucklandicus G. R. Gray, 1862, Ibis 4: 224—Auckland Islands.

Auckland and Campbell Islands (at Campbell Island, formerly on the main island but now restricted to small offshore islands).

FOGGO, M. N. 1984. Some observations on the southern subspecies of the New Zealand Pipit. Notornis 31: 1–5.

Anthus novaeseelandiae steindachneri Reischek
Antipodes Island Pipit

Anthus steindachneri Reischek, 1889, Trans. NZ Inst. 21: 388 — Antipodes Islands.

Antipodes Islands.

FOGGO, M. N. 1984. Some observations on the southern subspecies of the New Zealand Pipit. Notornis 31: 1–5.

Family **CAMPEPHAGIDAE**: Cuckoo-shrikes
Genus **Coracina** Vieillot

Coracina Vieillot, 1816, Analyse, p.37 — type (by subsequent designation) "Choucari" of Buffon = *Corvus papuensis* Gmelin (Cabanis, 1851, Mus. Hein, Th. 1, 1850–51, p.62).

39 **Coracina novaehollandiae** (Gmelin)
Black-faced Cuckoo-shrike

Turdus novae Hollandiae Gmelin, 1789, Syst. Nat. 1: 814 — "terra van Diemen" = Adventure Bay, Tasmania.
Colluricincla concinna Hutton, 1871, Cat. Birds NZ, p.15.

Throughout Australia and Tasmania; also Lesser Sunda Islands, New Guinea and Solomons, and probably conspecific with forms ranging to India and southeast Asia; southern Australian birds partly migratory. The subspecific identity of New Zealand records not determined.

About a dozen New Zealand records, mainly sight records: Motueka (1869); Invercargill (1870); Westport (about 1895 and 1931); Lake Ellesmere (1904); Greymouth (1914?); Okato (1914); north Kaipara Heads (Jan–Sept 1953); Himatangi (Jan 1955); Feilding (1965); Okuru (1966); near Rotorua (1987).

HUTTON, F. W. 1871. Catalogue of the Birds of New Zealand, p.15. Wellington: Govt. Printer.
TURBOTT, E. G. 1954. Record of Black-faced Cuckoo-shrike. Notornis 5: 253.
WILSON, R. A. 1955. Occurrence of Black-faced Cuckoo-shrike. Notornis 6: 119.

Genus **Lalage** Boie

Lalage Boie, 1826, Isis, col. 973 — type (by monotypy) *Turdus orientalis* Gmelin = *Turdus niger* Forster.

40 **Lalage tricolor** (Swainson)
Australian White-winged Triller

Ceblepyris tricolor Swainson, 1825, Zool. Journal· 467 — "Australia" (restricted to Sydney, New South Wales, by Mathews, 1930, Syn. Av. Austral., p.540).

Throughout Australia; vagrant to Tasmania; southern populations migratory.

One New Zealand sight record, Feb–June 1969, Macandrew Bay, Otago Peninsula.

McPHERSON, B. 1973. The first record of a White-winged Triller in New Zealand. Notornis 20: 46–48.

Family **PYCNONOTIDAE**: Bulbuls
Genus **Pycnonotus** Boie

Pycnonotus "Kuhl" Boie, 1826, Isis von Oken, 19: 973 — type (by monotypy) *Turdus capensis* Linnaeus.

***341 Pycnonotus cafer** (Linnaeus)

Red-vented Bulbul

Turdus cafer Linnaeus, 1766, Syst. Nat., ed. 12, 1: 295 — Cape of Good Hope, *ex* Brisson, error; type locality corrected to Ceylon, *apud* Stuart Baker, 1930, Fauna Brit. India, Birds, ed. 2, 7: 79.

Indian subcontinent, Sri Lanka, Burma and W. Yunnan.

Pycnonotus cafer bengalensis Blyth

Red-vented Bulbul

Pycnonotus bengalensis Blyth, 1845, J. Asiat. Soc. Bengal, 14: 566 — Bengal.

Himalayas from Uttar Pradesh eastwards through Nepal and Bhutan to eastern Assam, and southwards to Bengal. Introduced to Fiji, Samoa, Tonga, Hawaii and Australia (Melbourne area only, last reported 1942).

New Zealand: introduced to Auckland (deliberately or as a cage escape) in 1952; population possibly as high as 50 by 1954, and believed exterminated by the Department of Agriculture by 1955. However, since 1984 there have been reports from Auckland's North Shore, so that some of the original population may have survived, or a further introduction or introductions may have been made.

TURBOTT, E. G. 1956. Bulbuls in Auckland. Notornis 6: 185–192.

Family **PRUNELLIDAE**: Accentors
Genus **Prunella** Vieillot

Prunella Vieillot, 1816, Analyse, p.43 — type (by monotypy) "Fauvette de haie" Buffon = *Motacilla modularis* Linnaeus.

***342 Prunella modularis** (Linnaeus)

Hedge Sparrow (Dunnock)

Motacilla modularis Linnaeus, 1758, Syst. Nat., ed. 10, 1: 184 — "Habitat in Europa" = Sweden *ex* Fn. Svec.

Europe and western Asia; winters to Mediterranean and N. Africa.

New Zealand: introduced to both North and South Islands on several occasions between 1868 and 1882. Now present from

North Cape to Stewart Island. Breeding at Chathams, Campbell Island and Antipodes Islands, and present on Snares and Auckland Islands. Common south of Auckland in gardens, orchards and hedgerows; also in coastal and subalpine scrub (to 1500 m); rather rare in solid stands of forest.

MAUERSBERGER, G. 1977. Uber die Heckenbraunelle (*Prunella modularis*) in Neuseeland (Aves, Passeriformes, Prunellidae). Zool. Abh. Mus. Tierk., Dresden, 34: 101–126.

NIETHAMMER, G. 1971. Zur Taxonomie europaischer, in Neuseeland eingeburgerter Vögel. J. für Ornithol. 112: 202–226.

Family **MUSCICAPIDAE**: Warblers, Flycatchers, Thrushes, etc.

Subfamily TURDINAE: Thrushes and Allies

Genus **Turdus** Linnaeus

Turdus Linnaeus, 1758, Syst. Nat., ed. 10, 1: 168 — type (by subsequent designation, Gray, 1840, List Gen. Birds, p.27) *Turdus viscivorus* Linnaeus.

*343 **Turdus merula** Linnaeus

Blackbird

Turdus Merula Linnaeus, 1758, Syst. Nat., ed. 10, 1: 170 — *in Europae sylvis*; restricted to Sweden by Hartert, 1910, Vog. pal. Fauna, 1: 665.

Europe, N. Africa, western and southern Asia, Indian subcontinent (except SW), Sri Lanka, southern China. Migratory in northern part of range and in the far east.

New Zealand: introduced to both the North and South Islands several times during the 1860s and 1870s. Now widespread from North Cape to Stewart Island. Has successfully colonised Norfolk, Kermadec, Chatham, Snares, Auckland and Campbell Islands, and a stray has reached Antipodes Island. Common in suburban gardens, hedgerows, orchards, plantations and scrub, and widespread in native forest, reaching at least 1500 m above sea level. By far the most widespread species reported during the 1969–79 survey for the *Atlas of Bird Distribution in New Zealand*.

BULL, P.C. 1946. Notes on the breeding cycle of the Thrush and Blackbird in New Zealand. Emu 46: 198–208.

FLUX, J.E.C. 1966. Breeding of Song Thrushes and Blackbirds at St Arnaud, Nelson. Notornis 13: 142–149.

GURR, L. 1954. A study of the Blackbird *Turdus merula* in New Zealand. Ibis 96: 225–261.

NIETHAMMER, G. 1971. Zur Taxonomie europaischer, in Neuseeland eingeburgerter Vögel. J. für Ornithol. 112: 202–226.

ROBERTSON, H.A.; WHITAKER, A.H.; FITZGERALD, B.M. 1983. Morphometrics of forest birds in the Orongorongo Valley, Wellington, New Zealand. NZ J. Zool. 10: 87–97.

*344 **Turdus philomelos** Brehm

Song Thrush

Turdus philomelos Brehm, 1831, Handb. Naturgesch. Vog. Deutschl., p.382 — wanders in April and October through central Germany.

Europe, western and central Asia. Migratory in northern part of range; winters to northern Africa and southern Asia.

New Zealand: introduced to both the North and South Islands several times during the 1860s and 1870s. Now widespread from North Cape to Stewart Island, and has spread to Norfolk, Kermadecs, Chathams, Snares, Antipodes, Auckland, Campbell and Macquarie Islands, breeding on all except Antipodes and Macquarie. Common in gardens, hedgerows and orchards; especially common along farmland hedgerows, but scarce in native forest.

BULL, P. C. 1946. Notes on the breeding cycle of the Thrush and Blackbird in New Zealand. Emu 46: 198–208.

FLUX, J. E. C. 1966. Breeding of Song Thrushes and Blackbirds at St Arnaud, Nelson. Notornis 13: 142–149.

NIETHAMMER, G. 1971. Zur Taxonomie europaischer, in Neuseeland eingeburgerter Vögel. J. für Ornithol. 112: 202–226.

ROBERTSON, H. A.; WHITAKER, A. H.; FITZGERALD, B. M. 1983. Morphometrics of forest birds in the Orongorongo Valley, Wellington, New Zealand. NZ J. Zool. 10: 87–97.

Family **SYLVIIDAE**: Old World Warblers
Genus **Bowdleria** Rothschild

Bowdleria Rothschild, 1896, Novit. Zool. 3: 539, note — type (by subsequent designation) (Sharpe, 1897, Zool. Rec. 33: 57) *Synallaxis punctata* Quoy and Gaimard.

Note: P. R. Millener, and Olson (1990), have independently concluded that anatomical differences between *Bowdleria* and *Megalurus* are sufficient to justify separate generic status for *Bowdleria*.

OLSON, S. L. 1990. Osteology and systematics of the fernbirds *Bowdleria* (Sylviidae). Notornis (in press).

345 **Bowdleria punctata** (Quoy and Gaimard)

Fernbird

New Zealand. Originally widespread in swamp, fernland and low scrub on North and South Islands; well-defined subspecies on Stewart, Codfish and Snares Islands.

SIBLEY, C. G.; AHLQUIST, J. E. 1987. The relationships of four species of New Zealand passerine birds. Emu 87: 63–64.

Bowdleria punctata vealeae Kemp
North Island Fernbird (Matata)

Bowdleria punctata vealeae Kemp, 1912, Austral Avian Rec. 1: 124—Umawera,
Hokianga, North Island.

Now of limited range, restricted to a relatively few areas of
residual swampland and scrubland and, in some localities, scrub
adjacent to shorelines; still fairly plentiful in Northland and
parts of Volcanic Plateau. Present on Great Barrier Island and
Alderman Islands; formerly on Great Island, Three Kings.

Subfossil and midden records from widely distributed sites.

Bowdleria punctata punctata (Quoy and Gaimard)
South Island Fernbird (Matata)

Synallaxis punctata Quoy and Gaimard, 1830, *in* Dumont d'Urville, Voyage Astrolabe,
Zool. 1: 255; Atlas, 1833, pl.18, fig. 3—Tasman Bay, South Island.

Now restricted as in North Island to residual areas of suitable
habitat: mainly Nelson, Westland, Otago and Southland. Also
Open Bay Islands (subspecies unknown). Subfossil and midden
records from a few sites.

BARLOW, M. 1983. Territories of South Island Fernbirds (*Bowdleria punctata
punctata*). Notornis 30: 199–216.
BEST, H.A. 1979. Observations on habitat selection by South Island Fernbirds
(*Bowdleria punctata punctata*). Notornis 26: 279–287.

Bowdleria punctata stewartiana Oliver
Stewart Island Fernbird

Bowdleria punctata stewartiana Oliver, 1930, New Zealand Birds, 1st ed., p.451—
Stewart Island.
Bowdleria punctata insularis Stead, 1936, Trans. Proc. Roy. Soc. NZ 66: 312—Stewart
Island.

Stewart Island, and outliers except Codfish Island.

Bowdleria punctata wilsoni Stead
Codfish Island Fernbird

Bowdleria punctata wilsoni Stead, 1936, Trans. Proc. Roy. Soc. NZ 66: 312—Codfish
Island.

Codfish Island, west of Stewart Island.

Bowdleria punctata caudata (Buller)
Snares Islands Fernbird

Sphenoeacus caudatus Buller, 1894, Ibis. p.523—Snares Islands

Main island of the Snares group, where it feeds in penguin
colonies and on the open floor of *Olearia lyallii* forest.

BEST, H.A. 1979. Food and foraging behaviour of the Snares Fernbird. NZ J.
Zool. 6: 481–488.

346   **Bowdleria rufescens** (Buller)

Chatham Island Fernbird

Sphenoeacus refescens Buller, 1869, Ibis, p.38—Chatham Islands.

Note: Recent studies on the osteology of *B. rufescens* (P. R. Millener; Olson, 1990 in press), together with evidence from plumage characteristics, indicate that it is highly distinct from *B. punctata* and should be given specific status.

Formerly on Chatham, Pitt and Mangere Islands, extinct since about 1900. Recorded subfossil and midden.

FLEMING, C. A. 1939. Birds of the Chatham Islands, pt.1. Emu 38: 380–413; 492–509.

Family **PACHYCEPHALIDAE**: Whistlers and Allies
Subfamily MOHOUINAE: Whitehead and Allies
Genus **Mohoua** Lesson

Mohoua Lesson, 1835, Complements Oeuvres Buffon 9: 139—type (by monotypy) *Certhia heteroclites* Quoy and Gaimard = *Muscicapa ochrocephala* Gmelin.
Certhiparus Lafresnaye, 1842, Rev. Zool., Paris 5: 69—type (by original designation) *Parus senilis* Du Bus de Gisignies = *Fringilla albicilla* Lesson.
Clitonyx Reichenbach, 1851, Hanb. spec. Ornith. 1: 167.
Finschia Hutton, 1903, Ibis 1903: 319—type (by original designation) *Parus novaeseelandiae* Gmelin.

See Sibley & Ahlquist (1987, Emu 87: 63–66) and Keast (1977, Notornis 14: 50–58) for discussions of the relationships of this genus. Note: Buller (1882) placed *albicilla* and *ochrocephala* in the genus *Orthonyx*, now restricted to the two logrunners of Australia and New Guinea.

347   **Mohoua albicilla** (Lesson)

Whitehead (Popokatea)

Fringilla albicilla Lesson, 1830, *in* Duperrey, Voyage Coquille, Zool. 1 (livr. 15): 662 — Bay of Islands.

North Island only: mainland from Te Aroha and East Cape southwards; Little Barrier and Kapiti Islands. Successfully transferred from Little Barrier to Tiritiri Island (1989). Has colonised exotic pine forests in central North Island. Apparently now extinct on Rakitu (Arid) Island, east of Great Barrier, where last seen 1957 (Bellingham *et al.* 1982, Tane 28: 141–147). Subfossil from cave and dune sites throughout North Island.

GILL, B.J.; McLEAN, I.G. 1986. Morphometrics of the Whitehead *Mohoua albicilla* on Little Barrier Island, New Zealand. NZ J. Zool. 13: 267–271.

GIBB, J.A. 1961. Ecology of the birds of Kaingaroa forest. Proc. NZ Ecol. Soc. 8: 29–38.

MOEED, A.; FITZGERALD, B.M. 1982. Foods of insectivorous birds in forest of the Orongorongo Valley, Wellington, New Zealand. NZ J. Zool. 9: 391–403.

ROBERTSON, H. A.; WHITAKER, A. H.; FITZGERALD, B. M. 1983. Morphometrics of forest birds in the Orongorongo Valley, Wellington, New Zealand. NZ J. Zool. 10: 87–98.

48 **Mohoua ochrocephala** (Gmelin)
Yellowhead (Mohua)

Muscicapa ochrocephala Gmelin, 1789, Syst. Nat. 1: 944; based on "Yellow-headed Flycatcher" of Latham, 1783, General Synop. Birds 2: 342—Queen Charlotte Sound.

New Zealand: formerly widespread in South and Stewart Island forests, now well established only in Fiordland and at Arthur's Pass National Park; very rare or absent elsewhere. Subfossil from cave sites in northwest Nelson and a swamp site at Wanaka.

CUNNINGHAM, J. B.; HOLDAWAY, R. N. 1986. Morphology and head colour in the Yellowhead. Notornis 33: 33–36.

GAZE, P. D. 1985. Distribution of Yellowheads (*Mohoua ochrocephala*) in New Zealand. Notornis 32: 261–269.

READ, A. F. 1987. The breeding and flocking behaviour of Yellowheads at Arthur's Pass National Park. Notornis 34: 11–18.

49 **Mohoua novaeseelandiae** (Gmelin)
Brown Creeper (Pipipi)

Parus novaeseelandiae Gmelin, 1789, Syst. Nat. 1: 1013; based on "New Zealand Titmouse" of Latham, 1783, General Synop. Birds 2: 558—Dusky Bay (= Dusky Sound).

New Zealand: widespread in South and Stewart Island forests and scrub; on several islands off Stewart Island and in the Marlborough Sounds. No subfossil records.

CUNNINGHAM, J. B. 1984. Differentiating the sexes of the Brown Creeper. Notornis 31: 19–22.

GILL, B. J.; POWLESLAND, M. H.; POWLESLAND, R. G. 1980. Notes on the Brown Creeper (*Finschia novaeseelandiae*). Notornis 27: 129–132.

HENDERSON, N. M. 1977. Autumn and winter flocking behaviour of the Brown Creeper (*Finschia novaeseelandiae*). Mauri Ora 5: 75–88.

Family **ACANTHIZIDAE**: Australasian Warblers
Subfamily ACANTHIZINAE: Australasian Warblers
Genus **Gerygone** Gould

Gerygone Gould, 1841, *in* G. Grey, Journ. Two Exped. Discovery Northwest Western Australia, 2: 417—new name for *Psilopus* Gould, 1838, preoccupied by *Psilopus* Meigen, 1824.

Pseudogerygone Sharpe, 1879, Notes Leyden Mus. 1: 29—type (by original designation) *Gerygone personata* Gould.

Hapolorhynchus Reichenow, 1908, J. für Ornith. 56: 488—type (by original designation) *Pseudogerygone albofrontata* G. R. Gray.

Maorigerygone Mathews and Iredale, 1913, Ibis 1913: 437—type (by original designation) *Curruca igata* Quoy and Gaimard.

350 **Gerygone igata** (Quoy and Gaimard)

Grey Warbler (Riroriro)

Curruca igata Quoy and Gaimard, 1830, *in* Dumont d'Urville, Voyage Astrolabe, Zool. 1: 201; Atlas, 1833, Oiseaux, pl.11, fig. 2 — Tasman Bay, Cook Strait.
Gerygone flaviventris G. R. Gray, 1844, *in* Richardson and J. E. Gray (eds.), Zool. Voyage Erebus and Terror, 1 (Birds): 5; pl.4, fig. 1 — Bay of Islands.
Gerygone assimilis Buller, 1865, Essay on the ornithology of NZ: 9 — New Zealand.
Gerygone aucklandica von Pelzeln, 1869, Reise der Fregatte Novara um die Erde, Voegel: 65 — New Zealand.
Gerygone sylvestris Potts, 1873, Trans. NZ Inst. 5: 177 — near Lake Mapourika, Westland.
Pseudogerygone macleani Ogilvie-Grant, 1907, Ibis 1907: 545 — Mt Maungahaumi, northwest of Poverty Bay (2,000 feet altitude).

New Zealand: common throughout on North, South and Stewart Islands and on most offshore islands including the Three Kings group. Occurs up to 1400–1500 m a.s.l. Occasionally visits The Snares, but has not established. Subfossil at two South Island caves; no North Island subfossil records.

Formerly considered conspecific with *G. insularis* (Lord Howe I., extinct), *G. modesta* (Norfolk I.) and some Australian populations, but this no longer seems valid.

GILL, B.J. 1982. Breeding of the Grey Warbler *Gerygone igata* at Kaikoura, New Zealand. Ibis 124: 123–147.
GILL, B.J. 1982. The Grey Warbler's care of nestlings: a comparison between unparasitised broods and those comprising a Shining Bronze-cuckoo. Emu 82: 177–181.
GILL, B.J. 1983. Breeding habits of the Grey Warbler (*Gerygone igata*). Notornis 30: 137–165.

351 **Gerygone albofrontata** Gray

Chatham Island Warbler

Gerygone? albofrontata G. R. Gray, 1844, *in* Richardson and J. E. Gray (eds.), Zool. Voyage Erebus and Terror, 1 (Birds): 5, pl.4, fig. 2 — Chatham Islands.

Chatham Islands: present on Chatham (common in the south, rare or absent in the north), Houruakopara, Pitt, South East (abundant), Mangere (abundant), Little Mangere and Star Keys. A few subfossil cave, dune and midden records on Chatham Island.

DENNISON, M.D.; ROBERTSON, H.A.; CROUCHLEY, D. 1984. Breeding of the Chatham Island Warbler (*Gerygone albofrontata*). Notornis 31: 97–105.
ROBERTSON, H.A.; DENNISON, M.D. 1984. Sexual dimorphism of the Chatham Island Warbler *Gerygone albofrontata*. Emu 84: 103–107.

Family **MONARCHIDAE**: Monarch Flycatchers

Subfamily MONARCHINAE: Monarch Flycatchers

Genus **Myiagra** Vigors and Horsfield

Myiagra Vigors and Horsfield, 1827, Trans. Linn. Soc. Lond. 15: 250 — type (by subsequent designation) *Myiagra rubeculoides* Vigors and Horsfield = *Todus rubecula* Latham (G. R. Grav. 1840. List Gen. Birds, p.32).

352 **Myiagra cyanoleuca** (Vieillot)

Satin Flycatcher

Platyrhynchos cyanoleucus Vieillot, 1818, Nouv. Dict. Hist. Nat., nouv. ed., 27: 11 — Timor; error: Sydney, New South Wales *fide* Mathews, 1930, Syst. Avium Australasianarum, p.502.

Eastern Australia from Cape York to Tasmania; migratory from southern part of range to northern Queensland and New Guinea.

Vagrant to New Zealand: sight record, Hexton, near Gisborne, June 1963; one found dead, Motueka, Dec 1988.

BLACKBURN, A. 1963. The Satin Flycatcher: a new record for New Zealand. Notornis 10: 262–265.

Subfamily RHIPIDURINAE: Fantails
Genus **Rhipidura** Vigors and Horsfield

Rhipidura Vigors and Horsfield, 1827, Trans. Linn. Soc. Lond. 15: 246 — type (by subsequent designation) (G. R. Gray, 1840, List Gen. Birds, p.32) *Muscicapa flabellifera* Gmelin.

353 **Rhipidura fuliginosa** (Sparrman)

Grey/New Zealand Fantail

Australia; New Zealand (including Chathams); Norfolk Island; Lord Howe Island (extinct); New Caledonia; Vanuatu and Banks Islands; San Cristobal, Solomon Islands.

FLEMING, C. A. 1949. Pied Fantails. NZ Bird Notes 3: 188–190.

Rhipidura fuliginosa placabilis Bangs

North Island Fantail (Piwakawaka)

Rhipidura flabellifera kempi Mathews and Iredale, 1913, Ibis, p.441 — North Island, New Zealand.

Rhipidura flabellifera placabilis Bangs, 1921, Bull. Am. Mus. Nat. Hist. 44: 583. New name for *Rhipidura flabellifera kempi* Mathews and Iredale, 1913, preoccupied by *Rhipidura rufifrons kempi* Mathews, 1912.

Rhipidura flabellifera melandae (*sic*) Mathews, 1926, Bull. Br. Ornith. Club 47: 40. New name for *Rhipidura flabellifera kempi* Mathews and Iredale, 1913, preoccupied as above.

North Island and offshore islands. Common throughout both in residual forest and in settled districts wherever there are trees and shrubs; accepted modified conditions from the earliest days of European settlement. Scattered subfossil and midden records.

BLACKBURN, A. 1965. Breeding of the North Island Fantail. Notornis 12: 127–137.

McLEAN, I. G. 1984. Breeding by Fantails (*Rhipidura fuliginosa*) on Tiritiri Island. Notornis 31: 279–283.

McLEAN, I. G. 1989. Feeding behaviour of the Fantail (*Rhipidura fuliginosa*). Notornis 36: 99–106.

McLEAN, I. G.; JENKINS, P. F. 1980. Breeding and development of the New Zealand Fantail *Rhipidura fuliginosa*. Notornis 27: 105–113.

Rhipidura fuliginosa fuliginosa (Sparrman)
South Island Fantail (Piwakawaka)

Muscicapa fuliginosa Sparrman, 1787, Mus. Carlsonianum, fasc. 2, no.47 and pl. — "In Deserto Africano inter rivulum Heuj et Fontem Quamedacka" = South Island, New Zealand.

Muscicapa flabellifera Gmelin, 1789, Syst. Nat. 1: 943; based on "Fantail Flycatcher" of Latham, 1783, General Synop, Birds, 2, p.340, pl.49 — Dusky Sound, New Zealand *ex* Latham.

South Island; Stewart Island and outliers. Status as in the previous subspecies. A few scattered subfossil and midden records.

The species is dimorphic in the South Island, the proportion of "black" (melanistic) to "pied" birds varying locally; melanism is rare in the North Island subspecies.

CRAIG, J. L. 1972. Investigation of the mechanism maintaining polymorphism in the New Zealand Fantail, *Rhipidura fuliginosa* (Sparrman). Notornis 19: 42–55.

POWLESLAND, M. H. 1982. A breeding study of the South Island Fantail (*Rhipidura fuliginosa fuliginosa*). Notornis 29: 181–195.

Rhipidura fuliginosa penita Bangs
Chatham Island Fantail

Rhipidura flabillifera (sic) penitus Bangs, 1911, Proc. Biol. Soc. Washington 24: 41 — Chatham Islands.

Chatham, Pitt and South East Islands of the Chatham group. A few subfossil cave, dune and midden records in Chatham Island.

DENNISON, M. D.; DENNISON, T. C.; ROBERTSON, H. A. 1978. Notes on the Chatham Island Fantail. Notornis 25: 254–255.

DENNISON, M. D.; DENNISON, T. C.; ROBERTSON, H. A. 1979. Breeding of the Chatham Island Fantail. Notornis 26: 392–395.

FLEMING, C. A. 1939. Birds of the Chatham Islands, pt.1. Emu 38: 380–413; 492–509.

SIBSON, R. B. 1980. Why is the Chatham Island Fantail *penitus*? Notornis 27: 93.

Family **EOPSALTRIIDAE**: Australasian Robins

Genus **Petroica** Swainson

Petroica Swainson, 1830, Zool. Illustr., ser. 2, pt.8, pl.36 and text — type (by monotypy) *Muscicapa multicolor* Gmelin.

Miro Lesson, ?1830, Traité Ornith., livr. 5, p.389 — type (by monotypy) *Muscicapa longipes* Garnot.

Myiomoira Reichenbach, 1850, Avium Syst. Nat., pl.67 — type (by monotypy) *Muscicapa toitoi* Lesson.

FLEMING, C. A. 1950. New Zealand flycatchers of the Genus *Petroica* Swainson. Trans. Roy. Soc. NZ 78: (pt.1) 14–47, (pt.2) 127–160.

Subgenus **Petroica**

54 **Petroica macrocephala** (Gmelin)

New Zealand Tomtit

New Zealand. North, South, Stewart, Chatham and Auckland Islands (see under subspecies); on Snares Islands, an especially well-defined (black) subspecies. Still widely established in remaining native forests and scrublands, and has entered many exotic forests, but not a permanent inhabitant of gardens and settled areas.

Petroica macrocephala toitoi (Lesson)

North Island Tomtit (Miromiro)

Muscicapa toitoi Lesson, 1828, Man. Orn. 1: 188 — New Zealand.

North Island and certain larger offshore islands: Hen and Chickens, Little and Great Barrier, Kapiti. Subfossil from a number of caves (at one site possibly from midden debris).

BISSET, J. 1978. Song and breeding behaviour in the Pied Tit. Notornis 25: 246.
GIBB, J. A. 1961. Ecology of the birds of Kaingaroa Forest. Proc. NZ Ecol. Soc. 8: 29–38.
SKINNER, J. F. 1978. Status of the Pied Tit (*Petroica macrocephala toitoi*) in the Waitakere Range, Auckland. Notornis 25: 299–302.

Petroica macrocephala macrocephala (Gmelin)

South Island Tomtit (Ngiru-ngiru)

Parus macrocephalus Gmelin, 1789, Syst. Nat. 1: 1013; based on "Great-headed Titmouse" of Latham, 1783, General Synop. Birds 2: 557 — Queen Charlotte Sound, New Zealand, *ex* Latham.

South Island, Stewart Island and outliers, Solander Island. Subfossil from a few cave sites and a swamp (Pyramid Valley).

CLOUT, M. N. 1980. Comparisons of bird populations in exotic plantations and native forest. NZ J. Ecol. 3: 159–160.
CLOUT, M. N.; GAZE, P. D. 1984. Effects of plantation forestry on birds in New Zealand. J. Applied Ecol. 21: 795–815

Petroica macrocephala chathamensis Fleming

Chatham Island Tomtit

Petroica macrocephala chathamensis Fleming, 1950, Trans. Roy. Soc. NZ 78: 36 — Rangatira (= South-East) Island, Chatham Islands.

Chatham Islands: extinct since c. 1975 on Chatham Island; well established in residual forest and scrub on Pitt, Mangere, Little Mangere and South East Islands. No subfossil records.

FLEMING, C. A. 1939. Birds of the Chatham Islands, pt.1. Emu 38: 380–413; 492–509.

Petroica macrocephala dannefaerdi (Rothschild)
Snares Island Tomtit

Miro dannefaerdi Rothschild, 1894, Novit. Zool. 1: 688 — Snares Islands.

Snares Islands, inhabiting mainly the *Olearia lyallii* scrub that clothes much of the main island but also in tussock areas.

BEST, H. A. 1975. The Black Tomtit. Wildlife — A Review 6: 32–37.
STEAD, E. F. 1948. Bird Life on the Snares. NZ Bird Notes 3: 69–80.

Petroica macrocephala marrineri (Mathews and Iredale)
Auckland Island Tomtit

Myiomoira macrocephala marrineri Mathews and Iredale, 1913, Ibis, p.436 — Auckland Islands.

Auckland Islands: forest and scrub on Auckland, Adams, Ocean, Rose, Ewing, and Enderby Islands.

Subgenus Miro

355   ## Petroica australis (Sparrman)
New Zealand Robin

New Zealand. North Island, Little Barrier, Kapiti; South Island; Stewart Island and outliers. Mainly restricted to larger residual native forests, but also established in scrub and older pine plantations in some districts.

Petroica australis longipes (Garnot)
North Island Robin (Toutouwai)

Muscicapa longipes Garnot, 1827, *in* Duperry, Voyage Coquille, Zool. Atlas, 1, livr. 3, pl.19, fig. 1 (18 April); 1829, 1, livr. 13, p.594 (21 November) — Bay of Islands, New Zealand.

Native and older exotic forests of the western and central North Island (approximately between 37°50' and 40°S); Little Barrier and Kapiti. Subfossil and midden records from many localities, including areas well outside the present range (and, in the Far North, outside the historical range) of the subspecies.

GIBB, J. A. 1961. Ecology of the birds of Kaingaroa Forest. Proc. NZ Ecol. Soc. 8: 29–38.
PARKIN, C. H.; PARKIN, M. 1952. A North Island Robin nesting record. Notornis 4: 174.

Petroica australis australis (Sparrman)
South Island Robin (Toutouwai)

Turdus australis Sparrman, 1788, Mus. Carlsonianum, pt.3, no.69 — Dusky Sound, New Zealand.
Turdus ochrotarsus J. R. Forster, 1844, Descr. Animal. Itinere Maris Australis Terras, p.82 — South Island.
Miro bulleri Buller (*ex* Sharpe MS), 1906, Suppl. Birds New Zealand, 2, p.123 — Karamea Saddle, South Island.

South Island: native and older exotic forests of Nelson, where it reaches its greatest abundance; native forests of Fiordland; otherwise of restricted and local distribution (Marlborough, Canterbury and east Otago). Widely distributed subfossil and midden records, a number outside the present range of the subspecies.

CLOUT, M.N. 1980. Comparisons of bird populations in exotic plantations and native forest. NZ J. Ecol. 3: 159–160.

FLACK, J.A.D. 1973. Robin research—a progress report. Wildlife—A Review 4: 28–36.

FLACK, J.A.D. 1976. The use of the frontal spot and crown feathers in inter- and intraspecific display by the South Island Robin *Petroica australis australis*. Notornis 23: 90–106.

POWLESLAND, R.G. 1981. The foraging behaviour of the South Island Robin. Notornis 28: 89–102.

Petroica australis rakiura Fleming

Stewart Island Robin

Petroica (Miro) australis rakiura Fleming, 1950, Trans. Roy. Soc. NZ 78: 141—Jacques Lee Island, off east coast of Stewart Island.

Stewart Island and outliers (Jacky Lee, Green and the Wedge group).

356 ## Petroica traversi (Buller)

Black Robin

Miro traversi Buller, 1872, Birds New Zealand, p.123—Chatham Islands.
Miro traversi Hutton, 1872, Ibis, p.245—Chatham Islands.

Chatham Islands. Originally presumably on all the larger islands. By 1937 restricted to Little Mangere Island (Fleming 1939); when the Wildlife Service management programme began in 1976 the total remaining population (5 males, 2 females) on Little Mangere transferred to Mangere Island. Now established and breeding on Mangere and South East Islands. Subfossil from caves and dunes on Chatham Island; midden on Chatham and Mangere Islands.

CEMMICK, D.; VEITCH, D. 1985. Black Robin Country. Auckland: Hodder and Stoughton.

FLEMING, C.A. 1939. Birds of the Chatham Islands, pt.1. Emu 38: 380–413; 492–509.

MERTON, D.V. 1983. Chatham Islands Black Robin. Wildlife—A Review 12: 12–16.

Family ZOSTEROPIDAE: White-eyes

Genus Zosterops Vigors and Horsfield

Zosterops Vigors and Horsfield, 1826, Trans. Linn. Soc. Lond. 15: 234—type (by subsequent designation) *Motacilla maderaspatana* Linnaeus (Lesson, 1828, Man. Orn. 1: 286).

357   **Zosterops lateralis** (Latham)

Silvereye

Taxonomic studies, combined with banding studies on local migration, have not yet fully unravelled variation in this species, which extends round the border of the Australian continent from Western Australia to Cape York Peninsula. A western race (*gouldi*) and a resident race in the Capricorn and Bunker groups (Great Barrier Reef) (*chlorocephala*) are generally accepted, the remaining, i.e. eastern, south-eastern and Tasmanian forms being regarded as a complex of variable races under the following subspecies. Other subspecies on south-western Pacific Islands (New Caledonia, Loyalty, Vanuatu, Banks, Fiji).

Note: We follow the Australian *Atlas* in using the unqualified vernacular "Silvereye"; this species is alternatively known in Australia as the Grey-breasted (or Grey-backed) Silvereye. *Zosterops* elsewhere are commonly known as "White-eyes" (e.g. Japanese White-eye); the other Australian species are known respectively as the Pale Silvereye (or White-eye) (*Z. citrinella*) and Yellow Silvereye (or White-eye) (*Z. lutea*).

Zosterops lateralis lateralis (Latham)

Silvereye (Tauhou)

Sylvia lateralis Latham, 1801, Index Orn., suppl., p.55 — Tasmania (? or mainland).
A complex (see above) incorporating a number of described subspecies, ranging from the Cape York Peninsula through eastern Australia to South Australia and Tasmania. Migration in Australian populations is well established, especially in the Tasmanian population, but further north is apparently highly irregular; birds of southern origin, especially those from Tasmania, are recognisable by having richer and darker chestnut coloration on the flanks.

New Zealand was apparently colonised permanently by Silvereyes from southeastern Australia in 1856, when large numbers were first recorded; before this, noticed by explorers and settlers as early as 1832 (Milford Sound) and 1851 (Otago); the bird had not been known to the Maori, and on arrival in 1856 was given the name "tauhou" (meaning stranger). Now perhaps the commonest non-introduced passerine in New Zealand, being found in all settled districts in orchards and gardens, in exotic plantations, and in native forest and scrub. Has reached Kermadecs, Chathams, Snares, Auckland, Antipodes and Campbell Islands; a straggler to Macquarie Island. Colonised Norfolk Island (possibly from New Zealand) in 1904.

FLEMING, C. A. 1943. Notes on the life history of the Silvereye, based on colour-banding. Emu 42: 173–217.

KIKKAWA, J. 1961. Social behaviour of the White-eye *Zosterops lateralis* in winter flocks. Ibis 103a: 428–442.

KIKKAWA, J. 1962. Wintering Silvereyes at bird tables in the Dunedin area. Notornis 9: 280–291.

MEES, G. F. 1957, 1961, 1969. A systematic review of the Indo–Australian Zosteropidae (Pts. I, II and III). Zool. Verhandl., Leiden, 35: 1–204; 50: 1–168; 102: 1–390.

Family **MELIPHAGIDAE**: Honeyeaters
Genus **Notiomystis** Richmond

Pogonornis G. R. Gray, 1846, Gen. Birds, 1, p.123 — type (by monotypy) *Meliphaga cincta* Du Bus. Not *Pogonornis* Billberg, 1828 (Aves); cf. Mathews and Iredale, 1913, Austral Avian Record, 2: 40.

Notiomystis Richmond, 1908, Proc. U.S. Nat. Mus. 35: 634. New name for *Pogonornis* Gray, preoccupied.

358   **Notiomystis cincta** (Du Bus)

Stitchbird (Hihi)

Meliphaga cincta Du Bus, 1839, Bull. Acad. Roy. Sci. Bruxelles 6(1): 295 — Nouvelle-Zelande (= North Island, New Zealand).

Notiomystis cincta hautura Mathews, 1935, Bull. Br. Ornith. Club 55: 159 — Little Barrier Island, New Zealand.

New Zealand: recorded, living or subfossil, only from the North Island. Up to the early 1870s comparatively common in the southern parts of the North Island (as far north as the Waikato area), as well as on Little and Great Barrier Islands and Kapiti; a rapid decline then occurred and by 1885 the species had vanished from the mainland, Great Barrier and Kapiti, remaining only on Little Barrier Island. Subfossil records from Far North sand dune sites indicate that its original distribution included the whole of the North Island; subfossil from the King Country and Hawke's Bay. Causes of decline on mainland unknown. Successful transfers have recently been made to Hen and Kapiti Islands; also transferred to Cuvier Island but without success.

ANGEHR, G. R. 1984. Establishment of the Stitchbird on Hen Island. Notornis 31: 175–177.

ANGEHR, G. R. 1985. Stitchbird. Dunedin: John McIndoe and NZ Wildlife Service. 25pp.

CRAIG, J. L. 1985. Status and foraging in New Zealand honeyeaters, in Symposium on the Ecology of Honeyeaters, held at Auckland, April, 1985. NZ J. Zool. 12: 589–597.

CRAIG, J. L.; STEWART, A M; DOUGLAS, M. E. 1981. The foraging of New Zealand honeyeaters. NZ J. Zool. 8: 87–91.

RASCH, G. 1985. The ecology of cavity nesting in the stitchbird (*Notiomystis cincta*), in Symposium on the Ecology of Honeyeaters, held at Auckland, April, 1985. NZ J. Zool. 12: 637–642.

RASCH, G. 1989. Cavity nesting in Stitchbirds and the use of artificial nest sites. Notornis 36: 27–36.

Genus **Anthornis** Gray

Anthornis G. R. Gray, 1840, List Gen. Birds, ed. 1, p.15—type (by original designation) *Certhia melanura* Sparrman.

359   **Anthornis melanura** (Sparrman)

Bellbird

New Zealand. North, South and Stewart Islands, and many mainland offshore islands including the Three Kings; Chatham and Auckland Islands.

BARTLE, J. A.; SAGAR, P. M. 1987. Intraspecific variation in the New Zealand Bellbird *Anthornis melanura*. Notornis 34: 253–306.

Anthornis melanura obscura Falla

Three Kings Bellbird

Anthornis melanura obscura Falla, 1948, Rec. Auck. Inst. Mus. 3: 337—Three Kings Islands, New Zealand.

Three Kings Islands: in forest and scrub, throughout the group.

TURBOTT, E. G.; BUDDLE, G. A. 1948. Birds of the Three Kings Islands. Rec. Auck. Inst. Mus. 3: 319–336.

Anthornis melanura oneho Bartle and Sagar

Poor Knights Bellbird

Anthornis melanura oneho Bartle and Sagar, 1987, Notornis 34: 297—Poor Knights Islands, New Zealand.

Poor Knights Islands: throughout the group.

BARTLE, J. A.; SAGAR. P. M. 1987. Intraspecific variation in the New Zealand Bellbird *Anthornis melanura*. Notornis 34: 253–306.

SAGAR, P. M. 1985. Breeding of the bellbird on the Poor Knights Islands, New Zealand. In Symposium on the Ecology of Honeyeaters, held at Auckland, April, 1985. NZ J. Zool. 12: 643–648.

Anthornis melanura melanura (Sparrman)

Bellbird (Korimako, Makomako)

Certhia melanura Sparrman, 1786, Mus. Carls. 1(5)—Promontorium Bonae Spei (error = Queen Charlotte Sound, New Zealand).

Philedon dumerilii Lesson and Garnot, 1828, Voy. Coquille, Zool., 1, atlas, livr. 6, pl.21, fig. 1; and 1829, livr. 9, p.416, footnote; and 1830, livr. 14, p.644—Nouvelle-Zelande (= Bay of Islands, New Zealand).

Anthornis melanura incoronata Bangs, 1911, Proc. Biol. Soc. Washington 24: 23—Auckland Islands.

North, South and Stewart Islands and many offshore islands: present and often common throughout except on the mainland around and north of Auckland (previously also abundant on the mainland in Auckland and Northland but became locally extinct in these areas in the 1860s).* Occurs in forest and forest rem-

---

* In Northland may occur on the mainland as a stray opposite the offshore islands.

nants; also in exotic vegetation of orchards, gardens, etc., especially in the South Island, and in large exotic plantations. On the Auckland Islands, in forest throughout.

Subfossil and midden records from widely scattered sites in both North and South Islands.

CRAIG, J. L. 1985. Status and foraging in New Zealand honeyeaters. In Symposium on the Ecology of Honeyeaters, held at Auckland, April, 1985. NZ J. Zool. 12: 589–597.

CRAIG, J. L. 1985. Wing slots of bellbirds *Anthornis melanura* (Aves: Meliphagidae). In Symposium on the Ecology of Honeyeaters, held at Auckland, April, 1985. NZ J. Zool. 12: 431–432.

CRAIG, J. L.; DOUGLAS, M. E. 1984. Bellbirds in Auckland and Northland. Notornis 31: 82–86.

CRAIG, J. L.; STEWART, A. M.; DOUGLAS, M. E. 1981. The foraging of New Zealand honeyeaters. NZ J. Zool. 8: 87–91.

GAZE, P. D.; CLOUT, M. N. 1983. Honeydew and its importance to birds in beech forests of South Island, New Zealand. NZ J. Ecol. 6: 33–38.

Anthornis melanura melanocephala Gray
Chatham Island Bellbird

Anthornis melanocephala G. R. Gray. 1843, *in* Dieffenbach's Travels in New Zealand, 2, p.188 — Chatham Islands.

Formerly throughout the Chatham group; finally on Mangere Island; extinct since about 1906. Subfossil from caves and dunes on Chatham Island; midden on Chatham and Mangere Islands.

FLEMING, C. A. 1939. Birds of the Chatham Islands, pt.1. Emu 38: 380–413, 492–509.

Genus **Prosthemadera** Gray

Prosthemadera G. R. Gray, 1840, List Gen. Birds, ed. 1, p.15 — type (by original designation) *Merops cincinnatus* Latham = *Merops novaeseelandiae* Gmelin.

360 ## **Prosthemadera novaeseelandiae** (Gmelin)
Tui

New Zealand. North, South and Stewart Islands, and larger offshore islands (including, formerly, Three Kings); Kermadec, Auckland and Chatham Islands.

Prosthemadera novaeseelandiae novaeseelandiae (Gmelin)
Tui

Merops novaeseelandiae Gmelin, 1788, Syst. Nat. 1(1). 464 — Nova Seelandia (= Queen Charlotte Sound, New Zealand).

Meliphaga novaehollandiae Stephens, 1826, *in* Shaw, General Zool. 14: 259 — New Zealand.

Prosthemadera novaeseelandiae phoebe Kemp, 1912, Austral Avian Rec. 1: 124 — Umawera, Hokianga, New Zealand.

Prosthemadera novaeseelandiae kwini Kemp, 1912, Austral Avian Rec. 1: 124 — Auckland Islands.

Prosthemadera novaeseelandiae kermadecensis Mathews and Iredale, 1914, Austral Avian Rec. 2: 113—Sunday Island, Kermadec Islands.

North, South and Stewart Islands and larger offshore islands (including formerly Three Kings: recorded 1887); Kermadec and Auckland Islands. Widespread in forest and forest remnants. Present and breeding in some settled districts, including urban areas (especially greater Auckland), but mainly an occasional visitor in larger exotic plantations. In subfossil and midden deposits, abundant in both North and South Islands; predominant passerine in midden records.

BERGQUIST, C. A. L. 1985. Movements of groups of tui (*Prosthemadera novaeseelandiae*) in winter and settlement of juvenile tui in summer, in Symposium on the Ecology of Honeyeaters, held at Auckland, April, 1985. NZ J. Zool. 12: 569–571

BERGQUIST, C. A. L. 1985. Differences in the diet of the male and female tui (*Prosthemadera novaeseelandiae*; Meliphagidae), in Symposium on the Ecology of Honeyeaters, held at Auckland, April, 1985. NZ J. Zool. 12: 573–576.

BERGQUIST, C. A. L.; CRAIG, J. L. 1988. Competitive asymmetries, status, and breeding success of tui (Meliphagidae) at an established feeding station. NZ J. Zool. 15: 369–380.

CRAIG, J. L. 1985. Status and foraging in New Zealand Honeyeaters, in Symposium on the Ecology of Honeyeaters, held at Auckland, April, 1985, NZ J. Zool. 12: 589–597.

CRAIG, J. L.; STEWART, A. M.; DOUGLAS, M. E. 1981. The foraging of New Zealand honeyeaters. NZ J. Zool. 8: 87–91.

ONLEY, D. J. 1986. A method of ageing the Tui (*Prosthemadera novaeseelandiae*) and its use in assessing body measurements. Notornis 33: 45–49.

STEWART, A. M.; CRAIG, J. L. 1985. Movements, status, access to nectar, and spatial organisation of the tui, in Symposium on the Ecology of Honeyeaters, held at Auckland, April, 1985. NZ J. Zool. 12: 649–666.

Prosthemadera novaeseelandiae chathamensis Hartert
Chatham Island Tui

Prosthemadera novaeseelandiae chathamensis Hartert, 1928, Novit. Zool. 34: 204—Chatham Islands.

Chatham Islands: now rare on the main island, in moderate numbers on Pitt Island; common on South East Island; visitor to Mangere Island and Star Keys. Subfossil and midden on Chatham Island.

FLEMING, C. A. 1939. Birds of the Chatham Islands, pt.1. Emu 38: 380–413, 492–509.

Genus **Anthochaera** Vigors and Horsfield

Anthochaera Vigors and Horsfield, 1827, Trans. Linn. Soc. Lond. 15: 320—type (by subsequent designation) *Certhia mellivora* Latham = *Merops chrysopterus* Latham (Gadow, 1884, Cat. Birds Brit. Mus. 9, p.262).

361 **Anthochaera carunculata** (White)

Red Wattlebird

Merops carunculata White, Journ. Voy. New South Wales, ed. 1, p.240 — New South Wales cf. Mathews, 1925, Birds Aust. 12, pp.64–65.

Southeastern, southern and southwestern Australia, including coastal Great Australian Bight; performs altitudinal movements and at least partially migratory south to north.

Two New Zealand records: Matakana (about 1865) and Rahotu, Taranaki (1882).

BULLER, W. L. 1888. A History of the Birds of New Zealand, 2nd ed., vol. 1, pp.106–107. London: the author.

SIBSON, R. B. 1987. More Laishleyana: Red Wattlebird and White-faced Heron. Notornis 34: 81–82.

Family **EMBERIZIDAE**: Buntings, Cardinals, Tanagers, etc

Subfamily EMBERIZINAE: Buntings, American Sparrows

Genus **Emberiza** Linnaeus

Emberiza Linnaeus, 1758, Syst. Nat., ed. 10, 1: 176 — type (by subsequent designation) *Emberiza citrinella* Linnaeus.

*362 **Emberiza citrinella** Linnaeus

Yellowhammer

Emberiza citrinella Linnaeus, 1758, Syst. Nat., ed. 10, 1: 177 — "habitat in Europa"; restricted to Sweden.

Europe and W. Asia, wintering to SW and central Asia and N. Africa.

New Zealand: successfully introduced to both main islands during the 1860s. Now common from North Cape to Stewart Island, and has spread to the Chatham and Kermadec Islands. Strays have reached Lord Howe, Campbell and Snares Islands. Mainly a bird of open country, especially farmland with nearby scrub. Winter flocks are common where hay has been fed to farm stock, and may also appear in city parks and along tide lines.

HARRISON, J. M. 1955. New Zealand Yellow Buntings (Yellowhammers). Notornis 6: 176–177.

NIETHAMMER, G. 1971. Zur Taxonomie europaischer, in Neuseeland eingebürgerter Vögel. J. für Ornithol. 112: 202–226.

***363 Emberiza cirlus** Linnaeus

Cirl Bunting

Emberiza cirlus Linnaeus, 1766, Syst. Nat., ed. 12, 1: 311 — S. Europe.

Central and southern Europe (including southern England) to Mediterranean islands, Asia Minor and N. Africa. Mainly sedentary.

New Zealand: only two small introductions have been documented (7 birds to Otago in 1871 and 4 to Wellington in 1880–81), but probably others were made and not recorded. Remains by far the rarest of the introduced passerines (106 records during the 1969–79 *Atlas* survey cf. 8351 for Yellowhammer). Recent North Island records, sporadic and isolated, are from Ahuroa (North Auckland), Gisborne, Hawke's Bay and near Wellington. The species is more common in the South Island, especially in parts of Nelson, Marlborough, Canterbury and Otago. Most records are from farmland with hedge-rows or scattered scrub on slopes.

TAYLOR, T.J. 1978. The Cirl Bunting in Marlborough. Notornis 25: 249–251.

Family **FRINGILLIDAE**: Finches
Subfamily FRINGILLINAE: True Finches
Genus **Fringilla** Linnaeus

Fringilla Linnaeus, 1758, Syst. Nat., ed. 10, 1: 179 — type (by subsequent designation) *Fringilla coelebs* Linnaeus.

***364 Fringilla coelebs** Linnaeus

Chaffinch

Fringilla coelebs Linnaeus, 1758, Syst. Nat., ed. 10, 1: 179 — "Europe"; restricted to Sweden.

Europe, western and central Asia, and N.W. Africa; northern populations migratory.

New Zealand: introduced on several occasions during the 1860s and 1870s to both the North and South Islands. Now one of the commonest and most widely distributed birds throughout the three main islands of New Zealand, and it has spread to the Chatham, Auckland and Campbell Islands. This, the second most frequently recorded species in the 1969–79 *Atlas* survey, is common in city parks and gardens, farmland hedgerows and woodlots, orchards, scrub lands, pine forests and, to a lesser extent, native bush. Winter flocks occur on stubbles, and on pastures where hay has been fed to farm stock, and also along shore lines.

JENKINS, P. F.; BAKER, A.J. 1984. Mechanisms of song differentiation in introduced populations of chaffinches *Fringilla coelebs* in New Zealand. Ibis 126: 510–524.

MITCHELL, J.M. 1962. The bird problem in the natural regeneration of *Pinus radiata* in Kaingaroa Forest, New Zealand. Sylva 42: 4–10.
NIETHAMMER, G. 1971. Zur Taxonomie europaischer, in Neuseeland einge-burgerter Vögel. J. für Ornithol. 112: 202–226.
SIBSON, R.B. 1983. Winter flocking of Chaffinches in northern New Zealand. Notornis 30: 70–72.

Subfamily CARDUELINAE: Greenfinch, Goldfinch,
etc.
Genus **Carduelis** Brisson

Carduelis Brisson, 1760, Orn. 1: 36—type (by tautonymy) *"Carduelis"* = *Fringilla carduelis* Linnaeus.

*365 **Carduelis chloris** (Linnaeus)

Greenfinch

Loxia chloris Linnaeus, 1758, Syst. Nat., ed. 10, 1: 174—Europe; restricted to Sweden.

Europe, S.W. Asia, N. Africa; northern populations partly migratory.

New Zealand: introduced several times during the 1860's. Now common throughout both the North and South Islands; also present on Stewart Island, Chatham Islands and Norfolk Island, and has appeared as a straggler at Campbell Island and Raoul Island (Kermadecs). Particularly favours farmland shelter belts, edges of pine plantations, orchards and large gardens, but winter flocks range over open paddocks and along seashores.

GILLESPIE, G.D. 1982. Greenfinch feeding behaviour and impact on a rapeseed crop in Oamaru, New Zealand. NZ J. Zool. 9: 481–486.
McLENNAN, J.A.; MacMILLAN, B.W.H., 1985. The predators of eggs and chicks of Greenfinches in a mixed farming area in Hawke's Bay. Notornis 32: 95–100.
MacMILLAN, B.W.H. 1981. Food of House Sparrows and Greenfinches in a mixed farming district, Hawke's Bay, New Zealand. NZ J. Zool. 8: 93–104.
MacMILLAN, B.W.H. 1985. Breeding of Greenfinches in Hawke's Bay, New Zealand. Notornis 32: 85–93.
NIETHAMMER, G. 1971. Zur Taxonomie europaischer, in Neuseeland einge-burgerter Vögel. J. für Ornithol. 112: 202–226.

*366 **Carduelis carduelis** (Linnaeus)

Goldfinch

Fringilla carduelis Linnacus, 1758, Syst. Nat., ed. 10, 1: 180—juniper woods of Europe; restricted to Sweden.

Europe, central and S.W. Asia, N. Africa; northern populations migratory.

New Zealand: introduced to both North and South Islands on several occasions between 1862 and 1883. Now present throughout New Zealand, especially in orchards and farmlands, but scarce or absent at higher altitudes and in unbroken areas of native forest. Also present on Chathams, Snares and Auckland Islands, but has disappeared from Kermadec, Campbell and Antipodes Islands. Strays recorded from Norfolk and Macquarie Islands.

KEITH, K.; HINES, M. P. 1958. New and rare species of birds at Macquarie Island during 1951 and 1957. CSIRO Wildlife Research 3: 50–53.
NIETHAMMER, G. 1971. Zur Taxonomie europaischer, in Neuseeland einge-burgerter Vögel. J. für Ornithol. 112: 202–226.
SORENSEN, J. H. 1964. Birds of the Kermadec Islands. Notornis 11: 69–81.
WARHAM, J.; BELL, B. D. 1979. The birds of Antipodes Island, New Zealand. Notornis 26: 121–169.
WESTERSKOV, K. 1960. Birds of Campbell Island, NZ Dept. of Internal Affairs, Wildlife Publication No. 61. 83pp.

*367 **Carduelis flammea** (Linnaeus)

Redpoll

Fringilla flammea Linnaeus, 1758, Syst. Nat., ed. 10, 1: 182 — Europe; restricted to Norrland, Sweden, by Hartert, 1903, Vogel pal. Fauna, p.77.

Northern Eurasia and North America. Partial migrant; winters to southern Europe and Asia, and northern United States.

New Zealand: introduced to both North and South Islands on several occasions between 1862 and 1875. Now present from North Cape to Stewart Island in coastal sand dunes, farmlands, forest margins and subalpine scrub to at least 1750m above sea level, tending to be more common at higher altitudes than at sea level and in the South Island than the North. Has spread to Kermadec, Chatham, Snares, Antipodes, Auckland, Campbell and Macquarie Islands.

In the most recent New Zealand study of this species, Fennell *et al.* (1985) found that although in many characteristics the New Zealand birds deviated little from *C.f. cabaret* (Muller, 1776) (British Isles, and mountainous areas of central Europe), they could be differentiated from the latter race on the basis of other important characteristics; these authors accordingly recommended that "Redpolls in New Zealand should not be defined trinomially in terms of the European races". (For earlier discussions of the taxonomic status of the Redpoll in New Zealand, see Westerskov, 1953; Stenhouse, 1960b, 1962b; and Niethammer, 1971.)

FENNELL, J.; SAGAR, P. M.; FENNELL, J. S. 1985. Variation within the Redpolls of Canterbury. Notornis 32: 245–253.
FENNELL, J.; SAGAR, P. M. 1985. Variation between Redpolls in four southern New Zealand localities. Notornis 32: 254–256.
MERTON, D. V. 1970. Kermadec Islands Expedition Reports: A general account of the birdlife. Notornis 17: 147–199.
NIETHAMMER, G. 1971. Zur Taxonomie europaischer, in Neuseeland einge-burgerter Vögel. J. für Ornithol. 112: 202–226.

STENHOUSE, D. 1960a. The Redpoll and N.Z. agriculture. Canterbury Chamber of Commerce Agricultural Bulletin No. 366, 5pp.
STENHOUSE, D. 1960b. The Redpoll in New Zealand: Interbreeding sub-species. Nature 186: 488–490.
STENHOUSE, D. 1962a. A new habit of the Redpoll, *Carduelis flammea*, in New Zealand. Ibis 104: 250–252.
STENHOUSE, D. 1962b. Taxonomic status of the New Zealand Redpoll, *Carduelis flammea*: a reassessment. Notornis 10: 61–67.
WESTERSKOV, K. 1953. Taxonomic status of the Redpoll in New Zealand. Notornis 5: 189–191.

Family **PLOCEIDAE**: Weaverbirds
Subfamily PASSERINAE: Sparrows
Genus **Passer** Brisson

Passer Brisson, 1760, Orn. 1, p.36—type (by subsequent designation) *Fringilla domestica* Linnaeus.

*368 **Passer domesticus** (Linnaeus)

House Sparrow

Fringilla domestica Linnaeus, 1758, Syst. Nat., ed. 10, 1: 183—Sweden.

Europe and Asia (except E. and S.E. Asia), Nile Valley, N.W. Africa. Essentially sedentary.

New Zealand: introduced to both North and South Islands on several occasions between 1866 and 1871. Now ubiquitous from North Cape to Stewart Island wherever there are human habitations, and especially abundant in towns and in grain-growing and pig- and poultry-raising areas. Also occurs on Norfolk, Chatham and Snares Islands, and strays have reached Campbell, Auckland and Antipodes Islands.

BAKER, A.J. 1980. Morphometric differentiation in New Zealand populations of the House Sparrow (*Passer domesticus*). Evolution 34: 638–653.
DAWSON, D.G. 1967. Roosting sparrows (*Passer domesticus*) killed by rainstorm, Hawke's Bay, New Zealand. Notornis 14: 208–210.
DAWSON, D.G. 1970. Estimation of grain loss due to sparrows (*Passer domesticus*) in New Zealand. NZ J. Ag. Res. 13: 681–688.
DAWSON, D.G. 1972. House Sparrow, *Passer domesticus* (L.), breeding in New Zealand. Pp. 129–131 *in* Kendeigh, S.C. and Pinowski, J. (eds.) Proc. General Meeting of the Working Group on Granivorous Birds, IBP, PT Section. The Hague, September 6–8, 1970. Warsaw, 1972.
MacMILLAN, B.W.H. 1981. Food of House Sparrows and Greenfinches in a mixed farming district, Hawke's Bay, New Zealand. NZ J. Zool 8: 93–104.
MacMILLAN, B.W.H.; POLLOCK, B.J. 1985. Food of nestling house sparrows (*Passer domesticus*) in mixed farmland of Hawke's Bay, New Zealand. NZ J. Zool. 12: 307–317.
NIETHAMMER, G. 1971. Zur Taxonomie europaischer, in Neuseeland einge-burgerter Vögel. J. für Ornithol. 112: 202–226.

Family **STURNIDAE**: Starlings and Oxpeckers
Subfamily STURNINAE: Starlings
Genus **Sturnus** Linnaeus

Sturnus Linnaeus, 1758, Syst. Nat., ed. 10, 1: 167—type (by tautonymy) "Sturnus" = *Sturnus vulgaris* Linnaeus.

*369 **Sturnus vulgaris** Linnaeus

Starling

Sturnus vulgaris Linnaeus, 1758, Syst. Nat. 10, 1: 167—Sweden.
Europe and central and S.W. Asia; migrates to Spain, N. Africa, Iran and N. India.

Introduced to New Zealand: common on farmland and in urban gardens throughout. Non-migratory. Also recorded from Norfolk, Lord Howe, Kermadec, Chatham, Snares, Auckland, Antipodes, Campbell and Macquarie Islands.

BROCKIE, R.E. 1983. Starling (*Sturnus vulgaris*) roosts and flightlines near Wellington. Notornis 30: 217–226.
COLEMAN, J.D. 1974. The use of artificial nest sites erected for Starlings in Canterbury, New Zealand. NZ J. Zool. 1: 349–354.
COLEMAN, J.D. 1977. The foods and feeding of Starlings in Canterbury. Proc. NZ Ecol. Soc. 24: 94–109.
COLEMAN, J.D.; ROBSON, A.B. 1975. Variations in body weight, fat-free weights and fat deposition of Starlings in New Zealand. Proc. NZ Ecol. Soc. 22: 7–13.
EAST, R.; POTTINGER, R.P. 1975. Starling (*Sturnus vulgaris* L.) predation on grass grub (*Costelytra zealandica* (White), Melolonthinae) populations in Canterbury. NZ J. Ag. Res. 18: 417–452.
FLUX, J.E.C.; FLUX, M.M. 1981. Population dynamics and age structure of starlings (*Sturnus vulgaris*) in New Zealand. NZ J. Ecol. 4: 65–72.
MOEED, A. 1980. Diets of adult and nestling starlings (*Sturnus vulgaris*) in Hawke's Bay, New Zealand. NZ J. Zool. 7: 247–256.
NIETHAMMER, G. 1971. Zur Taxonomie europaischer, in Neuseeland einge-burgerter Vögel. J. für Ornithol, 112: 202–226.
ROSS, H.A.; BAKER, A.J. 1982. Variation in the size and shape of introduced starlings, *Sturnus vulgaris* (Aves: Sturninae), in New Zealand. Can. J. Zool. 60: 3316–3325.

Genus **Acridotheres** Vieillot

Acridotheres Vieillot, 1816, Analyse, p.42—type (by subsequent designation) *Paradisea tristis* Linnaeus.

*370 **Acridotheres tristis** (Linnaeus)

Common Myna

Paradisea tristis Linnaeus, 1766, Syst. Nat., ed. 12, 1: 167—"Philippines" error for (probably) Pondichery, *fide* Stresemann, 1952, Ibis 94: 515.
Afghanistan, Turkistan, India, Andamans, Sri Lanka; as the result of recent extensions of range or introductions has reached

much of S.E. Asia. Widely introduced and established (tropical islands in all oceans, Australia, New Zealand, South Africa).

New Zealand: introduced to both North and South Islands during the 1870s, Mynas persisted in the South Island (Nelson, Christchurch and Dunedin) only till about 1890. In the North Island they became common in Taranaki, Hawke's Bay and southern parts of the Auckland provincial area, and, during the late 1940s and early 1950s, they spread, almost explosively, throughout the rest of this area. They remain common, especially (but not exclusively) near human habitations, north of a line from Wanganui to Waipukurau, though odd birds, perhaps aviary escapees, occasionally appear further south (Hutt Valley, Wairarapa, Nelson and near Christchurch); have spread to off-shore islands, including Little Barrier.

BAKER, A.J.; MOEED, A. 1979. Evolution in the introduced New Zealand populations of the common myna, *Acridotheres tristis* (Aves: Sturnidae). Can. J. Zool. 57: 570–584.

BAKER, A.J.; MOEED, A. 1987. Rapid genetic differentiation and founder effect in colonizing populations of common mynas (*Acridotheres tristis*). Evolution 41: 525–538.

COUNSILMAN, J.J. 1974a. Waking and roosting behaviour of the Indian Myna. Emu 74: 135–140.

COUNSILMAN, J.J. 1974b. Breeding biology of the Indian Myna in city and aviary. Notornis 21: 318–333.

COUNSILMAN, J.J. 1977. Visual displays of the Indian Myna during pairing and breeding. The Babbler 1: 1–13.

CUNNINGHAM, J.M. 1951. The position of the Myna in 1950. Notornis 4: 66–67.

MOEED, A. 1976. Foods of the Common Myna (*Acridotheres tristis*) in Central India and in Hawke's Bay, New Zealand. Notornis 23: 246–249.

Family **CALLAEIDAE**: New Zealand Wattlebirds
Genus **Callaeas** J. R. Forster

Callaeas J.R. Forster, 1788 (March 27), Enchiridion, p.35 — type (by monotypy) Great Wattle Bird of New Zealand = *Glaucopis cinerea* Gmelin.
Glaucopis Gmelin, 1788 (July 25), Syst. Nat. 1: 363 — type (by monotypy) *Glaucopis cinerea* Gmelin.

371 **Callaeas cinerea** (Gmelin)

Kokako

New Zealand. At the time of European settlement, present in forest throughout, although early observations suggest habitat preferences within its range; a much wider original distribution indicated by subfossil records (see under subspecies).

HAY, J.R.; BEST, H.A.; POWLESLAND, R.G. 1985. Kokako. Dunedin: John McIndoe and NZ Wildlife Service.

WILLIAMS, G.R. 1976. The New Zealand wattlebirds (Callaeatidae). *In* Frith, H.J.; Calaby, J.H. (eds). Proc. 16th Int. Ornithol. Congr., pp. 161–170. Canberra: Australian Academy of Science.

Callaeas cinerea wilsoni (Bonaparte)

North Island Kokako

Glaucopis wilsoni Bonaparte, 1851, Consp. Gen. Avium, 1 (1850), p.368—New Zealand.

Found on European settlement in forests of the mid-northern, central and southern North Island (including Great Barrier Island); absent from extensive areas of the eastern North Island. Still well established in the now much reduced native forests of Northland (Puketi State Forest and neighbouring forest areas), and in central North Island native forests south to a line from East Cape to Cape Egmont. Successful transfers have been made to Little Barrier Island from populations threatened by felling, beginning in 1981. Subfossil records of this subspecies are particularly numerous, indicating that it was formerly present in many areas (especially coastal) which no longer provided suitable habitat at the time of European settlement; particularly abundant subfossil in Far North sand dune sites and King Country caves. Recorded also from a few midden sites.

LAVERS, R. B. 1987. Distribution of the North Island Kokako (*Callaeas cinerea wilsoni*): a review. Notornis 25: 165–185.
LEATHWICK, J. R.; HAY, J. R.; FITZGERALD, A. E. 1983. The influence of browsing by introduced mammals on the decline of the North Island Kokako. NZ J. Ecol. 6: 55–70.
O'DONNELL, C. F. J. 1984. The North Island Kokako (*Callaeas cinerea wilsoni*) in the western King Country and Taranaki. Notornis 31: 131–144.

Callaeas cinerea cinerea (Gmelin)

South Island Kokako

Glaucopis cinerea Gmelin, 1788, Syst. Nat. 1: 363—Queen Charlotte Sound, New Zealand.

Distribution on European settlement included western forest regions from north-west Nelson to Fiordland; also Banks Peninsula and, probably, large areas of beech forest adjacent to the mountains and subalpine scrub; in forest and scrub on Stewart Island. Recent records are so few and scattered that the subspecies may be close to extinction; recent unconfirmed reports from Stewart Island. Subfossil and midden records from widely distributed sites; one Stewart Island subfossil record.

CLOUT, M. N.; HAY, J. R. 1981. South Island Kokako (*Callaeas cinerea cinerea*) in *Nothofagus* forest. Notornis 28: 256–259.

Genus **Philesturnus** Geoffroy St.-Hilaire

Philesturnus Geoffroy St.-Hilaire, 1832, Nouv. Ann. Mus. Hist. Nat. (Paris) 1: 390—type (by monotypy) *Sturnus carunculatus* Gmelin.
Creadion, auctorum, not of Vieillot, 1816, Analyse nouv. Ornith., p.34 (cf. Mathews, 1925, Bull. Br. Ornith. Club xlv: 76).

372 **Philesturnus carunculatus** (Gmelin)

Saddleback

New Zealand. Like the Kokako, widely distributed in forests of North, South and Stewart Islands at the time of European settlement; also (unlike the Kokako) on many offshore islands. Much wider earlier distribution indicated by subfossil records.

WILLIAMS, G. R. 1976. The New Zealand wattlebirds (Callaeatidae). *In* Frith, H. J.; Calaby, J. H. (eds.), Proc. 16th Int. Ornithol. Congr. pp.161–170. Canberra: Australian Academy of Science.

Philesturnus carunculatus rufusater (Lesson)
North Island Saddleback (Tieke)

Icterus rufusater Lesson, 1828, Man. Orn. 1, p.355 — Bay of Islands, New Zealand.

Distribution on European settlement included the whole of the North Island; also Great and Little Barrier, Hen and Chickens and Cuvier Islands. By about 1950 it had been reduced to a single population on Hen (Taranga) Island: from there, under the Wildlife Service management programme beginning in 1964, it has been successfully transferred to: islands of the Chickens group (Lady Alice, Whatupuke: thence by self-introduction to Coppermine); to Cuvier Island; to islands of the Mercury group (Red Mercury, Stanley); to Little Barrier Island; to Kapiti Island; and to Tiritiri Island. Unsuccessful transfers to Motukawanui (Cavalli group) and Fanal Island (Mokohinau group). Subfossil records numerous and widely distributed; relatively few midden records.

ATKINSON, I. A. E.; CAMPBELL, D. J. 1966. Habitat factors affecting Saddlebacks on Hen Island. Proc. NZ Ecol. Soc. 13: 35–40.
JENKINS, P. F. 1978. Cultural transmission of song patterns and dialect development in a free-living bird population. Anim. Behav. 26(1): 50–78.
MERTON, D. V. 1965. A brief history of the North Island Saddleback. Notornis 12: 208–212.

Philesturnus carunculatus carunculatus (Gmelin)
South Island Saddleback (Tieke)

Sturnus carunculatus Gmelin, 1789, Syst. Nat. 1: 805 — Queen Charlotte Sound, New Zealand.
Creadion cinereus Buller, 1865, Essay New Zealand Ornith. p.10 — Banks Peninsula, New Zealand.

Found on European settlement throughout forests of northern, western and southern South Island; also Banks Peninsula, D'Urville and Stephens Islands, and Stewart Island and various outliers. By about 1950 apparently survived only on three of the South Cape Islands (to southwest of Stewart Island), but even here the accidental introduction of the ship rat (*Rattus rattus*) in 1963–64 made it necessary to transfer the remaining birds to smaller islands nearby (Big, or Stage, Island and Kaimohu Island). Since then successfully transferred to six other islands in the Stewart Island area: Betsy, Womens, Kundy, North, Motunui and Jacky Lee; unsuccessful transfers to islands in the Marlborough Sounds (Inner Chetwode, Maud). Numerous subfossil, and a few midden, records.

BLACKBURN, A. 1965. Muttonbird Islands diary. Notornis 12: 191–207.

Genus **Heteralocha** Cabanis

Neomorpha Gould, 1837, Synops. Birds Aust., pt.1 (pl.11 and text) — type (by virtual monotypy) *Neomorpha acutirostris* Gould. (*Note*: *Neomorpha* Gould has been suppressed under the Plenary Powers of the International Commission on Zoological Nomenclature, Opinion 514, 1958, in favour of *Heteralocha* Cabanis.)
Heteralocha Cabanis, 1851, Mus. Hein. 1: 218 — type (by original designation)
Heteralocha gouldi Gray = *Neomorpha acutirostris* Gould.

373   **Heteralocha acutirostris** (Gould)

Huia

Neomorpha acutirostris Gould, 1837, Synops. Birds Aust., pt.1 (pl.11 and text) — New Zealand.

New Zealand. Extinct. Recorded historically only from forests of the eastern and southern North Island (Raukumara Range and Turakina River south to Wellington) but, as indicated by subfossils (below), range probably included the whole of the North Island. Last generally accepted record 1907, but quite credible reports up to c.1920. Recorded from 19 subfossil localities from North Cape to the southern tip of the North Island (12 caves; 7 dune sites, of which all but one are possibly middens).

BURTON, P.J.K. 1974. Anatomy of the head and neck in the Huia (*Heteralocha acutirostris*) with comparative notes on other Callaeidae. Bull. Br. Mus. (Nat. Hist.), Zool. 27(1), 48 pp.
MEDWAY, D.G. 1968. Records of the Huia, North Island Thrush and North Island Kokako from the diaries of Joseph Robert Annabell (1857–1924). Notornis 15: 177–192.
PHILLIPS, W.J. 1963. The Book of the Huia. Christchurch: Whitcombe and Tombs.
WILLIAMS, G.R. 1976. The New Zealand wattlebirds (Callaeatidae). *In* Frith, H.J.; Calaby, J.H. (eds.). Proc. 16th Int. Ornithol. Congr. pp.161–170. Canberra: Australian Academy of Science.

Family **ARTAMIDAE**: Woodswallows
Genus **Artamus** Vieillot

Artamus Vieillot, 1816, Analyse, p.41 — type (by monotypy) Langraien (Buffon) = *Lanius leucorhynchus* Linnaeus.

374 **Artamus personatus** (Gould)

Masked Woodswallow

Ocypterus personatus Gould, 1841, Proc. Zool. Soc. Lond. 1840, p.149—"southern and western Australia" = York, Western Australia.

Mainland Australia (not Tasmania, but has reached King Island, Bass Strait); migratory and nomadic. Associates with the White-browed Woodswallow on migration and in breeding colonies (occasionally interbreeds).

One pair recorded New Zealand: Naseby Forest, Central Otago, January 1972–August 1973. The pair bred and reared two chicks; with them were associated 4 White-browed Woodswallows (see below).

CHILD, P. 1974. First breeding of woodswallows in New Zealand. Notornis 21: 85–87.

CHILD, P. 1975. The Central Otago wood-swallows. Notornis 22: 67–68.

DARBY, J. T. 1972. The Australian White-browed Wood Swallow in New Zealand. Notornis 19: 114–117.

375 **Artamus superciliosus** (Gould)

White-browed Woodswallow

Ocypterus superciliosus Gould, 1837, Synops. Birds Aust., pt.1, pl.1, fig. 2—"Interior of New South Wales" = Hunter River.

Mainland Australia; distribution as previous species (but usually predominating over that species in eastern Australia).

Four recorded at Naseby Forest, Central Otago, December 1971–July 1973, associating with the pair of the previous species.

CHILD, P. 1974. First breeding of woodswallows in New Zealand. Notornis 21: 85–87.

CHILD, P. 1975. The Central Otago wood-swallows. Notornis 22: 67–68.

DARBY, J. T. 1972. The Australian White-browed Wood Swallow in New Zealand. Notornis 19: 114–117.

Family **CRACTICIDAE**: Bell Magpies
Genus **Gymnorhina** Gray

Gymnorhina Gray, 1840, List Gen. Birds, ed. 1, p.37—type (by original designation) *Coracias tibicen* Latham.

***376** **Gymnorhina tibicen** (Latham)

Australian Magpie

Coracias tibicen Latham, 1801, Ind. Orn., Suppl., p.xxvii—New South Wales.

Australia and southern New Guinea.

New Zealand: two forms, the Black-backed Magpie *G.t.tibicen* (Australia except the southeast and southwest) and the White-backed Magpie *G.t.hypoleuca* (Gould, 1837) (southeastern Australia from southeastern New South Wales to South Australia, and Tasmania), were successfully introduced to both North and South Islands during the 1860s. The two subspecies now frequently interbreed: the Black-backed form is commonest (and least diluted by hybridisation) in central Hawke's Bay, but occurs less commonly and with many more hybrids among the White-backed Magpies in most other North Island districts, though it is rare near Wellington; in the South Island the Black-backed Magpie is virtually confined to North Canterbury, although hybrids are more widespread. White-backed Magpies with or without evident hybridisation have recently spread more widely over almost the whole country, but they are scarce (though still spreading) in the Far North, parts of southeast Waikato-Rotorua, northern Marlborough, Nelson, Westland, and parts of Southland.

The species prefers open farmland in New Zealand, with trees nearby for nesting; also on open river beds in bush country and in other open habitats (including some town and city parks) from sea level to 1700 m.

McCASKILL, L. W. 1945. Preliminary report on the present position of the Australian Magpies (*Gymnorhina hypoleuca* and *G.tibicen*) in New Zealand. NZ Bird Notes 1: 86–104.

WODZICKI, K. 1965. The status of some exotic vertebrates in the ecology of New Zealand. Pages 425–460 *in* Baker, H. G. and Stebbins, G. L. (eds.) The Genetics of Colonizing Species. New York: Academic Press.

Family **PARADISAEIDAE**: Birds-of-Paradise, Bower-birds and Piopios
Subfamily TURNAGRINAE: Piopios
Genus **Turnagra** Lesson

Turnagra Lesson, 1837, Compl. Buffon 8: 216 — type (by monotypy) *Tanagra macularia* Quoy and Gaimard = *Tanagra capensis* Sparrman.

377 **Turnagra capensis** (Sparrman)

Piopio

New Zealand. At the time of European settlement widespread, and in some districts probably abundant, in forest. The few recent records all require confirmation, and it is feared that both subspecies are extinct.

OLSON, S. L.; PARKES, K. C.; CLENCH, M. H.; BORECKY, S. R. 1983. The affinities of the New Zealand passerine genus *Turnagra*. Notornis 30: 319–336.

Turnagra capensis tanagra (Schlegel)

North Island Piopio

Otagon tanagra Schlegel, 1865, Ned. Tijdsch. Dierk. 3: 190—North Island, New Zealand.

Turnagra hectori Buller, 1869, Ibis, p.39—North Island.

Present in forest throughout, and even common, over most of the North Island on European settlement, but had all but disappeared by 1900; however, early records suggest that it was rare in Northland. Sight records (unconfirmed) claimed from: inland from Patea (1923), inland from Te Araroa (about 1927), between Gisborne and Wairoa (May 1947), Wanganui River (March 1950), Okataina, Waikaremoana. Subfossil and midden records, although few, are widely distributed over the North Island, including the Far North.

MEAD, W. P. 1950. North Island Thrush. Notornis 4: 3–6.

MEDWAY, D. G. 1968. Records of the Huia, North Island Thrush and North Island Kokako from the diaries of Joseph Robert Annabell (1857–1924). Notornis 15: 177–192.

Turnagra capensis capensis (Sparrman)

South Island Piopio

Tanagra capensis Sparrman, 1787, Mus. Carlson. 2, no. 45, pl.4—Dusky Sound, New Zealand.

Turnagra capensis minor Fleming, 1915, Proc. Biol. Soc. Washington 38: 121—Stephens Island.

On European settlement widespread in forested areas throughout the South Island; also Stephens Island. Although early records refer to it as "abundant" in a number of localities, it was "a fast expiring species" at the time of Buller's *Supplement* (1905). Unconfirmed sight records claimed from: west Nelson (January 1948), Southland (December 1947), Lake Waiuna, Fiordland (August 1962) and Fiordland (May 1963). Subfossil and midden records fewer than for the North Island, but widely distributed; one subfossil record from Stewart Island (i.e. outside the known historical range of the subspecies).

MEDWAY, D. G. 1976. Extant types of New Zealand birds from Cook's voyages. Part I: Historical, and the type paintings. Part II: the type specimens. Notornis 23: 45–60, 120–137.

Family **CORVIDAE**: Crows and Jays
Genus **Corvus** Linnaeus

Corvus Linnaeus, 1758, Syst. Nat., ed. 10, 1: 105—type (by tautonymy) "Corvus" = *Corvus corax* Linnaeus.

*378 **Corvus frugilegus** Linnaeus

Rook

Corvus frugilegus Linnaeus, 1758, Syst. Nat., ed. 10, 1: 105 — "Europa"; restricted to Sweden by Hartert (1903, Vog. pal. Fauna 1: 13).

Northern and Central Europe, W. and central Asia, E. Siberia, and north and central China. Northern populations migratory; winters to N. Africa, India and southern China and Japan.

New Zealand: introduced to Auckland, Napier and Christchurch during the 1870s. After an initial increase, the Auckland population disappeared about 1905, but the other two populations prospered. Now widely distributed on farmlands of the east coast of the North Island from Lake Tutira in northern Hawke's Bay to southern Wairarapa and, in smaller numbers, on Banks Peninsula and elsewhere in Canterbury. Smaller isolated colonies, many ephemeral, and stragglers, have been recorded in many parts of both islands and one bird from Chatham Island. The population reached its highest in 1978 (c. 30 000 birds), but has since been reduced by frequent poisoning by Pest Destruction Boards.

COLEMAN, J. D. 1971. The distribution, numbers and food of the rook, *Corvus frugilegus frugilegus* L. in Canterbury, New Zealand. NZ J. Science 14: 494–506.
BULL, P. C.; PORTER, R. E. R. 1975. Distribution and numbers of the rook (*Corvus frugilegus* L.) in the North Island of New Zealand. NZ J. Zool 2: 63–92.
NEITHAMMER, G. 1971. Zur Taxonomie europaischer, in Neuseeland eingeburgerter Vögel. J. für Ornithol. 112: 202–226.
PORTER, R. E. R. 1979. Food of the rook (*Corvus frugilegus* L.) in Hawke's Bay, New Zealand. NZ J. Zool. 6: 329–337.
PURCHAS, T. P. G. 1979. Breeding biology of rooks (*Corvus frugilegus* L.) in Hawke's Bay, New Zealand. NZ J. Zool. 6: 321–327.
PURCHAS, T. P. G. 1980. Feeding ecology of rooks (*Corvus frugilegus*) on the Heretaunga Plains, Hawke's Bay, New Zealand. NZ J. Zool. 7: 557–578.

Genus **Palaeocorax** Forbes

Palaeocorax Forbes, 1892, Bull. Br. Ornith. Club 1(4): 21 — type (by original designation) *Corvus moriorum* Forbes.

379 **Palaeocorax moriorum** (Forbes)

Extinct New Zealand Crow

Corvus moriorum Forbes, 1892, Nature 46 (1185): 252 — Chatham Islands.
Palaeocorax antipodum Forbes, 1893, Ibis 6(5): 544 — North Island, New Zealand.

Subfossil and midden from numerous sites (especially dune sites) in North and South Islands; one Stewart Island record. On Chatham Island abundant subfossil; also a few midden records.

BRODKORB, P. 1978. Catalogue of fossil birds (Part 5: Passeriformes). Bull. Florida State Mus. 23: 139–228.
DAWSON, E. W. 1958. Re-discoveries of the New Zealand subfossil birds named by H. O. Forbes, Ibis 100: 232–237.

SUSPENSE LIST

1. *Puffinus gravis* (O'Reilly, 1818)   Great Shearwater
   Reference: Jenkins, 1968, Notornis 15: 214–5.
2. *Ardea cinerea* Linnaeus, 1758   Grey Heron
   References: Buller, 1899, Trans. NZ Inst. 31: 28;
   Parkes, 1974, Notornis 21: 121–3.
3. *Haliaeetus leucogaster* (Gmelin, 1788)   White-bellied Sea Eagle
   Reference: Oliver, 1955, NZ Birds, 431.
4. *Crex crex* (Linnaeus, 1785)   Corncrake
   Reference: Buller, 1865, Trans NZ Inst. 1: 18.
5. *Porzana fluminea* Gould, 1842   Australian Spotted Crake
   Reference: Hutton, 1871, Cat. Birds NZ, 33.
6. *Gallinula chloropus indica* Blyth, 1842   Indian Waterhen
   Reference: Turbott and Scarlett, 1964, Notornis 11: 107–8.
7. *Calidris minutilla* (Vieillot, 1819)   Least Sandpiper
   References: Stidolph, 1953, Notornis 5: 115;
   Brathwaite, 1955, Notornis 6: 145–50.
8. *Calidris pusilla* (Linnaeus, 1766)   Semipalmated Sandpiper
   Reference: Sibson and McKenzie, 1967, Notornis 14: 84.
9. *Larus novaehollandiae novaehollandiae* Stephens, 1826
                                            Australian Silver Gull
   Reference: Dwight, 1925, Bull. Am. Mus.
   Nat. Hist. 52: 279–85.
10. *Apus apus* (Linnaeus, 1758)   Swift
    Reference: Gibb and Dunnet, 1969, Notornis 16: 204.
11. *Meliphaga chrysops* (Latham, 1801)   Yellow-faced Honeyeater
    References: Shaw, 1894, Trans NZ Inst. 26: 638;
    Oliver, 1955, NZ Birds, 512.
12. *Carduelis spinus* (Linnaeus, 1758)   Siskin
    Reference: Thomson, 1926, Wildlife in NZ, ii, 64–6.
13. *Acanthis cannabina* (Linnaeus, 1758)   Linnet
    Reference: Thomson, 1926, Wildlife in NZ, ii, 59–62.
14. *Corvus* sp.   Australian Raven
    References: Turbott, 1947, NZ Bird Notes 2: 106; Buddle,
    1947, NZ Bird Notes 2: 122.

Index of Common Names

Index of Scientific Names

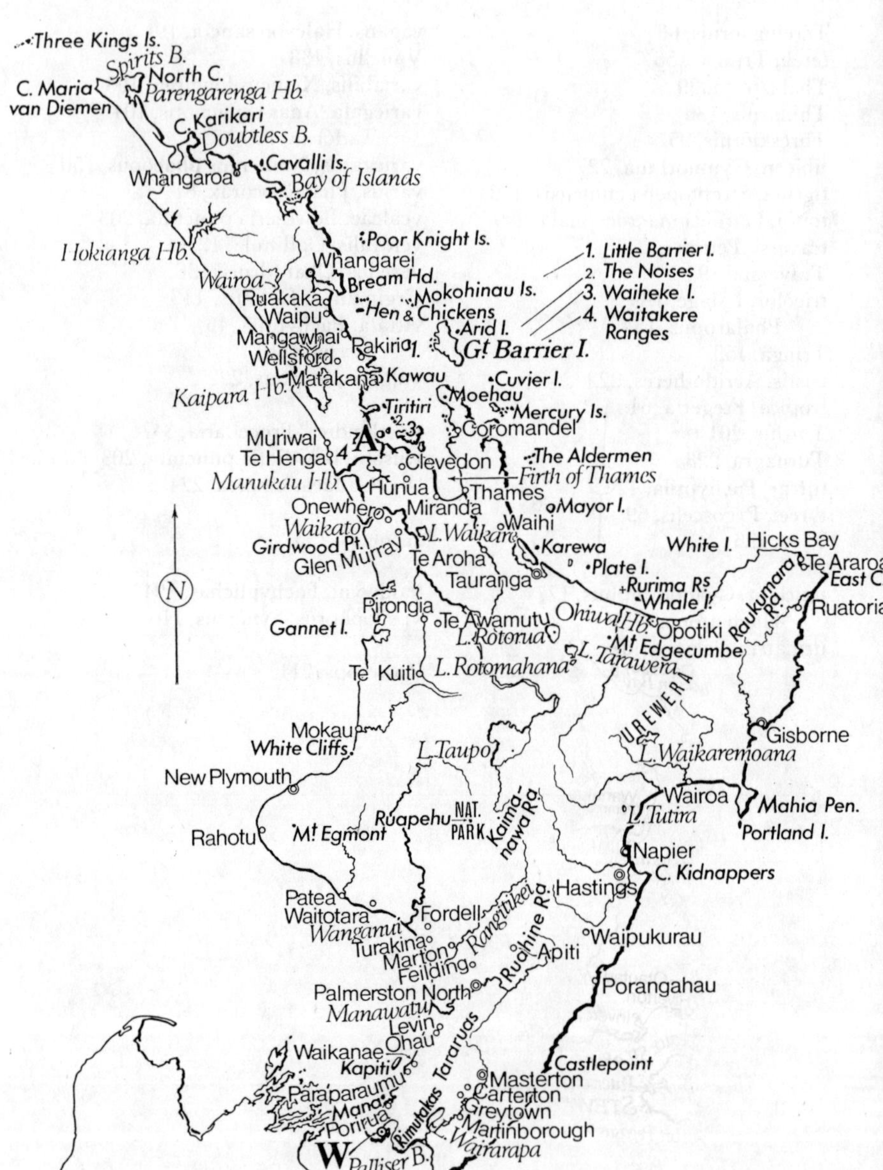

North Island

South and Stewart Islands

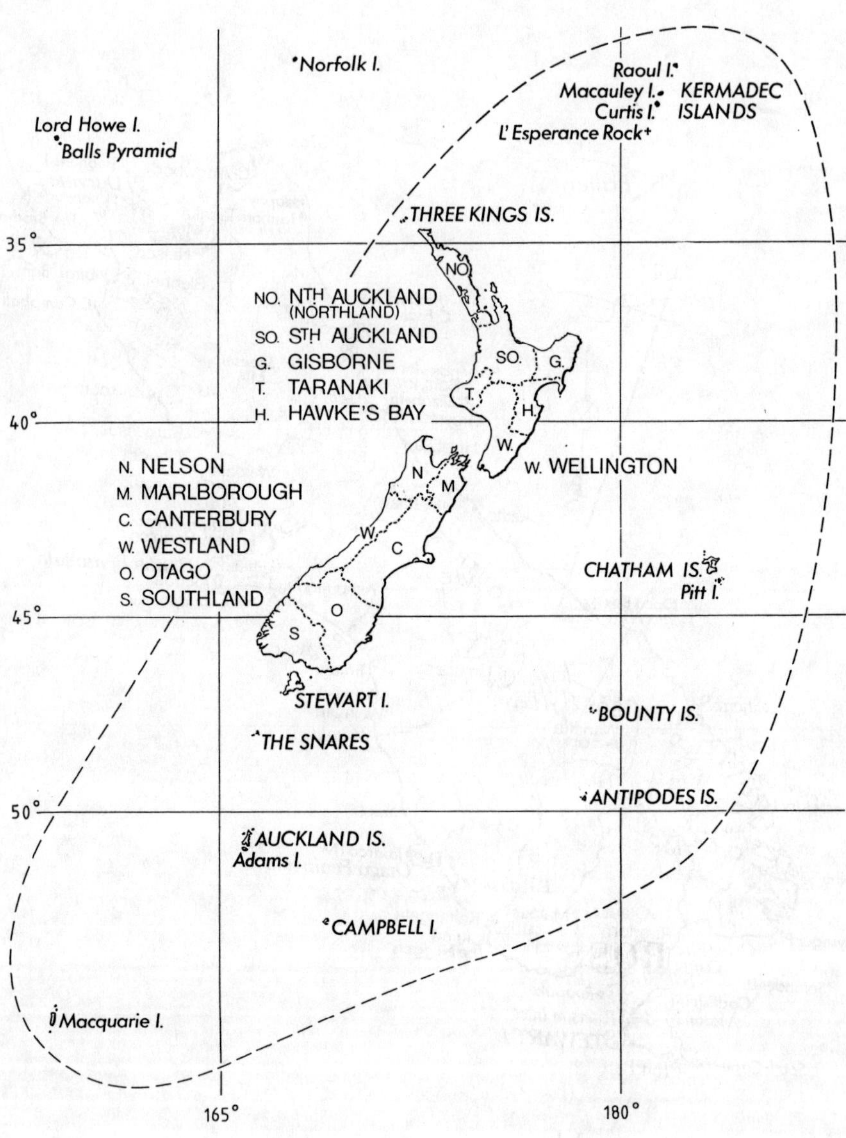

The New Zealand region

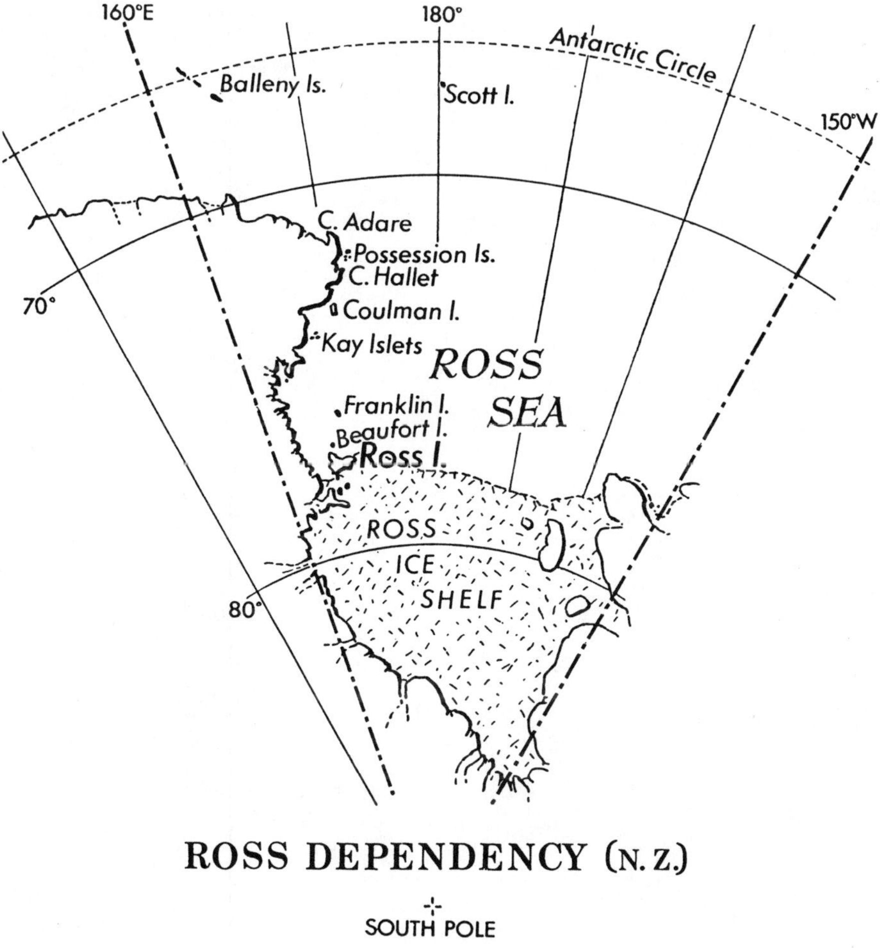

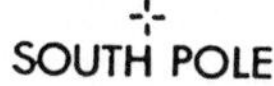

The Ross Sea area of Antarctica